## IN INTERLINE TICKETS

one coupon only to read "CHICAGO & NORTH WESTERN LINE"
is required over any one or more of the System railways named below:

MILEAGE

Chicago & North Western Railway ...... 8,402.28

Chicago, St. Paul, Minneapolis & Omaha Ry. .1,752.81

Total .................... 10,155.09

4650A

▬▬▬ INDICATES DOUBLE TRACK
▬ ▬ ▬ INDICATES LINES UNDER CONSTRUCTION

# The
# OMAHA ROAD

(Front Cover) Larry Fisher produced the cover painting of Omaha Road E-3 Class No. 602 in the 1950s with the eastbound *Viking*. The painting is based on a photo taken by Marshall "Pat" McMahon.

(Rear Cover) Early 1880s CStPM&ORy herald featured a map of the road including the four major cities listed in the corporate title. The "North Western Line" herald was used after 1882 when the Omaha Road became a C&NW subsidiary. *1881 Stillwater City Directory; courtesy of Washington County Historical Society.*

(Above) Omaha E-3 Class 4-6-2 No. 600 takes Train 508 upgrade out of St. Paul Union Depot and under Highway 12 in 1950. *Author's Collection.*

(Page 1) Train 508 rumbles over the Chippewa River bridge, a minute out of Eau Claire's station. *M.P. McMahon.*

(Opposite) D-6 Class 4-4-0 No. 76 poses at Stillwater, Minnesota, with her engineer and lady friends. The 1882 engine was scrapped in 1916. *John Runk; Minnesota Historical Society.*

# The OMAHA ROAD

## Chicago, St. Paul, Minneapolis & Omaha

### by Stan Mailer

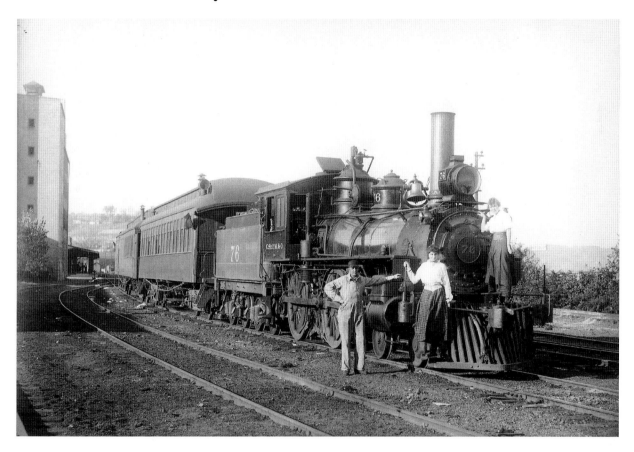

## Hundman Publishing, Inc.

13110 Beverly Park Road, Mukilteo, Washington 98275

# THE OMAHA ROAD

**Chicago, St. Paul, Minneapolis & Omaha**
By Stan Mailer

Copyright 2004 by Hundman Publishing, Inc.
Mukilteo, Washington

**Library of Congress:** 96-079703
**ISBN:** 0-945434-04-9

**Layout and Design:** Mike Pearsall,
Sandy Mewhorter and Jeffrey Koeller

**Contributing Editor:** Jeffrey Koeller

**Technical Adviser:** John Gaertner

**Photo Editing:** Kelsey Brigden

**Maps:** Connolly Design

Printed in Hong Kong

# TABLE OF CONTENTS

# SIDEBARS

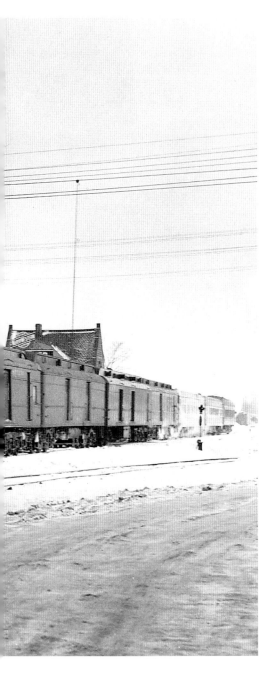

(Above) Train 513 awaits departure from the Superior depot on a cold January 21, 1956. Ahead lies passage over NP's St. Louis Bay bridge and a Duluth arrival. *Frank A. King.*

Two-year-old Omaha I-1 Class 4-6-0 No. 324 heads up the Marshfield freight in a beautiful snow covered action shot on November 30, 1905. *J. Foster Adams.*

# PREFACE

Omaha Road - officially the Chicago, St. Paul, Minneapolis & Omaha Railway Company, stood apart from its larger owner, Chicago & North Western Railway. It was much the rustic country cousin, reaching to Lake Superior in the north of Wisconsin and to Elroy, the original mainline's junction with C&NW. On the far west, Omaha completed a route between the Minnesota Twin Cities and Missouri River towns of Sioux City and Omaha, at the eastern end of the Union Pacific. It allowed for North Western penetration of the northern grain belt region in contest with old line rival Milwaukee Road. The Omaha was produced by several groups of investors intent on land grant gifts in three states. The combined effort opened southwestern Minnesota to the plow and Wisconsin forests to the gang saw. Still other ambitions put Omaha in Lake Superior ports for grain export, and Badger State lumber barons acquired tracts of first class pine for city construction far from the forests.

Grain and inbound coal were major traffic items for the Omaha Road, especially on the west side. Wisconsin's half was a declining farm and forest economy, and struggle for solvency by settler and railroad alike. By the mid-1950s, the entire system faced bankruptcy, and merger with C&NW brought some relief at the cost of many jobs. Today, after the sale to Union Pacific, far distant from the time C&NW contemplated the purchase of UP, the remains of Omaha press hard for survival. Precious little shows of CStPM&Os frugal touch on the landscape, now as far-removed as wooden pilots on Omaha Ten-wheelers.

A visit to Elroy (today without a railroad) in 1949 gave initial experiences in things Omaha. Two E Class 4-6-2s, doubleheaded and well-wiped, brought in day local 508. The two locomotives reflected better times, "When St. Paul had the say-so," as one employee put it. It was less so in 1949, and nonexistent today. Yet another adventure brought me to Adams, where an imposing 600-series super Pacific simmered on the point of an army troop train. Traveling to Altoona, Wisconsin, the mysteries of I-1 and K-1 Ten-Wheelers were laid bare. Certainly this gathering of high-headlight, brass numberboard equipped classics had it all over the parent road's rusting, but durable, R-1s. A rare I-23 Class 4-6-2 was another sign of a difference, the sole example on the Eastern Division. Finally, two years later, I found that a ride on this graceful engine to Drummond was a highlight of the summer of 1953... and the last summer for the I-2 Class.

Pioneer saw mills line the Eau Claire River in the city's early days. The Eau Claire and Chippewa Valley lumbering districts were a prime source of traffic for the new West Wisconsin Railway. *Eau Claire Public Library.*

# 1.

## WISCONSIN LOGS AND LAND GRANTS
### THE OMAHA BEGINS

Omaha's Wisconsin history includes nearly two decades of struggle for control of land grant forests, the chief way to pay for mid-19th Century Wisconsin railroads. There were plans for many lines, but relatively few came to fruition. East of the Mississippi and St. Croix Valleys, Wisconsin was seeing settlements in the high country of St. Croix County, and logging was in high gear. This country would eventually be the path westward for the Omaha. To the north, land grant timber beckoned to sawyer and investor alike. Wisconsin's land grant was to aid construction of a railroad "from Madison or Portage via Columbus northwesterly to the St. Croix River... to Superior and Bayfield." Shady politics played a part after the grant, but one paper road came forth in 1853: St. Croix & Lake Superior Railroad Company, with the grant to be shared with La Crosse & Milwaukee Railroad, grandfather of the Milwaukee Road. StC&LS got as far as meetings, subscriptions and a survey, but by 1855, Hudson, Wisconsin, was confident that the southern terminus of the StC&LS would be located there.

Daniel A. Baldwin, a real estate investor, had holdings in North Hudson, at Lake Mallilieu, which divided Hudson and North Hudson. Baldwin was engaged in frontier businesses, and was attracted to the railroad project. A New Yorker by birth, he was caught up in the StC&LS scheme and spent the next 20 years in St. Croix County. StC&LS failed in the Panic of 1857, but ignited railroad interest in the region, leading to the Omaha's first ancestor in 1863; the Tomah & Lake St. Croix Railroad. Baldwin was to participate in its activity. T&LStC had as subscribers many lumbermen of the Chippewa Valley. Several were close to local politics, and successfully mixed their business skills with the road's requirements. A railroad offered transportation year-round, not possible with even major northern rivers. The two main streams were the Chippewa River and the Red Cedar River, passing through Eau Claire and Menomonie. Both rivers and cities influenced the coming of the T&LStC. Here, a mainline with local traffic available could be a success.

In 1864, the land grant was enlarged, but that didn't stimulate sales of T&LStC securities. Daniel Baldwin brought a new contract in January 1866, and the road's directors gave him a free hand. Baldwin also traveled eastward (and twice to Europe) in search of funds. On April 5, 1866, T&LStC was rechristened West Wisconsin Railway Company, with Baldwin negotiating further. Baldwin engaged Jacob Humbird as the railroad's builder, March 26, 1867, after a meeting in New York. Baldwin had split his life between New York and Hudson and, after securing Humbird as

builder, Baldwin managed an 8% mortgage in England.

Jacob Humbird had become a railroad contractor in the very dawn of such activity. A Pennsylvanian by birth, he last worked in Brazil, contracting for Emperor Dom Pedro II on a 40 mile line through the Sierra del Mar mountains. The work lasted from 1859 to 1866, cost $8 million and claimed 14 tunnels in 11 miles, with 4.5 miles in tunnels. Humbird prospered from his Brazilian adventure. While on a long holiday, he was introduced to Baldwin, and the two contracted for West Wisconsin's first 32 miles, Tomah to Black River Falls. Humbird was alleged to have received $250,000 in preferred stock, and $375,000 cash.

West Wisconsin Railway was incorporated with capital stock of $4 million, while Humbird advanced funds to complete the first part. His security was a construction lien on the finished roadway. Baldwin's European success produced an 8% indenture dated August 28, 1868, in the amount of L800,000 Sterling. Issuance of L200,000 for 60 miles completed would be followed by a like amount for 100 and 140 miles respectively.

Black River Falls had awaited a railroad for twelve years. Now its paper, *The Banner*, was finally able to report headway toward the village of 2,000 on the Black River. The new railroad skirted primitive sawmills in the lowlands, its rails fresh off Great Lakes steamers. The WW left Tomah near today's Milwaukee Road depot, near Highway 12. Farther north and a century later, the original Tomah-Warrens grade has become County Highway "0." Yet, in a haunting, undisturbed section in a forest glade, the work of 125 years ago can still be viewed south of Warrens.

Tracklaying began in September 1868, with a mile a day achieved ideally. By year's end, Milwaukee & St. Paul Railway would be operating the new road as a branch, which continued until May 7, 1871. M&StP received 50% of the proceeds. Their annual report for the first year stated "brings us no new business, or any which we could not get without it..." Trackage to Augusta was completed by December 1869. The Black River Bridge, extensive for the times, was completed the previous August 17; its abutments are still intact. The village of Humbird, 18 miles away, greeted its first train in October 1869, where the road met hilly terrain. The road skirted the hills, providing a route fully 100 miles shorter than Milwaukee & St. Paul's own Twin Cities line (Minnesota Central). Grades to Eau Claire were moderate from the east, and within the city, two major bridges were constructed, over the Eau Claire River and the Chippewa River. Beyond lay another river, the Red Cedar, at Menomonie. By 1870, before the WW reached the St. Croix River banks, there were four major bridges in place.

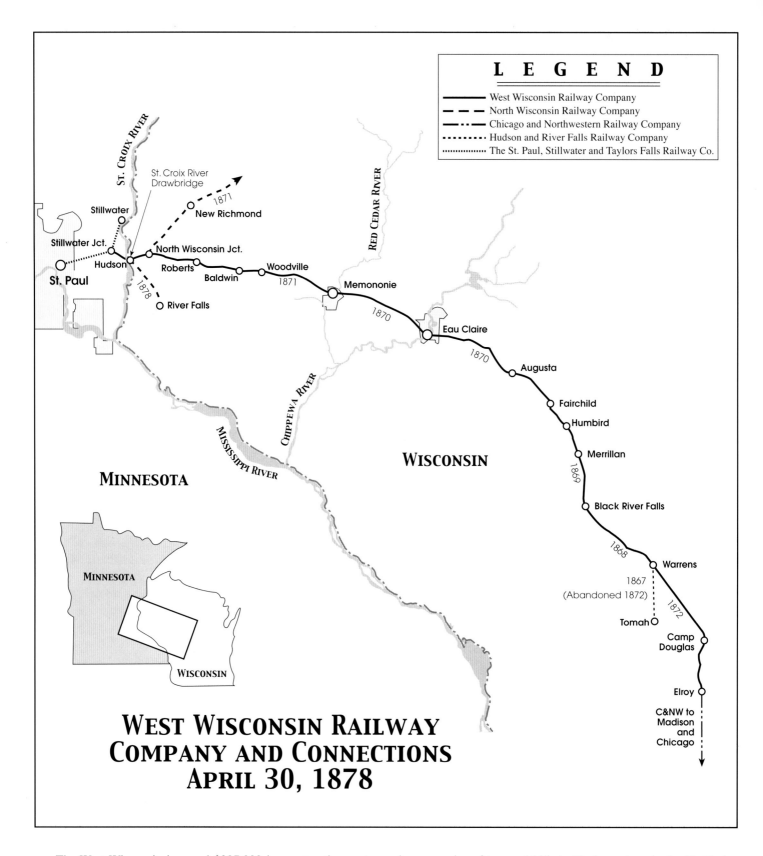

**LEGEND**

———— West Wisconsin Railway Company
– – – – North Wisconsin Railway Company
–·–·– Chicago and Northwestern Railway Company
········· Hudson and River Falls Railway Company
·············· The St. Paul, Stillwater and Taylors Falls Railway Co.

St. Croix River
St. Croix River Drawbridge

Stillwater
New Richmond
1871

Stillwater Jct.
North Wisconsin Jct.
Hudson
Roberts
Baldwin
Woodville
1871
1878
River Falls

St. Paul

RED CEDAR RIVER

Memononie
1870

Eau Claire
1870

Augusta

Fairchild

Humbird

Merrillan
1869

WISCONSIN

Black River Falls

1868

MISSISSIPPI RIVER

CHIPPEWA RIVER

MINNESOTA

Warrens

1867
(Abandoned 1872)

1872

Tomah

Camp Douglas

MINNESOTA

WISCONSIN

Elroy

C&NW to Madison and Chicago

# WEST WISCONSIN RAILWAY COMPANY AND CONNECTIONS APRIL 30, 1878

The West Wisconsin incurred $397,000 in construction costs in 1869, while earning nearly $60,000 ($30,000 in each: freight and passenger). By the end of 1870, only 23 track miles had been laid between Eau Claire and Menomonie. 1871's program included grading the "Mountain Division" between the Chippewa and St. Croix Valleys. Here the road ascends a long hill west of Knapp to the Dunn-St. Croix County line, past "Humbird's Point." It then crested the summit between Wilson and Hersey and wound

down a series of terraced hills to Hudson, deep in the St. Croix River Valley. This portion, revised twice, presents operating problems to this day. It was J.B.G. Roberts, brother-in-law of Jacob Humbird, and also a native of Cumberland, Maryland, who was responsible for the final surveys of 1867. Roberts, like Baldwin, left his name on a village in St. Croix County.

WW's first modest shop was located in Eau Claire, together with a depot and other essentials. The city vied with Hudson for the facility which spelled business for the finalist. Daniel Baldwin had other plans, especially for his land in Hudson. Hudson realized the route to the St. Croix shore would affect them greatly, and would include two greater bridges, the Lake Mallilieu trestle and the St. Croix River swing span. By early 1872, the two bridges were in place and operating. The swing span crossing included one mile of timber structure.

The Hudson bridges had to be adjacent to acceptable grades down to the river, thus sites were considered at Stillwater, Hudson and west of River Falls. Steep banks precluded other sites. Construction absorbed two million feet of timber in the St. Croix span, and the work required six months, beginning June 15, 1871.

Upstream, Stillwater argued against the new bridge on the St. Croix. They felt threatened by the final prospect, as it would wall off their river boat economy and the important log rafts that moved regularly downstream. Stillwater attempted to get legislation passed to prevent any bridge over the river below the city's corporate limits.

An injunction was handed down Friday, June 30, 1871, and the following Saturday discussions accompanied the thump of a pile driver, despite several log rafts trapped at Stillwater's booms. It was a near repeat of Abraham Lincoln's Rock Island case, but here steamboaters and loggers opposed the railroad in "The War of Hudson Bridge." Stillwater's staunchest were still riled over losing the West Wisconsin crossing, and having the final site block their river. Stillwater's lawyers tried to serve paper on WW officials, but the latter evaded the legal weapon. WW later agreed to a circuit court meeting, cleverly timed to allow completion of pile driving in mid-river. What followed was mob action at the bridge site.

Stillwater's "navy" included the steamer *Knapp*, reconnoitering at the bridge as the work gang stepped up activity. Both sides sent for reinforcements, and five "enemy" steamers converged on the bridge site to harass the driving of piles. A picked bridgeman deftly pulled off the choke ropes put about the piles, but was soon overwhelmed by loggers. The next day, the steamer *Minnesota* stood by the work, roiling the waters about the pile driver's barge, then they hijacked the pile driver. It nearly ended in hostilities, but another day saw cooler heads prevailing. Stillwater baron Isaac Staples was anxious to settle, and met with Baldwin, Humbird and retinue, to arrange a bridge that would allow heavy log traffic. Peace then reigned on the St. Croix.

West Wisconsin faced competition from another railroad built from St. Paul to Duluth. The Lake Superior & Mississippi Railroad was completed in 1870, and a branch entered Stillwater to feed grain to Duluth. It was financed largely by Minnesota interests, and Stillwater had the first of three roads at riverside. LS&M ultimately became St. Paul & Duluth Railroad, and finally, the Northern Pacific.

The Baldwin-Humbird partnership took control of the West Wisconsin on May 1, 1871, and bought its first new engines from Baldwin Locomotive Works of Philadelphia (not related to Daniel Baldwin). Numbers 10 and 11 were built in March 1871, named *D.A. Baldwin* and *J. Humbird*, the first of 20 "three-dome" 4-4-0s, a common choice in Wisconsin at the time. They cost $10,000 each.

Seven more came that first year, while Wason of Springfield, Massachusetts, built ten passenger coaches. The engines were named *Geo W. Clinton*, *L.J. Foley*, *Matt H. Carpenter*, *J.G. Thorp*, and *Wm. Wilson*. The so-honored notables on wood cabsides were lumber barons, politicians and men of local power. One hundred freight cars soon arrived from the east to complement the shiny Baldwins.

The West Wisconsin required an entry into St. Paul, which became an intricate final chapter of construction. A state charter for another line with another name in Minnesota spawned the St. Paul, Stillwater & Taylor's Falls Railroad Company, of December 1869, born of St. Paul & Sioux City Railroad promoters. This was a plan to link St. Paul with the St. Croix villages, controlling much of the area's commercial ambitions. Stillwater had visions of competing directly with St. Paul in that time. The 19.8 mile Stillwater Road also built a 3.5 mile line from Stillwater Junction (later Siegel) down to the west approach of WW's St. Croix River bridge, the true intent of the Stillwater Road. Among its principals were A.H. Baldwin, R.F. Hersey and Isaac Staples of logging and land circles. Yet another small railroad, St. Croix Railway & Improvement Company was incorporated on August 4, 1872. This appendage was extended from Stillwater Switch, 1.2 miles south of Stillwater, to present day Bayport, then called South Stillwater. Aided by the StPS&TF, the line was operated by the Stillwater Road from its inception, and was just 2.10 miles long. Finally, WW was able to claim 63.10 miles beyond its swing bridge, ending at Westminister Street in St. Paul. With the testing of the St. Croix River bridge and the Lake Mallilieu trestle, excursion trains

(Right) Stillwater, Minnesota, about 1875, was the site of numerous saw mills which generated a large amount of St. Croix River traffic. (Below) Stillwater, looking north from near the old railroad depot circa 1910. Isaac Staples' home is on the bluff in the backgroud, above the State Prison. Both: *Minnesota Historical Society.*

(Above) A view of C.C. Smith's original wood St. Croix River crossing is shown circa 1875. The original trestle was later filled to become the contemporary mainline, as were many early WW trestles after the line was able to afford the secondary work. (Below) The first iron bridge at Hudson was installed in the 1890s. Minneapolis contractor Winston Brothers employed several Omaha Road locomotives to complete the work. The photos were taken from the Minnesota side, looking northeast. Both: *St. Croix County Historical Society.*

bore down on Hudson and St. Paul in January, 1872.

With a railroad to the Twin Cities now in operation, attention focused on the second half in Wisconsin: extension to Lake Superior. Just as WW built past the site of North Wisconsin Junction (later Northline), a Wisconsin corporation, North Wisconsin Railway Company, was legalized on November 17, 1871. An affiliated building firm, the Lake Superior Lumber & Land Company, began grading the first 14 miles northward, reaching New Richmond in 1872. This was in exchange for $70,000 of capital stock, first mortgage 10% bonds, par value $222,000, plus town bonds valued at $51,700. The building firm sold out to D.A. Baldwin, and probably Jacob Humbird, on December 17, 1872. Baldwin eventually acquired all of NW's outstanding capital stock and assumed title to the property. A new issue of bonds was then given to Lake Superior Lumber & Land Company to settle construction debts. Later, sale of land grant bonds raised money for the NW's completion. The promise of exceptional timber north of St. Croix County occupied ambitious minds, like Daniel Baldwin, and recently arrived attorney John Coit Spooner, formerly of Madison, Wisconsin.

Spooner's arrival in Hudson in the days of a completed railroad to Wisconsin's interior could hardly have been coincidental. He then began his duties for the West Wisconsin, a post he held for twelve years. Spooner was immediately elected to the state legislature, a watchdog position for his associates in lumber, land and railroads. He was 28 when he arrived, with a long career ahead of him, including elevation to the U.S. Senate in January 1885. His most important ally in 1870-1872 was perhaps the greatest Wisconsin power in logging and politics, Philetus Sawyer.

The years 1871-1872 were active for the "pre-Omaha" roads, and important St. Paul men were eyeing events around Hudson. The banking community in St. Paul was also the financing "other half" of the North Wisconsin, the bankers tracing back to the days of the Minnesota Valley Railroad. Also, in 1870, the West Wisconsin's charter was expanded to Wisconsin's southern boundary. It precipitated a struggle with Tomah, Wisconsin, of no small legal significance.

The Minnesota men associated with the North Wisconsin, who also invested in the St. Paul & Sioux City RR, were J.W. Bishop, Horace Thompson, Amherst Wilder, Russell Blakeley, J.C. Burbank, Samuel F. Hersey, J.L. Merriam, Elias F. Drake, and A.B. Stickney. The NW then had D.A. Baldwin's 840 shares in the undertaking as well. Philetus Sawyer eventually acquired shares of the NW, finished only as far as New Richmond in 1870-1872. Thus, NW was the center of attention during the 1870's depression years.

D.A. Baldwin's scheme for the West Wisconsin shops bore fruit on his North Hudson plat, on the Willow River's north bank. There was a seven stall roundhouse, two shop buildings, offices and the elegant residence of Mr. Baldwin. The new shops employed variously about 100 men in both locomotive and car work. As an institution, Hudson Shops lasted until the merger with C&NW in 1957.

Simultaneous actions of West Wisconsin and Chicago & North Western Railway were aimed at linking the two companies at Elroy, Wisconsin. C&NW's construction company, the Baraboo Air Line, was extended north from Madison, into the valley of the Baraboo River, a winding stream with surrounding high bluffs. The Baraboo Air Line would make a junction with the WW and be a jump-off for a connection with the Winona & St. Peter Railroad. While BAL struggled with three tunnels west of Elroy, WW was faced with a 900 foot bore through a high ridge, six miles north of Elroy. C&NW had readied five acres for the Elroy terminal, and the final rails were laid December 23, 1872, in ghastly weather of polar temperatures and heavy snowfall.

Tomah was bypassed by the creation of a straight mainline and the townsfolk resented it. On the last Sunday in November, 1872, WW sent an abandonment crew into Tomah to pull up the stub, now a useless appendage. An irate citizenry menaced the work. Legal proceedings cited great injury to its commerce. In the end, a vacant grade ran ten miles to Warrens, and Camp Douglas became a new WW station. The representative for Tomah in the legislature introduced a bill requiring relaying the track, and the bill was approved by the Governor on February 18, 1873. The railroad resisted and the matter went to the court.

The case brought John C. Spooner to argue for the railroad. In the end, Spooner and the West Wisconsin prevailed, the new line established as legal. The WW was now 177.4 miles long in Wisconsin, and 19.8 miles leased in Minnesota, with another 3.5 miles to Stillwater, Minnesota. In 1872, WW carried two mortgages, part of which covered the Warrens-Elroy line. There were also land grant bonds. This comprised the entire mainline, which is in operation to this day.

Ties to the Milwaukee & St. Paul were severed, and with it the operation of non-WW equipment. Transferred to WW were two "14 inch engines," numbered 1 and 2. These pioneering machines may have been Baldwin "Flexible Beam" engines, possibly procured by Jacob Humbird from the North Pennsylvania Railroad in his home territory. Engines 10-16 were "15 inch" engines of Class B-1, three-dome Baldwins of 1871. In 1872, two 4-6-0s arrived from Baldwin: Nos. 17-18, both "16 inch" engines. By August, 1873, there were 20 Baldwins on the property, all 4-4-0s except for Nos. 17 and 18. It began the tradition of classifying Omaha Road power by cylinder diameter. All of the Baldwins in that time had a 24 inch stroke. Few improvements were made on motive power in the depression-struck 1870s. Jacob Humbird personally purchased North Wisconsin No. 1, an unusual, low-drivered 4-6-0 from Pittsburgh Locomotive Works. It was named *Cumberland*, for Humbird's Maryland home town. Long afterward, this old engine was a switcher at Worthington, Minnesota, and was off the roster by 1905, Humbird returned to the Mayoralty of Cumberland in the 1880s.

Both WW and NW companies fell with the Panic of 1873. After the crash, Chicago's William H. Ferry acted for the New York bondholders who actually operated the road. Ferry presided as trustee until October, 1876, when control was returned to the company. The receiver was again called in June, 1877, to March, 1878, the date of foreclosure sale. It was operated in that period by Ferry, who was associated with C&NW's Minnesota expansion. In 1874, the State of Wisconsin delivered the federal land grant related to the St. Croix-Bayfield-Superior railroad, and also granted lands to another firm which lay between the Bayfield and Superior branches of the NW: Chicago & Northern Pacific Air

West Wisconsin Railway No. 13, the *L.J. Foley*, eases across the original wood truss Black River bridge at Black River Falls. The locomotive was built in October 1871, one of 21 three-domed Baldwins on WW's roster. This design was common on Midwest railroads in the early 1870s. *State Historical Society of Wisconsin.*

An eastbound passenger train, complete with Wason-built rolling stock and a Baldwin 4-4-0, pause on the Red Cedar River bridge at Menomonie, Wisconsin, in 1875. A prime logging stream, the Red Cedar was Knapp, Stout & Company's main transport route from its cutting sites near present-day Rice Lake. Tainter Lake is just upstream from the bridge, an important log storage point for KS&Co. In 1881, Omaha incorporated the Cedar Falls & Northern Railway line to the KS&Co mill at Cedar Falls. *Lou and John Russell.*

Headquarters for the West Wisconsin were built on D.A. Baldwin's land at North Hudson. This faded print depicts 4-4-0 No. 12 *Geo. W. Clinton*, with railroaders in fashionable garb, posing in front of the headquarters building. Included from left to right are: E.S. Graves, Clerk, Auditor's Office; A.H. Baldwin, Vice President; A.C. Peck, Master Mechanic; Harry Baldwin, Clerk; David Humbird, Cashier and Paymaster; J.H. Hull, Superintendent; William James, Auditor; George H. Daniels, Roadmaster; John James, Clerk, Auditor's Office; George S. Marsh, Superintendent's Office; W.S. Wright, Chief Bookkeeper; S.A. Quale, Clerk, Land Office; A.L. Clark, Secretary; C.A. Cosgrove, Chief Train Dispatcher; and D.A. Baldwin, President. *State Historical Society of Wisconsin.*

Looking north toward North Hudson, WW's great wood trestle at Hudson spanned the Willow River, at Lake Mallilieu, until the 1881 line relocation called for its removal. After crossing the high bridge and entering North Hudson, the mainline turned 180 degrees and headed south back toward Hudson (out of the picture to the upper left), finally swinging west across the St. Croix River bridge into Minnesota. The low-level causeway and bridge in the background carried road traffic from Hudson to North Hudson (see detail map on page 127). *St. Croix County Historical Society.*

# Daniel A. Baldwin 1810-1877

**From *The Ashland Press* June 30, 1883**
**By Sam S. Fifield, Editor and Proprietor**

To Daniel A. Baldwin, perhaps more than to any other man, do the people of "The New Wisconsin" owe a debt of gratitude, for the energy, capital and brain, that was necessary, to push this road as well the "West Wisconsin" to success. Others may rightfully divide the honors with him, perhaps, still had his part been left out, we should today be wishing for the iron track instead of witnessing the incoming of the engine and cars over the bars of steel that now stretch across the great northern water shed from the Father of Waters to the King of Lakes. When he took hold of the enterprise it was dead. Others had expended their energies in vain and failed. They did not posses the confidence in the future, the pluck, nor the required skill to make their efforts successful. With most of them the holding of the franchises, and the organizing of the railroad companies, simply meant a venture – a bold speculation. But with Mr. Baldwin and his associated Mr. Humbird, it was a bonafide transaction. They meant business from the start and when they took hold of the road, it brought to its management the necessary push and nerve to build it.

In writing a history of this really wonderful man, we regret exceedingly that we have been unable to learn more of his early life and his career previous to his coming to Wisconsin, for it would add much to the interest of his biography.

He was born in Spencertown, Columbia County, New York, on March 7, 1810. He was the son of a farmer and spent his boyhood days upon the farm, doing the hard work and drudgery that usually falls to the lot of farmers sons. He managed, however, to attend a school in winter and gain a fair education. He finally began the study of law, and leaving the farm, taught school to pay his way. He was at length admitted to practice, but his labors had been so close, that his health failed him and he was obliged to seek outdoor labor, something that would serve to build up and strengthen him physically. He engaged in contracting and building and in a few years, he accumulated a large property in what is now the depot grounds of the Erie Railway in Jersey City. A portion of this property he sold and in the trade he obtained a large interest in Western property, consisting of town lots in Hudson, pine lands, etc. This transaction occurred in 1855-1856. This interest was what first turned his attention to Wisconsin, and brought him to the state. He soon after became interested in the old St. Croix & Lake Superior Railroad, and also the Tomah & St. Croix, afterwards the West Wisconsin. In promoting these two enterprises he spent over 20 years of the best part of his life, working as but few men can work, day and night, in season and out of season, pushing and lifting, and by mere force of will, making headway against every obstacle that could possibly be thrown in his way. He went to Washington and labored there like a giant, finally securing the additional four sections of land per mile, to the original grant, which aided so materially in securing capital with which to begin the great work. It is stated upon undoubted authority that during this struggle at the Nation's Capital, he spent some twenty nights in sleeping cars traveling between Eastern cities and Washington. He would not give up when all was discouraged and ready to desert the scheme, and finally was rewarded by success. It was the turning point that secured the ultimate building of both roads.

Mr. Baldwin, from the force of events, was unfairly tested as a financier and manager of a great enterprise. He had to meet and overcome the whirlwind of panics and "Potter Laws," hard times, adverse legislation, and almost every obstacle that could have possibly been thrown across his path. But for his bulldog tenacity he would have laid down his burden long before he did, but he was a man of iron will and seldom gave way to other's judgment, or took their advice. He was not what can be fairly termed an opinionated man, for he always listened to others, and weighed well their words but he only made up his decisions from the weight of evidence as it presented itself to his mind. He was firm to a fault, and his associates had hard work to get along with him at times. But he had his good side, for when relieved from cares of business he was as kind and generous hearted as a man could be. It was only when crossed or opposed by perplexing hindrances to his plans, that the lion within him was aroused. In the building of the land grant roads he was working, or course, for a profit for himself, but his greatest ambition was to be instrumental in developing the great Northwest. But he could not stand the strain forever, and when he had exhausted every resource and made a gallant fight for over 20 years, he stepped down and others took up the task and have now finished the great work.

He returned to New York in 1876, having sold out his interest in the North Wisconsin to H.H. Porter, Senator Sawyer and others. But the siege had been too much for him and he broke down under the terrible strain of care and disappointment. On the 3rd of December, 1877, he was found dead. The sad particulars of his death, familiar to all who knew him we shall not repeat. It was a sad ending of a life of hardship and toil. But his monument, the great railways of Northwestern Wisconsin, will for ages remind the people that he lived, and in his life was useful to his fellow man.

Line Railway Company. The Air Line was another scheme locally created to obtain the land grant. It actually began as the first Wisconsin Central Company, graded from Richmond, Illinois, to Jefferson, Wisconsin, in the 1850s. It is still partially visible near Elkhorn. Also named Chicago, Portage & Superior Railroad, it was to cross the state diagonally toward the northwest. The Omaha-CP&S struggle reached its climax in 1882.

The WW receivership also faced repairs to a major bridge, or replacement in the case of the Black River Falls span, costing $200,000. In the short time of eight years, the iron rails on the bridge were worn out, and steel replacements were authorized by the state railroad commissioner. The work was completed in January 1878. In the summer of 1878, one Andrew Sheppard requested a 1,400 foot siding five miles east of Black River Falls to accommodate his humble sawmill. It was yet another name along the WW mainline, derived from a sawmill, like Lowery's, Warren's, Rudd's, and Wright's. Decades later there was a tower at Sheppard for trains going to Black River Falls.

WW's trusteeship for the first mortgage bondholders ended in September 1876, the company again taking control of its own affairs. It was in this time that Henry Hedge Porter, David Dows and Walston H. Brown formed a purchasing committee to obtain the property of the WW. Porter's own biography is as follows:

"In December, 1874, the West Wisconsin Railroad was about (to fail) to pay interest on its bonds due January 1, 1875. This prospective failure threatened to make bankrupt the principle owners of the railroad's stock. I happened to be in New York at that time and the holders of the stock urged me to purchase the whole issue for one hundred thousand dollars and to reorganize the company. I believed that it would be greatly to the advantage of the Chicago & North Western Railway, of which I was then an active director, to take this railroad, as I considered it an important connection. As there was not time to consult with the other directors, my associates and I purchased the road on our own account."

Porter then tendered the WW to the C&NW at the buying price, believing it to be in their best interest to take it, but C&NW's directors differed, "most feeling that they had too much railroad already."

Porter and associates then organized the Chicago, St. Paul & Minneapolis Railway Company, soon to acquire the several small lines which were to become Omaha Road property. The difficult trail of finance was to lead to a successful end, but it excluded Daniel A. Baldwin, former president and veritable founder of the West Wisconsin Railway.

Daniel Baldwin usually wintered with his wife and son in New York's Gramercy Park Hotel, far from his fine home along the St. Croix River. He weathered the financial storm of the 1870s, at one time holding two-thirds of the West Wisconsin's stock. He and his son A.H. Baldwin were in control, after the presidency of Horace M. Ruggles of New York in the late 1860s. After the derangement of the 1873 panic, Baldwin's fortunes began to sink, and his ambitions were frustrated. After the Porter-Dows-Brown purchase, Baldwin lost influence, and became demoralized, then contracted Bright's disease. One Saturday night in December, 1877, Baldwin left his home and traveled to Hoboken, New Jersey. Sunday morning a body was found in the livery barn of Enoch Greenleaf, identified as Baldwin's, dead by hanging. He was identified via a North Wisconsin pass in his effects. Thus ended tragically a promoter's life, much like that of Massachusetts lawyer David M. Kelly of the nearby Green Bay & Minnesota Railroad - by his own hand.

Like a struggling handmaiden, the North Wisconsin Railway made little progress beyond New Richmond after the depression years. Another 24 miles of track were laid to Clayton in dense, mixed forests, the site of Jacob and John Humbird's first sawmill in 1875. The St. Paul & Sioux City Railroad executives were concerned privately about the Wisconsin Land Grant, and if it should lapse without a taker. NW would fit well into their expanding StP&SC empire. Securing the grant proved to be an elusive goal and, in 1873, the NW was sold to Baldwin and Humbird. John A. Humbird, son of Jacob, became its president. Afterwards, the NW lay unextended until 1878 and better times. Operationally, on January 8, 1876, the St. Paul, Stillwater & Taylor's Falls entered into agreement with NW to jointly operate the two roads. Oddly enough, the two were separated, with trackage rights required over the WW. The NW agreed to furnish ten cars and one passenger coach, while the other company ponied up one locomotive (probably a Taunton 4-4-0) and cars for New Richmond-Hudson-Stillwater service. The WW obligingly granted trackage rights to NW/StPS&TF between North Wisconsin Junction (later Northline) and the St. Croix River drawbridge. Costs included a car levy and a shared telegrapher's wage.

A.B. Stickney, Vice-President and Superintendent of the Stillwater Road, informed his board of spotty traffic available in March of 1876. It was similar to steamboats on the upper St. Croix River, the Stillwater Road's chief competitor. Stickney, a sharp competitor, had the steamer *Lulu* built to compete in the railroad's name. In seeking the new business, Stickney advocated the nearby Hudson & River Falls Railway Company, eventually built in 1878. The 11.7 mile H&RF required another "run-through" formality over the West Wisconsin, to connect with its parent, the Stillwater Road! Thus arranged, the three branches equaled a "mini-system." Stickney went elsewhere in time, finally becoming president of Chicago Great Western Railway.

The first Hudson & River Falls train rolled into the college town of River Falls in October 1878, with proper formalities and the locomotive *Hudson* in charge. *Hudson* was a Taunton, possibly coming from the Stillwater Road. H&RF was leased by StPS&TF and financed by Horace Thompson, E.F. Drake and Amherst Wilder, all of whom were St. Paul & Sioux City Railroad Company investors and officers.

Wisconsin properties of the soon-to-be Omaha Road were being molded into a new corporation while the StP&SC-Stillwater Road remained separate. In November 1878, the Stillwater Road entered into an agreement with the new Chicago, St. Paul & Minneapolis Railway Company, successor to WW, to operate its trains over CStP&M between North Wisconsin Junction and Hudson for the benefit of the old H&RF-NW schedules. Thus arranged, the lean years and financial juggling around Hudson began to form the ultimate product that was to become the Omaha Road. Ahead lay the union of small companies, plus the formation of the Minnesota half of the Omaha in the next five years. *The Royal Route* was well on its way.

West Wisconsin's North Hudson facilities originally included a seven stall round-house. This view shows a construction crew and several new Baldwin 4-4-0 engines, all built in 1871. From left to right are: No. 12, *Geo. W. Clinton*; No. 14, *Matt. H. Carpenter*; No. 10, *D. A. Baldwin*; and No. 11, *J. Humbird*. *State Historical Society of Wisconsin.*

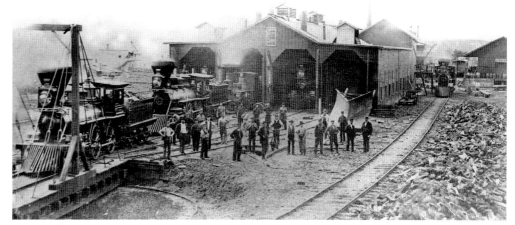

The WW's Eau Claire enginehouse was located on the site of Omaha's final city depot. Several Baldwin 4-4-0s flank an ancient construction engine, probably acquired from the North Pennsylvania Railroad by Jacob Humbird for the WW. *William O'Gara Collection.*

North Wisconsin Railway No. 1, *Cumberland*, was built in 1877 by Pittsburgh Locomotive Works for Jacob Humbird, who sold the 35 ton C-1 Class 4-6-0 to NW during financially hard times. It carried a lease plate, unusual for the times, "Leased from Jacob Humbird." The 55" drivered loner became a switcher in the 1890s and was retired in 1912. *Alco Historical Photos.*

(Above) Taunton-built in 1871, Hudson & River Falls engine No. 2, *Hudson*, is shown on the hand powered turntable at River Falls. Engines such as this came from StPS&TF and StP&SC and served the road in the 1870s-1880s. These tough engines withstood pioneer railroading in Wisconsin and were later sold to short lines and loggers. (Below) A turn-of-the-century scene depicts the arrival of Omaha D-4 class 4-4-0 No. 44 at the River Falls depot. The 1881 Baldwin was retired in 1920. Both: *University of Wisconsin - River Falls.*

(Above) Willow River Mills stood along the St. Croix River at Lake Mallilieu and was controlled by D.A. Baldwin. *St. Croix County Historical Society.* (Below) West Wisconsin Railway engine No. 21, *T.C. Pound*, one of the standardized Baldwin 4-4-0s of the 1870s, weighed less than 40 tons. *State Historical Society of Wisconsin.*

Minnesota Valley Railroad was a St. Paul & Sioux City predecessor. Here an MV train eases past an early water tank, made of stonework, on the old "high line" in Mankato. The engine may be No. 13, inevitably of Taunton make. The print is from a stereopticon slide from the 1870s. *State Historical Society of Wisconsin.*

# 2.

## GOPHER STATE PIONEER

**W**est of the St. Croix, the 1850s saw another land grant to assist in populating the Minnesota prairie and providing it with transportation. The federal government granted lands to the Minnesota Territory for railroads, one of which was Root River Valley & Southern Minnesota Railroad Company, incorporated March 2, 1855. The name covered two routes, finally split into Minnesota Valley Railroad Company and Southern Minnesota Railroad Company on March 4, 1864. In its checkered history, RRV&SM became the SM May 23, 1857. Following in the wake of the 1857 panic, the SM defaulted on interest payments for its state aid bonds, and was sold to the newly-formed State of Minnesota October 16, 1860.

Authorization for a railroad came to the Minnesota River valley through an amendment to a special act creating RRV&SM. It authorized a line from St. Paul to the south bend of the Minnesota River, and then to the southern boundary of the territory, to the mouth of the Big Sioux River (Sioux City). Scant material progress was made until 1865. Previously, some 37 miles were graded and some work continued through the Civil War years. Finally, in March 1864, a new firm acquired the assets: Minnesota Valley Railroad Company. Horace Thompson became the president for MV's first year. He was a leading banker in St. Paul, and made financial accommodations for nearly all the railroads sponsored by the St. Paul & Sioux City Railroad. Other names that appeared were Sibley, Bigelow, Blakeley and Merriam, all connected with Twin Cities businesses. Elias F. Drake, one of the few true railroad experts, hailed from Ohio and held presidencies of Dayton & Xenia and the Dayton & Western. He acquired the first railroad equipment, brought by barge into St. Paul, for Great Northern's ancestor railroad. Drake was thereafter to serve 16 years as president of the St. Paul & Sioux City Railroad Company, the Minnesota Valley's successor.

Mankato, Minnesota, had looked forward to a railroad since 1855. Required was the all-important land grant to resurrect the old MV, since the old Root River Company had stalled, and Horace Thompson aggressively went after the prize in Washington. It fueled the advance of the new firm, ably aided by politician William Windom, for whom a town was named along the line to Sioux City. At the time of the May 1864 land grants, applied to both Wisconsin and Minnesota, the state of Iowa also received a grant of ten sections to the mile. This aided construction from Sioux City to the south line of Minnesota, and was conferred upon Sioux City & St. Paul Railroad Company, an Iowa organization of January 1865. The Iowa company had its board split between Iowa and Minnesota, with an Iowan, J.C.C. Hoskins, as its first president. Ambitious Sioux City entrepreneurs worked to create an important transshipment center on the Missouri River. SC&StP stretched 148 miles, from St. James, Minnesota to Sioux City, including a 25 mile segment between Sioux City and Le Mars via Iowa Falls & Sioux City Railroad (later Illinois Central) trackage rights.

E.F. Drake proposed to build the old MV/StP&SC portion to St. James, Minnesota, to meet the road's other half, with banker Horace Thompson as its treasurer. The new organization completed the road to St. Peter, Minnesota, in summer 1868, and later the same year, to Mankato. Equipment from eastern sources was transshipped from La Crosse, Wisconsin, via barges as early as 1865. One engine, *Mankato*, arrived that year, along with an odd steamcoach, *Shakopee*. The latter was built by the Columbus and Indianapolis Railway and first ran July 6, 1865. Several more Taunton-built 4-4-0s arrived in 1865-1866, among them *Le Sueur, Belle Plaine* and *St. Peter,* brought ashore from barges. After June 1867, locomotives were delivered by rail via Milwaukee Road pioneer Minnesota Central.

To bring about its own steamboat connection with the east, and while just 22 miles of the old MV was in place, the road extended trackage on the south bank of the Mississippi two miles to West St. Paul, to South Wabasha Street. A small yard and freight house served the location after 1867, later called Fillmore Avenue Yard. In April of that year, MV appointed Judson W. Bishop as Chief Engineer, a post he occupied for eight years. Bishop oversaw completion of the line to St. James, 122 miles southwest of St. Paul, where Bishop's road met the Sioux City & St. Paul Railroad. The MV also appointed Mr. John F. Lincoln as its Superintendent from 1867 to 1880.

During Bishop's time, another extension eastward was made in concert with the Minnesota Central (later Milwaukee Road). The new 5.2 mile line bridged the Mississippi River and ran eastward from the junction with the Minnesota Central to the site of St. Paul Union Depot. A joint operation from its beginning in 1869, the line is still in use under modern ownership.

MV's final days involved grading away from St. Peter, on the Minnesota River, and through the town of Kasota. This small junction town, surrounded by quarries, made the connection with the Winona & St. Peter Railroad, C&NW's other Minnesota property. MV built its road far up the side of the steep valley in Mankato, occupying Fourth Street, vacated for the railroad. Extensive trestles carried the road to the present grade southwest from Mankato. The city received its first passenger train October 10, 1868, hauled by 4-4-0 *St. Paul* (No. 7). It was built by Taunton a month earlier.

In 1903, General Bishop recalled a grassland beyond Mankato in 1868, unbroken by the plow. The "General," John Merriam and

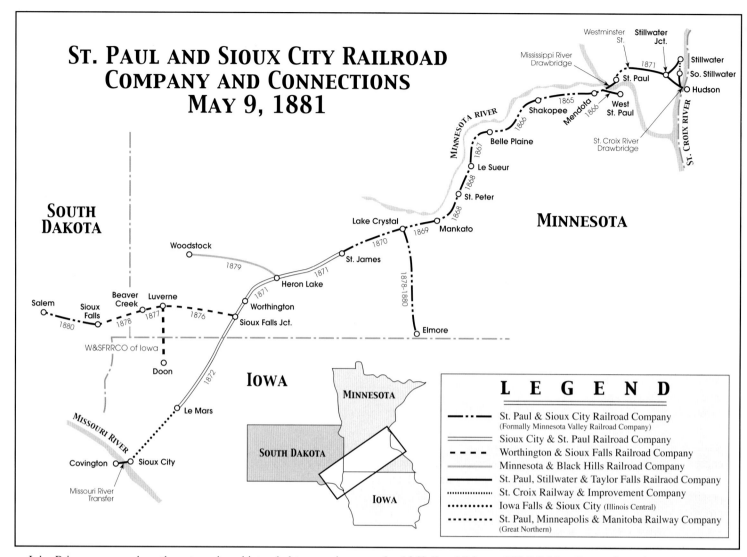

## ST. PAUL AND SIOUX CITY RAILROAD COMPANY AND CONNECTIONS MAY 9, 1881

**SOUTH DAKOTA**

**MINNESOTA**

Westminster St.

Stillwater Jct.

Mississippi River Drawbridge

Stillwater

So. Stillwater

St. Paul

Hudson

1871

MINNESOTA RIVER

1865

Shakopee

Mendota

1866

West St. Paul

St. Croix River Drawbridge

ST. CROIX RIVER

1866

Belle Plaine

1867

Le Sueur

1868

St. Peter

1868

Lake Crystal

1869

Mankato

Woodstock

1879

1870

1878-1880

St. James

1871

Heron Lake

Elmore

Salem

Sioux Falls

Beaver Creek

Luverne

1871

Worthington

1880

1878

1877

1876

Sioux Falls Jct.

W&SFRRCO of Iowa

Doon

1872

**IOWA**

Le Mars

MISSOURI RIVER

Covington

Sioux City

Missouri River Transfer

**MINNESOTA**

**SOUTH DAKOTA**

**IOWA**

### LEGEND

—··—··— St. Paul & Sioux City Railroad Company
(Formally Minnesota Valley Railroad Company)

═══════ Sioux City & St. Paul Railroad Company

– – – – Worthington & Sioux Falls Railroad Company

────── Minnesota & Black Hills Railroad Company

━━━━━ St. Paul, Stillwater & Taylor Falls Railraod Company

·············· St. Croix Railway & Improvement Company

•••••••• Iowa Falls & Sioux City (Illinois Central)

•–•–•–• St. Paul, Minneapolis & Manitoba Railway Company
(Great Northern)

John Prince, surveyed southwestward, and intended to experience the land grant country stretching 150 miles toward the Missouri River. At the time, only a mail carrier's path to several cabins existed in the open grassland.

In January 1869, the road changed its name to St. Paul & Sioux City Railroad Company, just as construction was completed in the Minnesota River Valley. The line makes a steady climb past Minneopa Park, a local recreation spot, until prairie land is reached. On October 8, 1869, the odd *Shakopee*, half locomotive and half coach, steamed into Mankato's new station, bulging with dignitaries and directors amid admiring crowds.

The SC&StP, the alter ego of the road to Omaha, began to extend its line southwestward in the spring of 1871, with Messrs. Merriam and Brown resigning as directors to accept the contractor's role on March 2, 1871. The Sioux City road then issued land grant 8% bonds, dated August 1, 1871, in the amount of $2,800,000, and the road conveyed 550,000 acres in Iowa and Minnesota to Trustees E.F. Drake and A.H. Rice. Land sales would bring proceeds, while the road retained $175,000 of the land grant bonds, a portion of which were sold at a discount. SC&StP also held $20,000 in the Worthington & Sioux Falls Railroad Company, built in 1876-1878, and some real estate, plus grain elevators along the SC&StP. During 1871, grading was completed to the connection with the Iowa Falls & Sioux City (Illinois Central), which was in position to accept SC&StP trains

by 1869. In addition to IF&SC, New Jersey financier John I. Blair backed several neighboring railroads converging on Sioux City, just ahead of the Omaha Road predecessors. Blair had substantial holdings in land companies and town sites as well as C&NW, and Sioux City & Pacific Railroad, a strategic route up the Missouri River. SC&P was an outgrowth of interest in locating Sioux City on one of five proposed branches of the Union Pacific, which would diverge from UP's mainline near Fort Kearney, Nebraska, as provided in the 1857 land grant act.

The contract into which the two St. Paul-Sioux City roads entered called for StP&SC to turn over to the SC&StP all rights pertaining to the StP&SC in Minnesota, including the St. James-state line segment. It gave all land grant assets to the construction company. The entire line was due for completion at the end of 1872. SC&StP had E.F. Drake as its President. Two Bostonians, G.H. MacKay and A.H. Rice, may have influenced the Sioux City roads to invest in Taunton-built motive power. Some 42 of the Massachusetts engines were active on the western lines.

St. James, Minnesota, was created at the junction of the two related companies. Actually, the town was fixed as near 120 miles out of St. Paul as possible. St. James was named by its first settler, James Parrington, and it grew quickly to a population of 300. The line had 2,400,000 shares of common stock, but 15 directors owned a majority of its securities. They were again St. Paul bankers and their names were found on the Tauntons as well as on distant depots of small towns on the prairie.

Immediately after completion, the road to Sioux City suffered severe economic setbacks, despite comparative ease of construction across the flatlands. The prairie weather assaulted the new road, winter coming with a ferocity which virtually halted operations. New settlers whose accommodations were hardly up to it, were seriously endangered. The railroad had to employ numbers of hapless new settlers to shovel mountains of snow off the line, so that relief could be shipped in to those very people. Imperative was the need to bring in firewood from the Minnesota Valley, the cold as intense and merciless as a polar storm. St. James was hard hit, as it had no natural cover in its flatland location.

The winter of 1872-1873 was no easier. With the line opening to Le Mars, a larger territory was served, but it became a liability in another harsh winter. By November 1872, a three-day snowfall and high wind paralyzed transport. Nearly 100 souls were overtaken, their lives snuffed out by smothering cold and lethal snow, the severity greater than the previous winter. Portions of summer work were dedicated to cut widening and snow fence installation. The combined companies suffered heavy financial loss, as weather sealed off revenues at a critical start-up time. Another disaster loomed in the form of the fabled grasshopper plague, which extended the effect of the 1873 depression, and stripped desperately needed grain crops from the land. Politically, the granger movement swept the grain belt, curtailing further railroad earnings. Chief Engineer Judson Bishop was forced to engage in anti-insect warfare or face ruin. Recovery only came in 1876, as the promise of Minnesota's great fertile soils beat back pessimism and despair, and growth resumed. The Thompson group worked to forge an empire in the new Missouri valley, while the gangsaw whined in northern forests, producing lumber for towns on the flatlands.

In the midst of the 1870s, the StP&SC found it necessary to protect itself from competition, especially from the Chicago, Milwaukee & St. Paul Railroad. The Milwaukee's march into South Dakota was coming via its north Iowa line, and all were conscious of Black Hills gold after 1873. To maintain a line haul and avoid transfers, the Sioux City road embarked upon branch-building. In the spring of 1876, the St. Paul & Dakota Railroad Company was organized by the Sioux City roads, with two-thirds of its stock held by StP&SC, the balance by SC&StP. A name change came on June 23, 1876, to Worthington & Sioux Falls Railroad Company, and construction began that summer from Sioux Falls Junction (later Trent), 28 miles to Luverne, Rock County, Minnesota. Sioux Falls had its new railroad by August 1878, 59 miles out from Trent, just south of Worthington.

A branch was begun in 1879 from Luverne southward to Doon, Iowa, 28 miles. The "Bonnie Doon" was authorized by its Iowa charter to be extended to the Big Sioux River, down the gentle valley of the Rock River. It was never extended further toward its Sioux City goal and finally expired in 1933.

Another hopeful branch came forth in 1879, as the Minnesota & Black Hills Railroad Company. It was the fabled hills of South Dakota, which tantalized railroads and brought midwestern lines to the limits of their western expansion. M&BH was built from Heron Lake, Minnesota, to Woodstock, completed by July 18, just five weeks after organization. The 44 mile line was further extended 11 miles to Pipestone in 1884. Another extension was made beyond Sioux Falls to Salem, 40 miles into McCook County's grassland. The last segment into Mitchell, South Dakota, was completed in 1887. It was founded in 1879, ironically named for Milwaukee Road's president. The Dakota boom brought lots of settlers, furthered by Milwaukee Road actions, and by climactic conditions. Drought set in by 1887, which intensified in 1889, curtailing settlement and gain by railroads. The Omaha Road predecessors pushed into Mitchell too late for a share in a dubious boomtime.

Throughout the 1870s, StP&SC continued to maintain a locomotive shop at Shakopee, Minnesota, which cared for "west side" power even after the 1872 fire, in which five engines were badly

Pioneer "steam coach" *Shakopee* operated in early times for Minnesota Valley Railroad. It was purchased in Ohio and first operated in July 1865. The coach was created by W. Romans from an Osgood-Bradley car built in Worchester, Mass. *Minnesota Historical Society.*

damaged. By 1879, need for a larger shop was arranged on 40 acres in St. Paul, the work completed in 1880. The new shops were connected to the mainline near the road's Mississippi River bridge and remained there through CStPM&O operation. Later additions by the Omaha brought the roundhouse to 36 stalls of four different lengths. St. James had 19 stalls by comparison. Sioux City, in turn, had a 38 stall roundhouse which maintained motive power for the Nebraska and the Iowa & Minnesota divisions. The district became the Western Division by the 1930s, when repair work was divided with St. Paul Shops.

The C&NW line to Elmore, Minnesota, began as Des Moines & Minnesota Railroad, later Des Moines & Minneapolis, a three foot gauge line which expired financially in 1879 at Callanan, Iowa, 58 miles north of the capital. The final 66 miles to the state line came in 1882, to meet a St. Paul & Sioux City branch to Elmore on nearly flat terrain. The StP&SC's Elmore line was 41 miles long, and was completed in 1880. It tied the two state capitals together by 1882.

Bustling Sioux City had competition from Omaha, Nebraska, to the south and Yankton to the north. In 1869, the year the Union Pacific was completed, Omaha capitalists organized the Omaha & North Western Railroad Company. This road was to build a line from Omaha to the mouth of the Niobrara River, a point about 30 miles west of Yankton on the Missouri River. The O&NW built the first 25 miles from Omaha to Blair, and in fits extended its line to Tekamah, 17 miles further, by September 1876. Sioux City had reason to fear encirclement to its west. Omaha and Yankton, with allied railroad lines, could potentially strangle Sioux City's new steamboat commerce up the Missouri River and, after 1873, affect the Black Hills carrying trade.

Foreclosure came to the O&NW, and the sale followed on December 2, 1878, to Union Trust Company of New York. The trust company conveyed the railroad to the Omaha & Northern Nebraska Railroad Company, a reorganization. The road was then extended to Oakland in 1879, and a sale was made on November 29, 1879, to StP&SC subsidiary Sioux City & Nebraska Railway Company "for the benefit" of the StP&SC. Part of the city of Omaha's interest in the O&NW-O&NN project was to "conquer" northeastern Nebraska and draw the agricultural commerce of the Logan Valley, and the territory west of Sioux City, plus Dakota and Dixon Counties, to the south.

A more colorful and obscure railroad was destined to connect northeastern Nebraska with Sioux City, but without benefit of a sought after bridge. The Covington, Columbus & Black Hills Railroad Company, an unusual 3' 6" narrow gauge line, was incorporated under prevailing, misguided concepts of economics rampant in the 1870s. CC&BH was 26 miles long, built from Covington, opposite Sioux City, to Ponca, Dixon County, and was completed in 1876. Like many other slim gauge lines, CC&BH aimed for endings in distant Black Hills gold camps, or as far as its money could reach.

The promise of a coal seam in Dixon County prompted interest in building to Ponca,which coincided with Black Hills fever. Many of the directors were substantial Sioux City businessmen. Stockbooks were opened January 31, 1875, in Covington, an unsavory town which, in time, slid into the Missouri River. Wayne County was its avowed goal by December 1876, on the route to Columbus, Nebraska, and the Union Pacific. It was "thence to the

Minnesota Valley Railroad No. 6, *Henderson*, came in October 1867, serving well into Omaha ownership. It became St. Paul & Sioux City No. 206, then Omaha No. 206. It was sold in 1897 to W. Stoddard of St Paul. *Minnesota Historical Society*.

new Golden Eldorado of the Black Hills." Nearby Cedar County's newspaper issued a supplement, in German, in favor of voting bonds for CC&BH. Bond issues went for the railroad in both Dixon and Dakota counties. It won their names on cabsides of two identical Mason "Bogie" locomotives, possibly the road's only power. They were 0-6-6-T engines, which were arranged with a swivelling forward engine truck pivoting on a ball joint above the truck's center. Locomotive *Dakota* arrived via SC&StP at Sioux City in August 1876, built the previous month at the William Mason Machine Works. Mason was founded in the 1820s as a textile machine manufacturer. *Dakota* was CC&BH No. 1, later becoming StP&SC No. 47, then Omaha No. 247. *Dixon* was Stockton & Ione (California) No. 1, but was rebuilt and resold with new "trucks" as an 0-6-6-T, arriving on CC&BH November 1876. The S&I engine originally was an 0-4-4-T, obscuring proper identification. It became CC&BH No. 2.

*Dixon* proved to be hard to land in Nebraska. Embarkation on a transfer steamer nearly had the little engine in the Missouri mud. Safely ashore, *Dixon* was immediately fired up to relieve *Dakota,* much in need of repairs. CC&BH was completed to Ponca in September 1876, and received its first two passenger cars, a coach and a baggage-mail-smoker, from Wason of Springfield, Massachusetts. Both arrived on standard-gauge trucks, and were "wheeled" before landing. The coach seated 54 with the smoker having longitudinal seating, facing the center. The railroad built 20 flat cars and box cars in the fall. Schedules were posted, and the above little train was off to Ponca at 7:30 AM.

CC&BH's General Manager reported that 100 miles of extension were funded to date. Rumors were afoot linking them with Illinois Central ambitions, still others naming O&NW as a suitor. County bonds were acquired during an excursion to Ponca in 1876's fall, and the press was invited to view the flat land, narrow gauge from the Wason coach. Conditions were far from ideal in mid-January 1877, as the road encountered six foot drifts, overwhelming for the low-drivered Mason Bogies. The small company was unable to make headway as an independent and moved toward foreclosure on October 22, 1879, in the interest of the StP&SC. CC&BH was formally conveyed to E.F. Drake, President of StP&SC. At year's end, Drake and his wife conveyed the road to Sioux City & Nebraska Railroad Company, a Nebraska corporation organized December 18, 1879, in the interests of the StP&SC. In 1880, the road was widened to become a branch of SC&N.

SC&N possessed the following mileage in 1880:
Omaha (Farnham Street) to Oakland, Neb: 57.7 miles.

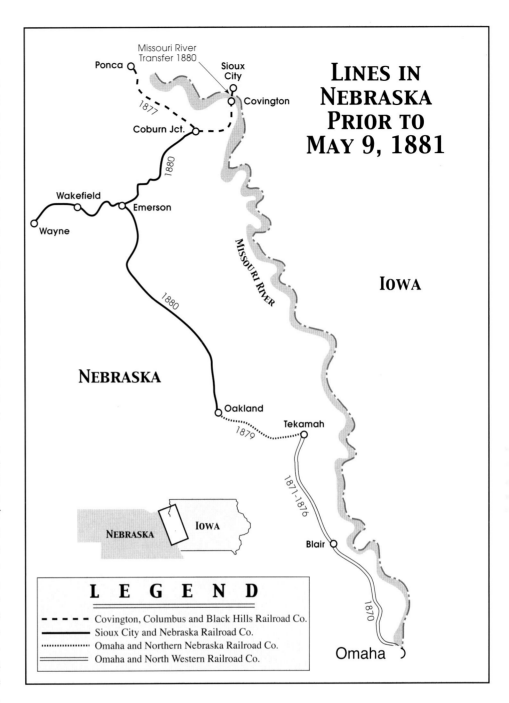

LINES IN NEBRASKA PRIOR TO MAY 9, 1881

**LEGEND**

- – – – – Covington, Columbus and Black Hills Railroad Co.
- ———— Sioux City and Nebraska Railroad Co.
- ·············· Omaha and Northern Nebraska Railroad Co.
- ═══════ Omaha and North Western Railroad Co.

Covington to Ponca, Neb: 25.8 miles.
Oakland to Coburn Junction, Neb: 53.5 miles.
Missouri River Transfer (ferries) 1.3 miles.

In March 1880, SC&N was conveyed to StP&SC, including lines under construction, with the Emerson Junction-Wayne segment of the Norfolk line completed into Norfolk in 1882.

Expansion of the Nebraska lines followed, beginning with the bottleneck of the Missouri River Transfer, the standard gauge ferry system replacing CC&BH's service. Spurs to the riverbank on both sides completed the 127 mile road to Omaha. Thus, the StP&SC had in place most of the Omaha Road's later possessions in Nebraska just before CStPM&O was formed. Branches were built later to Crofton (1883-1906) and Bloomfield (1886-1890) north of the Norfolk line.

The Norfolk line was reminiscent of CC&BH's aims to reach the Union Pacific at Columbus, Nebraska. Grading started in 1880, with promises of a shorter (by 60 miles) connection to UP, bypassing C&NW's middleman status.

(Above) Omaha No. 229 was built by Taunton as Sioux City & St. Paul No. 9, *Geo A. Hamilton*, in August 1872. The well-polished engine is ready for an inspection trip in St. Paul circa 1892. *State Historical Society of Wisconsin.*

(Right) Omaha No. 229 was sold in 1900 to E.H. Hobe Lumber Company, and put to work at Knox Mills, Wisconsin, until sold to Marinette, Tomahawk & Western Railroad some years later. *Minnesota Historical Society.*

(Below) St. Paul & Sioux City No. 8, *Sioux City*, was built by Taunton in 1869, eventually becoming Omaha No. 208. It was rebuilt into an 0-4-0 in 1886, and was finally retired in 1909. *William F. Armstrong Collection.*

Supplies for the extensions were tardy in arriving, and labor was scarce in the summer of 1881. It was "boom time" according to the Sioux City *Journal,* and every "St. Paul Line" (local parlance for SC&StP) engine was heavily engaged in freight service, notably the lumber movement to the Great Plains. Only occasionally could power be spared to deliver iron to "the front." New engines were purchased to cover the new lines in the summer of 1880. They were the last Taunton 4-4-0s to come, twelve in number, each weighing 33 tons. Transfer boats last used by the Burlington at Plattsmouth, Nebraska, began to work cars across the Missouri to Covington. The Sioux City locomotive shop converted the two CC&BH Mason Bogies to standard gauge and employed them locally as ferry switchers. The first Council Bluffs-St. Paul night express was scheduled to arrive in Sioux City in mid-July 1881, its southbound counterpart due at 3:57 AM the following day. In turn, daylight trains were scheduled for 7:25 AM and 7:40 PM, respectively.

Sioux City rumors had Union Pacific acquiring the Norfolk line. It proved to be a vain hope just before the Omaha Road was formed. In the end, organization caught up with overtaxed rail gangs, and a large labor force was brought to Covington, and the Omaha Road began to conquer northeast Nebraska's majestic hills. Four steep grades lay ahead, with wide lowlands between the knobs. Tracklaying halted at Apex, 17 miles out of Norfolk, in March 1882. The Omaha was expected to enjoy "lake freight" penetration of central Nebraska, bringing coal, salt and heavy hardware deep into UP territory. A junction with Blair's Fremont, Elkhorn & Missouri Valley Railroad in the vicinity would also strengthen the Omaha's thrust. Ultimately, a joint depot for UP and Omaha was built in "uptown" Norfolk, while FE&MV built its depot, offices and roundhouse at South Norfolk.

Changes to the former O&NW line at Florence, just north of Omaha, began in 1881. That year's floods heavily damaged the original line close to the Missouri River floodplain, undermining it extensively. Work extras crowded the operable part of the branch, where washed-out track was held up by tie pile cribs, requiring slow running. Much of the repairs sapped progress on the Norfolk line, also delayed by slow rail delivery. The line was raised out of the river floodplain and made deep cuts across new terrain for six miles. The Florence cut-off shortened the old line, but excavation reached 80 feet in clay deposits. Grades, however, were reduced by one-half. It cost more than the grading of the Norfolk line, while smallpox epidemics scattered laborers. North of Oakland, in the Logan Valley, track had to be raised for nine miles after spring washouts.

The Omaha consolidation of 1880 was nearly at hand. Still working its transfer boats, *President* and *John F. Lincoln,* across the Missouri River at Sioux City, the four-car capacity boats were operated singly. Shifting sandbars and ranging river levels plagued the boats in warm weather, and a winter bridge was put across the ice in season. On Covington's side, federal engineers fought shifting banks with willow sapling mats, but in time, the village was all but washed away, some say payment for sinful living in its streets. In March 1882, the *Lincoln* set a daily record by crossing 105 cars. Bright new CStPM&O "Lumber Line" box cars rumbled into Sioux City with a three-way routing choice for incoming cars (SC&P, Covington Transfer, Sioux City local). At Harry Hall's Sioux City restaurant, the Omaha also made regular deliveries of Lake Superior Whitefish and Mackinaw Trout.

Sioux City's alternative winter ice bridge was a temporary pile structure locked in river ice, with piles 15 feet into the river bottom. Cuts made into the riverbank to facilitate reconstruction had to be cleared each year to allow for the work. It also required constant vigil to ward off shifting masses of ice. The Omaha risked the winter bridge's perils to maintain traffic to Nebraska. It would be a long time before a permanent bridge could be built.

The perils of the ice bridge soon became apparent. On December 31, 1881, the ice gorge carried away 300 feet of bridge, taking it into deeper water, thereby cutting the St. Paul-Omaha mainline. Regular Ponca and Omaha-bound trains were

Taunton-built in 1871, Sioux City & St. Paul No. 1 carried the famous (to Omaha history) name *E.F. Drake.* The engine became Omaha No. 221. In 1891, Sioux City & Northern bought the engine. SC&N (later Great Northern) was a competing route northeast out of Sioux City to the Twin Cities. *Nebraska State Historical Society.*

# MASON BOGIES ON THE OMAHA
## STANDARD GAUGED CC&BH POWER

The Omaha inherited two 3'6" gauge Mason "Bogie" engines from the Covington, Columbus & Black Hills Railroad. The pair were built in 1876 and were converted to standard gauge when the Omaha widened the railroad. They worked at Sioux City most of their existence, performing switching duty related to the cross-river ferries.

(Right) Omaha No. 247 is at 7th and Howard Streets in Sioux City, between switching assignments. It was later sold to the Riverside Land Company. *State Historical Society of Wisconsin.*

(Above) No. 248 became the property of Pacific Short Line Company in 1890. It is shown shuttling PSL coaches across the temporary Missouri River bridge. The new Omaha bridge can be seen in the distant background.

(Right) The two engines came to an abrupt end on September 18, 1896, when they were reunited in a head-on collision staged at Riverside Park in Sioux City. The photographer caught the moment of impact! Both: *Sioux City Public Museum.*

made up in Covington for a week thereafter. In March of 1882, nearly to the spring resumption of ferry service, the ice again moved, pressing down on the structure's upstream side. The railroad stationed a crew on the structure, actively working to break up the oncoming ice, to save the bridge for just one more day. Ferries were steamed up in anticipation of the bridge's loss, great slabs of ice 14 feet thick grazing the boats' hulls as they carried downstream.

On the last day it was decided to cross some of the backed-up carloads by kicking them at speed across the weakened bridge, as an engine's weight was excessive. The Ponca-bound mixed train was shoved onto the bridge, its pushing engine making a fast stop, short of entering the structure. Then something happened to befoul the day. A grinding crash brought the free-rolling cut of cars to a splintering halt. The rear truck of the leading car was jerked out, dropping the skidding carbody onto bridge rails, the loads behind shoving the catastrophe onward. The second box car, a tie load, slid off its trucks and landed roof-down on the ice. A third car lodged vertically against the bridge's side, while the Ponca combination car lost a truck into the mush ice below.

The bridge withstood the onslaught well, but succumbed to the ice on January 4. Again, 300 feet were carried out on the Iowa side, a carload of ties floating off behind the other wreckage. Crews were put on the remainder and all iron and stringers were salvaged. Management pronounced the winter bridge a success, while looking forward to an eventual permanent span. It came in

1888, a four-span Coopers E-30 structure, each span 400 feet long. Caissons were 99 feet deep (below surface of high water), with 8,974 tons on each pier. Designed by G.S. Morison and E.L. Corthell, it continued to carry Omaha Road trains from Sioux City into Nebraska until abandonment of those lines. Purchase of the location by Burlington Northern on December 4, 1981, brought a competitor's dream to the site of the old crossing. A modern $14 million structure was built, equally high above the controlled Missouri River mud.

Sioux City and its railroads considered a Union Station, like many upcoming communities. The idea was raised in hard times, for SC&StP suffered a financial loss in 1881's disastrous winter, due to snow removal costs and line closure. One report cited $200,000 in losses due to plowing out the mainline, which postponed the grand idea of a transport citadel until stronger times.

Progress at Sioux City included new yard trackage, several new buildings, a coal dock and excavation of bluff land north of the shops. Material taken from the high banks behind the shops was used to fill in railroad land elsewhere. More shop buildings were promised for 1882. Carshop forces completed the sleeping car *Minneapolis* on July 10, 1881, which immediately left for St. Paul, to be used as a temporary pay car on the Eastern Division. At year's end, cars of an entire passenger train rolled out of the paint shop, to be run as one train. They were painted bright yellow, very much the pride of the shops, and were lettered *Chicago, St. Paul, Minneapolis & Omaha*.

Sioux City, Iowa, was once known as the "steamboat capital of the upper Missouri River." In this waterfront scene from Second and Pearl Streets circa 1870, the steamers *Zephyr* (far right) and *North Alabama* keep company with two unidentified vessels at the busy steamboat dock. Sioux City entrepreneurs, benefited by the Black Hills gold rush, worked the provisioning trade well up the river during 1868-1875. The town was also an important river ferry transfer point between Iowa railroads and lines in Nebraska prior to building a permanent railroad bridge. *Sioux City Public Museum.*

(Above) Four-year-old F-5 No. 266 is ready to depart Great Northern's original Minneapolis Union Station in 1896 with Train 4, the *Badger State Express*, for Chicago. The 67" drivered Schenectady products were the first series of fast passenger 4-6-0s on the Omaha Road. The Ten-Wheeler was retired in December 1928. *National Railroad Museum.* (Below) E-3 Class No. 94 was a one-of-a-kind 1883 Baldwin, shown in St. Paul shortly after delivery. The 57" drivered engine was retired in 1926. *Robert H. Graham Collection.*

(Above) The St. Paul & Sioux City roundhouse and machine shop at Shakopee, Minnesota, depicted about 1875, were considered "temporary" until more permanent facilities could be constructed elsewhere. StP&SC completed its new locomotive shops in St. Paul near Western Avenue in 1880. StP&SC was subsequently conveyed to the Omaha and the shops became a primary operation. (Below) Shop transfer engines found work making roundhouse movements with dead locomotives. Shown on the St. Paul Shops turntable, 0-4-0T shop goat No. X-0 (1st) was built by Grant in August 1869. Formerly engine No. 233, it was scrapped in 1910. Both: *Minnesota Historical Society*.

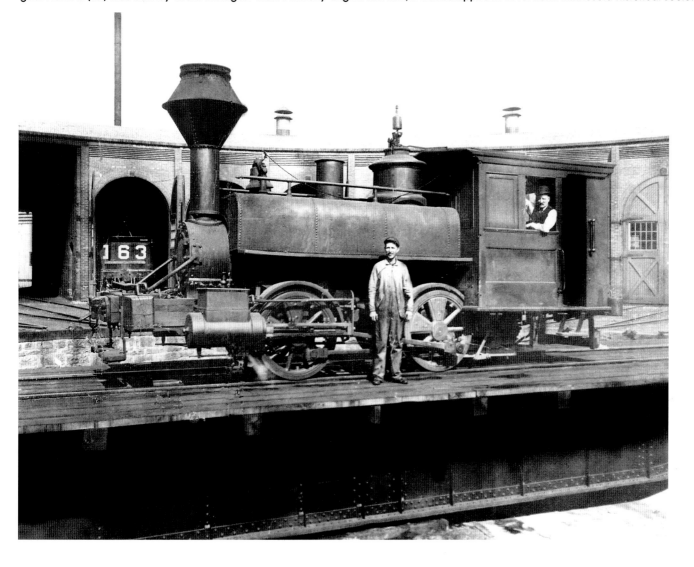

St. Paul in the 1860s served as a junction between Mississippi River traffic and newly constructed railroads. At center is the depot of James J. Hill, entrepreneur and promoter of Great Northern Railway's ancestor. At left is the freighthouse of LaCrosse & Milwaukee Railroad, tied to end-of-track at La Crosse and a steamer monopoly. Nearby, the region's first locomotives and cars were unloaded from steamers scant years before, some for St. Paul & Sioux City predecessor Minnesota Valley Railroad (trackage would be to the right, out of view). This photo is looking eastward toward Dayton's Bluff from present day Robert Street. *Minnesota Historical Society.*

# 3.
# OMAHA IN THE EIGHTIES

West Wisconsin Railway's bankruptcy sale was held in Madison, Wisconsin, on March 1, 1878, where Henry Hedge Porter, David Dows and Walston H. Brown purchased the property. A reorganization plan was published May 2, and the road was conveyed to Chicago, St. Paul & Minneapolis Railway Company, a Wisconsin corporation, organized April 30, 1878. CStP&M's directorate included Porter, Dows, Spooner and others of the C&NW group interested in the marriage of Omaha Road to the North Western... the "radical faction." Porter, Dows and Brown owned outright or represented a majority of security holders of the defunct WW, and were allied with this faction. Philetus Sawyer was also tied to the CStP&M, with distinct interests in the land grant forests.

Porter was another "State-of-Mainer" by birth, coming west to Chicago in 1853. He found a position as a clerk in the young Galena & Chicago Union Railroad, the seminal line of C&NW. He rose in the hierarchy, then shifted to another road, finally entering Chicago business as a financier. A partner of Michigan lumber baron Jessie Spaulding after the Civil War, Porter sold his interest to Philetus Sawyer. Sawyer and Porter were experienced in timberland dealings, and they joined the cadre concentrating on the fruits of the St. Croix Land Grant.

Porter and Chicago banker Samuel M. Nickerson invested in Michigan timberlands and, by 1869, Porter became a director of the First National Bank of Chicago and of the Chicago & Rock Island Railroad. In C&RI, Porter was to associate himself with John F. Tracy and Ransom R. Cable of Rock Island, Illinois, on the eve of the Great Chicago Fire and the Pestigo Fire (Pestigo is 42 miles north of Green Bay). Both events destroyed some of Porter's investments, who was also seriously affected by the 1873 Panic, normalized by 1878, the year Porter and associates bought the West Wisconsin and North Wisconsin railroads.

According to Porter's biography, he and Sawyer were involved in purchasing the Wisconsin Farm Mortgage Company, which held interlocking parcels and claims interfering with the Omaha Road land grant in 1880. They resold their claims to operating lumbermen over the next five years at ten times the original cost. Porter went on to speculate in competing railroads, such as the St. Paul & Duluth (the reorganized Lake Superior & Mississippi). He and his associates doubled their money in the purchase of Minneapolis & St. Louis Railroad. Steel mills, coal, railroads, iron ore lands, mines and lake boat repair yards were investments found in Porter's 1880 portfolio.

Porter's other associates in the Omaha Road and the North Western were people like Roswell P. Flower, New York member of Congress, later Governor of New York, and a Wall Street magnate. John Tracy was President of the Rock Island and a C&NW

Director in the 1870s. Dows was a New York banker and a broker of considerable means. William H. Ferry moved up through banking circles and was G&CU President in the 1860s and, by 1874, was receiver of the West Wisconsin. Ferry died in 1880, leaving CStP&M's Presidency in mid-1878. Henry Porter then succeeded him, helping to pilot the company through difficult times to consolidation. CStP&M reiterated its traffic agreement of April 27, 1876 (with the WW), to be binding until May 1, 1918. Trackage rights agreements around Hudson were also continued.

Creation of Minneapolis Eastern Railway Company was a direct result of CStP&M and Milwaukee Road's interest in penetrating the Minneapolis milling district. Rapid development of flour milling on the properties of Washburn-owned Minneapolis Mill Company gave an edge to Minneapolis & St. Louis as the exclusive carrier; M&StL was Washburn-controlled too. ME's first President was J.R. Bassett. Initially, ME was to build and operate a line from Minneapolis to St. Paul, connecting with other carriers and mills. Actual trackage never exceeded a flour and grain terminal road, but it succeeded in gaining access to Washburn's property. ME was incorporated October 25, 1878, and possessed 1.78 mainline miles and 2.3 miles of sidings. By 1952, ME had 3.5 track miles, and operated ex-Omaha M-1 Class 0-6-0 switchers.

The St. Paul Union Depot Company was organized in 1879 to provide and maintain a facility for all the city's railroads. Tenants included: Milwaukee Road; St. Paul & Sioux City; St. Paul, Minneapolis & Manitoba; St. Paul & Duluth; Northern Pacific; StPS&TF; and CStP&M. The incorporators were each road's General Managers, including Frank B. Clarke for the CStP&M. In 1940, the list of roads entering and sharing the great station were Milwaukee Road; Great Northern; Northern Pacific; CB&Q; Soo Line; Chicago Great Western; Rock Island; and Omaha Road.

The elaborate layer cake of the Omaha Road began to take shape in spring 1880. The Directors met in New York City April 16, and John C. Spooner, General Counsel for the new company, presented a draft of the Articles of Consolidation. It provided for merger of the CStP&M and NW companies, an action unanimously adopted. Previously, on March 3, Elias F. Drake, John Merriam and Amherst Wilder of St. Paul, were elected Directors of CStP&M at a Hudson meeting. Of significance was the election of Philetus Sawyer to fill the Vice-President's post, succeeding W.H. Ferry. A month later, on May 25, 1880, consolidation took place and Chicago, St. Paul, Minneapolis & Omaha Railway Company was formed. Porter, Drake and Wilder had brought the StP&SC into the new organization March 1, 1880, an act the Hudson newspaper referred to as "triunification." On April 12, 1879, the North Wisconsin had reorganized and held a director's election, at which time Jacob Humbird and Henry Porter held a majority of its stock. After the new ownership of North Wisconsin rearranged financing, it was extended northward to Cumberland, toward significant forest lands coveted by the Porter-Humbird-Sawyer group. Tracklaying halted for the winter in December 1869, just beyond Chandler. One source indicated that Philetus Sawyer owned one-fourth of NW's stock, becoming its president for its important years of construction. Sawyer's eyes were very much on the excellent stand of white pine in the grant, the largest and most valuable publicly owned land in Wisconsin. Other railroads were interested in it too, namely: Wisconsin Central; Chicago, Milwaukee & St. Paul; and Milwaukee, Lake Shore & Western. CM&StP (Milwaukee Road) masterminded the Chippewa Valley & Superior Railway to run from the Mississippi Valley to Lake Superior. Eau Claire lumbermen like Jim Thorp were involved, as well as New York philanthropist Ezra Cornell, whose land holdings lay adjacent to the St. Croix grant. The group exemplified the combinations of ambitious men, native and distant capitalist alike, attracted to Wisconsin's northern forestland. CV&S was built in 1882 as a CM&StP holding from Reed's Landing, Minnesota, and operated over a pontoon bridge across the Mississippi River.

Philetus Sawyer (1816-1900) mixed lumbering and politics at an opportune time in Wisconsin, with his investments centered around Oshkosh. He entered the state and national government to ensure his own best interest (logging) by spearheading improvements in local waterways, paving the way for prosperity in eastern Wisconsin lumbering. From a humble, hard beginning, Sawyer rose to power and influence in the Republican Party, serving from 1865 to 1893 in Madison and Washington. The firm of P. Sawyer & Son was a leading Oshkosh mill, producing over 5,000,000 feet of lumber in 1862. Sawyer's Chicago outlet was through William O. Goodman, later Sawyer's son-in-law. Together, they forged Sawyer-Goodman Lumber Company (in 1880). Their saw mills in Marinette, Wisconsin, churned out some 30,000,000 feet per year, supporting Chicago retail dimension yards, daily loading 50 cars for the western trade. Sawyer's next arena was to be the St. Croix pineries.

The formation of CStP&M required expansion of its securities. The foreclosure of WW was bid in at $1,500,000 in accord with a reorganization plan, the deed delivered May 2, 1878. Among other steps, a 999 year lease covered the Hudson swing bridge, with CStP&M being required to maintain it, together with an annual rental for the mainline from the bridge to Stillwater Junction (later Siegel). Temporary arrangements assisted the road in regaining financial strength.

CStP&M's capital stock was $5,000,000 with $1,000,000 in preferred. As merger took place many small construction company names disappeared into the main body of completed lines. More were to come as the road built new branches and improved its physical plant, assisting trackside industries.

Consolidation also spelled new equipment purchases after the 1870s to supplant overworked rolling stock. Twenty-three engines arrived for the "west side," seven of them Baldwins built in 1880. The order covered the last power for StP&SC (No. 62, renumbered to CStPM&O No. 262), and terminated orders for Taunton locomotives. Sioux City's shops built several types of cars while receiving 100 new box cars from an outside source. Repairs on

"bad order" cars were speeded, and 6,000 tons of steel rail arrived. The acute engine shortage kept loaded cars from reaching their destinations, leaving the cuts of cars standing on sidings. The road went from feeble motion in the 1870s to a burst of activity in 1880.

Construction of new lines in 1880 reflected interest in expanding business along existing routes. The initial thrust of Black River Railroad Company was only 4.5 miles toward Neillsville from Merrillan, Wisconsin, on the Eastern Division mainline. BR was organized March 2, 1878 to build northeasterly to the Clark County seat. Original officers were locals, including Milwaukee land speculator James L. Gates. The original company was unsuccessful, and on November 27, 1880, Black River's franchise was purchased by the Omaha Road. It wasn't until 1890-91 that the Omaha extended the line another 22 miles to Marshfield and a connection with Milwaukee, Lake Shore & Western Railway (MLS&W became C&NW property on August 19, 1893). The Marshfield extension, incorporated as Neillsville & North Eastern Railway Company, was also sold to the Omaha on April 22, 1884. This company possessed some right-of-way, but performed no construction work, and was conveyed to the Omaha for $1. Two other Eastern Division branches were the result of major sawmills and their owners desire for rail connections. The Menomonie Railway Company was incorporated April 8, 1879, to serve the city of Menomonie, Wisconsin, and the Knapp, Stout & Company milling district. MR was a three mile long access road following the Red Cedar River's west bank. Some of the branch right-of-way was on KS&Co land, and the lumber firm settled for a cash adjustment. Officers of the original road were locals, "Captain" William Wilson of the lumber company prominent among them. KS&Co was consolidating its Red Cedar Valley holdings and, in 1882, began work on the Cedar Falls & Northern Railway Company, duly incorporated September 22, 1881. CF&N was a 2-1/2 mile road connecting Cedar Falls Manufacturing Company, a new acquisition of KS&Co at Cedar Falls, north of the Omaha mainline and the city of Menomonie. The Omaha bought the road at a cost of about $20,000.

Knapp, Stout & Company closed out their operations and the CF&N was abandoned in 1902, the same year CM&StP removed its 4.3 mile connection to the mill site. Today, a large dam is located at Cedar Falls. West of Menomonie's rail yards, an extensive brickmaking industry, Wisconsin Pressed Brick Company, flourished for many years as an important on-line business. Menomonie Railway Company was conveyed to the Omaha on June 3, 1893, after ownership by CF&N for 10 years.

Another strategic short line built in the Omaha's interests was Eau Claire Railway Company, a circuitous route to Shawtown, having steep grades and sharp curves down to the river level south of the city, to the mills clustered about Half Moon Lake. ECRy was brought forth June 23, 1879, to operate formally within the city, from West Eau Claire's depot. Cost was $30,000 when transferred to CStP&M in 1880. A special ordinance was required as the line crossed many streets. It was all in R.F. Wilson's addition to the city, the 6th Ward. A contract was made to handle lumber and freight to the junction with CStP&M at $1 per car, the agreement to run ten years. A second contract between H.H. Porter and ECRy had the 2.7 mile line ready for use in six months, complete

(Above) The original St. Paul Union Depot served all of the major railroads entering the city. (Right) Omaha Road's city ticket office was located in the Nicolet Hotel. Advertised service was nearly overwhelming. Both: *State Historical Society of Wisconsin.*

with customers. This was vital, as within three years CM&StP (Milwaukee Road) arrived in Eau Claire via Shawtown to share the trade. ECRy was executed by prominent names in Eau Claire logging circles, including Orrin Ingram, W.A. Rust and S.W. McCaslin. ECRy was conveyed to the Omaha on June 3, 1893.

In the spring of 1880, Chicago, St. Paul & Minneapolis, through its top investors, secured 40,000 shares (controlling interest) in St. Paul & Sioux City Railroad, soon to be the Western Division of the Omaha. At this time, the St. Paul Shops served the road's west side, and plans were made for similar facilities in the Eau Claire area. In a time of single management for the property, CStP&M also planned replacements for its major bridges over the Eau Claire, Chippewa and Red Cedar Rivers. The list of needed improvements from 1879 pointed up the need to lessen the steep summit grade near Hersey, Wisconsin, and to widen the final cut at Wilson. It was the first of several similar episodes on the "Mountain Division" between Knapp and Baldwin.

Another need was to fill trestlework between the St. Croix River swing span and the Wisconsin shore. The 1879 summer brought a contract for starting on the right-of-way west of the

(Above) Omaha predecessor St. Paul & Sioux City located its main locomotive repair facility two miles west of St. Paul Union Depot on the Mississippi's north bank. Known as "St. Paul Shops," the 1880 facility included a 20 stall roundhouse. Ten stalls were added in 1887, with the final ten stalls added in 1892, completing a full circle (the roundhouse is behind and left of the water tank). In the foreground is the joint Milwaukee Road-Omaha bridge. An Omaha passenger train has just whistled for closure of the swing span before proceeding to Union Depot. (Below) The tower at Cliff regulated the ancient shared trackage agreement between the Omaha and Milwaukee Road, dating back to Minnesota Valley/Minnesota Central days. This route was Milwaukee's first entry into St. Paul, in 1866. The Omaha train is powered by F-8 No. 259 in 1921. Both: *Minnesota Historical Society*.

Chippewa River's new bridge. Another 200 miles of steel rail was to be laid, with ballasting proceeding apace over the entire road. Black River's wood span was rebuilt in 1878, and the new Red Cedar and Chippewa spans were completed by 1881.

Eau Claire in summer 1879, looked to a promise of new, fast-train service and a notable new station. H.H. Porter's new organization took hold of a weary property and strengthened it with better train service. One town suffered though, as the new "Limited" no longer stopped at Baldwin's eating house, a decade-old custom. Chicago-St. Paul fare was $14.00, a drop in price. A year later, a Day Express and a Night Express graced Omaha's rails, both ways, every day. The Day Express left St. Paul at 1:35 PM, arriving in the Windy City the next day at 7:00 AM, with one hour removed from the previous schedule. It was rumored that a new St. Paul-Black River Falls turnaround would connect with Green Bay & Minnesota Train 2 at Merrillan, due at 10:25 AM, and again with GB&M Train 1 in the afternoon.

The Chippewa River iron bridge renewal was announced August 21, 1879. Five piers and two abutments were to be made of Mankato-quarried stone, after assessments were made of stone around Wilson, and of quarry stock at Winona, Minnesota. The four spans were 180 feet long each, with two 90 foot sections replacing wood trestle work at the ends. Stonework took the most time, as each piece was cut and fitted in the cofferdams on the river bottom. Piers were 17x50 feet at the bottom, tapering to 17x25 feet, and measuring 54 feet high in the tallest example. Mr. Porter and entourage arrived in September 1879 to view the work, two months before the bridge iron began to arrive. It was completed in May 1881, with the customary testing procedure. The veteran "tech reps" of Lehigh Bridge & Iron Works, Rochester, NY, watched as three of the heaviest engines drawing a train of flat cars eased onto the structure. Each flat car had a load of moist earth aboard, and the train stretched the bridge with 205 tons on each span. The same process was repeated on the Eau Claire River bridge, several miles away, beginning in mid-June 1881.

The Eau Claire River bridge also replaced a wood unit with a four-span feature on Mankato stone piers, having two 80 foot and two 150 foot spans, also built by the Rochester firm. This span eliminated a difficult set of curves and grades built in 1870. Parts of the original grade are visible today, leading away from Altoona, the Eastern Division's major division point.

Altoona's beginnings were nearly those of Fall Creek, some 8.8 miles farther east. Fall Creek is located 96 miles from Elroy and from Minneapolis, but Eau Claire prevailed in harboring this first division point. Space in Eau Claire was limited, adequate chiefly for the city's depot. As early as July 1879, a mayoral committee from Eau Claire met with CStP&M officials regarding the large terminal. Messrs. Porter, Ferry and Winters, plus the Chief Engineer, met with various land and lumber barons to determine an acceptable site. Eau Claire was finding that the railroad contributed considerably to its prosperity, as employees traded and settled in the city. It saw the move to Fall Creek as undesirable, but argued that such industry would be better found outside the city limits. Fall Creek extended free land much as modern cities do to attract industry. Eau Claire countered by offering $1,000, stipulating that the general shops be located on the land, to be four miles or less from Eau Claire's depot. Thus, near a small station

called Sunnyside, on level and spacious grounds, Altoona, Wisconsin, was established.

Altoona was at first renamed East Eau Claire, but billing mistakes prompted a change, and the Pennsylvania name prevailed. The yard itself would be 6,000 feet long and 350 to 700 feet wide. In time, a 20 stall roundhouse would be the centerpiece. The new and final name dates to 1882, just as the work was completed. Altoona aided extension of the Chippewa Falls & Northern Railway Company, Omaha's direct connection between Eau Claire and the Lakehead. Over $3,500,000 was expended in 1882 for major yard construction at Altoona and Elroy (roundhouses included), with additional buildings at St. Paul Shops, together with new structures and grounds obtained at both East and West Minneapolis yard locations. William Babbington piloted the first westbound Altoona-St. Paul train out of the new yard on May 13, 1882. He also operated new Baldwin engine No. 48, a D-4 Class 4-4-0 onto Altoona's turntable on October 2, 1882. Babbington was a pioneer railroader who retired in 1912.

Chippewa Falls & Northern was arranged to operate from Chippewa Falls to the Chicago Junction wye just south of Spooner. It built 14.5 miles from Chippewa Falls to Bloomer in 1881, and was conveyed to the Omaha Road on February 13, 1882. In the same year, CF&N pushed 37 more miles from Bloomer to Haugen, and finished to Chicago Junction in 1883.

Upon completion of the line to Superior, the Omaha chose to construct its own road between Chippewa Falls and Eau Claire, alongside locally-built Chippewa Falls & Western Railway, in operation since 1874. Eventually to become the property of Wisconsin Central, CF&W was the brainchild of Thaddeus C. Pound, another transplanted Pennsylvanian, who came to Chippewa Falls in 1856, advanced to President of Union Lumber Company in the city, and entered "logger's politics" by 1864. Aimed northward, CF&W and Pound had the land grant in mind. The building of CF&W had Wisconsin Central varnish running on the Omaha Road to St. Paul (until late 1884), the trains turned over to Omaha crews. In turn, Omaha got rights to Chippewa Falls and a temporary connection to its own new construction north of the city. Thus, Omaha served Chippewa Falls and its mills during the lean years of the 1870s, but didn't buy the route. Finally, when financial strength was adequate, Omaha formed the Eau Claire & Chippewa Falls Railway Company, 10.5 miles long, between the two rival cities and put together its own line.

Beginning in the 1850s, with a scheme to connect Chicago with the Lakehead and the eastern end of the Northern Pacific, the original Wisconsin Central was able to grade portions of its line in Wisconsin. After 1857, it became Chicago & Northern Pacific Air Line Railway, and finally, Chicago, Portage & Superior on June 10, 1874. CP&S was actively engaged in competing for the prize of the land grant and 250,000 of its acres, allegedly worth $5,000,000. Air Line president A.A. Jackson of Janesville and A.B. Schofield of New York were among its principals, but progress was spotty. In April 1881, Jackson had engineers in the field surveying to a point called Veazie (near today's Trego) from Superior in a dead heat with Omaha forces. CP&S had the grant, but Omaha's land and lumber barons were intent on its capture.

The Air Line had several problems to face when it contracted to build its first 65 miles from Superior, not the least of which was

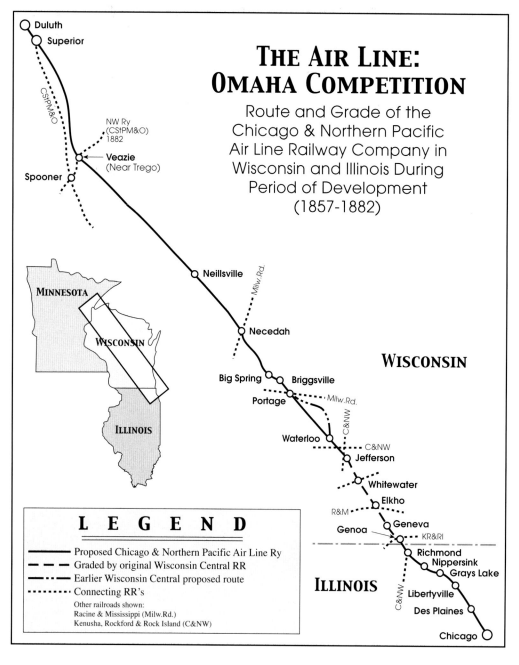

# THE AIR LINE: OMAHA COMPETITION

Route and Grade of the Chicago & Northern Pacific Air Line Railway Company in Wisconsin and Illinois During Period of Development (1857-1882)

**WISCONSIN**

**ILLINOIS**

**MINNESOTA**

**WISCONSIN**

**ILLINOIS**

## L E G E N D

———————— Proposed Chicago & Northern Pacific Air Line Ry
– – – – – Graded by original Wisconsin Central RR
–·–·–·– Earlier Wisconsin Central proposed route
·········· Connecting RR's

Other railroads shown:
Racine & Mississippi (Milw.Rd.)
Kenusha, Rockford & Rock Island (C&NW)

*Map labels: Duluth, Superior, CStPM&O, NW Ry (CStPM&O) 1882, Veazie (Near Trego), Spooner, Neillsville, Milw.Rd., Necedah, Big Spring, Briggsville, Portage, Milw.Rd., Waterloo, C&NW, C&NW, Jefferson, Whitewater, Elkho, R&M, Genoa, Geneva, KR&RI, Richmond, Nippersink, Grays Lake, Libertyville, C&NW, Des Plaines, Chicago*

de facto existence of the Omaha at Chandler and Trego. Omaha supplied its advancing railheads from St. Paul and Hudson, while the Air Line relied upon the port of Superior and the lakes, a distinct shortcoming. Air Line contractor Horace G. Angle immediately advertised for 2,000 men. New Yorker Angle had a deadline of May 9, 1882, and extension beyond the original date set by the state legislature for bestowal of the coveted land grant, the contractor's paycheck. The work went on feverishly, with the Omaha construction mostly paralleling and, in many instances, crossing the Air Line grade in the latter half of 1881. Omaha forces also worked southeastward from Superior, and in autumn completed crossing the Amnicon River on a 700 foot bridge.

Milwaukee Road historically attempted to land the great prize, and in 1881 joined the Omaha to take the grant away from the Air Line. Lawyer John C. Spooner worked in Madison to revoke the CP&S grant. He succeeded in raising sufficient doubt that Omaha's opponent would finish on time, and on January 10, 1882, entered into a contract with the Milwaukee, in which the latter received one-quarter of the land grant and trackage rights to

Superior. Spooner approached the Air Line to buy $2,000,000 of the ailing company's stock for $200,000. A.A. Jackson agreed to sell out, but the action left the contractor high and dry. Labor riots occurred along the Air Line's grades, as workers faced the loss of jobs deep in the woods. An answer came from Governor Rusk in the form of militia suppression of lawlessness, but editors and onlookers favored relief for the beleaguered graders. In the end, Omaha prevailed, and the sputtering dream of the Air Line nearly faded away, save for lawsuits.

After the fall of the Air Line, the Milwaukee-Omaha pact was broken, and the former sued. Litigation continued into the 1890s, but a Milwaukee sponsored northward thrust was to compete in Eau Claire and Chippewa Falls as a result. Milwaukee reached Duluth in 1900 over NP trackage rights.

Completion to the Lakehead at Bayfield and Superior opened the Omaha to eastern connections in 1883-1884, linking St. Paul with both ports and the Eastern Division. At trackside, the business was logging, and mills began to rise along the old North Wisconsin at nearly every town. North of New Richmond, home of John Glover's Willow River Lumber Company, lumbermen lost little time installing sizable mills and acquiring a timber supply. Clayton had a new 60,000 foot capacity operation. Turtle Lake was host to S.F. Richardson's operation. Cumberland had a large works, on a nearby island, run by Griggs & Foster. Barronett was another, financed by old line Mississippi River lumberman Chancy Lamb, with Eau Claire's D.R. Moon and W.A. Rust. In 1881, the same group established Shell Lake Lumber Company, six miles south of Spooner, with Lafayette Lamb as president. SLLCo saw the need for a pioneer narrow gauge line to bring in its logs. Both Barronett and Shell Lake had Frederick Weyerhaeuser and F.C.A. Denkmann as investors, along with the Joyce family of Lyons, Iowa. Southbound Omaha log extras supplied these operations until many of them moved farther north into timberlands closer to Lake Superior.

The city of Superior was a product of the booming 1850s, which breathed life into many northern towns. The prospects of Superior and Duluth increased with the opening of the locks at Sault Ste. Marie and access to the lower Great Lakes. The two rival towns were the farthest west of the lake ports and looked to railroads for inland commerce. Duluth's first railroad was Lake Superior & Mississippi, ironically having investors later interested in the Omaha Road. Jay Cooke, a prominent Philadelphia financier was an early Duluth developer. Superior-Chicago commerce developed by lake steamer in 1856, while Omaha's prospects for rail trade came after it pushed into Superior in late 1882. Omaha Road's grand excursion to Superior was held June 7, 1883, a round trip from Eau Claire and St. Paul, complete with steamboat rides to Duluth. Dinner was served overlooking the bay, a full view of the cities guaranteed. But when regular service began, Omaha's conductors faced a 172 mile run each work day.

As the Omaha worked to complete its system, several accidents occurred in 1880-82 at Hudson. A North Wisconsin train broke in two on the steep approach to the St. Croix bridge in July 1880. Conductor John Cosgrave and his brakemen were separated from engineer John Drummond and fireman Dennis Curley, who plunged toward the open drawbridge. The engine and nine cars rolled off the approach onto a log raft which happened to be passing through the draw at the moment. The raft was destroyed, and the entire train and 40 ton engine went into 30 feet of water. The train wreck narrowly missed the towboat *Silver Lake*. Curley and Drummond jumped beforehand. It required two barges equipped with derricks to raise the engine between them, finally lashed between the barges and beached at Hudson.

In February 1881, heavy snows stalled Omaha service in St. Croix County east of Hudson. A four engine team muscled a snowplow through to the stalled *Night Express* between Roberts and Hammond. Cuts drifted shut immediately after clearance, the blockade lasting many days. Snow reached depths of 15 feet, and firewood was scarce. It was an extension of the four day blizzard experienced west of St. Paul. The battle was won, only to become a surging flood in 1881s spring.

Twelve months after the St. Croix bridge wreck, it was Isiah Trider's fate to be called to duty at Hudson. On a Sunday morning in July 1881, a "wild" freight (extra) went on duty at North Hudson with two locomotives and 43 cars eastbound. Engineers

Mike Sullivan and Webb Griffith eased their engines into motion, up the curving, climbing line out of North Hudson toward Northline shortly after 9:00 AM. The flour-laden extra paused on the flats 4-1/2 miles east of Hudson to wood up, leaving the train's rear unprotected, as all were engaged in loading tenders with wood. Conductor Frank Fowler was anxious to reach Roberts, 6-1/2 miles farther, to meet an opposing train. Handbrakes hadn't been set and somehow a coupler link snapped.

(Above) Early coal chutes were formidable structures. Omaha D-11 Class 0-6-0 No. 187 is dwarfed by the Altoona facility. (Below) The 1881 roundhouse at Altoona is shown about 1909. I-2 Class 4-6-2 No. 382 rolls onto the short turntable, soon to be inadequate as newer, larger power arrived. Both: *Author's Collection.*

Then, 14 cars plus a caboose began to roll quietly away from the train, headed downgrade, a hill of 80 feet to the mile. The defection went unnoticed for several critical moments.

Discovery came belatedly; the horrified extra crew set out the balance of the train and pursued the runaway cars. It was impossible to stop them. Northline's operator telegraphed Hudson of the peril when the runaway passed his station, but Hudson's agent was not at his telegraph key (St. Paul's man was). The speeding cars reached the Lake Mallilieu high bridge, and there they were seen by a waiting second extra, standing at the North Hudson depot, with 45 cars and Baldwin 4-4-0s Nos. 2 and 30. As whistles blew and crewmen scattered, the runaway smashed into the standing engines, and poor Isiah Trider, who stuck to his engine.

Trider, a Nova Scotian, tried to back his engine out of harm's way. He paid for his perseverance with his life, attempting at last to jump from the cab window just as the wreck engulfed him. Flour and dust hung in the summer air, mixed with steam from the broken engines. The still-moving mass of wreckage finally plunged through a small trestle over the Willow River's mouth, opposite the Comstock Mill. Trider's family resided in Nova Scotia, the engineer coming west a year before, to work for another road with his son. He had been on the Omaha, among many Irishmen there, for only two months.

To resume service, sluice gates on the Willow River were opened to lower 17 feet of water over the wreckage. Temporary track was attached to the mill siding as a "shoo-fly" to reopen the mainline. It had been a very costly Sunday.

Later in 1881, an extensive project was underway to alter Hudson Hill and the great loop to the site of Trider's death. The westbound descending grade was made to drop more directly toward Hudson's station, requiring extensive rock-cutting and the elimination of the great trestle over Lake Mallilieu. The new grade, Hudson to Northline, averaged just over 1%, but it cut off North Hudson from the mainline. Hudson's newspaper condemned the great trestle as an eyesore, the larger town now relieved of its northside competition. The River Falls train could now run into St. Paul without long delays at North Hudson, which had been a traditional stop since Daniel Baldwin's time. The date of changeover was October 13, 1881.

Shortly after arrival in Superior, the Omaha Road organized Superior Short Line Railway Company, incorporated in February 1884. SSL constructed 6.30 miles from SSL Junction to West Superior, plus branches at West Superior and Conner's Point (SSL owned no equipment). The Omaha operated the line as part of its own system, together with the Superior Street Line and the Connor's Point Extension. Superior Short Line Railway Company of Minnesota was incorporated on September 19, 1885. The object was to maintain a connection with the St. Paul & Duluth Railroad in downtown Duluth. The two Short Lines were consolidated May 13, 1895, then sold to the Omaha on August 1, 1895. Omaha gained direct access to their Rice's Point yard, beginning in July 1885, by using Northern Pacific's St. Louis River drawbridge, built through a February 27, 1873 Congressional grant.

Two transfer railway companies were formed in 1883. The Lake Superior Terminal & Transfer Railway Company in Superior, and Minnesota Transfer Railway Company in the Twin Cities. LST&T was organized to operate within Douglas County, Wisconsin, as a transfer road. Incorporated October 17, 1883, LST&T ownership was divided between: St. Paul, Minneapolis & Manitoba (GN in 1890); Northern Pacific; Eastern Railway of Minnesota (a GN affiliate); St. Paul & Duluth; Duluth, South Shore & Atlantic; and the Omaha. Minnesota Transfer Railway was organized to operate in Ramsay, Hennepin and Anoka Counties of Minnesota. It was a product of J.J. Hill, S.S. Merrill, E.W. Winter, Herman Haupt and W.H. Truesdale (StPM&M, CM&StP, Omaha, NP and M&StL Officers respectively). The two transfer companies worked to centralize carloadings passing through local bottlenecks.

The Ellsworth extension in Wisconsin was 13 miles beyond River Falls and came in 1885. The original law of 1874 called for the North Wisconsin to build its line to Prescott, Wisconsin, or some point on the Mississippi River in Pierce County, Wisconsin. This was altered by the Wisconsin legislature to compromise the destination to be Ellsworth, same county. It was acceptable to the governor, and the extension was put into operation November 9, 1885. Surveyors did their work in the spring of 1885, the earthwork following shortly thereafter.

Concurrent with Omaha's general progress, motive power continued to arrive, chiefly from Baldwin, a few each quarter. Nos. 41 through 100 inclusive were built between November 1880 and March 1886. With some exceptions, most were 4-4-0s. Omaha's first 0-4-0 was regarded as a technical breakthrough by reporting journalists; engine No. 36 had 15 inch cylinders and 48 inch drivers. The successful switcher generated reorders, and Nos. 50-53 inclusive came in October 1881. Another four came in the spring of 1883 (Nos. 90-93), and in 1882, Manchester built two switchers (Nos. 107 and 108) completing factory purchases of the type. Several of the "yard goats" were used at Eau Claire and the yard at Altoona, when the young facility began the work of marshalling Eastern Division carloadings. Altoona frequently dispatched double-headed trains in the heavy traffic brought to the road in the fall of 1882, the passenger trains running with up to eight packed coaches. Riding in the rear coach of one train, eight gentlemen from New York and England were on a pleasure trip to the Rockies, soon to enjoy the Omaha's own hill country west of Eau Claire. A great shipment of Montana stock passed eastward in the same season, and in winter four cars of Black Hills silver bullion (234 bars per car, or 22,750 lbs. each, for a total of 91,000 lbs.) rode the Omaha to Elroy and Chicago.

In the 1880-1883 Omaha Road consolidation period, business, however brisk, came at a cost. Rate wars persisted in driving down revenue no matter the traffic volume. Aggression by the Milwaukee Road in entering NorthWestern's territory (the Omaha included) finally brought about action by the cautious parent of the Omaha. In 1878-79 the counsel of William K. Vanderbilt kept the North Western carefully solvent in boom times. The son of the famed commodore was the NorthWestern's largest stockholder by 1880, and became an Omaha Road securities holder in the same period. Vanderbilt suggested expansion and improvement of existing physical plant together with dividend payment after conditions improved for C&NW. But expansion required more money and, by 1884, the road's debt grew to 125 percent of the 1880 figure. Financing the Omaha Road purchase was done through debentures (a debt without mortgage), while newspapers

(Above) An Omaha F-5 Class Ten-Wheeler, No. 265, rolls the *Badger State Express* eastward across the original Chippewa River iron bridge at Eau Claire, Wisconsin. Built to replace a wooden structure and completed in May 1881, the new bridge consisted of five "Mankato stone" piers and two abutments, with four 180 foot spans and two 90 foot girders at each end. *Gisill Collection.* (Below) The size of the 1881 structure is further exemplified in this view of Omaha F-8 4-4-0 No. 252 eastbound with a six car Limited. *Author's Collection.*

Baldwin 0-4-0 No. 36 was built in July 1879 and received quite a write-up in Eau Claire's newspaper upon arrival. The *Journal* felt that the cutting-edge of technology had arrived with the switcher and its advanced wheel arrangement. Due to the low height of the tender, the backup light was positioned on the cab roof. No. 36 was sold to Hicks Loco & Car Works in 1899. *William O'Gara Collection.*

Omaha 4-4-0 No. 57 arrived from Baldwin in 1881, a D-5 Class that came at the time of the railroad's formation. The polished engine was photographed at Spooner in 1888 with quite a "crew" (including a baby). No. 57 was scrapped in 1913. *State Historical Society of Wisconsin.*

The first 4-6-0s on the roster were 1872 Baldwins, Class C-2 Nos. 17 and 18, built for the West Wisconsin. No. 18 is at St. Paul about 1884, set up for switching duty with a footboard pilot and a tender mounted backup light. *State Historical Society of Wisconsin.*

reported that Vanderbilt had decided upon the Omaha purchase for C&NW in 1882 when visiting St. Paul. Ashland's progressive editor, Sam Fifield, reported that Vanderbilt practically controlled the road, especially when Porter's group sold out their Omaha Road holdings.

The role of the Rock Island in the sale of Omaha reflects the complicated activity of the period. R.R. Cable, H.H. Porter and David Dows held Rock Island securities, while William Vanderbilt held Union Pacific, Rock Island, C&NW and Burlington stock. Cable, a native of Rock Island, Illinois, was identified with Rock Island railroad almost from the beginning. In 1883 he became President of RI. New Yorker Dows was a director of RI and the Omaha when C&NW acquired a majority interest in Omaha Road stock. Porter, Dows and John Tracy were associated with RI when Tracy was its president until the early 1870s, and also possessed substantial C&NW holdings.

C&NW conservatism in not acquiring the Omaha in the 1870s (as H.H. Porter had counseled) was to cost dearly. The Porter group's building of the Omaha sale was packaged to attract the highest bidder or the railroad most likely to be damaged by its sale. At the same time (early 1882) the Rock Island was working to perfect its Twin Cities entrance. The linkage included Burlington, Cedar Rapids & Northern, and Minneapolis & St. Louis, reaching from West Liberty, Iowa, to Minneapolis over "The Albert Lea Route." The Omaha steered much of its wheat traffic to the Rock Island via this route, instead of delivering it to the C&NW at Elroy, Wisconsin. This act reinforced the collective desire to sell the Omaha Road to C&NW at a handsome profit.

The roughness of the old West Wisconsin showed through the new facade during the 1880s. In summer of 1879, Baldwin 4-4-0 No. 27 ran through an open switch with nine cars at Fall Creek. The engine was later sold to John Humbird's White River Lumber Company ( Mason, Wisconsin). The next summer, 25 cars went off when a backing freight got in the way of a following train. One engine was demolished.

Wrecks with snowplowing engines were frequent as the light power often derailed after ramming drifts at speed. On Lakeland Hill (west of the St. Croix), one engine left the track and plunged 100 feet, killing two men. In the hideous 1880-1881 winter, Baldwin 4-4-0s Nos. 41-43 arrived, but on December 30th two engines collided, nearly negating the numbers. No. 43 was the last Chicago, St. Paul & Minneapolis-owned engine; all others came lettered for the final company, CStPM&O.

As a new night express carried perishables over the Eastern Division in 1881, the emigrant trade burgeoned. Hundreds of Manitoba-bound settlers passed through on the Omaha, just as new coaches arrived for Train 1. They were equipped with Baker car heaters. The night trains each received new diners, while in August one L.A. Stiles, Eau Claire agent, absconded with company money. Under cover of a trip to his Humbird home, Stiles passed down to Madison to intercept about $2,000 in a previously shipped trunk. Stealthy Mr. Stiles reached Texas before he was apprehended and returned in mid-September to face the wrath of the Omaha. Company theft didn't end there. That winter two conductors were arrested on government embezzlement charges. Still, accidents continued, especially in the hilly district west of Knapp, where helper and double-the-hill railroading prevailed.

In the late 1880s, plans were drawn up to improve the difficult St. Croix County line with several track relocation projects. In 1882, however, Omaha invested in 60 lb. rail for its mainline from Hudson to Eau Claire, and on the Western Division, from St. Peter to Lake Crystal. This investment may very well have been overseen by H.H. Porter, as he helped develop the Illinois Steel Company, a key rail supplier.

In 1884, the Omaha contributed to another competitor's rise as a rudimentary Soo Line arose at Cameron, Wisconsin, in Barron County. Omaha supplied the new company with ties cut near Cable, while rail was unloaded at the Washburn dock, shipped from Chicago via steamers. In a few years, the small Turtle Lake-Bruce road became a thorn in the Omaha's side, as it competed for Liverpool-bound flour and grain business.

Advertising in the 1880s period had a menu furnished to newspapers for "The Royal Route," touting the finest dining cars in the world for Minneapolis-Chicago service. There were $30,000 Pullman Palace Hotel cars, three of which were named *Duluth*, *Eau Claire* and *Chippewa Falls,* running in 1886's key trains. In March 1886, *Eau Claire* was inspected by the public and press at Eau Claire, together with new coaches and a diner. The great cars were finished in Cherry, outfitted with mirrors and olive brocade seat covers, while Spanish Mahogany prevailed overhead. Brass and nickel shone everywhere in Eau Claire, one of six sleepers with 28 large double berths, equipped with electric bells in smokers and saloons. A special trip was offered on "The Royal Route" to Chicago aboard Eau Claire and cohorts, to experience the evangelist Jones. The new trains moved in quick time, as competition solidified between the Milwaukee, the WC and the North Western Line. One hour was clipped off the schedules over the mainlines, as all knew of the new Chicago, Burlington & Northern water level line under construction. Omaha's overnight *Shore Line Limited* left Minneapolis at 7:00 PM, arriving in Chicago 12 hours later, in studied elegance.

When C&NW built its Mankato & New Ulm Railway, downgrading the older line through Kasota and St. Peter in 1891, a more spacious Mankato depot was required, and Western Division headquarters were moved from St. James to Mankato. Thus, with the new route in place, C&NW and the Omaha could transfer passengers and baggage in the larger town instead of at Kasota. In 1896, the Omaha eliminated its old 4th Street line high above the business district and entered the new station near the Minnesota River. The high line through Mankato's residential district was subject to city ordinances, which governed speeds, and greatly delayed passenger trains. Grade changes were also in store for the long hill westward through Minneopa Park and Cray, a location on the level prairie beyond the Minnesota Valley.

Significant line changes were put into effect in St. Croix County, Wisconsin, also known as the "Mountain Division," beginning in 1889. St. Paul contractor Shepard, Siems & Company began to straighten out the mainline just west of Wilson, working downgrade toward Woodville and Baldwin. The original WW grade was typical in its hurried approach to line completion, but quite adequate for short trains and 25 MPH speeds. Work in 1889 produced a virtually straight descent, averaging 0.5% gradient eastbound from Woodville to Hersey. To this day much of the old grade is intact, except for roadway in

Woodville's village limits. The original line made a 180 degree, then a 90 degree reverse curve, exiting the village westbound and converging with the present line several miles west of town. The original alignment is flanked by an 1889 revision. The final mainline lies alongside, built in 1912-1913.

In 1880, the Omaha contracted with the St. Paul, Minneapolis & Manitoba (GN in 1890) for trackage rights from Westminster Street Switch to GN's old Minneapolis depot on Washington Avenue North. The agreement was to continue for 99 years unless terminated by mutual consent. Omaha's yearly rental was 2-1/2 percent of total evaluation. In 1880, the lines used consisted of single and double track, changed to two main passenger and two main freight tracks from Westminster Street Switch to University Switch. Two tracks from University Switch to Omaha's West Minneapolis Yard, plus several sidings were also utilized. In 1886, another contract was made, amended in 1912, granting the Omaha use of GN's famous Stone Arch Bridge and its passenger tracks from University Switch through Minneapolis Union Station, to a junction with the Omaha at Third Avenue North. Omaha was granted use of five tracks at the depot plus the terminal building itself.

In conjunction with improvements at Baldwin and Hudson, a second track was extended between Westminster Street in St. Paul and Stillwater Junction in 1883. Another addition of double track was completed from Stillwater Junction (later Siegel), to

North Wisconsin Junction (later Northline) in 1886, creating a St. Paul to Northline double track mainline (the St. Croix River drawbridge remained intervolved, or gauntlet, trackage).

Further expansion in Nebraska came in 1886, when Northeastern Nebraska Railroad Company constructed 21 miles northwest from Wayne. In 1890, an additional 21 miles was built from Randolph to Bloomfield as Randolph & Northeastern Nebraska Railroad Company. The two roads were conveyed to the Omaha in 1888 and 1890 respectively.

Another trackage rights agreement was sealed in the case of the Le Mars-Sioux City (Iowa) segment. The paper trail led from Omaha's SC&StP predecessor to Iowa Falls & Sioux City Railway (Illinois Central) and onward, requiring a new document after October 1, 1887. Omaha was thereby a legal tenant of the IF&SC trackage to run its trains the 25 miles between Le Mars and Ninth Street in Sioux City.

Legal incorporation for a Missouri River crossing at Sioux City came in November 1872, when Sioux City Bridge Company was authorized. A charter was granted by an Act of Congress, approved August 15, 1876, with little activity for just over a decade. On June 6, 1887, control of the Sioux City Bridge Company was transferred to C&NW and CStPM&O and construction began. On November 26, 1888, the first train crossed the new bridge, the last span of which was completed on the 20th. Maintenance of the bridge and its approaches was done on behalf

F-2 Class 4-6-0 No. 195 pauses near the coal chute at Milston, Wisconsin, 12 miles east of Black River Falls, with a westbound freight train in the 1890s. Omaha's F-2s came in 1892-1893 from Schenectady and lasted in service into the 1930s. No.195 was retired in 1937. Link and pin couplers are still in use here, but the box cars are AIR BRAKE equipped. *State Historical Society of Wisconsin,*

(Above) An Omaha Road passenger train is posed on the new Black River Falls iron bridge, built to replace an earlier wooden structure. (Below) Omaha I-1 Class 4-6-0 No. 324 crosses the bridge with a freight train headed north toward the sharp curve at the bridge's end. The original West Wisconsin route through Black River Falls was reduced to local traffic when the Omaha completed its 1903 mainline cut-off. The WW line north of town was abandoned in 1912. Both: *Van Schaik; State Historical Society of Wisconsin.*

of SCBCo, with the Omaha and CB&Q holding operating rights over this high crossing. With a substantial new link to its Nebraska lines, the Omaha entered into a long-term agreement with the Blair-owned Fremont, Elkhorn & Missouri Valley Railroad. The "Elkhorn" was given trackage rights between Blair and Omaha, and joint use of the North Omaha terminal. This continued when C&NW acquired FE&MV in 1901.

Omaha appointed a new General Manager on November 16, 1885. Edwin W. Winter had heretofore been Assistant President, appointed by Mr. Porter upon consolidation of the Omaha Road. The old office was abolished at the same time, but Winter remained to fill the GM's position. He was a Vermonter by birth (1846) and came west to Illinois to settle in those expansive times. In 1868-73, he gained experience on Union Pacific construction, finally coming to the West Wisconsin via C&NW at Porter's request. Winter had been General Superintendent of the WW by 1879, in the receivership. Winter would have both Operating and Traffic Departments reporting to him. By July 1896, Winter had moved on to President of Northern Pacific.

Mainline improvements in 1885 ticketed the Black River bridge for replacement. Situated on a sharply curved line opposite the city of Black River Falls, Wisconsin, it was anticipated locally that a line would eventually be built bypassing the city, something of a deflation for the municipal ego. Instead, a new iron bridge was scheduled to replace the wood original. Work began in September 1885, and line changes were made to raise trackage six feet to lessen grades. Reported cost was $25,000. Stonework was actively pushed through October as Chicago steel gangs arrived to erect the new spans alongside the old bridge. The city's depot was moved to accommodate the new alignment.

While the Omaha revised its line at Black River Falls, activity surrounding an iron deposit east of town promised a mining and smelting boom in Jackson County. In 1856, an iron company was formed, known as "the German Company," which raised an iron furnace at New Denamora, just north of Black River Falls. The German immigrants were unsuccessful, and the site was abandoned. The "iron mound" was revived in the mid-1880s, when Ohioan James E. York offered to complete a 50 ton capacity blast furnace costing $30,000. York Iron Company was built at the site, going into blast in late 1885. The charcoal iron operation netted an unimpressive 5 tons of pig iron, at a time of economic recession. The "syndicate of Minneapolis capitalists," backing York, were financially ensnared in legal proceedings, John Humbird allegedly sued the iron makers over contract abrogation. York, which became affiliated with Spring Valley Iron & Ore Company, ceased operation in 1892. Omaha Road built a spur to the site, even supplying a tank loco for local switching.

Concurrently, the Black River Falls Lumber & Iron Company was chartered December 2, 1885 by lumbermen C.A. Goodyear of Tomah, W.T. Price of Black River Falls, and others, with capital stock of $1 million. The road was to build 40 miles eastward to Goodyear's mills, near Mather. The object was to supply the new iron furnace with wood fuel (charcoal). Goodyear's log operation moved northward a decade later (1895).

The 1880s witnessed a general movement of Omaha's offices into St. Paul closer to its shops and operating centers. Hudson, however, remained home to the passenger car fleet, with appro-

priate skills residing there. Omaha's general office in St. Paul was a fire victim on January 18, 1889. Rebuilding brought a new structure, completed the next summer. The building was used until 1917.

Hudson Shops suffered numerous fires, some more serious than others. Nearly all related to paint, varnish and oils, so important to outshopping a coach fleet. Several "editions" of coach and paint shop buildings went up in flames, their vulnerable wood construction forfeited before final brick structures arose. Adventures in heroism on the job took place as men risked their lives to save their smoldering projects, dragged frantically out of the blazing sheds. Omaha lost its pay car this way in the spring of 1886, but two coaches were saved. Craftsmen would have to begin again after fire damage was righted, creating their popular art for the traveling masses. In between the excitement, Hudson's Master Car Builders presided baronially over 85 coaches and 900 freight cars annually. They searched for defects and safety violations, or just plain wear and tear. In 1890, extensive improvements at Hudson cost $200,000 for brick and stone buildings, many of which still stand.

The wood machine shop was 80x300 feet, full of planing mills, special saws and mortising machines for car construction. One end of the shop was devoted to patterns and cabinet making tools. The wheel shop was 80x436 feet, well-lighted by a glazed monitor roof. Another building was an iron and blacksmith shop, where blacksmiths toiled over 17 fires and two steam hammers, while other machines devoted to heating red and white-hot iron into useful shapes. The freight car repair shop was 85x262 feet. The passenger car shop was 109x203 feet. Identical were two paint shops, part of which was a tin shop. Other buildings were used for brass cleaning, upholstery and storage. Two 70 foot transfer tables served the main buildings, the pit for one being 246 feet long. All buildings were steam heated.

John Coit Spooner in the 1880s decade had less time to devote to his family and home in Hudson. He was kept in Madison twelve years, steering the Omaha through its gestation period, appearing as a lobbyist for the road in court over the land and logging affairs. He gained in status and, in January 1885, he was elected to the U.S. Senate. The small (130 lbs.) Senator from Wisconsin replaced Angus Cameron in Washington, and he eventually settled in New York, a close friend of Philetus Sawyer.

In 1890-91, Omaha extended its road from Neillsville to Marshfield, Wisconsin, establishing joint terminals with the Milwaukee, Lake Shore & Western Railway. MLS&W's Rhinelander line reached Marshfield just before the road became a C&NW possession. The Omaha-MLS&W junction united two halves of a pre-merger system, providing a lumber outlet toward the Mississippi and the southwest, away from northern Wisconsin. A junction with the Omaha Road meant that the combined roads could reach Lake Michigan at Manitowoc from St. Paul, competing with the Green Bay Route and Wisconsin Central. MLS&W and Omaha could also supply Marshfield's several mills with raw materials.

In the same region, Omaha acquired Nathaniel Foster's 36.6 mile line from Fairchild to Mondovi, Wisconsin, completed in 1890. Begun as Fairchild & Mississippi River Railway Company and organized in 1885, Foster's road struck out for the river's

The York Iron Works at Black River Falls had an impressive blast furnace and pig iron stock piles. Note the five tall-height Omaha "Charcoal Cars" just behind the standard-height cars at the lower right. The engine may be leased from, or assigned by, the Omaha. *State Historical Society of Wisconsin.*

York Iron Works, an important Omaha customer of the late 1800s, is shown in this high angle view. *State Historical Society of Wisconsin.*

edge and a Chicago, Burlington & Northern connection. Soon reorganized, the new incorporation planned to reach northeast to Rhinelander and a connection with Soo Line (officially, Sault Ste. Marie & Southwestern Railway Company), forged on July 16, 1887. It was evident that Foster found Omaha services in Fairchild less than satisfactory, with oppressive rates on lumber. A route to the Mississippi could open a new southwestward marketing scheme via Winona for his lumber. Reversal of fortune put the Fairchild-Mondovi line in Omaha hands by April 1, 1891, finally conveyed to the Omaha on June 3, 1893.

Nathaniel Foster was no stranger to building timber-hauling railroads. He began logging near Green Bay, migrating to Fairchild in 1876. Foster built the Chicago, Fairchild and Eau Claire River Railroad into his timberland northeast of Fairchild by 1882. This effort was powered by two Porter tank engines. Next, two unusual Dickson Manufacturing Company 0-6-2t locos arrived, named for offspring Willie and Gracie May. Foster's empire covered stores, grist mills, farms and a basic railroad covering his logging requirements. In the late 1890s, the cutover lands were sold to willing immigrant farmers, whose sparse claims hardly made them prosperous. After Foster's trees were gone, he rebuilt the logging road into a comparative airline, christening it Fairchild & North Eastern Railway in 1898. Thereafter, F&NE operated secondhand Omaha Road engines and coaches. The line achieved common carrier status, building to Wisconsin Central at Greenwood, and finally to Owen, 38 miles.

In 1912, Foster furthered his ambitions by building the last common carrier in Wisconsin, the Fairchild & North Eastern extension to Cleghorn, 15 miles south of Eau Claire. The 80 year

old magnate planned to reach the Milwaukee Road at Caryville to settle a territory devoid of railroads. Completion of the extension came just as World War I broke out in Europe, while English settlers clustered around villages Foster hoped would grow steadily. The roller-coaster line required the best of F&NE power in 1914, including an unmatched pair of 2-6-2s in logging weights and dimensions. One was a Lima, the other a Vulcan. One is still operable on a tourist carrier at Laona. The region of the three Foster-built lines never prospered as the F&NE faced very hard times in the 1920s. Reorganized again as the Central Wisconsin Railway, control of the road left Fairchild for Chicago. N.C. Foster died in 1923 at age 89, his commercial empire having long since decayed. By 1928, the Caryville Extension (which halted at Cleghorn) was abandoned, this being the shortest-lived common carrier in Wisconsin. By 1929, Foster's shortlines were memories, just overgrown rights-of-way through the cutover.

A legacy of the Foster empire lasting to the present is the outstanding photography of J. Foster Adams, a relative of N.C. Foster. Adams was responsible for an enduring collection of F&NE and Omaha Road photos, plus local scenes at Fairchild beginning in the 1890s. Adams later lived in rustic manner in Idaho, returning at least once to Fairchild and the Omaha Road in 1922. He became affiliated with Angelus Studios in Portland, Oregon, in 1914, and recorded many more west coast railroad scenes on 8x10 inch glass plates and smaller film negatives. His classic locomotive photos and action scenes represent literally the dawn of railroad enthusiam's union with photography. His proximity to the work of Van Schaik of Black River Falls is unrecorded. They must have known of each other.

Omaha operated 25 miles between Sioux City and LeMars, Iowa, over Illinois Central trackage rights. The IC-Omaha junction at LeMars called for a magnificent depot, now long gone. The sign on the jointly owned Union Depot had raised letters proclaiming, "ILLINOIS CENTRAL - CHICAGO ST. PAUL MINNEAPOLIS AND OMAHA RAILROADS." *Author's Collection.*

Omaha's Missouri River Bridge was opened December 5, 1888 to replace the river ferries between Sioux City, Iowa, and Covington, Nebraska. It was designed by G.S. Morrison and E.L. Corthell. (Above) An Omaha Road passenger train descends the Iowa side approach after crossing the bridge in 1901. Behind the train is the Silberhorn Packing Company, a later location of Armour & Company, and finally, Cudahy Packing Company. The Sioux City Rapid Transit right-of-way parallels the Omaha tracks. *Sioux City Public Museum.* (Left) An Omaha passenger train, with Class E-7 No. 154 on the headend, is just entering Iowa. *State Historical Society of Wisconsin.*

Baldwin delivered fourteen D-4 Class "Eight-Wheelers" in three groups, two engines in 1878 and the others in 1881. The handsome 57" drivered engines had 17" cylinders and weighed 37-1/2 tons with 13,000 lbs. tractive effort. (Above) The left side portrait of No. 65 was taken in 1907, eight years prior to retirement. (Below) Ten D-5s and fourteen D-6s, near duplicates of the D-4s, followed the D-4s onto the roster in 1881-1883. D-6 No. 81 was built in 1882, and was retired in 1910. Both: *J. Foster Adams.*

Twenty-three E-6 Class engines came in four groups from Schenectady in 1886-1888. They had 18" cylinders and 63" drivers, as did the following fourteen E-8s built in 1888. Omaha E-6 No. 130, at Fairchild in 1905, has a snow plow for winter service. The 1886 locomotive was retired in 1927. *J. Foster Adams.*

Baldwin delivered six E-2 Class 4-4-0s in 1882. The speedy and graceful 57" drivered engines were prevalent on the best of the "Limiteds." No. 73 is at Fairchild in April 1906. *J. Foster Adams.*

(Above) Class E-2 No. 74 is posed with the Mondovi local at Fairchild, Wisconsin, about 1905. The Mondovi line was N.C. Foster's first mainline carrier, which soon fell to the Omaha when his concept of a Burlington connection for Fairchild faded. The E-2s made fast work of Trains 269-270 over the 37 mile branch. (Below) Engineer Hennegen, on the ground, and fireman Olsen stand for the camera with Class E-8 No. 161 at Fairchild in September 1903. The 1888 built engine was retired in 1935. Both: *J. Foster Adams*

# Fairchild & North Eastern Railway

Fairchild & North Eastern began in the early 1880s as a logging road in Fairchild, Wisconsin, by Nathaniel Foster. The line ran through Foster's lands in Clark County. After the timber was removed, the road was upgraded to common carrier status, and land was offered to settlers.

(Right) In 1883, two tank-type machines were ordered from Dickson Mfg Co. They were named *Willie* and *Gracie May*, for Foster's children, with the initials of the then current company, Chicago, Fairchild & Eau Claire River Railway, painted on the sides. *Author's Collection.*

(Right) F&NE became a refuge for well-used Omaha rolling stock and several old Taunton 4-4-0s. Ex-Omaha No. 211, F&NE No. 7 was an 1870s survivor sold to the road in 1890. It's shown at Fairchild in May 1902. *Author's Collection.*

(Below) F&NE No. 8, was another Taunton engine, formerly Omaha No. 231 built in 1876, purchased by N.C. Foster in 1898. *J. Foster Adams.*

(Above) The town of Willard was located about midway to Owen, on F&NE's north end. A Czech settlement and a pickle works took root on Foster's cutover land. The depot stood into the 1970s.

(Left) F&NE acquired Taunton 4-4-0 No. 9 from Weyerhaeuser's Hawthorne, Nebagamon & Superior Railroad in 1898. It was built in 1880, previously No. 257 on the Omaha. Both: *Author's Collection.*

F&NE 2-6-2 No. 12 is shown at the Fairchild depot in 1922. By this time, Nathaniel Foster's empire had shriveled to pre-common carrier status, but still had its heaviest engines, Nos. 11 and 12, acquired a decade earlier. No. 12 was later sold to Laona & Northern Railway in Forrest County, where it remains. *J. Foster Adams.*

Mason depot, on the Bayfield line, still exists today as a museum. However, in 1910, an Omaha E-5 Class 4-4-0 No. 122 brought the day local into town, a dozen miles southwest of Chequamegon Bay. *Author's Collection.*

# 4.

# BAYFIELD - FARTHEST NORTH

Bayfield's snug port proved to be shelter from westerly gales, reason enough for its founding. It was named in the original land grant maneuvers of the 1850s, equal to Superior's clout to the west. Bayfield never became as important as Superior, but in neighboring Washburn's eyes, Superior was an arch competitor bent on dominating the lake-rail trade for a century. Washburn flowered as a special inland port for grain and coal, but only for a few bright years.

North Wisconsin Railway built northward to Chequamegon Bay with redoubled purpose. Chief Engineer John W. Remington arrived in Ashland in late August 1880, immediately setting out for Long Lake (later Lake Owen), 40 miles south. NW's end-of-track lay just north of present-day Cable, and Remington's forces were poised to complete the lake connection, to secure a large portion of the land grant. Construction in 1879 followed the Namekagon River's course northeast, away from Superior Junction (later Trego) and past Veazie of Air Line fame. Accomplishments in 1878 included 17.20 miles built from Clayton to Cumberland, named for Jacob Humbird's old Maryland hometown. Chandler was reached in 1879, a railhead shantytown earning bad marks that year as an entertainment center. Chandler today displays evidence of more orderly times, as extensive gravel pits lined Omaha's trackage past the site of bawdiness.

Chandler is several miles north of Spooner, the ace division point on the north end. Spooner began to grow after 1882, in time hosting a 22 stall roundhouse, an extensive yard and office building. Cable next served as the north end of construction in 1880-1881, no less the roughhouse of stories.

Grading became tougher on the edge of forests above Cable. The hilly district required approximately one million yards of earth moved toward the White River Valley, where two 700 foot trestles, 80 and 60 feet high, were built. The steel replacement bridges still stand, trackless in the wilderness, spanning "18 Mile Creek" at Grand View. The line then curved downgrade through Bibon swamp and crossed the White River south of Mason, and continued to Ashland Junction. Omaha reached the Lake Superior watershed seven miles north of Cable and 820 feet above Chequamegon Bay. Rough contracting, performed by Messrs. Rossiter and Brown of La Crosse, continued along the shore of the bay toward Bayfield in late 1882. The chief contractor for the line in Bayfield County was C.C. Smith, another La Crosse railroad builder and maker of several significant Mississippi River crossings. Smith was also responsible for the Ashland Railway Company work, a 4.38 mile Omaha subsidiary between Ashland Junction and Omaha's Ashland station. It was incorporated June 28, 1882, and included a 1.31 mile long waterfront industrial branch reaching docks and lumber mills. It allowed the railroad to use its new "Lumber Line" box cars, which actually were convenient specialized unit trains a century before the term arose. Omaha established an enginehouse and a depot in the first year.

Omaha's thrust required extensive land grants to be sold for expansion money, and as the line was completed northward, the state released parcels of land for sale. Much of the pineland territory behind Bayfield was purchased by Bayfield's R.D. Pike and associate E.F. Drake (of St. Paul and the Omaha Road), allegedly for $690,000. It was the beginning of a mill at Washburn and of the Washburn & North Western Railway, just one of entrepreneur Pike's ventures. Another member of the Omaha team was John A. Humbird, son of Jacob, whose immediate interests included acquiring timberlands and erecting a new mill at Mason, Wisconsin. One of the co-investors with Fredrick Weyerhaeuser, Humbird was associated with the old North Wisconsin Company and operated a sawmill at Clayton, the latter requiring new timber resources. Humbird and the Weyerhaeuser interests opened the Mason plant instead, Humbird becoming President and manager of the sprawling White River Lumber Company. A decade after an 1894 fire, Weyerhaeuser sold the rebuilt mill to Edward Hines.

Wisconsin's northernmost railroad was just beginning operations in mid-1883. Bayfield-Ashland service was scheduled twice a day, at a time when Governor Jeremiah Rusk and Railroad Commissioner Nils Haugen arrived aboard a two-car special. The Bayfield line possessed some of the Omaha's finest scenery as it wound along the marshlands and cliffs bordering Chequamegon Bay. Governor Rusk came north to enjoy the brisk air and issued patents on 102,589 acres to the Omaha Road in Douglas and Bayfield Counties, while paint dried nicely on Bayfield's new depot. Lake Superior now had a direct connection with St. Paul, Omaha, Nebraska, and the far west.

Other notables came and went in the railroad's business: Marvin Hughitt, President of Chicago & North Western in the key years; John Coit Spooner, able lawyer for the Omaha; Edwin Winter, President of subsidiary Ashland Railway, and Assistant President of the Omaha Road. Mississippi River lumber baron Chancy Lamb (of Clinton, Iowa, and Weyerhaeuser interests) arrived "en familia" at Ashland's Chequamegon Hotel, a huge firetrap owned by the Wisconsin Central railroad. Lamb had ties to the White River Lumber Company and was closely attended by co-investor John Humbird.

Humbird, Winter, Spooner and W.H. Phipps (Omaha's Land Commissioner) helped form the Bay Land & Improvement Company, which incorporated the townsite of Washburn in 1882, together with R.D. Pike, S.H. Peavey and C.H. Pratt of Minneapolis. Their aim was to invest in the location of the great new Omaha dock complex, which began to take form in 1883, and was completed in 1886. The new village was named for

Cadwallader Colden Washburn (1818-1882), whose business and political career closed just as the Omaha neared the bay. Washburn had a key role in shaping Minneapolis into a leading flour milling center, and it was fitting that the flour and coal port should bear his name. C.C. Washburn was engaged in Wisconsin and Minnesota politics and business, and he made a fortune in the process. Born in Livermore, Maine, he began his business life with partner Cyrus Woodman at land speculation in Mineral Point, Wisconsin, in the 1840s. A lawyer, he went to Washington in 1855 when his two brothers were serving in Congress. After a full tour of duty in the Civil War (he raised a cavalry regiment and rose to Major General), he settled in La Crosse, reentering politics in 1866. Ten years before, his relative Dorilus Morrison, of Minneapolis, involved C.C. and his brother William Drew Washburn in the waterpower at St. Anthony's Falls. By 1867, the Washburns and Morrison owned Minneapolis Mill Company, a key but risky venture in the heart of the flour district. At the same time, C.C. entered Wisconsin politics, serving again in Congress until his election as Governor in 1871. In 1873, he left politics to concentrate on the Minneapolis flour boom. His successes were set back by the explosion of his new Washburn "A" mill on May 2, 1878, only four years old. Eighteen men died in the blast, and many other mill buildings were wrecked, crippling the new, important industry. His last years were spent managing the mill company, of which he had been President since 1865.

Bayfield native, Captain R.D. Pike, entered business and dealt in several enterprises, including a sawmill. Pike's small steamer *Favorite* was chartered in 1883 and toured the Apostle Islands with grandees aboard, putting into Basswood Island to examine its brownstone quarry. His passengers and friends were significant in the Omaha Road's history: Henry M. Rice, Elias F. Drake, Ambrose H. Wilder and John L. Merriam. The St. Paul moguls were interwoven in many paths of commerce, while Pike and Rice were linked, naming Bayfield after Lt. Henry W. Bayfield of the Royal Navy, who surveyed Lake Superior in 1823-1825. Basswood, Wilson and Stockton Islands each had brownstone quarries, supplying a warm brown building and facing stone after 1869, with examples raised in many Omaha Road towns plus

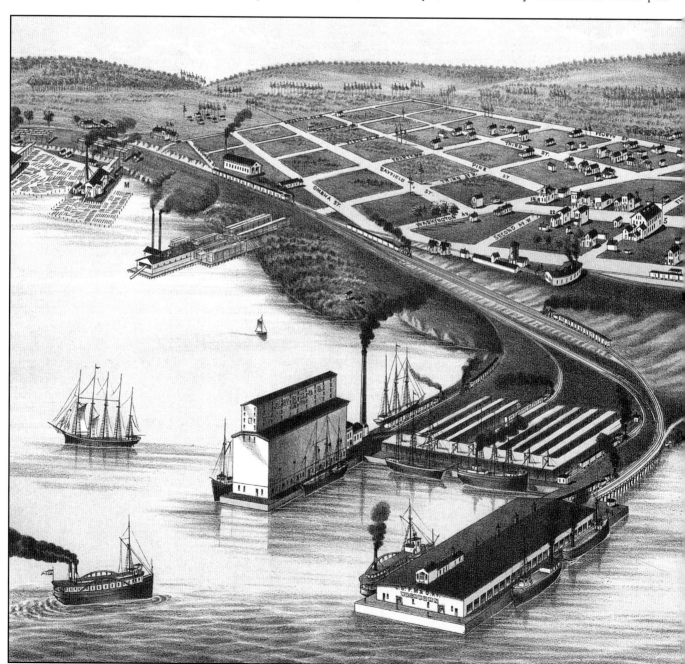

Chicago and Milwaukee. One boost in sales was a negative one: the 1871 Chicago fire. Milwaukee's city hall received its stone from Basswood's quarry, along with many north country buildings of note. Houghton Point, several miles north of Washburn, had a quarry operated by Fredrick Prentice in the 1890s. This work nearly supplied a great obelisk, 115 feet high, for the Columbian Exposition, but the endeavor failed. The remainder went into Ashland buildings. Houghton quarry closed in 1897.

Omaha's forces began work on a dock complex at Washburn to compete with the Superior and Duluth terminals of the St. Paul & Duluth Railroad, archenemy in the St. Paul-Lake Superior trade. Construction progressed between 1883 and 1886, and produced a 1,000,000 barrel grain elevator 1,000 feet offshore. Coal piers and dock houses were erected, with an all-important water depth of 24 feet just offshore. Timber came from nearby tracts and was cut at Ashland's Union Mill. The elevator itself was designed by George Moulton & Company, Chicago, a prominent midwest builder. Moulton had examples standing in Duluth, and soon the firm had 200 men at work.

The elevator was 84 feet by 225 feet and 149 feet high from the waterline, built on massive cribbing filled with stone. 160 piers and an additional 5,000 cubic feet of stone completed underwater details. Some 36,000 feet of oak planking and 24,000 lbs. of sheet iron went into the project. The elevator had 100 storage bins. Sioux City Engine & Iron Works supplied the elevator engine. It was a 700 HP tandem-compound single crank giant, with cylinder dimensions of 24x36x44 inches. The flywheel weighed 12 tons and the bandwheel was 13 feet in diameter. Steam came from two 120 lb. pressure boilers, topped off with a 150 foot tall smokestack, the second highest in Wisconsin at the time. This machinery could empty 240 cars per day, six cars at a time, with 12 spouts loading two vessels simultaneously. At a cost of $225,000, construction crews finished on March 17, 1886.

The railroad chose F.H. Peavey & Company as Washburn's operator. On February 7, 1886, the first 75 cars of grain arrived from Omaha stations at Bancroft, Lyons and Oakland, Nebraska. This shipment served as a machinery test. Peavey, incidentally, ran 24 elevators along the Omaha that year, becoming one of the road's major shippers. The first modest cargo was loaded at Washburn on May 6, aboard the *City of Fremont*, aptly chosen as a reminder of an important North Western town. It was early enough in season for the incoming steamer *Winslow* to encounter ice near Bayfield. Unable to dock there, *Winslow* came into Washburn and took on Buffalo-bound flour. Several problems arose almost immediately. A dock strike in mid-1886 over wages erupted, and Omaha hired strikebreakers, Italians from Ashland, and violence flared. Ashland and Bayfield militia units were summoned, but the original labor force of St. Paul men prevailed. The dock was closed until a truce was called. In June, steam barge *James H. Shrigley* landed 4,000 barrels of salt (for meat packing), but encountered another strike, again over hourly rates. Several more steamers were diverted to Ashland before all was peaceful. The second set of problems were far more serious and involved the complex business of rates, routes and competition.

Twin Cities traffic enjoyed phenomenal growth in the early 1880s, enough to encourage the development of Omaha's lake port at Washburn. Some roads, including the Rock Island (which was linked to Omaha as a prospective merger partner), saw its flour-hauling business balloon to four times its 1880 receipts.

A construction boom in 1878-1882 brought more rail routes into the Twin Cities as the northwest grew, but rates on the Chicago-St. Paul routes remained low as more roads were built. During the unstable (for rates) 1880s, the North Western had to contend with the lower rates of the St. Paul & Duluth, which maintained the lowest rates to Lake Superior, staying out of rate pools. The lower rate shackled Omaha's Washburn port route until such agreements over rates could be settled, an elusive goal. It was a period in which rates were made and broken overnight. Pools were developed in attempts to equalize traffic and protect investments. For the Omaha, the C&NW and Washburn, the chal-

**(Left)** This "Bird's Eye View" lithograph of Washburn and harbor, originally published by Norris, Wellge & Company of Milwaukee, depicts the grain elevator, coal dock and merchandise dock as they existed in 1886. The depot and roundhouse were located, appropriately, along Omaha Street. *Author's Collection.*

(Above) The Washburn coal dock with its elaborate unloading apparatus as seen from the top of the 149 foot tall grain elevator. (Below) The Omaha grain facility nears completion in this 1886 view looking toward the brick power house and frozen Chequamegon Bay. Both: *Washburn Historical Society.*

Washburn, Wisconsin, with a deep water harbor on Chequamegon Bay, became a grain port for the Omaha, with grandiose plans to compete with Duluth-Superior, 60 miles to the west. The shorter haul by water would lure business to this more easterly port, so said the promoters.

(Above) Proudly lettered for the C.St.P.M.& O. Ry. Co., the grain elevator is shown from the Merchandise Dock just after completion in 1886. It was operated by F.H. Peavey & Company. Unfortunately, after about twenty years of service the elevator fell into disuse, a victim of railroad rate wars with the Twin Ports trade, and was torn down beginning in 1910.

(Left) Elevator power was supplied by a Sioux City-built steam engine. Both: *Washburn Historical Society.*

lenge was to capture a large piece of the flour trade.

When C&NW took control of the Omaha, it insisted the Washburn route be outside traffic agreements like the St. Paul & Duluth. StP&D's rates were five cents per hundred-weight (CWT) less than Omaha's, and such differences caused traffic to go to the Minnesota line and undercut parent C&NW in its all-rail route to Chicago. The rates were made equal to StP&D's in May 1885, and temporarily settled the Washburn vs. Duluth-Superior rate problem. But, further complications arose as several new roads took advantage of lower interest rates, which funded new construction. Northern Pacific reached Ashland in May 1885, and William Drew Washburn's Minneapolis, St. Paul & Atlantic Railway, ultimately the Soo Line, was building east from Turtle Lake, Wisconsin. Several routes were also operating across southern Minnesota and Iowa to Chicago, carrying off grain and flour. Thus, Omaha had problems filling the Washburn facility.

One market at Bayfield that did improve and began to feed company coffers was the vacation trade based on the fine, unpolluted air of Lake Superior. Bayfield's *Island View* hotel was "the largest hotel in north Wisconsin," fully equipped with electric bells and telephones. Bayfield claimed a maximum temperature of 75 degrees, which attracted those of adequate means to summer in "Lake Superior ozone." General Passenger Agent T.W. Teasdale pushed such trade from his St. Paul office. Business lasted into the early 1930s. Teasdale's office released a booklet about Bayfield as a resort, sending two St. Paul journalists to magnify Bayfield attractions. At one time, Omaha indicated interest in founding a mammoth family resort, much like Ashland's Chequamegon Hotel. Hay fever sufferers found special rates helpful when Omaha announced $7.00 fares for up-Saturdays-down-Sundays bargains. The booklet, *Midst The Pines,* eulogized Washburn's place as "Offspring of the union of land and water transportation, result of absolute commercial requirements." Certainly the Omaha so hoped.

Madeline Island, just offshore from Bayfield, was also a vacation-land on the rise. Colonel Fredrick M. Woods of Lincoln, Nebraska, came to Madeline Island in the early 1890s, and left "Nebraska Row" in his wake, a series of friends and relatives' summer homes. His following continued into the 1980s to alleviate summer's pollen aggravations for Lincoln natives.

Washburn's facilities survived into the 1920s, but the grain elevator came down prior to World War I, its influence on lake transportation seemingly marginal. The six stall enginehouse was quiet by 1930, and the once busy switch engines disappeared in favor of mixed train and wayfreight service. For a while, coal was landed at Washburn for Barksdale, DuPont's explosive plant south of town, which became Washburn's chief, if spotty, employer. The small terminal steadily wound down operations in favor of Ashland-Bayfield locals, which ran down to the dock for occasional inbound lake cargos. Inevitably, in 1925, the Washburn switch crew was notified of their job's abolition, including the "Barksdale Scoot," a little-known suburban service between Washburn and Barksdale.

Passenger service on the Bayfield line in the l9th Century amounted to a 25 mile local run that went to work at Bayfield's two stall enginehouse and modest depot about 8:30 AM. It was variously arranged to meet Ashland-Spooner mainline trains at Ashland Junction, and finally settled for transfer of passengers and head-end business at Ashland station. During the Barksdale boom, the branch had up to four runs daily.

An all-out Lake Superior blizzard on March 2, 1904, caught one noon arrival from Bayfield at Washburn and nearly buried it. The engine and baggage car were dug out, and attempted to run further, but stalled at Ashland Junction in heavy snowfall. Northern Pacific's westbound train, minutes before heading for Iron River, stalled in drifts eight miles west and was relieved many hours later. That same year, Lake Superior had record sheets of ice. Passengers arriving at Ashland requested adequate visiting time, and shopper-commute schedules were examined by the Omaha. Occasionally, Washburn or Bayfield would complain about timing, but until the mixed train won the day, the branch train began and terminated at Bayfield.

Among the many special cars and trains that ran in the summer to Bayfield, that of Chicago Great Western president Alpheus Beede Stickney arrived in August 1906. Earlier, Stickney arranged for the Omaha to handle his private car on Train 4 from St. Paul to Menomonie for a banker's convention. Stickney, a competitor of the Omaha, savored Lake Superior's breezes and brought his daughters to escape from St. Paul's hot summer.

Barksdale was developed by E.I. DuPont Company, and addressed midwestern mining's need for dynamite. The new factory town lay 4.5 miles south of Washburn and midway between Michigan and Minnesota ore bodies. The site was picked for safety purposes by Colonel W.G. Ramsay, acting in behalf of DuPont in 1902. The next year, the Atlantic Manufacturing Company purchased the Ramsay property as a DuPont subsidiary, and began clearing the site of timber. Ashland contractors put up over 80 buildings, using Houghton sandstone, and bricks from Menomonie Pressed Brick Company. By February 1905, there were 11 miles of narrow gauge horse-drawn tramways constructed to move explosives. The works opened that month and, by the spring of 1905, the first three cars of commercial explosive were shipped to the waiting mines. Washburn's newspaper claimed that miscreants celebrated the event by cracking a local safe with nitroglycerine, which did little to promote stability.

There immediately rose a need for passenger service to and from Barksdale to accommodate work forces. Plant officials, in late 1904, called upon Omaha's St. Paul office to promote a commuter service, albeit just four miles, from mushrooming Washburn. Omaha insisted on 100 paid patrons per day for the special five cent fare. Omaha's new *Dynamite Limited*, with two vintage repainted cars, carried but 75 workers in the beginning. This continued into the automobile era, in good times and bad. Employment was highest in both World Wars, which boosted the commuter service. Proposals to extend the Ashland Street Railway with a Van Depoele trolley line to Barksdale never materialized. Barksdale finally closed in November 1971. Today, it is an empty, overgrown wood lot.

By August 1915, and up to America's entry into World War I, Washburn was a boomtown full of speculators and construction workers with a need for housing. DuPont employed over 1,500 workers, and Omaha had to provide 20 coaches for Trains 273-276 (inclusive), hauled by a larger than usual engine, possibly an I-1 Class. Despite the heavy power, it required doubling the hill

(Above) Washburn was created in 1882 by Omaha railroad officers and investors in the Bay Land & Improvement Co. This view from the top of the grain elevator shows acres of stumps awaiting final clearing. *Washburn Historical Society.*

(Left) The Washburn depot is shown with one of Omaha's 1883 Baldwin 90 series 0-4-0 switchers posed with friends. *W.E. Chase Collection.*

(Below) The 90 series 0-4-0 and a rebuilt "West Side" Taunton 4-4-0 are ready for dock duty at Washburn's 1883 six stall roundhouse. The facility was closed in the 1920s.

to Barksdale. Five trains were run daily, usually in two sections on a ten minute headway. And in December, Omaha loaded a special train of Washburnians to see the film *Birth Of A Nation* at Ashland, probably using the same commuter coaches. On the negative side, Omaha Operator N.A. Cowing "jumped ship" to take a more promising position at the dynamite plant.

The prewar period reflected high times in 1910, when Northwestern Fuel Company shipped a large amount of coal and occupied two Washburn switch crews and 70 men on the Washburn Dock. This was a time in which 40 to 70 cars of coal were loaded daily, in a nine hour work day. A year before, locals requested passenger shelters for the Pike and Sioux Spurs, some five miles south of Bayfield. Salmo happened to be the midpoint between the two, and the applicants tried to bargain for further conveniences. Passenger Agent Thayer's survey uncovered that Pike contributed about six daily passengers, too little to warrant moving Salmo's station. Pike was finally eliminated as a stop, but Sioux Spur, with much more business, received a box car body depot. Save for one boy riding to Washburn's school, most patrons north of Washburn were quarrymen in that prewar time. Pike, Houghton, Nash, and Sioux Spur (which nearly became Guernsdale) were diminished, while Salmo (site of a state fish hatchery) remained in name. Pureair, 2.1 miles south of Bayfield, was added in the 1920s. If not lost due to local economics, they faded away in favor of paved roads and the auto.

Despite layoffs of car knockers (who repaired "powder box" dynamite dedicated box cars) and a temporary layoff for the Barksdale-Washburn crew in 1924, Omaha continued passenger service with 4-4-0s and two coaches. A turnaround wayfreight and switch train presided over freight work with a combination coach at the rear. Some jobs still originated at Washburn (at least to Barksdale) in 1927, but the terminal's days were numbered. Barksdale's mid-1920s work included making Pyrotol, a stump-blowing explosive recanted from old military stock. Barksdale exported some 32,000 lbs. to Birchwood (on the Park Falls Line) to clear land for settlers in Washburn, Rusk and Barron Counties. As the stumps blew away, Omaha was granted permission to abandon an old connection with the Wachsmuth Lumber Company, the last affiliation with Bayfield's Dalyrimple regime in 1925. At nearly the same time, a Chippewa pageant in the Apostles, starring 400 Native Americans, drew a large crowd that filled Omaha coaches. The fare was $2.50.

On the eve of the Great Depression, literally days away from Black Tuesday, Omaha reassigned a switch train to Washburn for increased coal and pulpwood loadings. Northwestern Fuel Company received the bulk of coal shipments, unloaded at the aging dock. After the economic crash, the silence at Washburn brought inevitable layoffs. Both Ashland and Washburn roundhouses, six stalls each, were closed, their antiquated, air-operated bucket coaling stations retired upon inspection by B&B Foreman Gunderson in 1934. Elsewhere, the company gathered up long unused trackage at factories vacant since the Armistice. Yet in 1930, the "Devil's Hole," one mile south of Bayfield, required filling. It was a 61 foot deep ravine that required a culvert and 22,000 cubic feet of fill, administered grandly by side dump cars loaded by steam shovel. There was always a need for maintenance, even on branchlines.

Complaints regarding passenger service arose in the late 1920s. The problem was to provide connections with Spooner-Ashland mail service on Trains 363-364 by rearranging the six trains numbered 181-186 to Bayfield. At the same time, Omaha faced a deficit of $1,000 a month (in late 1931), as ridership averaged only five per train, and mail revenues were not compensating. All over the railroad, observed the Public Service Commission of Wisconsin, there was a tremendous falling of revenues. The Omaha failed to pay interest on its debts by $2,416,288, while cutting operating expenses over $3,000,000 below the previous year's figure. It was necessary to cut everywhere to maintain services. Finally, after several adjustments, which failed to raise revenues, the six runs were abandoned by a Public Service Commission order of March 21, 1934, and a bus was substituted. Mixed Trains 181-182 became the final mode of travel on the road to Bayfield. As a sop to patrons, switching would be restricted to southbound operation only. Engineer W.T. Stevens, age 69, had run the first train to Bayfield on October 12, 1883, and was present for the beginning of mixed service as engineer.

With the loss of branch passenger service, Omaha and Northern Pacific jointly applied to close Ashland Junction station. The first attempt came on December 28, 1931, as the station business was too light. The facility was maintained for passengers changing trains to and from Bayfield (from Ashland-Spooner trains), but with ridership down, the need for a building disappeared. The roads substituted "custodial" management for the depression years. In March 1938, Northern Pacific chose to discontinue the station, with Omaha assenting. In 1937, 68 fares were generated along with 12 Less-Than-Car-Load shipments, earning $51.40. Bus service had bypassed the lonely station, soon to be dismantled in favor of a tiny shack foreign to passengers, but still familiar to mixed train crews bound for Barksdale, Washburn and Bayfield.

Gas-electric cars were introduced in the late 1920s on Bayfield trains after a study concluded a motor car could be used on the branch in the summer. Shipments of fish were expressed from Bayfield (in 1926) and influenced the final decision to put on a motor car. In October 1928, a 70 foot turntable was installed at Bayfield, in anticipation of the new motor cars and Class I-1 and K-1 4-6-0s. Washburn's newspaper heralded motor car No. 2003's arrival on August 1, 1929, which would revolutionize scoot service. After September 1, the 2003 went over to Ashland-Hudson usage, but may have returned the next summer. Apparently, this was the pattern for the remainder of branch passenger service to 1934. The passenger train abandonment study of 1933 was written in red ink and, unhappily, the big 600 HP dual engine motor car consumed more costly fuel than a steam engine (figures were $992.34 versus $340.53 for steam coal in 1933).

Problems with mail deliveries plagued the Bayfield run until the spring of 1934. Then on Saturday, March 31, 1934, a few souls boarded the scoot at Ashland for its final run, along with Mrs. O.A. Brenske, a veteran of the first train of 1883. That initial trip had been on flat cars, with benches for the throngs riding to a Washburn lumber camp. This time, the consist was simply a two car train that clattered off to Ashland Junction, curving northward into a land of cattails and pines, and was shortly swallowed up in Chequamegon Bay mists.

(Above) One of Omaha's three rebuilt 4-4-0s handles the passenger "Scoot" near Washburn. This train ran between Bayfield and Ashland. *Chick Sheridan.*

(Left) Omaha provided suburban service from Washburn to the DuPont explosive plant at Barksdale using vintage coaches for the 4.4 mile commute. *Washburn Historical Society.*

(Below) In the 1890s, several brownstone quarries were worked at Houghton, 3.6 miles north of Washburn. The building stone was used in various towns along the Omaha, as well as Milwaukee and other cities. *Washburn Historical Society.*

(Right) Bayfield County features tough winters with substantial snowfall, and many drifts had to be shoveled out by hand as this scene near Washburn testifies.

(Opposite page) Omaha K-1 No. 107 is switching freight cars at the Washburn water tank. The "flanger" car coupled in behind the tender will clear the snow from inside the rails.

(Below) At the same location, snow has piled up behind the tender of No. 107 after backing down-wind with its short, flanger equipped consist. The "day after" a snowstorm in the Northland always brings cold, clear weather as depicted by these photos from the 1930s. All: *Chick Sheridan.*

(Right) Omaha Class I-1 No. 103 brings a mixed train into the Washburn depot on a cold winter morning. This train went around the bay to Ashland and returned several hours later.

(Below) Engine No. 230 plows out one of the sidings at Washburn. The K-1 Class 4-6-0 was a familiar engine on the branchline. Both: *Chick Sheridan.*

(Above) Digging out after the great blizzard of February 1922 required the use of Omaha's rotary snowplow. No. R-200, a Cooke machine, chews out a siding near the Hayward depot.

(Left) The rotary takes a breather at Spooner after clearing snow from the same storm. Both: *Chick Sheridan.*

Washburn turns out en masse to greet old warrior General John J. Pershing upon his return from the Apostle Islands vacationland. *Chick Sheridan.*

(Above) In the midst of the Great Depression, Civilian Conservation Corps workers from Chicago muster outside their train at Washburn, prior to being trucked to project campsites. The CCC provided indigent men with jobs planting trees and other seasonal work in the local forests. *Chick Sheridan.*

(Right) During the summer of 1930, gas-electric No. 2001 operated out of Bayfield in an attempt to economize services. The 1929-built motor car later became a limousine coach in Ashland-Hudson *Namekagon* train operations. *L.T. Williams.*

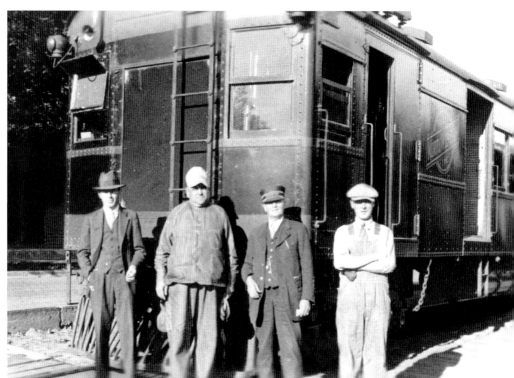

Bayfield's depot was the northernmost on the Omaha Road. *Chick Sheridan.*

(Above) I-1 No. 362 rolls past the abandoned Washburn roundhouse, by this time reduced to three stalls, with a strawberry grower's extra of National Refrigerator Car Company express reefers in the early 1930s. This local attempt to market fruit was unsuccessful.

(Left) Bayfield's old two stall engine house lasted until the 1980s. Bayfield also had a hand powered 70' turntable. Both: *Chick Sheridan.*

(Above) The conductor begins his accounting work inside Omaha combination car No. 423, which was a regular on the Bayfield-Ashland mixed Train 181. (Right) The interior of the classic car reflects 19th Century charm. (Below) The car is flanked by weeds at the Bayfield depot. All: *H. Markwiese.*

(Above) Omaha Class I-1 No. 356 is in charge of mixed Train 181 at Washburn, but the days of steam are numbered in this 1950s view. At this time, the ancient wood combine was still present on the rear. *Mike Runey.* (Below) Bayfield's humble mixed train became active around noon. Revenue was equally basic, with pulpwood piled high in battered gondolas. Here, Omaha K-1 No. 203 is shown easing combine 423 back to the depot. *H. Markwiese.*

# THE BIBON CONNECTION

Omaha's sometime partner after 1900 was Duluth, South Shore & Atlantic Railway, which vacated its Northern Pacific trackage rights in 1892 to complete its own route to Duluth via Lake Nebagamon. A transfer station was located at Bibon (pronounced Bib-un), just south of Mason, on Omaha's Ashland-Trego line. Here, Omaha's two each-way-daily passenger trains rolled to a stop above the South Shore's new line, impatiently awaiting passengers, often bound for St. Paul. The DSS&A thereby gained access to Ashland and Bayfield, and Omaha reached the teeming Copper Country. The dark side included the inability of the two roads to faithfully make connections at Bibon, which caused some lengthy exchanges.

In January 1907, missed connections led to an ultimatum from the Post Office, which imposed a twenty minute wait between trains. Finally, the mails were discontinued, leaving only the passenger baggage transfer. Both roads had strived to be on time, but South Shore Train 8 and Omaha Train 66 (northbound *Twilight Limited*) had a history of missing each other. Omaha had a group of trains arriving and departing at Spooner about 7:00 PM each night, and Train 65 evidently became Train 66, the northbound counterpart, compromised if Train 65 was late. Superintendent T.W. Kennedy worked to erase Bibon from the Omaha's scheduled stops and issued instructions to annul Train 65's Bibon halts unless the westbound DSS&A train was in sight.

In May 1907, C.E. Lytle of the DSS&A was chagrined when Omaha left an influential Marquette citizen in the dust of the Bibon platform after DSS&A Train 5 arrived eight minutes late. The Michigander was bound for St. Paul, and Lytle sent two messages to request Train 65 to await Train 5, but Omaha upheld its edict. The *Twilight Limited* carried one less fare that afternoon.

Omaha passengers on Train 66 had a sympathetic conductor when it came to the Bibon transfer. H.C. Schultz saw to it that those unfortunate enough to be stranded at lonely Bibon rode into Ashland with him to be returned the next day to try again. His instructions were not official, but were verbal from his predecessor, a Conductor Towey. This railroad gallantry was not to continue, as St. Paul and Spooner officialdom got wind of such events and, in February 1920, C.D. Stockwell required Schultz to cease carrying passengers without proper tickets, or to pay their fares into Ashland. A year later, on December 24, 1922, Conductor Peabody empathized with passengers for Saxon, Wisconsin, and Ironwood, Michigan, who missed South Shore's Train 8. Peabody was in charge of northbound Train 66 (also late) and, on that Christmas Eve, he rearranged the tickets to read "via C&NW/Ashland." Peabody was challenged as to his authority for the act, for in F.R. Pechin's judgement, passengers should have paid for the 20-miles to Ashland, although Omaha's Train 7 (on the mainline) caused the delay.

Omaha and South Shore found a way to compete for fast meat shipments into Upper Michigan via Bibon in February 1911. Chicago-Upper Peninsula meat traffic took another day to reach the boomtowns, and Sioux City-St. Paul-Bibon routings were potential alternatives. C.E. Lytle of DSS&A addressed Omaha's T.W. Kennedy on the subject, proposing to take advantage of time and distance, and sought Omaha's cooperation. It was a connection ripe with difficulties, as northern weather operating problems worked against the union.

DSS&A freight No. 64 was retimed to pass Bibon eastbound around 8:00 AM, to make the pick up and deliver the meat cars into Michigan points six hours earlier than a Chicago routing. The match ran into trouble almost immediately, as

Omaha's Trains 74 (St. Paul-Spooner) and 76 (Spooner-Ashland) experienced delays. Extreme temperatures caused air brake problems, adding to the headaches. Car service agents, checking 15 cars at random, found unreasonable delays, plus the meat cars were not given preferential handling over the Omaha. A connection at Superior was considered, but unworkable. DSS&A wound up giving Omaha a three-hour leeway at Bibon, but both roads feared the Soo Line would acquire the business.

In November 1913, Omaha Train 74 was delayed at Northline five hours by a derailed car. The Bibon connection was again compromised. C.D. Stockwell wrote to Traveling Engineer E.R. Gorman regarding Extra 325, noting the Class I-1 had stalled and doubled its train into Drummond enroute to Bibon and Ashland. Engineer Conolly filled out his doubling report, the delay beginning two miles north of Cable. The 4-6-0 was dragging 11 loads and 48 empties (1,410 tons) in intense cold. Extra 325 was considered overloaded for the conditions. Omaha men also found that a Cudahy Car Lines reefer (No. 4054, loaded with meat for Houghton) contracted a case of "sticking air" or acute brake problems, which caused the doubling episode.

Engineer Conolly had the 325 again on November 24, 1913, and asked for an assist out of Bibon by Train No. 69, as the reported temperature was well below freezing. No. 325 this time had 9 loads and 48 empties. Delay was 35 minutes. In February 1918, Train 74 was handled by a Class J Mikado, bringing 1,118 tons to Spooner, but too late for Bibon's time. It was almost necessary to order a short hop with only the meat cars to maintain the connection. Omaha traffic men stated the meat was going via the Great Northern to Superior from Sioux City as a result of the delay record.

While reasonable timing may have

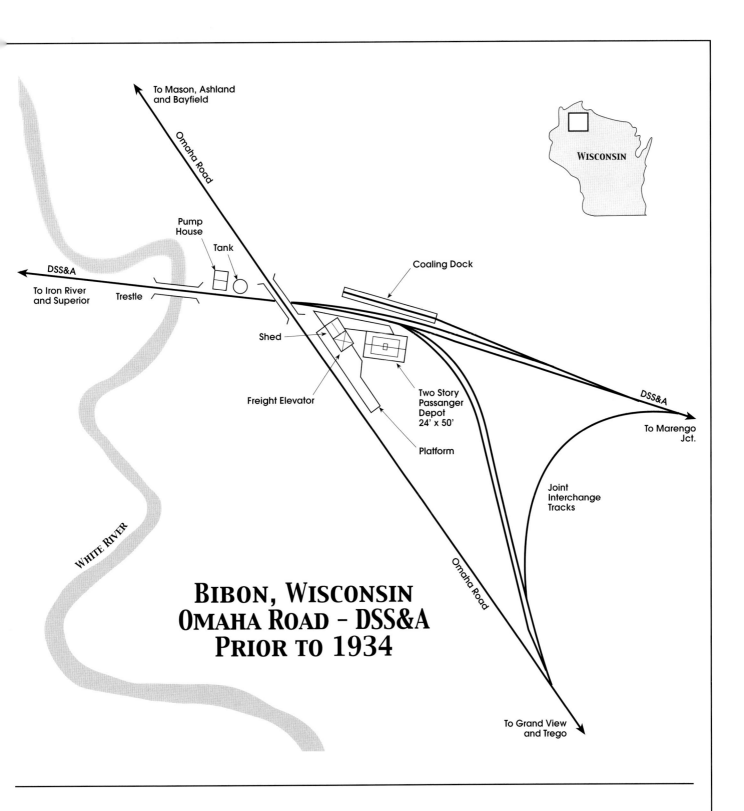

To Mason, Ashland and Bayfield

Omaha Road

Pump House

Tank

DSS&A
To Iron River and Superior

Trestle

Coaling Dock

Shed

Freight Elevator

Two Story Passanger Depot 24' x 50'

Platform

DSS&A
To Marengo Jct.

Joint Interchange Tracks

WHITE RIVER

WISCONSIN

Omaha Road

To Grand View and Trego

## BIBON, WISCONSIN OMAHA ROAD – DSS&A PRIOR TO 1934

occurred, in October of 1919, a copper country meat dealer appealed for on-time arrival, stating that the Bibon connection was competing with Chicago, Milwaukee & St. Paul-Copper Range Railroad, which arrived earlier. Stockwell assured that his division was not responsible, that Train 74 was delayed at St. Paul four hours, or still further down the Omaha. Lytle of the DSS&A indicated that Omaha was steadi-

ly failing its customers. Occasionally, Omaha crews spotted the reefers on the wrong track at Bibon. Difficulties continued as late as 1933, when the running time Spooner-Bibon was 2-1/2 hours for a 5:00 AM arrival. Further problems centered on maintenance of reefer car heaters, charcoal stoves (later oil-fired), and decisions were made to run Omaha heaters through on DSS&A. To some

extent, fruit loadings came from the far west, with heaters installed at St. Paul. The Bibon connection was finally terminated in June 1934, when DSS&A abandoned its 75-mile Marengo Junction to Superior East End mainline through Bibon and Lake Nebagamon in favor of trackage rights over Northern Pacific-Wisconsin Central (Soo Line) via Ashland.

(Above) Omaha joined the C&NW in their roundhouse at Ashland's east end after abandoning their own Ashland engine servicing facilities in the 1930s. Omaha Class I-1 No. 106 is nearest the turntable on the left. C&NW R-1 Nos. 178 and 291 stand outside the shop building. These are three of the oldest R-1s, built in 1901, and still serviceable in this 1948 view. C&NW Class E-2 4-6-2 No. 2903 is at the right on Train 116. Today, this site is devoid of railroad activity, but Omaha's six stall roundhouse still exists near 12th Ave West. *Ed Selinsky.*
(Below) M-1 No. 18, built by Alco in 1912, represents Omaha's lone assignment at Ashland in 1950. M-1 No. 9 also worked the job, the two engines kept on the roster just for this assignment. No. 9 was retired in June 1953, while engine No. 18 lasted until June 1956, when it was replaced by a diesel switch engine. *D. Kotz.*

Class I-1 No. 316 sports new paint, thick tires and a tender from a G-3 4-4-2 in this view at the Hayward depot. It's wartime, so the 40 year veteran will serve a few more years before retirement in November 1950. The photographer claimed never to have seen No. 316 before or since, as it was not a north country native. Train 69 will depart after coupling to its train. *L.T. Williams.*

Finale for Omaha's Bayfield line saw C&NW GP7 No. 1599 bringing in the last train in a driving snowstorm. C&NW ceased activity in the Ashland area when it abandoned the old Milwaukee, Lake Shore & Western line north of Antigo in 1981, and the remaining Ashland switch engine was terminated in January 1982. *Chick Sheridan.*

# LOGGING ROADS ALONG THE OMAHA
## NORTH COUNTRY CUSTOMERS

**North Wisconsin Lumber Co.** Omaha's Bayfield Line had several sizable lumber mills along its length, some of which were linked to Weyerhaeuser interests. Hayward, Wisconsin, was named for the efforts of Anthony J. Hayward and lies some 25 miles northeast of Spooner on the Namekagon River. A Michigander, Hayward visited the site as a timber cruiser and noted its potential in 1880. He was once associated with Senator Philetus Sawyer in his lumber activities, and located timber tracts for the Oshkosh lumber baron. Hayward established a hold on standing timber and a small mill, and sought financial backing from Laird, Norton & Company of Winona, Minnesota. The result was the North Wisconsin Lumber Company, founded in November 1880, with Hayward having one-third interest.

Hayward's operation expanded to a $450,000 capitalization in June 1882, but "big mill" ran into financial trouble and soon needed Fredrick Weyerhaeuser's aid. The mill continued until 1902, with the lumber going to Minnesota, Iowa and Dakota points. Previously, Weyerhaeuser bought 70,000 acres of Omaha timberland for North Wisconsin Lumber Company. In 1902, Hayward's mill passed to Edward Hines Lumber Company of Chicago, part of the larger sale of Weyerhaeuser properties in Wisconsin. The mill closed in 1912, reopened in 1914 under new ownership, then finally expired in May 1922 after being destroyed by fire.

Hines also built logging lines in the Hayward area in the early 1900s. By 1910, this included the Hayward Northern & Lake Superior Railroad. The "H&N" ran over Omaha trackage from the mill site for about 3/4 of a mile, then branched off just north of Hayward, and headed north to Barnes, extending almost to Iron River. Years later, a pulpwood siding at the site of the old junction was still called the "H&N" by Omaha men.

**White River Lumber Company.** Located at Mason and active from 1882 to 1913, WRLCo was a prosperous lumber mill owned by Chancy Lamb, Fredrick Weyerhaeuser and John A. Humbird (son of West Wisconsin Railway builder Jacob Humbird), who became President and Manager of the company. WRLCo was a customer of both the Omaha Road and Duluth South Shore & Atlantic Railway, which passed through Bibon, two miles south of Mason. WRLCo had several cutting locations in central Bayfield County, including lands along DSS&A between Bibon and Iron River. The mill burned in 1894, but it was rebuilt and in 1904 was sold to Edward Hines. WRLCo operated narrow gauge logging lines out of Cusson, Delta and Sutherland on the DSS&A, connecting them via a third rail laid inside the South Shore's standard gauge tracks. This rail operation also fed logs to Hines' mill in Iron River, as did the Washburn, Bayfield & Iron River Railway.

White River Lumber Company was a sprawling operation located along the Omaha at the south side of Mason, Wisconsin. *Author's Collection.*

## Drummond & Southwestern Ry.

Located 25 miles north of Hayward, Drummond was the site of the Rust-Owen Lumber Company, which remained the longest of the Bayfield County mill-rail operations. Co-founder John S. Owen arrived in Eau Claire in 1873, and by 1879, cruised into a majestic stand of 81% pine, one of the state's best. Four partners promptly formed Rust-Owen Lumber Company in April, 1882: Frank H. Drummond, Frank W. Gilchrist, (of Alpena, Michigan, also of Gilchrist Transportation Company, a steamboat line on the Great Lakes); Owen, of Eau Claire; and Ralph C. Rust. They purchased more than 45,000 acres from the Omaha, ultimately acquiring 80,000 acres. Frank H. Drummond managed the mill site, the town bearing his name.

Rust-Owen Lumber Company chartered the standard-gauge Drummond & Southwestern Railway in 1891, and logged west of the town site. There was also a flume built to Lake Owen, once called Long Lake, where the Owen family still maintains a summer residence.

Drummond & Southwestern's curious motive power was noteworthy, selected from the Pittsburgh Locomotive Works, unusual for a logger's choice. The first engine was a 2-6-0, and the second was a 4-6-0. One Shay loco succeeded another, and rolling stock consisted of about 100 Russell logging cars. D&S was chartered as a common carrier, later relinquishing this status to become a private logging road. In 1924, a crossing was installed to permit D&S to cross the Omaha to the east for a final logging show, lasting until

1930. Several Rust-Owen Lumber Company buildings still stand at Drummond, west of the Omaha's depot location, itself razed. Drummond & Southwestern had 30 miles of track.

## Washburn & North Western Ry.

Just south of Washburn, along Van Deventer Bay, C.C. Thompson Lumber Company built a large mill that was served by the Omaha. North of this complex, A.A. Bigelow & Company was at the east end of the Washburn & North Western lumber road, one of several intriguing log lines that penetrated Bayfield County's forests in the 1880s-1890s. Many were three foot gauge like the W&NW. The 30 mile Bigelow road reached into the tangle of narrow gauge lines in the interior, which emptied the woods of marketable trees.

(Above) Rust-Owen Lumber Company operated its Drummond & Southwestern Railway on both sides of the Omaha in the Drummond area. D&S purchased road power from Pittsburgh Locomotive Works, the largest of which was 4-6-0 No. 3 built in 1897. *Alco Historic Photos.*

(Left) Shown with crew posing in camp, engine No. 3 displays a number of changes including an electric headlight, a straight stack, a third dome and a standard pilot. *G. Goodwin Collection.*

79

**Bayfield Transfer Railway** was perhaps the most colorful line created on Chequamegon Bay. BTRy was brought to near reality by the ambitious William F. Dalyrimple, a native of Warren County, Pennsylvania. By the 1870s, Dalyrimple and brother Oliver had real estate holdings in Milwaukee, St. Paul and Bayfield, plus vast wheatlands (28,000 acres) just west of Fargo in the Dakota Territory. Oliver experimented with winter wheat crops in their "bonanza farm" investment, which led to an interest in transportation to move their crops away from the Red River Valley.

The marketing of Dalyrimple's wheat was linked to a railroad idea, which would terminate at a Lake Superior port. Bayfield appeared to provide the ideal location. Lake vessels could call at a port farther east than Duluth-Superior, promoting the same idea Omaha brought forth at Washburn. A beachhead railroad was incorporated on July 26, 1883, to be 3.86 miles long northward to Roy's Point, a candidate for Dalyrimple grain elevators and docks. Progress was glacial in the seven remaining 1880's years, while Dalyrimple's health steadily failed as he ran operations from distant Pittsfield, Penn. H.C. Hale was appointed Manager in the early 1890s, and he had BTRy running by April 1893. It was extended west under several names (the Bayfield Harbor & Great Western Railway and the Bayfield, Superior & Minneapolis Railroad), each being six miles and a separate entity. The 1902 roster included two locos

(one was Omaha's old No. 24, a C-4 Class 4-4-0 built in 1873), two coaches and 19 flat cars. Total mileage was 16.52 miles with one 625 foot trestle. BH&GW carried the mail to Red Cliff (Indian Reservation) six times a week. A full-blown railroad was planned at one point to run southwest to Hinckley or Stillwater, Minnesota, to accept grain shipments from Dalyrimple's Dakota wheatlands.

The Dalyrimple dream wound down by 1912, and Bayfield's Wachsmuth Lumber Company began operating the railroad for its only true function: a logging line. By 1914, Omaha engines were on BTRy trackage switching loads of fish for the Booth & Company plant, as BTRy was not running. Omaha risked losing the fish business to Duluth, and its crews crossed Washington Street in pursuit of the carloadings. An Omaha report stated that BTRy had degenerated into a logging railroad and much of its mainline had been taken up by August 1918, with Wachsmuth now its owner. The line halted operations and was abandoned on September 1, 1924, its records decaying in the old Booth Fisheries building, which had formerly been the BTRy station

**Washburn, Bayfield & Iron River Railway. The "Battleaxe"** was a standard gauge, steeply graded line running west out of Washburn. Begun in 1897 and completed in 1899, WB&IR ended 34 miles away at Iron River, a noted area milltown. Christened the "Battleaxe," in line with a tobacco-oriented outlook, WB&IR was heavily involved in court

actions, and its principals suffered fines for their pains. Bayfield County had pledged aid and looked forward to settling WB&IR land with farmers. In early 1902, the line was offered to the Weyerhaeuser concern for a scrap price. WB&IR was in receivership when it was purchased by Northern Pacific in June 1902, despite reservations by NP management. Logging ceased by 1903, and marginal operations barely supported mixed train service before World War I. In 1922, it was cut back to Coda, nine miles from Iron River, and that was torn up in 1927. Thus, Omaha had the peninsula to itself for the remainder of the railroad era.

**Ashland, Siskiwit & Iron River Railway** crossed the Omaha at Nash, ending at a log dump in the shallow waters of Chequamegon Bay. The three foot gauge AS&IR reached about 50 miles northwest, ultimately to Siskiwit Lake, but lasted just nine years.

**Washburn Area Mills.** Several small mills were operated near the town, including Kenfield & Lamoureaux, S.S. Vaughn, South Shore Lumber Company, Duluth Log Company, and Bonnell Shingle Company. A few miles beyond Houghton Point, Brown & Robbins Lumber Company operated a railroad from forest to dock near Omaha trackage at the mouth of the Onion River. It was three foot gauge and employed both "rod" and Shay-geared locomotives, lasting from 1899 to 1903. Most of the dock operations employed tugboats to transport logs to Ashland or Washburn in booms.

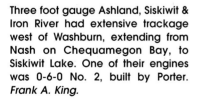

Three foot gauge Ashland, Siskiwit & Iron River had extensive trackage west of Washburn, extending from Nash on Chequamegon Bay, to Siskiwit Lake. One of their engines was 0-6-0 No. 2, built by Porter. *Frank A. King.*

## "Farthest North" Railroad

The record for the farthest north of any Wisconsin railroad falls to the Apostle Islands operations of John Schroeder Lumber Company. Schroeder bought the property of R.D. Pike in 1905, beginning hardwood cutting on Oak Island shortly thereafter. Schroeder's operation on Michigan Island was active from 1920 to 1922, with 10 miles of track laid from a dock at the island's south end. Work on Outer Island began in 1923, lasting into 1930, with trackage reaching 38 miles. Outer Island had a 650 foot dock, and logs were moved to Schroeder's Ashland mill as tows behind the tugboat *Ashland*. Interestingly, Schroeder leased C&NW rail for the isolated lines, which employed Shay-geared power. Federal surveys of the Apostle Islands National Lakeshore after 1970 uncovered a cab and headlight off a Schroeder company Shay locomotive, scrapped on the island in 1930-31.

(Left) Schroeder Lumber Company had extensive operations on Michigan Island and Outer Island in the 1920s. The removal of Outer Island rails has begun in this 1930 scene.

(Below) Outer Island's dock and log dump in 1930. The logs would be towed across the bay to Schroeder's Ashland mill by tugboat. Both: *Chick Serridan.*

**Minneapolis, St. Paul & Ashland Railway: The "Peerless."** Beyond Ashland Junction, a curious competitor crossed Omaha's Bayfield line near Nash: the ambitiously named Minneapolis, St. Paul & Ashland Railway. Discussions in Twin Cities circles in January 1895 centered on building a 125 mile road utilizing Minneapolis' new Belt Line and Soo Line trackage rights.

The scheme allegedly was to relieve Ashland of Chicago railroad domination, i.e., C&NW-CStPM&O. Ashland's development and markets had not accrued to the Twin Cities, but the MStP&A would change the equation. The Peerless (named for popular chewing tobacco) would use the Soo Line to St. Croix Falls, then head toward Shell Lake, ending at Ashland.

Land sales and development accompanied interest in vast hardwood and hemlock stands along the MStP&A's proposed route. Directors included Ashland newspaper editor Sam Fifield, ambitious for further growth in his "new north." Others of interest were: W.R. Sutherland, pioneer Ashland lumberman; Robert Laird McCormick, of the Laird, Norton & Company; and Weyerhaeuser affiliates W.R. Bourne, recently losing his Barronett mill to fire, and C.H. Pratt of Superior & South Eastern Railway's early history. MStP&A was designed to threaten the Omaha's Ashland line as well as give the South Shore and Soo Line access to Ashland. Hardly loyal to the Omaha, Spooner's newspaper stated the railroad would help develop the underpopulated

cutover lands then coming on the market. It was enough to send Omaha's business car to Ashland with the General Manager and staff to discuss the matter with Weyerhaeuser investors. Omaha appeasement brought unhappy Ashland a revival of a recently cancelled night train, yet the county voted bonding for the new road.

The Peerless, which interchanged cars with Omaha at Ashland, had rolling stock agreements with two car builders in 1896 and 1898, and leased an engine from the St. Paul & Duluth, the Omaha's nemesis. Actual construction was just 24 miles, Ashland to DSS&A (near Sutherland), with a proposed and mapped extension southward to the Hayward area, as well as promises to build into Sawyer County forests. The Peerless expired in 1912.

(Above) Minneapolis, St. Paul & Ashland Railway ordered 2-8-0 No. 10 from Brooks in 1899, but it was apparently never delivered, instead going to the Quincy, Omaha & Kansas City Railroad. *Author's Collection.* (Below) Caboose No. 2 stood for its official portrait at St. Louis, Missouri, one of seven such cars and 50 logging flats purchased by the fledgling railroad from AC&F in 1899. *American Car & Foundry.*

# THE NORTH END
## Showing Principle Lumber Roads and Connections

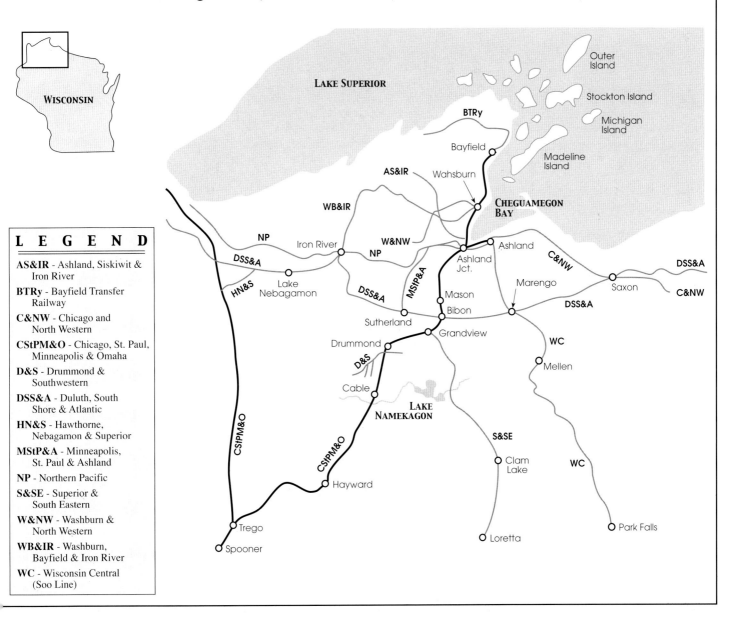

WISCONSIN

LAKE SUPERIOR

Outer Island

Stockton Island

Michigan Island

BTRy

Bayfield

AS&IR

Wahsburn

Madeline Island

CHEGUAMEGON BAY

WB&IR

W&NW

NP

Iron River

NP

Ashland

C&NW

DSS&A

DSS&A

C&NW

DSS&A

HN&S

Lake Nebagamon

DSS&A

MStP&A

Ashland Jct.

Mason

Marengo

Saxon

Sutherland

Bibon

DSS&A

Drummond

Grandview

WC

D&S

Mellen

Cable

CStPM&O

CStPM&O

LAKE NAMEKAGON

S&SE

WC

Hayward

Clam Lake

WC

Trego

Park Falls

Spooner

Loretta

### LEGEND

**AS&IR** - Ashland, Siskiwit & Iron River

**BTRy** - Bayfield Transfer Railway

**C&NW** - Chicago and North Western

**CStPM&O** - Chicago, St. Paul, Minneapolis & Omaha

**D&S** - Drummond & Southwestern

**DSS&A** - Duluth, South Shore & Atlantic

**HN&S** - Hawthorne, Nebagamon & Superior

**MStP&A** - Minneapolis, St. Paul & Ashland

**NP** - Northern Pacific

**S&SE** - Superior & South Eastern

**W&NW** - Washburn & North Western

**WB&IR** - Washburn, Bayfield & Iron River

**WC** - Wisconsin Central (Soo Line)

The Washburn & North Western narrow gauge line, owned by A.A. Bigelow & Company, had 30 miles of trackage running west out of Washburn. W&NW 2-8-0 No. 7 is at the head end of a substantial log train in this 1890s view at Cozy Corners. *H. Peddle Collection.*

This is one of J. Foster Adams' amazing action shots from the glass plate era. An freight "extra" is down from Altoona with Class I-1 No. 328 on the headend. The new power - free steaming, robust and speedy - dominated the Omaha's Eastern Division. Built in 1903, No. 328 was retired in the late 1940s. *J. Foster Adams.*

# 5.

# IMPROVING THE ROAD

In the 1890s, Omaha made its final extensions. In the west, the former Covington, Columbus & Black Hills narrow gauge railroad was built from Ponca to Newcastle, 10.2 miles in 1893. An accompanying 18.4 miles was added in 1907 to Wynot, Nebraska, about 15 miles short of Yankton, South Dakota. The line skirted the Missouri River, reminiscent of the narrow gauge's desire to reach the Black Hills and serve the Missouri River trade in a time long past.

Another branch was extended from Madelia, Minnesota, to Fairmont, 29.3 miles in 1899, parallel to, and about 15 miles west of, the Lake Crystal-Elmore branch. The line served central Watonwan County, the new railroad taking the name Watonwan Valley Railway Company, a Minnesota corporation organized to build the road in January 1899. The property was conveyed to the Omaha Road on December 4, 1899.

Omaha organized Des Moines Valley Railway Company of Minnesota, also in 1899, to push another line northwest from the Western Division mainline. DMV entered Cottonwood and Murray Counties south of Tracy on the C&NW. The work ended at Currie, at the head of the Des Moines River's West Fork, 38 miles from Bingham Lake, the junction town. The line was finished in August 1900, but sold to the Omaha on June 4, 1900.

As the Omaha pushed out of the depression of the mid-1890s, a series of projects were implemented to improve the mainline. Most pressing was the need to double-track the Eastern Division, a project that began in 1900 between Altoona and Eau Claire. A second track was also constructed between Worthington and Sioux Falls Junction (Trent, later Org). The Black River Falls Cut-Off, built east of the city and river crossing, augmented the new program and contributed to higher train speeds through Wisconsin. The 5.7 mile Cut-Off was completed on May 10, 1903, eliminating 326 degrees of curvature, and about two miles of grades for mainline trains. On November 4, 1911, the Black River Falls-Vaudreuil (later Levis) by-pass was finished, and the old iron bridge and sharp curves related to 25 MPH railroading in town were abandoned. More double-track was installed between Spooner and Superior Junction (Trego), in service by 1906. A line change in Juneau County, "where there were numerous sharp and several reverse curves rendering the operation of the road unnecessarily difficult and expensive," took place in mid-1897. Still another statement, " the line may be greatly improved in alignment," was filed with the Secretary of State's office for a line change between Humbird and Fairchild in July 1900.

Of the "Limited" passenger trains that passed daily over the Eastern Division, The *North Western Limited* introduced parlor car operation by 1897. The luxury service included two superb 68 foot cars, *Minneapolis* and *St. Paul,* costing $18,000. The pair were painted Pullman green, with gold trim, finished in St. Jago mahogany, with ceilings in dark olive, pierced with six large Pintsch gas chandeliers. Both cars had 22 revolving chairs with large windows opposite, velvet carpets, mirrors of proper size, and capacious smoking rooms.

Sister trains in 1893 included the *Badger State Express*, a daytime flyer, and the *Atlantic Express,* a close connection with morning trains out of Chicago for the east. The *Chicago Special,* a solid through-train, made the time in 16 hours in 1893, splendid with Pullman and Wagner sleeping cars. On the north end, it was Trains 91-92 between Eau Claire and Ashland, equipped with reclining chair cars. New coaches arrived, some to occupy places of cars taken by mishaps. The Wagner sleeper *Germania,* damaged in a mishap on the Western Division in February 1892, was again placed in service at Chicago several months later.

The advent of the speed game on the Omaha prompted newer and more powerful locomotives. Several types of 4-6-0 Ten-Wheelers were in evidence by the late 1880s, operating chiefly in freight service. Competition heated the need for faster power, as passenger schedules were tightened steadily. No longer adequate was the 63" drivered 4-4-0 type engine, which reached its zenith with the E-8 Class of 1888, weighing 46 tons in working order. The last of the class, No. 173, carried 140 lbs. of boiler pressure, but produced only 14,688 lbs. of tractive effort, inadequate for the oncoming period. In 1890-1892, the Omaha entered the "Ten-Wheeler age" beside parent C&NW and remained taken with the type for many years.

Other companies began their programs with wagon-top boilered engines designed over closely-spaced drivers. The Omaha engines had drivers of 59", an odd size for freight service, unlike competitor Milwaukee Road's 63" drivered types. A variation of Omaha's F-2 Class was the E-9 series, Nos. 174-179, a probable star in the speed game in the 1890s. The first movement toward specialized passenger power (driver size, firebox size and depth) was the F-5 Class, identical in wheelbase dimensions to the F-2's, but with 67" drivers. Nos. 263-266, used on the Omaha's Limited trains, weighed about 63 tons and achieved 18,600 lbs. tractive effort. The closely-related E and F series (engines of 18" and 19" cylinder diameter) finally reached another high point in early 1896, not with a 4-6-0 for heavy passenger duty, but with a "Fast Mail" design 4-4-0 of herculean proportions, the F-8 Class.

The North Western's speed game on its Galena Division, versus such formidable competitors as the Burlington Route, required drastic action, and the demand brought larger 4-4-0s into use. Several experimental 4-4-0s and 4-6-0s were tried (including some compounds) to 1893, but out of this research came big, fast A, B, and C Class, 75" drivered Fast Mails. The A Class came to

C&NW in August 1895, after the deep depression years of 1893-1894. This type weighed just over 65 tons, carried 190 lbs. of steam pressure and performed so well that Omaha ordered three similar engines. Nos. 275-277 arrived and entered service in April 1896, probably at first between Elroy and Altoona, on Trains 5-6, *The North Western Limited*.

The St. Paul *Globe* reported the Omaha drew great pride from its new fleet-footed mail train service. On January 20, 1899, on a Sunday press run, General Passenger Agent Teasdale and C.J. Gray sampled the mettle of the F-8 Class speedsters, in a private car attached to Train 2, the *Fast Mail*. By that date, Omaha had received another seven of the big 4-4-0s, Nos. 255-260 and 278. There would be another four added by January 1900 to complete the class. Teasdale and friends experienced a hot box near Eau Claire, but once there, they enjoyed the opportunity to inspect the new engine and the equally new Eau Claire depot. Train 2 made Chicago in ten hours, and the passengers had the option of either enjoying a chair car until the Duluth-Chicago sleeper was attached, or staying put. Within days Train 9, the westbound *Fast Mail*, set a record between Eau Claire and Roberts, over both ideal and rugged terrain, running off 36 miles in 59 minutes. The entire 194 mile run from Elroy to St. Paul was made in 198 minutes. It was also noted that special trains had attained higher speeds, but the *Fast Mail* was 42 minutes late into Elroy, over the North Western's Madison Division. The Omaha brought it into St. Paul on time.

Two new sets of bright yellow cars were turned out of Hudson Shops for Trains 1 and 4, the *Badger State Express*, in mid-1899. The fleet had full-width vestibules, steam heat and gas lights. Hudsonians were advised to see for themselves, and perhaps experience the observation-buffet, supplied with adequate cigars and liquid refreshments. These trains had a history of stopping at Augusta for the Eau Claire County Fair in September of each year, even in the time of the Spanish-American war. In the bitter cold (minus 40 degrees), Omaha moved its February troop trains off for Jersey City, New Jersey, in five sections. The troops went on to Manila via the Indian Ocean and Singapore.

Faster and better North Western service to St. Paul continued in the spring of 1901. The *Fast Mail* again set a form of record, when it scissored past Fairchild seven minutes late. A long, straight roadway northward through Kempton to Augusta was the scene of some particularly fast running. The engineer at the throttle of what had to be an F-8 set off to reclaim his record. Ahead was 11 miles of level, straight roadway. He snatched up the exact time from the Fairchild operator as he opened up speed. Nine miles ahead, Augusta's operator held his watch at trackside and looked south. In minutes, a cloud of springtime dust rolled up behind the express, growing larger and more imminent, obscuring the onlooker's view. Train 9 roared past Augusta and was immediately lost in the distance, closing in on Fall Creek and Altoona. The speed was enough to drag barrels and boxes off the platform in its wake. Train 9 made up the time and gained a reputation that distant early morning.

While fast trains became the rule on the long, lonely stretches of Eastern Division mainline, the company was engaged in evaluating several sets of 4-6-0s, chiefly for freight service. Two experimental "pilot models" of contemporary dimensions came in

November 1897, from Schenectady Locomotive Works, classified as F-7. The new arrivals weighed 78 tons, with 63" drivers, and measured 60-1/2 feet long over tenders. In this period, serious studies were made on the C&NW concerning the traditional narrow firebox, which was carried between frames, and the more modern concept of a wide firebox above the drivers. Motive power men were always conscious of the center of gravity on the new designs, which might offset previously successful characteristics. The F-7s put forth about 24,000 lbs. of tractive effort, nearly twice that of 4-4-0s of 1898. Moderate speeds were also available to handle fast freights. F-7 steaming characteristics were satisfactory enough to bring a similar class two years later. The hot summer of 1898 brought a crop of F-9 Class 4-6-0s, Nos. 279-288, which were a lighter version of the preceding F-7 pair, weighing 110,900 lbs. on drivers. A year later, with better economic times, the combined "North Western Line" began investing in the slightly heavier G-1 Class for the Omaha and C&NW's equivalent R Class engines.

The advent of the wide firebox, an engineering breakthrough of no small significance, was about to sweep the North Western. Work on a still heavier Ten-Wheeler for freight service was to have a great impact. At the time of C&NW's final R Class deliveries in the Fall of 1900, an engine of 82 tons (127,500 lbs. on drivers) was being perfected. This design would be equipped with piston valves, and possessed a grate area of 46.27 square feet versus 28.54 square feet of the R Class. This 63" drivered fast freight design would become the most reliable and valuable medium duty engine on the system for over 40 years. C&NW ultimately acquired 350 R-1s over a 12 year timespan, while Omaha stocked 69 I-1s, and an additional 26 K-1s, a modified I-1.

Omaha's first I-1s came in July 1901, accompanied by three G-2s, 4-6-0s of a far different character. The G-2 Class enjoyed far less success in its passenger service role, curiously bearing consecutive builder's numbers with the I-1s. If Omaha had in mind an exhaustive design contest to settle the narrow versus wide firebox discussion, it came at this time. The first I-1s, Nos. 302-304, were followed by G-2 Nos. 305-307. The G-2s came with a unique cylinder saddle design, common to several other roads, distinguishable by a single piece valve and cylinder head cover. Further, they were to run on 69" drivers, another unusual feature not native to the Omaha. They weighed just under 80 tons. While the I-1s immediately met with success and were duplicated several times, the G-2s finally went out to the Nebraska Division, and were scrapped in the late 1920s.

Evaluation of the G-2 Class, in May 1902, centered on recording No. 305's performance. The big Ten-Wheeler sported a box on the pilot deck that extended over one cylinder. This housing sheltered a man who read the valve events, pressures and timing. No. 305 went onto the level stretch west of Eau Claire, speeding in from Elk Mound at a rate tantamount to flying. The G-2s, similar to Northern Pacific's P-2 Class 4-6-0, went through extensive testing on the Eastern Division mainline.

More than a decade before the G-2s, Omaha invested in another NP design for more basic work: helper service out of St. Paul. The first 2-8-0 used by the Omaha was No. 214, equipped with a slope-back switching tender. It arrived in May 1890. The engine was followed in November 1891 and June 1893 by H-1 Nos. 211

(Above) An obliging fireman provides smoke for photographer Adams as Class F-9 4-6-0 No. 285 slows to a crawl at Bridge 178, outside Fairchild, Wisconsin. The fire is conveniently choked with fresh coal, the pop valves are lifting, and the crew is determined to be immortalized in the gangway on July 6, 1902. The F-9 Class, Schenectady products of 1898, lasted into the 1930s. (Below) With bell ringing and enginemen posed, Omaha 4-4-0 No. 162 heads a way freight near Fairchild on June 28, 1905. Fourteen 63" drivered Class E-8s were built by Schenectady in 1888, with No. 162 being retired in March 1927. Both: *J. Foster Adams.*

and 267 respectively, duplicates of NP's F-l Class, 50" drivered "Octopods" by Baldwin. They all weighed 75 tons and worked several grades, including Hudson Hill.

One difficulty presented early on with the I-1s and R-1s was the plight of the fireman facing the wide grate, long before the Godsend of the early 1920s came - the single "Butterfly" air-operated fire door. Omaha men operated the earlier chain doors, alternately firing each half of the big grate, supplying 200 lbs. of steam pressure, to make over 30,000 lbs. of tractive effort. Eventually the I-1s received superheaters and many other straightforward improvements.

While I-1s enjoyed success through 1903, one of the G-2s (No. 307) got into trouble on the mainline speedway, at Kempton. Located on a sandy, low lying, flat stretch, the lonely station was often plagued with flooding problems. Such was the case early in September 1903, as a special Duluth-bound "extra" passed over the system, picking up passengers on C&NW's Madison Division below Elroy. The special was due past Kempton about 3:00 AM, but a torrential rain struck 100 miles of Omaha track between Elroy and Eau Claire. Minutes before, an eastbound Duluth-Chicago train passed Kempton at reduced speed, but the extra passenger was not so lucky.

In minutes, a torrential downpour choked culverts and overflowed trackside ditches, even as track patrols were looking for problems. A farmer later reported his inability to see four feet from his door just before the excursion train approached Kempton. Proceeding at 25 MPH, Engineer Del Brewer ran G-2 No. 307 into water that covered 400 feet of track. The Saturday morning special crashed into the soft roadway, piling coaches at right angles. No. 307 remained upright, its tank tearing off and plowing into the quagmire. One passenger and two others riding the platforms were killed.

Omaha's mainline was cleared within hours, and new track was built through the site. Two of the C&NW coaches were burned, with total losses running to $75,000. This had been a near repeat of an accident south of Fairchild, in September 1902, in which engine No. 255 struck soft track and toppled on her side. It had not been a bright start for the new Schenectady power and their trains.

The area around the Kempton wreck remained a problem for the Omaha in following years. Once again, on October 29, 1908, fall rains damaged the mainline. The westbound *Chicago-Duluth Limited* running at night at 40 MPH, with brand new I-2 No. 371, ran into a washout, derailed and turned completely around, bunching against its tender. The cars skidded through the soft spot, finally halting at odd angles. Nine passengers were injured.

Back in 1891, Omaha's engineer corps worked on an intriguing alternative to the St. Croix County route. They proposed a connection between N.C. Foster's old Mondovi line and the Ellsworth branch. This was to run via El Paso and Rock Elm, two hamlets in Pierce County, Wisconsin. Engineer O. Vedder was not enthusiastic about the possibilities, as he felt the region was extremely rough. Several alternate surveys ended with the same conclusion: 100 foot high trestles would be needed, and this was felt a poor substitute for the problems of the existing mainline. In a time of intense competition, a shorter route was a motivation. The prospect excited the towns of Ellsworth, Durand and

Mondovi, but by the summer of 1891, the issue lay dormant.

The growing community of North Hudson, clustered around the Omaha car shops, divulged its ethnicity in 1892. The population of 345 was divided into 97 Germans, 57 Norwegians and 54 Irishmen as chief groups. What had been a profoundly Irish company was now moving toward inclusion of skilled craftsmen from other nations. Irishmen continued to be counted behind the throttles, along with Yankees. Conductors continued to be Anglo-Saxon in origin and nature.

At the turn-of-the-century, Omaha had as its General Manager W.A. Scott, appointed when the company discontinued the office of General Superintendent. On June 5, 1899, James Truman Clark was elected Second Vice President. Clark started with the Illinois Central, switching to the North Western in the mid-1880s. In March 1903, jurisdiction was extended to the Operating and Construction Departments of the Omaha. Ex-Canadian A.W. Trenholm came to the Omaha in 1880 from his native Nova Scotia and the Intercolonial Railway. He became a Division Superintendent in 1893, then General Superintendent and finally rose to General Manager until May 1916, when he was promoted to Vice-President and General Manager.

At one time, the Omaha maintained a "Confidence Book" that dealt with the personal conduct of its workers. Several case histories from the 1897-1898 period are of interest. One involved the operator at Knapp, who was discharged as he left his station without permission while Trains 80 and 83 were to be blocked to meet at Knapp. The trains had to be stopped at Hersey and Menomonie Junction, and given caution cards. The operator claimed to be sick, but later in the year, he was discharged for using improper language over the wire, and refusing to comply with the dispatcher's instructions. His general insubordination belied his grade as a "good operator." Michael Donnelly, a St. Paul office worker, was later promoted to operator at Wisconsin Valley Junction and Camp Douglas. Donnelly "failed to raise a block signal" after Train 4 had departed.

In the summer of 1903, in keeping with several other mainline roads, the Omaha acquired its first Pacific type 4-6-2 engines. Omaha's I-2 class, Nos. 371-375, was introduced in May 1903, destined for the Eastern Division and the *North Western Limited*. The I-2 was the first Pacific type on the North Western Line, predating the L Class lignite burner No. 1453 of July 1908. The Omaha engines arrived at Elroy in June 1903 for a two week break-in. Previously, No. 373 was tested between Chicago and Milwaukee, making several successful runs in the high-speed territory on passenger trains. The new engines were all in service by mid-July, "guaranteed to draw 10 sleepers at the rate of 70 MPH," according to the Elroy paper.

Lineside papers continued their praise of the I-2, referring to the "new monster locomotives... largest, heaviest and most expensive of any running out of the Twin Cities." The I-2s had 75" drivers, piston valves similar to the I-1, 21"x 28" cylinders, and an overall weight of 206,500 lbs., or just over 103 tons. Grate area was 47 square feet, compared to the I-1's 46 square feet. The locomotives measured 72 feet over couplers.

Comparatively, Northern Pacific's Q Class 4-6-2s (Nos. 280-286) were similar, but rode on 69" drivers and weighed 97-1/2 tons. Both employed the Rushton trailing truck, not repeated in either case due to the improved Cole truck's availability.

The fast rise of the I-1 4-6-0 as Omaha's prime freight power in the first decade of the 20th Century is illustrated in dispatcher's records. On December 8, 1904, I-1 No. 311 assisted by sister I-1 No. 321 worked a westbound extra up Knapp Hill as far as Wilson. Engine 321 then returned to Knapp for another assist westbound. The next extra again had No. 321, with No. 325 working hard past Humbird's Point, a scenic location just east of Wilson. Other I-1s that day running between Eau Claire and Hudson on freights were Nos. 316, 322 and 327.

Sometimes the I-1s got into trouble. In June 1906, No. 316 was proceeding through Wascott on the Superior line. It was a Wednesday morning, and everything was fine until the crown sheet in the firebox dropped, blasting hot water and steam into the left side of the cab. Brakeman Ambrose Sales and Fireman Charles L. Stevens were badly scalded, but managed to jump. Engineer Robert Hanson was unhurt, however. The injured were taken to the Spooner Red Cross Hospital for recovery from painful burns.

Omaha's total bonded debt on December 31, 1901, was $25,831,324.41, of which $24,167,800.00 was outstanding, and the balance ($1,663,524.41) was held in the treasury. Other actions that year were the acquisition of the Minnesota & Wisconsin Railroad, 15.7 miles, and the Chippewa Valley North Western Railroad Company, 12.5 miles. Line changes comprised 7.9 miles: a major change between Fairchild and Humbird, Wisconsin; 1.2 miles between Boardman and Burkhardt in St.

Croix County; and another 1.6 miles between Clayton and Turtle Lake in Polk County. There were 14.7 miles of grade changes at seven other locations in Wisconsin, and the combined actions moved 558,700 cubic yards of earth and 39,000 cubic yards of rock. Twelve steel bridges, five stone culverts and eight iron pipe culverts were built, replacing 1,042 feet of wood bridging. The line was shortened 828 feet; curvature was reduced 226 degrees, 58 minutes, and 11-1/2 miles of grades ranging from 0.7% to 1%, were reduced to less than 0.6%. Another 5000 feet of line at 0.9% was reduced to 0.7%. In the process of leveling and lining, 23 wood bridges were replaced with steel and stone culverts or with steel bridges. Still another 4,569 feet of earth fill permanently replaced wood bridges.

Building construction, in 1901, included the 50x800 foot Minneapolis freight house, plus two-story extensions and improvements on brick buildings at St. Paul Shops. There were also new depots erected at Hersey, Boardman, Barronett and Minong, in Wisconsin, plus Belle Plaine, Grogan and Lake Wilson, in Minnesota.

Omaha's rail-change program continued, and 108 miles of 60 lb. rail was replaced with 80 lb. rail. A new yard at Barronett replaced the ruins of the fire-ravaged original, including a new depot and turntable. In Minneapolis, the Omaha purchased about 23 acres of property between First Street North and the Mississippi River from Plymouth Avenue to Twentieth Avenue North. At Sioux City, Iowa, more property was being acquired to extend and enlarge the shops and yards.

Omaha operated three classes of transfer 2-8-0s, beginning in 1890, with H-1 Class No. 214, followed by Nos. 211 (in 1891) and 267 (in 1893), all Baldwin-built. In 1898 and 1901, Baldwin delivered four H-2 engines, Nos. 209, 210, 228 and 229. Class H-3 Nos. 216 and 217 came in 1905 from Alco. All rode on 50" drivers and came with slope back tenders. H-2 No. 209 was delivered in October 1898. *Author's Collection.*

Originally No. 267, Class H-1 No. 227 is on the verge of retirement at St. Paul on June 8, 1927. The design was identical to Northern Pacific's F-1 Class of 1888. In June 1928, the H-1s were displaced by the arrival of four heavy 0-8-0 switchers. *Robert H. Graham.*

To accommodate the heavier power that was arriving, new steel turntables were installed at Minneapolis and St. James, in Minnesota, as well as at Spooner and Itasca, in Wisconsin.

Equipment purchases included 12 locomotives, 2 parlor cars, 27 refrigerator cars, 50 vegetable cars, 30 flats and 5 cabooses, at a total cost of $238,909.69. The Omaha, in 1901, operated 1,590.61 miles of track.

West of Blakeley, Minnesota (north of Mankato), improvements were made to 2.75 miles of line along the Minnesota River, as seven wood bridges were removed and the gradient improved. Six reverse curves were eliminated and curvature was decreased some 122 degrees 27 minutes. Also, more buildings were constructed. At Prince Street in St. Paul, a two-story 40x468 foot brick freight house replaced a wood structure. East St. Paul had six stalls added to its engine house, while on St. Paul's west side, a one-story 40x104 foot brick freight house arose. Hudson Shops received a new 102x234 foot paint shed. Spooner's new depot measured 32x234 feet and was of frame construction, with an accompanying frame baggage and express building.

In 1901-1903, the work at Sioux City was extensive. This included grading of new land for yard additions and constructing a new 15 stall roundhouse with a 70 foot turntable suitable for I-1 and I-2 Class power (23 additional stalls were added to the roundhouse by 1910). There were also three buildings over 250 feet long for machinery; a boiler and blacksmith shop, a large storehouse/office, as well as an electric transfer table. The company also erected an elevated coal dock with a 188 foot sloping trestle, with a height of 47 feet. It lasted well into the 1930s.

Later, in 1906, further improvements were in order when the new yard at Plymouth Avenue was completed at Minneapolis.

Also that same year, a start was made on a new yard at Harvester Works in St. Paul. Omaha realigned trackage at Lake Crystal, Minnesota, between Bingham Lake and Windom in 1906, and relocated an old problem, the track between Ottawa and St. Peter, plus the Minneopa Park realignment.

Between orders for its first Pacific types for passenger service, Omaha emulated C&NW, in early 1906, by receiving four Atlantic type 4-4-2 engines, based on the current C&NW D Class designs, the first of which arrived in late summer 1901. C&NW got 91 Ds between 1901 and 1908, most having Stevenson valve gear, weighing 86 tons loaded, with 81" drivers. The G-3s, as Omaha classified them, were representative of the "middle" group of C&NW power, and were equipped with Alligator crossheads. G-3 Nos. 367-370 were followed in June 1906 by Nos. 364-366, going to work on the Eastern Division, powering several mainline trains.

In May 1907, another order of I-2 Class 4-6-2s arrived from Alco, Nos. 376-378. The new I-2s came with an improved trailing truck that set all subsequent orders apart from the pioneer 371-375. It was a built-up improvement over the inboard bearing truck, a design by American Locomotive Company's F.J. Cole. The key was the outside-mounted journals, giving the necessary stability. The G-3 4-4-2s had received a truck with limited lateral motion, with many familiar features. Both trailing trucks were used by Alco in the early 1900s. The new I-2s weighed 5500 lbs. more than the earlier engines. The pioneer Pacifics numbered 17 engines, Nos. 371-387 inclusive. The last examples, in December 1910, came with Walschaert valve gear. Whatever the power Omaha employed on its Limiteds, the fast-running territory on the Eastern Division was east of Eau Claire, where speed was the order of the day.

Omaha's first departure from the elegant engines of the early 1890s were the F-8 4-4-0s like No. 255 shown on a local passenger train on September 5, 1904. Characteristic of the class was the extended wagon-top boiler. Other features included a clerestory cab, shotgun stack and 73" drivers, the first on the railroad. The 1898 Schenectady engine was retired in May 1933. *J. Foster Adams.*

Fourteen F-8 Class 4-4-0s came from Schenectady in 1896-1899. No. 251 lacks the clerestory cab roof in this April 1906 view at Fairchild. The engine was in service until 1933. *J. Foster Adams.*

(Above) By the early 1930s, the F-8 Class was beginning to fade, but four superheated examples continued to work light runs (Nos. 257, 258, 259, 276). No. 257 displays several improvements, at Minneapolis in 1932, including a welded tender tank and Andrews tender trucks. *Robert H. Graham.*

(Left) The last F-8s worked trains between Merrillan and Manitowoc, via Wausau-Eland-Appleton Junction for parent C&NW. No. 257 is shown at Eland in 1940, not long before being retired. *Neil Torssell.*

91

(Above) Pristine G-1 No. 294 is shown near Fairchild on the "Marshfield Freight" on July 23, 1904. Similar to C&NW's R Class, thirteen G-1 Class engines came from Schenectady in mid-1899 and January 1900. The arrival of the I-1 Class will soon eliminate such narrow firebox engines from all but the basic jobs on the Eastern Division. The last four of the 63" drivered G-1s were cut up in mid-1935. (Below) Production of the I-1s began in 1901 and continued through December 1910, by which time there were 69 of the 63" drivered engines. No. 336 was at Fairchild in October 1906, just four months after delivery. Both: *J. Foster Adams.*

Another Omaha thrust to search out the virtues of the Ten-Wheeler was the dual service concept that could extend to a 69" drivered, narrow firebox design, competing with the I-1. Three Class G-2 engines, Nos. 305-307, came in May 1901, just prior to the delivery of the I-1s. (Above) G-2 No. 307 has the *Badger State Express* behind the drawbar at Fairchild, Wisconsin. Although the G-2s were experimental, they apparently had enough stamina to handle the Limited's seven car consist. (Below) The left side view of the engine was taken on November 26, 1903. No. 307 was retired in March 1929. Both: *J. Foster Adams.*

# OMAHA TEN-WHEELERS
## THE LONG LINE OF EVOLUTION

(Right) Omaha's F-2 Class had 19" cylinders, 59" drivers and even drive wheel spacing. Eighteen arrived in 1892-1893 from Schenectady. No. 196 is shown at Fairchild, Wisconsin. It was retired in December 1929.

(Below) Five E-4 Class 4-6-0s came from Schenectady in August 1885, with 18" cylinders and 57" drivers. Relegated to branchline duty by the 1920s, Nos. 95-99 were all scrapped in 1927. Engine No. 97 was photographed at the Hudson depot after getting a fresh clean-up of signal oil applied to the boiler jacket. Both: *J. Foster Adams.*

(Right) The lone example of the F-3 Class was No. 226, Baldwin-built in August 1893. Photographed at Mankato, Minnesota, in the 1920s, it had 55" drivers and a slope back switcher tender. It was retired in 1929. *John Tesky Collection.*

(Left) Schenectady delivered four 67" drivered Class F-5s in July 1892. The last survivor in passenger service, No. 266, was at Sioux City, Iowa, on September 27, 1928, a few months before retirement. *Robert H. Graham.*

(Below) Two F-7 Class 4-6-0s came from Schenectady in 1897, 63" drivers and underslung springs, plus the all important extended wagon-top boiler. In 1922, a rare photo depicts No. 273 taking water at Omaha. The engine was retired in 1930. *J. Foster Adams.*

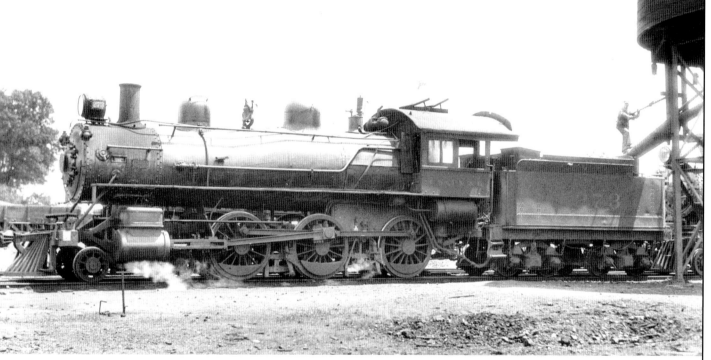

The Omaha ordered ten F-9s, Nos. 279-288, with curious 59" drivers. Delivered in 1898 by Schenectady, they featured clerestory cab roofs and the final version of CStPM&O corporate initials on the tender. All ten engines were retired in 1933-35. *Alco Historic Photos.*

# OMAHA TEN-WHEELERS
## CLASS I-1: THE ULTIMATE 4-6-0

In the spring of 1901, the North Western completed its exploration of 4-6-0 designs for freight service and ordered the product of their deliberations: C&NW's first R-1 arrived from Schenectady in April, and 20 were present by year's end. Omaha's first I-1s (Nos. 302-304) arrived in the summer of 1901, curiously bearing the lowest of that years builder's numbers. The principle feature of the R-1/I-1 design was its wide firebox, then coming into general use. The new engines had a grate area of 46 square feet, 17 more than the G-1/R Classes of 1898. Aside from the larger heating surface, the boiler shells were very nearly the same. Lastly, the newcomers had innovative piston valves, previously found less than perfect due to lubrication problems. At the same time, competitor Milwaukee Road acquired 65 heavy Baldwin compound 4-6-0s, also boasting 45 square feet of grate area. Milwaukee would field still heavier 4-6-0s destined to compete in freight service between Chicago and the Twin Cities. Elsewhere, two other contenders for the trade, the Chicago Great Western and Chicago, Burlington & Quincy, chose Prairie types, also with wide fireboxes, to do the same work. Modernized with superheaters during the early 1920s, the R-1/I-1 program proved to be a solid one as the majority of the engines operated well into the diesel era.

(Right) Omaha's first three I-1s arrived in July 1901 with 5,400 gallon tenders. Almost a year later, No. 302 halts at the Fairchild, Wisconsin, depot, while the crew and a few "sports" pose for the camera.

(Below) Also at Fairchild, No. 345 was built in July 1906, part of the 336-345 number group. It featured a 7,500 gallon tender and alligator crossheads. By this time, the lettering scheme had evolved to using large, road numbers on the tender sides. Engine No. 345 was retired in August 1954. Both: *J. Foster Adams.*

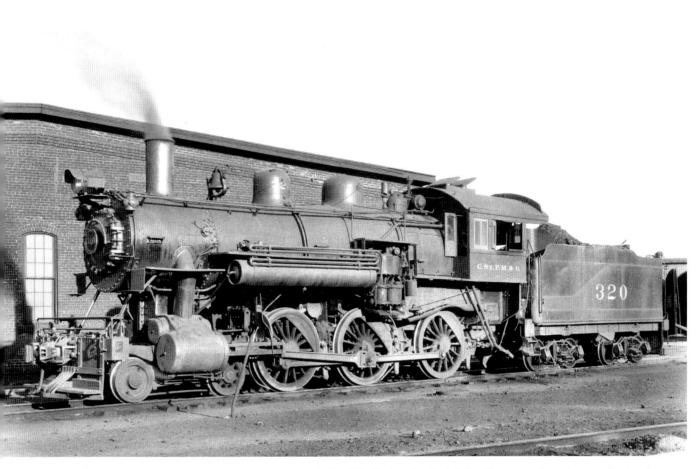

(Above) Sitting alongside the Altoona roundhouse in 1941, I-1 No. 320 displays the last style of large road numbers on the tender. The 1903 Alco product was from the third group of I-1s and was retired in September 1945. *Harold Du Bal Collection.* (Below) At Hudson on October 16, 1938, I-1 No. 353 is set up for winter operations with a flanger plow. The final tender lettering scheme is represented, featuring the parent road's "ball and bar" herald. The 1907 engine was in service until August 1954. *Robert H. Graham.*

Known as the "Zenith City," Duluth, Minnesota, in its heyday was a vibrant, growing lakehead community with ties to the richest iron-ore deposit in America, plus the established grain and lumber industry. Union Depot, with its huge train shed, is at left center, while the Omaha's depot appears in the right center distance. *Author's Collection.*

# 6.

## DULUTH, SUPERIOR AND SPOONER

Deep in St. Croix woods, the "Superior branch" was studded with many log landings or junctions with logging roads. There were several lines out of Hines station, 22 miles from Duluth. David Tozer's St. Croix Timber Company railroad and Edward Hines' own road were neighbors. The Weyerhaeuser firm ran a mill at Nebagamon, and the largest stumpage acquisition ($580,000 worth) nearly doubled their holdings with 1/2 billion board feet purchased from the Omaha. Weyerhaeuser subsidiary Hawthorne, Nebagamon & Superior Railroad ran 7-1/2 miles out to the Omaha at Hawthorne. The road operated until Edward Hines bought the property, at which time some of its locomotives were transferred to Park Falls, and the HN&S was abandoned.

Hines bought approximately 300 million standing feet of pine in 1902 in western Bayfield County. The Omaha was involved to the extent of leasing rail and rolling stock to Edward Hines, a common practice. The logger set up a six stall enginehouse three miles west of Hines station to house leased engines (an LST&T 0-6-0 and ex-PRR 2-8-0s). The timber cut was often as much as 36 cars per day, and this would be transferred to Hayward for finish-milling. Other logs went to Stillwater, Minnesota.

Duluth traffic rose enough by the end of the century to cause the Omaha to pronounce the Superior line foremost, a shift from the original importance of the Ashland-Bayfield line. It was the track location and interlocking plant construction at Trego that rendered the road to Chequamegon Bay the junior. In 1885, when Pullman Palace cars were seen at the Twin Ports, they were thinly patronized. The great cars were deleted that year because Duluth-Superior was still growing, and the Missabe wealth was only beginning to flow. On the Omaha, and near the HN&S interchange in late 1895, the company excavated to both produce fill for Itasca Yard and to widen the space available for trackage at Hawthorne. In 1897, approval came for improvement between Spooner and Superior Junction.

Spooner's beginnings as a town date from 1882, as the last parts of the North Wisconsin Railroad were completed in a territory that became Washburn County in 1883. The Chandler location was not level enough for development as a yard or townsite, and thus the choice was five miles south. In the end, Spooner responded to the railroad's requirements for a division point. The 1890s Depression, however, didn't help Spooner's growth. One ex-Canadian storekeeper, 12 years in Spooner, elected to return to the old country.

Spooner's first hotel, an Omaha creation, served meals to crowds of passengers who left the cars for north country cuisine. The Omaha's roundhouse, coal chute and yard were the center of activity in the comparatively new town, now shaken by economic troubles. Nonetheless, Spooner would weather the storm. By December 1893, the local newspaper called upon General Superintendent W.A. Scott to generate a great depot worthy of the town, hardly the first time Scott, of St. Paul Headquarters, was so buttonholed. It was promised, but had to await better times.

During the mid-1890s disruption, Omaha conductors on passenger trains were reassigned from their hard-won positions at a moment's notice, like men "working extra." The general displacement was also manifested by 16 engines entering storage at Spooner due to a lack of business. One machinist returned to New York State after his Spooner layoff. In June 1894, the American Railway Union struck, and as Omaha was covered in agreements with the brotherhood, it was idled. Spooner was soon full of unused engines and men. The action centered on sympathy for the Pullman strike, and Omaha men were discharged for refusing to handle the cars. In sympathy, ARU's Spooner Lodge went out in full, some 300 strong and quiet prevailed.

As the strike continued in July, St. Paul-Minneapolis experienced car shortages, which shut down shippers. On the Omaha, all trains continued on the mainline, and on time, except for the *North Western Limited*. There were no trains to and from Duluth. Spooner's ARU chapter was entertained by the Spooner's Athletic and Concert Company, a benefit performance for the strikers. After the Indian club and horizontal bar act, ARU publicly thanked the athletes for their support. In time, the Omaha men returned to work at their old positions.

Spooner in 1894 also found A.W. Trenholm of the Omaha the president of the Spooner Loan & Building Association, engaged in real estate work. The firm was prosperous over the previous year, while banks weren't. Roadmaster T.H. Hillman was another officer. Henry H. Porter, en route with Marvin Hughitt, Scott and Trenholm, used the Omaha business car, with a long stop at Spooner. Porter frequented the Omaha in the 1890s in the affairs of his iron and steel empire, which became part of United States Steel Company in 1901. It was also the time for state fisheries car No.1, the *Badger*, to distribute small fry trout, bringing those less important than Porter to reside near northern waters.

Fires around Spooner brought another anxiety in September 1894. The nearby communities of Shell Lake and Barronett were hard hit. Barronett was wiped out, the loss estimated at $275,000. Spooner was threatened, barely saved by a hard fight on the part of townspeople and the Omaha, which suspended traffic for three days. Some special trains were dispatched to evacuate fire victims of Shell Lake, threatened by a southwesterly firewind. It had a parallel on the St. Paul & Duluth, the "Skally," in Minnesota.

# LINES IN WISCONSIN

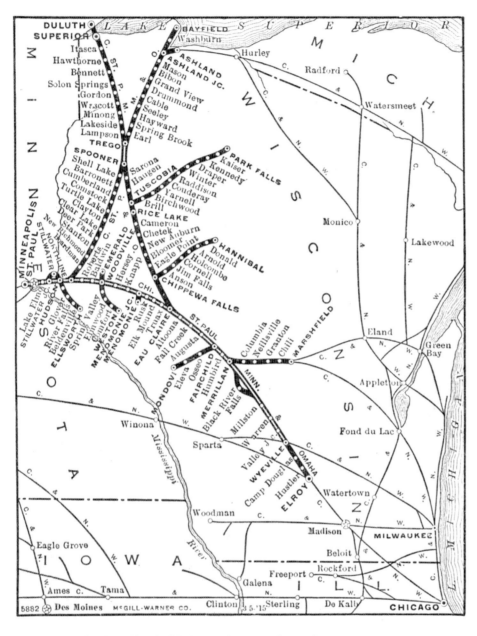

(Above) Produced by McGill-Warner Company for the Omaha public timetable dated June 25, 1924, this map features the "great Omaha X," an image created when mapping the Eau Claire-Superior line and the route from Bayfield to Northline (three miles east of Hudson) with their crossing at Spooner-Trego. *Author's Collection.*

to Allouez, then began the fast run southward. The big F-8 was up to the task, as the time for the Itasca-Spooner leg, 66 miles, was run in 65 minutes. The Itasca-Eau Claire lap was performed in 154 minutes, which included three stops, and a considerable wait at Spooner's important station. The Holts made the mainline Limited with just ten minutes to spare.

In the depressed mid-1890s, Spooner experienced a loss of jobs, with scores of men affected. Many wrote back to Spooner's hometown newspaper from remote posts, including the western divisions of the Northern Pacific, discussing their adventures. By 1904, the road was borrowing men for an unprecedented rush of business at Superior. Trainmen were enlisted from the Iron Range roads, as pulpwood and winter coal needed transport to inland markets. Large pulpwood cuts were being shipped to new paper plants, which had supplanted the pine log harvest in many Wisconsin towns. The activity took place the same year as 52 new block signal stations were established on the Northern District (lines north of Eau Claire and Northline) at a cost of $15,000. A year later, the Northern line was host to the great 25 carload Marshall-Wells Paint Train, the largest consignment of paint to one firm ever shipped to the Northwest. The cargo weighed 950 tons.

Spooner finally got its new depot, in the fall of 1902. In 1903, the division's Bridge & Building Department moved into the new second floor. Spooner was satisfied, especially as the new bulletin board gave all trains a full billing. The great Spooner Railway Eating House, an imposing building of wood, was shifted westward toward the town in 1902. A quasi-railroad operation, the house had its supplies carried in Omaha baggage cars at a reduced charge. Five years later, billing was required as the old way constituted a free ride for the news company, which ran the institution. In 1929, the Union News Company, the ultimate operator, discontinued its dining room as uptown restaurants cut into the railroad trade. Such institutions were disappearing nationwide. The large old wooden hotel building, once moved west, was moved again. Final disposition wasn't until the 1960s, when it was torn down.

The Trego-Superior Junction upgrading included building a second track to Spooner. The Trego interlocking tower was built into a depot in 1906, and Hall signals controlled the territory in between. The gravel pit at Chandler was used for coal storage in 1902-1903, hoarded for Omaha's own use that winter. It was the same year that the Omaha employed E-4 Class 4-6-0s Nos. 97 and 99 as helpers at Spooner. The 49 ton engines were manned by "sometimes paper editor" Frank Hammill, who worked southbound drags to Shell Lake with the F-4s. Hammill ultimately

There, engineer James Root succeeded in saving scores in the famous Hinckley Fire. Omaha's loss at Barronett was $8,000, mostly buildings. The yard was the subject of replacement in the early 1900s.

The line to Superior had been improved to the point of inviting a speed event, but not for sheer pleasure. In 1903, George H. and William A. Holt of American Lumber Company were anxious to get to their dying mother's bedside in Chicago. Engaging the Omaha to run a special from Duluth to Eau Claire, the railroad had idle equipment from the *Twilight Limited* available. The engine was equal to the task: F-8 No. 251, with Conductor Kelly and Engineer William Frazer in charge. No. 251 eased cautiously

became Spooner's mayor, and bought the town's newspaper. Hammill used his clout to push for a big shop at Spooner, mixing journalism and valve oil to acceptable consistencies. Jack Farrell was another Irishman on the helpers. There was also James Killoran, assigned to Washburn, while Thomas Riley was assigned to passenger trains. Conductors Fearney, Sharpe and Owen O'Connor were present and accounted for.

Log trains filled many dispatch sheets at Spooner. The Mason-New Richmond job ran log flats to the Glover mill. A Grand View-Chippewa Falls drag brought out still more. An Itasca-Superior Junction operation was another consisting of rumbling flat cars with great pine logs aboard. Another turnaround job ran between Spooner and Cumberland, one that elicited competition among trainmen for the work. Amid the log extras in 1903, a new *Twilight Limited,* splendidly appointed and equipped with a parlor-observation car, was available to the Duluth traveler. The *Limited,* Trains 63-64, left St. Paul at 4:25 PM and arrived at Spooner at 7:20 PM. Spooner then dispatched an Ashland-bound section, Train 65, for a 10:10 PM arrival. The Duluth train arrived daily at 9:59 PM. In March 1903, however, a log train met the *Twilight Limited* in a collision a mile above Hayward in a blinding snowstorm. Fireman Frank Boehm was killed when the logger failed to clear the oncoming passenger train.

Occasionally, errors in messages spelled the difference between safety and disaster. On September 28, 1906, Train 64, with engine No. 252, an F-8 Class, struck a washout one mile north of Rockmont. The track was undermined for two feet, and while the engine passed over the spot, the tender, combination car and parlor car went into the void. The combine turned upside down. Two company officers were aboard and sustained injuries, along with three passengers. Engineer John Cameron had observed all due caution in running engine No. 252, to the extent of coming to a full stop before proceeding slowly into the imperiled area. The trouble was that the message read to be on the lookout for washouts one mile south of Rockmont, not north. Both Cameron and section men were ready for trouble to the south.

As service to Duluth rose in importance, the Spooner outpost burgeoned. In 1904, Omaha put on its new *Duluth Limited* to coordinate with the *Badger State Express* eastbound at Eau Claire. A return trip could be effected aboard a connection with the *Twilight Limited* to Spooner. A library car and two 12 section sleepers were available on the newcomer. The *Duluth Limited* had its troubles with schedule-keeping, larger power not withstanding. Blizzards in the north dictated double-heading, with speeds in such weather hardly breathtaking. Spooner gathered more importance when foundations were laid for long engine stalls at its roundhouse. It meant large power was coming.

Winters at Spooner, in May 1915, also included running perishable cars into the roundhouse to save them from abysmal temperatures. Cold of 20-50 below was not unknown. Yet in 1915, the house required attention as engines froze in their stalls due to the building's poor condition. It was questionable if there would be improvements that year, yet a 90 foot steel turntable was installed in the summer. There was also discussion regarding the

Competition for Omaha came from Lake Superior & Mississippi Railroad, shown in this 1870s view at Duluth. LS&M opened trade between the Twin Cities and Twin Ports, later becoming St. Paul & Duluth, and then Northern Pacific. *Minnesota Historical Society.*

installation of false floors in perishable cars to circulate warmer air inside.

North of Spooner, in June 1916, was the territory of the Ten-Wheeler. One bit of evidence, a "flimsy," survives to give notice of a few trains and men's passage near Minong: "To Conductor and Engineer of Extra 203 North (K-1 4-6-0 No. 203) at Minong. 10:01 AM, No. 61 will meet Extra 237 South (K-1 No. 237), Conductor King, at Sauntry, and Extra 203, C.E. Johnson, at Solon Springs and take siding at Solon Springs and pull by and back in." Also, March 23, 1916, 10:19 AM: "No. 96 D.M. Enockson will wait at Lakeside until 10:55 AM for Extra 222 South (I-1 4-6-0 No. 222), C.F. Johnson, and meet No. 61 Lowe at Wascott." Another read: "Second No. 73, Gillen, will meet Extra 360 North (I-1 No. 360), P. Calhoun, at Barronett." I-1's 357, 321, 105 and K-1's 183 and 240 were also running on the line.

In 1925, the Omaha at Spooner was handling a brisk pulpwood trade, and practically every station northward had great stacks of logs as a backdrop, the gondola and flat car representing the means of transport. The largest operators were Northern Pulp & Timber Company, with landings at Lampson, Young's Spur, Lakeside (100,000 feet) and Minong (150,000 feet). NP&TCo was a Duluth-based firm, with several local jobbers. Another operator in the thinning northwoods was Sampson & Link, also at Minong, who banked tons of logs at nearby Gordon and Wascott. Goodwin & Gilbert, still another woods operator, contracted for cedar posts. Bennett was another site, which held 75,000 logs in March 1925 for Northern Pulp & Timber. To the east, on the Ashland line, logs were readied for the mills at Trego, Earl and Spring Brook. Spooner itself had a greater pulpwood load than ever for shipment. In that same month, a great pine in Forest County named "King Tut" was cut. Tut possessed 467 growth rings, and was left standing for 45 years beyond its discovery, as it was too big for the then existing mills. Save for a few areas, Wisconsin pine was nearly extinct.

Spooner, its roundhouse burdened with a number of I-1, K-1 and F-2 Ten-Wheelers used to handling log trains, suffered a setback May 8, 1925. A fire destroyed the old eight stall frame section, and three locomotives had their cabs burned off. The fire was discovered at 6:45 AM, with a prompt response, but little could be done. Attempts were made to pull the engines out with cables, but their cabs burned despite the effort. Loss was $30,000. The cabless engines went to St. Paul Shops for repairs. The newer brick additions bracketed the fire on either end, and the replacement was well along by the fall.

Spooner, in the mid-1920s, had several passenger trains, but only one was a through train to Duluth-Superior. True, there were trains beginning and ending there, like Train 98 from Eau Claire in the afternoon, and a combined run up just after seven to the Lakehead. The *Duluth-Superior Limited* (Trains 511-512), overnight from Chicago, was the premier service. It carried the separate numbers 93-94 north of Spooner, sharing the road with the *Duluth Express*, Trains 95-96, the daily run that coordinated with Trains 403-404 from Milwaukee, over the new line.

Train service adjustments loomed for the summer of 1925. The changes took into account the automobile traffic eroding the new resort business, even causing layoffs for Omaha men. The new *Arrowhead Limited* was to make its first run on June 1st, leaving Duluth daily at 9:15 PM for Chicago. The *Arrowhead* would operate in summer months only, catering to the tourist into October. Afterward, it would be replaced by Trains 65 and 97. Competitor Mohawk Bus Lines began to run Duluth-Spooner-Eau Claire with large and commodious vehicles.

When the Omaha merged its Northern and Eastern Division, at first naming it the Wisconsin Division, headquarters were moved to Eau Claire. C.D. Stockwell became the new division's Assistant Superintendent in October 1925. The movement included the old Northern's dispatchers at Spooner and Itasca, the relocation a typical one for railroaders. The shakedown inevitably put one man off; W.K. Neal went to Portland, Oregon, to become a Traveling Agent for the road. As the transplants and their families settled into life at Eau Claire, I-1 and J Class helpers were active out of Knapp, often scorching ties, where firemen cleaned their engine's fire (cinders and coals would be dumped into ash-pans, allowing the fires to breathe better).

As the largest Omaha power came to dominate Wisconsin Division trains, the business of fire cleaning was specified at Altoona. The General Manager suggested doing away with the practice at Knapp and Lakeland Junction, eastbound. The tie bill for fire damages was running to $140 annually. The damage also caused train delays, as engine crews would elect to drop ashes when on the spot. Motive Power Chief Gorman offered that ash-pan water spray was now available to quench potential fires.

During the era of the United States Railroad Administration, Omaha acquired four heavy Mikados from Schenectady, Nos. 422-425. The 320,000 lb. machines were the first 63" drivered Mikes on the roster. They were followed by six more built by Richmond, a division of American Locomotive Company, delivered in January 1921. The J-2s came equipped with stokers; Nos. 422-425 (straight USRA designs) had Standard stokers, while Nos. 426-431 carried Duplex Stokers. Operation of J-2s by the mid-1920s seems to have been largely an Eastern Division affair, mostly on the Elroy-St. Paul mainline and at times on the Marshfield line.

In February 1921, Spooner's agent at the depot was given authority to employ an inspector from 3 PM to 11 PM. Passenger trains were rearranged in the early evening. Train 65, the *Twin City Passenger*, had to be inspected, with air, steam and signal lines cut (uncoupled), the train switched and light cleaning was performed. Train 20 supplied some cars for Train 66 bound for Ashland, and Train 98 was to be switched and readied for the next day's round trip, requiring cleaning. The northbound *Twilight Limited*, Train 64, was broken up with a mail car going on to Ashland. The *Chicago Limited*, Train 93, was also inspected. Another train required a mail car cut in, and Train 93 had inspection and a dining car cut off. The work was considerable and a request was made for three carmen at the depot over 2-1/2 hours. The work included servicing refrigerator car heaters in slack time over the shift. The reefers required careful tending with heaters to prevent perishables from freezing in the frigid winter temperatures. One year later, Spooner was caught in a still famous blizzard, which raged on February 22, 1922. The company's Cooke-built 1888 rotary snowplow, usually stabled on the Western Division, was summoned to clear the northern Wisconsin lines out of Spooner. Digging out was a major effort.

(Above) The Omaha reached Duluth in 1885 and established passenger and freight depots at 5th Avenue and Commerce Street. The small depot at right sports a "Royal Route" sign for the discerning traveler. On the other side of the depot, the road's Limited is ready for departure. The Omaha freight depot is the large building to the left. In time, the mud flats were filled with more industry. In the distance, Minnesota Point protects the harbor of Duluth and Superior. *Wayne C. Olson Collection.* (Below) Omaha passenger Train 96, the *Chicago Express*, is shown departing the Itasca depot in the 1920s. The train, which boasted an observation-cafe car between Eau Claire and the Lakehead, will arrive in downtown Duluth in 45 minutes. *Author's Collection.*

In 1920, Omaha defined the difference between a "switch engine" and a "switch train." It made a difference in the pocketbook, as a switch train carried lower pay scale for its crew. The difference branded the Cornell job a switch train, but work at Rice Lake and Ashland remained switch engines.

Assignments of locomotives in 1927 included a large compliment of older switch engines, used chiefly east of St. Paul. They matched in modest quantities the large roster of North Western 0-6-0s built during the World War I period, Omaha followed suit with three designs. In September 1917, the M-2 Class arrived, nine strong, weighing 173,000 lbs. This design was actually heavier than the second series (USRA M-3 Class) that weighed 163,500 lbs. In 1927, the M-2's (Nos. 46-54 inclusive) and M-3's (Nos. 75-82 inclusive) worked mostly on transfers and some helper assignments, with Nos. 77-80 and 83 used at Itasca and the Duluth-Superior terminals. Omaha created a special variation of the M-3 USRA type in February 1921, Nos. 83-86 inclusive. They came with large C&NW standard road-style cabs and tenders similar to the M-2 Class, carrying 6,500 gallons of water and 10 tons of coal. On the Western Division, where the older M-1 Class switchers were found, St. James and St. Paul (Western Avenue) utilized three M-3 Class newcomers.

1927 was the final year for Omaha's H Class 2-8-0s to dominate heavy Twin Cities work. All were regulars on transfer and helper assignments and around East St. Paul. In August and September 1928, eight heavy M-5 Class 0-8-0s (Nos. 60-67 inclusive) took over the hard work of helping eastbound drags toward Hudson and coping with the hills. The M-5s weighed 239,000 lbs. each and put forth 58,400 lbs. of tractive effort. Some of the 2-8-0s were moved to outlying terminals such as Sioux City. Nos. 209, 210, 216, 217, 228 and 229 survived, but H-1 pioneers 211 and 227 (formerly 267) were scrapped in 1928.

While retired General John J. "Black Jack" Pershing was received by an admiring crowd at Washburn in 1924, President Calvin Coolidge arrived at Spooner in mid-June 1928 to establish his northwoods White House at Winneboujou, in Douglas County. His special train arrived at Spooner at 6:30 AM, with grade crossings guarded by Omaha employees, and switches on the mainline spiked for the passage. The special went to Superior, then they motored to Brule. The President's wife arrived sometime later on the DSS&A at Winneboujou. After being seen occasionally in the area, and with some fishing luck, Coolidge passed through Spooner on August 2 at 9:30 AM southbound, the President and family waving from the back platform. Up ahead, Engineer Emory LePage and Fireman George Plahn assumed responsibilities and delivered "Silent Cal" to the mainline at Eau Claire.

An Omaha work train headed by K-1 No. 356 is anchoring a pile driver on the dock flanking Commerce Slip in Duluth. Accessed from Omaha trackage (to the left), the tracks on this dock were laid in 1891 and were Omaha owned. The caboose is blocking tracks known as the *Commerce Tracks*, which were jointly owned by NP (3/4) and Omaha (1/4). They ended at 5th Avenue (behind the large building) and were used to access the docks along the city's waterfront southwest of here. In the background, M-3 No. 78 brings a cut of cars past the Omaha passenger depot. The author was on-hand to observe this scene along with the photographer on October 20, 1955. *Wayne C. Olson.*

(Left) Omaha's 1897 depot in Duluth was designed by Chicago architect Charles S. Frost. This view shows the north side of the structure, away from the tracks.

(Below) The depot's east end with its curving platform and shelter roof as seen in the 1940s. Both: *William F. Armstrong.*

The Duluth depot in the late 1950s has activity by both tenants. C&NW switcher No. 1237 has delivered Train 510, the *Chicago Limited,* to the depot prior to its early evening departure. The train arrived earlier in the day as the *Duluth-Superior Limited.* The passenger cars were serviced at the 5th Ave coach yard, and the train was turned at Garfield Ave. At right, Duluth, Winnipeg & Pacific's Rail Diesel Car No. D-301 awaits its run to Fort Francis, Ontario. *A. Robert Johnson.*

(Above) Alco delivered in 1921, Class M-3 Nos. 83-86 were "copies" of the USRA engines, but had M-2 type cabs and tenders. Shown switching cars near the Duluth depot on September 18, 1951, No. 85 was retired in May 1954. *Charles Winters Collection.* (Below) M-3 No. 85 switches cars at Omaha's 8th Avenue merchandise warehouse in Duluth in 1948. Wholesale grocers Gamble-Robinson and Arrowhead Grocery occupied the 80 x 918 foot structure, which was completely rebuilt after a disastrous fire in July 1904. Omaha's original dock and warehouse were constructed in 1886. *C&NWRy.*

(Above) Class F-10 No. 22 was built by Baldwin in July 1902. Photographed in Duluth on June 3, 1935, the 51" drivered 0-6-0 was retired in March 1945, after nearly 43 years of service. *Robert H. Graham.* (Below) Class M-3 No. 78, a grimy Duluth fixture, faces its final winter of operation in 1955-56. The engine was built for the United States Railroad Administration in July 1919 and assigned to the Omaha as part of a group of eight 0-6-0s, Nos. 75-82. The tenders later had their coal bunkers narrowed for "clear vision." It was retired in June 1956. *Frank A. King.*

(Inset) John Vachon, photographer for the government "Farm Service Administration," climbed the Great Northern grain elevator concrete annex in August 1941 to record Northern Pacific's great drawbridge over St. Louis Bay, connecting West Superior with Rice's Point. The "Wisconsin Draw" swing bridge is in the immediate foreground, with the "Minnesota Draw" in the background. The Omaha gained access to Duluth and their own yard and engine terminal on Rice's Point via trackage rights over the 1885 built structure, which was double-tracked to the Minnesota Draw in 1908. *Library of Congress.*
(Main picture) In the last year of Omaha steam operations in the Twin Ports, 2-8-0 No. 218 negotiates Northern Pacific's remarkable timber trestle with a transfer run from Itasca to Rice's Point yard on a warm day in May 1956. Movements over the drawbridge were governed by NP rules and, during open navigation season, trains were limited to 1355 feet in length, or the equivalent of "twenty-six average freight cars, road engine, caboose and one helper engine." The train shown here is very close to the limit with 27 freight cars, a caboose and a road engine. Speed was restricted to 20 MPH. The north end of the GN grain elevator annex buildings can be seen at the far left behind the "Wisconsin Draw" bridge. *Wayne C. Olson.*

(Above) Duluth Elevator Company, commonly known as the Sawyer System, built three large wood frame structures on Omaha's West Superior dock in 1887. Omaha 4-4-0 No. 211, decked out in fresh paint and polished trim for the day's occasion, poses along with dignitaries and railroad officials in front of house No.1, probably at the time of completion. The 1870 Taunton was built for St. Paul & Sioux City as *Medelia*. It became Fairchild & North Eastern No. 7 in 1890. *H. Peddle Collection.* (Below) Globe Elevator Company purchased the elevators in 1894, the enormity of which is apparent in this 1908 view. F.H. Peavy Company operated the system. Northwestern Fuel Company coal dock No. 3 occupied the dock's north end (far left). *K.E. Thro Collection; UW - Superior.*

(Above) Duluth and Superior possessed great lines of weedy, but serviceable trackage, empty at times, but always filled to capacity in grain rush autumns. There were always switchers shepherding the heavily laden box cars, a tradition from the beginning in the 1870s. In this 1948 view, "Zulu" No. 218 works West End yard in Superior, originally established in 1886, when Omaha built an 1,100-foot dock at the site. The 12 track yard was used for interchange with LST&T and also served Globe Elevators, which were closed in 1988. Globe house No. 3 is in the left background. The Farmers Union Grain Terminal Association elevators are at the right. *C&NWRy.*
(Below) Class Z No. 218 is about to depart from Itasca with a transfer run to Duluth on October 21, 1955. Two of the 2-8-0 Consolidations arrived on the Omaha in July 1913. They were being used extensively in the Twin Ports area by the 1950s. *Stan Mailer.*

111

(Above) The Omaha replaced the original wooden depot at West Superior in 1891, with this Charles Frost designed brownstone, brick and masonry structure, seen here in 1948. The railroad changed the name of the station to *Superior* in 1903. *C&NWRy.* (Below) Omaha Class E No. 509 is on the point of Train 513 at the Superior depot in 1955. Traffic on Ogden Avenue will have to wait until business is finished and the *Fast Mail* departs for the St. Louis Bay bridge and a 12:15 PM arrival in Duluth. A city ordinance prohibited blocking any street crossing for more than ten minutes, except in the case of an unavoidable breakdown. *Frank A. King.*

(Above) Omaha J Class 2-8-2 No. 401, second from the left, keeps company with a number of transfer and switching engines at Itasca on June 3, 1935. During the slack years of the Great Depression, motive power was often stored outside. *Robert H. Graham.*
(Below) Regularly assigned Duluth-Superior engines, Nos. 218 and 76, rest inside the Itasca roundhouse, while 2-8-2 No. 393 rides the 90 foot turntable on June 19, 1948. The 1894 roundhouse had 15 stalls, while the three stalls at the right were added in 1898. After a fire in 1918, the doors and roof of the original structure were rebuilt, the roof becoming the newer monitor style. *C&NWRy.*

(Right) In 1899, the Omaha built a large wood frame grain elevator on the Itasca dock, just south of the merchandise warehouse, the end of which can be seen to the right of the photo. Cargill Elevator Company purchased the elevator in 1930, the same year the concrete storage annex was completed. (Below) This 1948 view from the boat loading side shows the entire facility, including the brick power plant and smoke stack at the south end of the elevator. Both: *Author's Collection.*

(Above) Located on the north end of the Itasca dock, Omaha's 80 x 1500 foot brick merchandise warehouse was completed in 1896. This view of the east side, looking north, was probably made for the 1917 Valuation records. At left is the pump house, which provided fire protection. *John Gaertner Collection.* (Below) M-3 No. 76 is working at the Cargill grain elevator with the morning switch crew in 1948. Itasca's mill yard had a capacity of 250 loaded cars and 70 empties. The elevator was closed in 1962. *C&NWRy.*

(Above) Train 513, the *Fast Mail,* along with its southbound counterpart, the *Arrowhead Limited,* connected Eau Claire with the Twin Ports. In steam's last decade, E Class No. 500 surges northbound with nine cars, including two lightweight coaches, north of Eau Claire in 1950. *Mike Runey.* (Below) Wayfreight 103 canters along near Haugen, several miles north of Rice Lake, enroute to Spooner on June 15, 1955. Rebuilt to Class J-A in January 1939, 2-8-2 No. 406 was delivered by Alco in 1916 and retired in 1956. *Bruce Black.*

The sharp cold of a Duluth winter brings forth photographer's smoke from Class Z No. 218, as it moves a wintertime drag of loaded DM&IR ore jennys away from Rice's Point, toward the NP drawbridge and Itasca yard on New Years Eve, 1955. From time-to-time, all-rail winter shipments of iron ore went over the Omaha via Spooner and Altoona to Chicago area destinations. *Wayne C. Olson.*

(Below) Spooner-bound Train 103 is approaching New Auburn, Wisconsin, north of Eau Claire, with J-A No. 411 as power. Omaha rebuilt 24 of their 2-8-2s to Class J-A, including two Js acquired from C&NW during WWII. No. 411 was rebuilt in 1937 and retired in 1956. *M.P. McMahon.*

(Above) Spooner, Wisconsin, looking north from the water tower in the 1920s, shows the three story Spooner Hotel and imposing Omaha depot. The south end of the depot had a restaurant known as the "Beanery," which lasted until 1929. Extensive rip-tracks and a materials yard can be seen above the depot to the right, while the elevated coaling facility is in the middle-background. (Below) A ground level view of the track side of the hotel and the north end of the 1892 depot. Division offices were located in the depot's second floor until the new Wisconsin Division headquarters were moved to Eau Claire in 1925. Both: *William O'Gara Collection.*

(Above) Located 6.4 miles north of Spooner, Trego tower and depot, pictured in 1908, was originally called Superior Junction. It controlled the line to Superior, on the left, and the Bayfield line, on the right. The small depot was used by passengers transferring between Eau Claire-Duluth trains and Twin Cities-Ashland trains. *Sawyer County Historical Society.* (Below) M-2 No. 54 was part of a group of nine Alco engines delivered in 1917, which followed parent C&NW's specifications and class designation. Five of the engines were retired in 1949-1950, while No. 54 and the others lasted until June 1956. The engine is shown at Spooner on September 1, 1947. *Ken L. Zurn.*

(Above) The Spooner engine terminal in 1947, showing the concrete coal chute and sand tower. At this time, the Omaha was still delivering company "lake coal" in drop bottom gondolas, as evidenced by the steel cars on the left. The depot is in the distance, behind the coal chute. To the right, Class I-1 No. 360, still equipped with a wood pilot, is coming from the roundhouse. *William F. Armstrong.* (Below) On July 1, 1955, Class M-3 No. 86 rides Spooner's 90 foot turntable, installed in 1905 to replace a smaller table. The 0-6-0 switcher was a 1921 product of Alco and would be retired within a year, in June 1956. *Bruce R. Meyer.*

(Above) Southbound Train 104 clatters out of Spooner yard for Altoona in the 1950s. On the back side of the coal chute, engine smoke indicates the presence of a way freight, waiting for clearance to depart for either Park Falls or Hudson. *C&NW Ry.* (Below) Dieselization came to Spooner by May 4, 1956. Yard duties that day were assigned to EMD SW8 diesel switcher No. 127, which also ran that month on the Park Falls line. A pair of C&NW GP7s ease past, on their way to Altoona. *William F. Armstrong.*

On March 3, 1956, J-A No. 413 approaches the Highway 53 overpass at Sarona with a freight train in the last months of steam. The 413 is dirty and rusting, reflecting neglect which befell Omaha power "after Chicago had the say-so." The aging J-A is just weeks away from retirement, and the railroad from near bankruptcy. *Marvin Nielson.*

(Above) Later in the day, on March 3rd, No. 413 met a wayfreight in charge of 2-8-2 No. 440, shown taking water, at the village of Bloomer, where both trains will make set-outs. Engine 440 was formerly C&NW No. 2363, acquired in 1943 when Omaha traded two 2-10-2s to C&NW in exchange for a pair of Class J Mikados. (Below) After switching is completed, No. 413, with bell ringing, backs three cars up to tie onto its train. Within minutes, the train will head for Chippewa Falls, 15 miles to the south. Both: *Marvin Nielson*.

A big F-8 4-4-0 does some heavy braking coming into Hudson from the East Hill. The train is probably No. 9, the *New Limited*.
*St. Croix County Historical Society*

# 7.

# THE PROBLEM WITH HUDSON HILL

Thirty years after Jacob Humbird completed the West Wisconsin, operating problems on Hudson's grades nagged the company. The significant line change in the 1880s made an acceptable average of one percent eastward, and a comparable 1.2 percent on the Minnesota side. A high bridge seemed unattainable, as the valley was too wide. Still, Wisconsin Central's mainline was put across a narrow upstream valley near Somerset, Wisconsin. Omaha had to live with its problem, while one on-line newspaper offered electrification as a panacea.

On March 12, 1907, several irregularities brought about a serious accident. Engineer Ed Moe and Conductor Moriarity started their train downgrade, only to lose control, their sluggish brakes unresponsive. Engine 309 (an I-1) and the uncontrolled mass descended upon the Hudson depot and a hapless switch crew working coaches, and a passenger train. Extensive damage and injuries resulted. Trackage was blocked for hours, and Trains 63, 64 and No. 1 were detained. Train 64, the northbound *Twilight Limited* to Duluth and Ashland, returned to St. Paul and was redirected over the Soo Line to Turtle Lake and the northline. Mainline trains were detoured over Milwaukee Road to Camp Douglas, a standard procedure.

Superintendent T.W. Kennedy had stop boards ordered from Hudson Shops to be installed 3/4 miles on either side of Hudson depot. He also ordered conductors and brakemen to be out on top going downhill into Hudson from both directions, to make sure all brakes were in good working order. Departmental communications criticized the slow detouring of passengers, as well as the difficulties clearing the wreck site. Others stressed interest in safer methods of operation.

Kennedy further detailed the wreck in terms of the delays to Omaha's passengers, as the three trains due at Hudson were improperly handled. Train 63 (again *Twilight Limited,* down from Spooner) should have been detoured via Turtle Lake as had Train 64. He also stipulated that no trains be allowed west of Northline when a train was standing at the depot. Trains 1 and 63 had been standing on either side of the wreck and passengers should have been taken to a hotel. As it was, there were two available coaches west of the wreck, which should have been used to convey passengers to St. Paul. Those in charge at the wreck also chose to transfer baggage, mail and express at the same time, eliciting ugly comments from the passengers. In rebuttal, it was stated the wreck clearing had progressed up to engine 309's tender, with the engine itself set to one side so it could clear a passenger train alongside. The track site was completely cleared at 4:00 AM. It was decided to move Train 63 by the wreck site, but engine 309

had settled back toward the passing track, fouling it by one inch. It was necessary for the wrecker to make another lift before the *Limited* could pass.

Afterwards, stringent rules were brought into play, and movements were carefully analyzed. No passenger trains were permitted to leave Northline until the depot block was cleared, not even helpers running light. Shortly, Mr. M.M. Keating, an Omaha traveling engineer, made a set of investigations addressing the main issue: malfunctioning air brakes.

Mr. Keating's report highlighted some of Omaha's problems in the inspection of cars and their brakes. Sampling freight trains coming down Hudson Hill, he found many cars to have poor braking power. He also found a number of non-air brake cars with brakes in poor condition. Keating inspected Extra 325 North, an eastbound 50 car train, at East St. Paul before departure, and found the brakes in deplorable shape. The brakes on ten cars would not operate at all, five had excessive piston travel and another five were without air, having never been brought up to standard by 1907. Keating let the train go after adjusting piston travel on the five cars, 35 operative brake sets doing the work of 50. He understood the brakes were not well-cared for at the "Head of Lakes," i.e., Superior. The head brakeman, a new man, had instructions to set ten brakes near Stillwater Junction, while the conductor and head brakeman stayed in the caboose. The novice had no idea where to release the brakes, so the offending cars were dragged headlong into Hudson. Keating went on to ride and examine several other trains, including Extra 317 West, Extra 314 East and Extra 320 West, all I-1 powered freights. Extra 317, with 1,200 tons and 36 loads, had 35 air brake cars, one piped, two cutout (no defect cards) and six with brakes that would not apply due to dirty triple valves, some uncleaned up to 20 months. Extra 314 consisted of 20 loads, St. Paul to Hudson. The brakes on three cars would not work, five had too much piston travel, but this was rectified before leaving St. Paul. Extra 320 had 36 loads and four empties, of which 29 had good brakes. Keating found that of all the cars, C&NW's and Omaha's, were the worst offenders. He attributed the March wreck to poorly-maintained brakes, recommending the use of retainers, about ten cars worth descending the hills, and a speed of 20 MPH between Northline and Stillwater Junction. An inspection bottleneck was found at Harvester Works, where the northline cars were transferred and where few inspections were made.

Keating concluded that further training and better rules to offset future difficulties were in order. He also recommended larger capacity air pumps, "...the same as we now have on our new Class I-1 engines..."

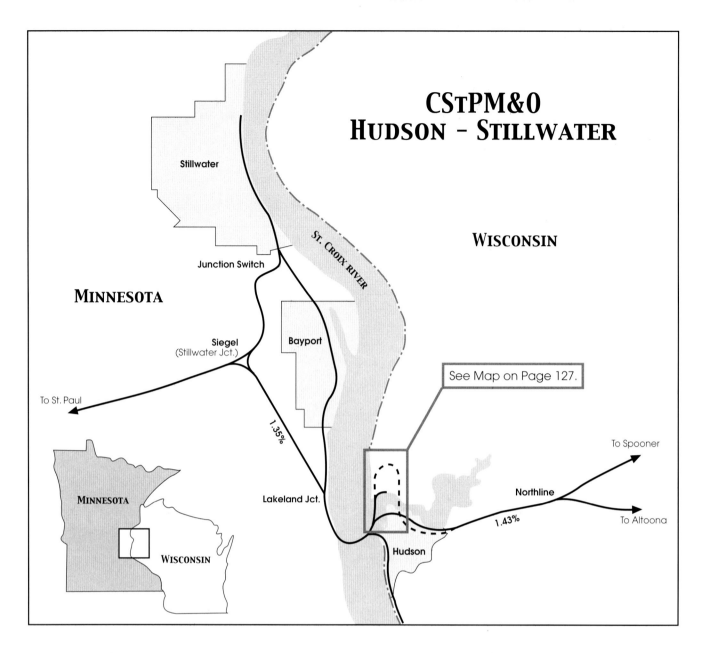

**CStPM&O**
**HUDSON - STILLWATER**

WISCONSIN

MINNESOTA

Stillwater

Junction Switch

ST. CROIX RIVER

Siegel
(Stillwater Jct.)

Bayport

See Map on Page 127.

To St. Paul

1.35%

Lakeland Jct.

To Spooner

Northline

1.43%

To Altoona

Hudson

MINNESOTA

WISCONSIN

Another accident occurred on August 17, 1907. Extra 327 West became a statistic upon descent of the east hill at Hudson. The rear end brakeman observed the train had stopped in the clear at Northline for 20 minutes and did not know why. The I-1 whistled off, reaching 20 MPH, and the rear end man set several handbrakes, then felt the air brakes go on. He was worried about the train breaking in two with too many hand brakes set. Near the first overhead bridge (over tracks), engineer Jalmer whistled for brakes. The brakeman proceeded to "club" three more cars when they struck Train 67 at the Hudson depot. Jalmer and Extra 327 were rolling about 35 MPH with 44 loads and one empty when they plowed into Train 67's caboose, just west of Hudson's east standpipe. The extra's crew consisted of two green brakemen, Engineer Jalmer, Conductor E.T. White, and new men, Peterson and Warner: All received marks for the incident. Superintendent Strickland observed that carelessness caused the wreck, and underscored the poor brake inspection and car work related to it.

Keating's work also included the presence of a Westinghouse representative, and several car and engine specialists from the Omaha. In August 1907, motive power men such as J.J. Ellis were busy putting ten new I-1s into service, however, they would short-

ly concentrate on the hill, beginning a series of tests there. By year's end, the team of traveling engineers recommended all trains move down the two hills with air brakes only, and trainline pressure held above 70 lbs. The use of retainers was debated further, but the thinking was to make the descent entirely without assistance to the regular train brake. Also, above all, car repairs were to be enforced.

Safety on Hudson's hills continued to be a problem. In January 1911, a report claimed that freight trains observing proper rules of the road were tied up for as long as six hours trying to move west from Northline. New rules brought about by the 1907 accidents were hampering operations. Due to these rules, eastbound freights were taking up to four hours to move between Lake Elmo and Hudson. The sheer number of trains in the district prevented getting over the road within the 16 hour law.

One example was an eastbound freight passing Lake Elmo, and a westbound passenger train passing Roberts. The freight train had to be held at Stillwater Junction, as it was a risk to allow it to proceed further east: the train could go to Lakeland Junction, just west of the drawbridge, before "fouling" the westbound passenger train's progress over the bridge, but there was the chance

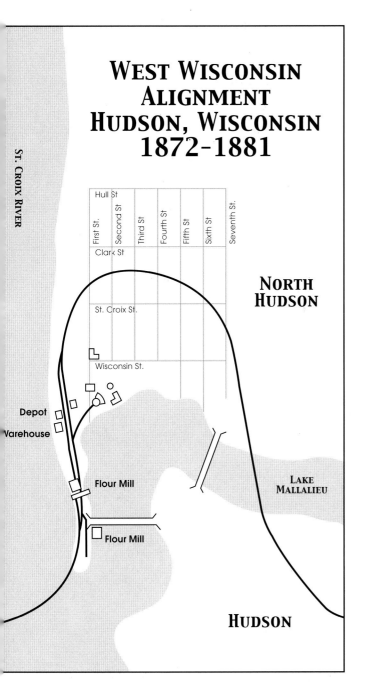

# WEST WISCONSIN
ALIGNMENT
HUDSON, WISCONSIN
1872-1881

ST. CROIX RIVER

Hull St
First St.
Second St
Third St
Fourth St
Fifth St
Sixth St
Seventh St.
Clark St

NORTH
HUDSON

St. Croix St.

Wisconsin St.

Depot
Warehouse

Flour Mill

Flour Mill

LAKE
MALLALIEU

HUDSON

helper service. The powerful hill climbers weighed 162 tons, or 324,200 lbs. compared to the J's 302,000 lbs. The pair were classified J-1 and had several restrictions: top allowable speed was 25 MPH, and they spent most of their time within four miles of the Hudson depot. Even after spending one third of their careers in this service, they were still limited to the same speed even when assisting passenger trains. Tonnage ratings for J Class Mikes in May 1926 included the use of an assisting J-1 on the hill: 2,600 tons between St. Paul and Northline (three miles east of Hudson). The figure implied that either engine was exerting its 64,356 lbs. of tractive effort on trains climbing away from Hudson.

The J-1s were equipped with a special lateral motion device, essentially a free driving box on the first pair of drivers, which could compensate for sharp curves. The first set of drivers could move much as the lead truck did, almost a 4-8-2 in application, negotiating a 16 degree curve. A blessing indeed was the air-operated fire door and power reverse, making the exacting work of holding maximum tractive effort easier. Perhaps the short movements of three to four miles for assignments influenced the deletion of a superheater, then just coming into wide favor.

Times were when helpers assisted foreign road trains. The Milwaukee Road met with trouble in May and June 1920, and had to reroute onto the Omaha, from St. Paul to Camp Douglas. Congestion on Hudson Hill was materially increased as 12 car Limiteds were shoved upgrade by the two J-1s. Milwaukee's F-3 and F-4 Class passenger engines were assisted by the 491. The year before, many delays were in evidence, due to the application of Rule 99 between Northline and East St. Paul. Virtually every train was delayed ten minutes. There were also problems hearing train whistles when a freight rattled through, the din muffling the all-important passing of signals in the hill district. The helper engine was often detailed to move back and pick up the flag man, as it saved time. In November 1919, a record was set as some 1,474 trains moved over the intervolved track of Hudson's bridge the first 20 days of the month, an average of one train every 19 minutes. There were also up to eight helper movements across the bridge. The spaced-train district at Hudson was bettered somewhat by Hazel Park-East St. Paul activities, but switch engines darting off the mainline constituted a hazard. It was heads-up railroading throughout the old Stillwater Road territory. For the men on the J-1s, there was a request for a 20 minute lunch period, especially for the fireman (J-1s were hand-fired, a man-sized task), to be set between 4-1/2 to 6 hours duty. Motive power chief E.R. Gorman concurred.

In 1926, rules for the hills were meticulously designed and inevitably based on tragic accidents. Trainline pressure was required to be on the mark, and westbound trains arriving at Northline made full stops. The rear end crew was required to examine the last cars for brake set-ups and for full-release positions. Car weights were required to be calculated into brake retaining valve settings for adequate brake control when descending. After the brakes were released at the foot of the grade, with a 20 lb. reduction, feed valves had to be reset to 70 lbs. Other precautions were also designed to prevent wheel sliding when the train proceeded. The monitoring of speed and trainline pressure was required at all times. Such were the detailed, tedious conditions on the big hill district.

that the brakes would not hold on the hill. The passenger train had to pass Hudson and the "intervolved" (a.k.a. gauntlet) track on the St. Croix River drawbridge, or be held at Northline. The difficulty lay with the volume of short trains over this segment of the hills, compounding the problems of dispatching. Freights would stand at Northline for hours and could not back out of Hudson's yard due to the passage of others. The cost was heavy, but happily, there were no "air losses" on Hudson Hill. By February 1913, however, Bulletin 383 told all crews in charge of eastbound freights of more than 15 cars to stop at Stillwater Junction and turn up the sufficient number of retainer valves to ensure holding down the hill. Another headache began in 1913, when engineers rebuilt the St. Croix swing bridge.

Standardization of Omaha's heavy power was interrupted by two legendary 2-10-2s built by Baldwin in September 1917. Essentially a lengthened Class J Mikado, but with 57 inch drivers, Nos. 491 and 492 were designed to master Hudson's hills in

The steep hills at Hudson proved to be a bottleneck in the age of steam. To ease the problem, Baldwin delivered two J-1 Class "Santa Fe" type 2-10-2s to the Omaha in August 1917. Reflecting standardization on the C&NW, Nos. 491-492 looked like lengthened J Class 2-8-2s but with 57" drivers. The big engines replaced 2-8-0 Consolidations and had clear vision tenders with narrowed coal bunkers for hill running. The pair were a fixture at Hudson until WWII, when they were traded to C&NW and converted to 0-10-2s for Proviso hump yard duty. (Above) No. 492 pauses, between helper assignments, next to Hudson's three stall wooden roundhouse. *A.R. Johnson.* (Below) The 492 simmers on the Ellsworth line, near the Hudson depot, in the late 1930s. *Robert H. Graham.*

(Above) A K-1 Class 4-6-0 waits in the clear, while J-A No. 417 shoves past on the rear of an eastbound freight headed uphill from Hudson. The helper will cut off on the fly at Sono Junction or at Roberts. All three classes of 2-8-2s were employed in helper service after Omaha's 2-10-2s were traded to C&NW. *A. Robert Johnson.* (Below) In summer 1949, Class E-3 No. 600 holds in front of the Hudson depot with Train 515, the *Victory*, while the helper engine hustles to tie onto the rear of the train for the push across the St. Croix River drawbridge and up the 1.35% grade on the Minnesota side of the river. On the weed covered ready track at right, the *Namekagon* coaches await their 9:15 AM departure to Ashland. *Ken L. Zurn.*

(Above) Hudson's famous helper station centered on the small roundhouse shown in this wintery scene with a Class J 2-8-2 awaiting its turn to boost tonnage out of the valley. The wooden bridge on the left is for vehicle access to the depot. *M.P. McMahon.* (Below) At Lakeland Junction in June 1954, Class E No. 504 descends the 1.35% grade on the Minnesota side of the St. Croix River with Train 508, the *Viking*, by this date reduced to just three cars. The Bayport-Stillwater branch heads off to the right. *Harold Van Horn; Lou Schmitz Collection.*

(Above) Some railfans were lucky. Engineer-collector-photographer Harold Van Horn of Hudson stays aboard K-1 No. 243 as his fireman takes on some "lake coal" at Hudson's 200 ton Ogle concrete coal chute, put into operation in 1946. The 1.43% eastbound ruling grade rises in the background, but Van Horn's crew will switch the shops this afternoon of October 26, 1955. The track on the left goes to Omaha's North Hudson car shops. *Stan Mailer.* (Below) Prior to assisting an eastbound freight train on August 22, 1955, J-A No. 407 takes on water at the Hudson tank, located between the roundhouse and the depot on the Ellsworth line. *Lou Schmitz.*

On August 22, 1955, Lou Schmitz recorded J-A No. 407 pushing (in reverse) on the rear of an eastbound Wisconsin Division freight train. (Above) The train has cleared the drawbridge as the caboose and helper engine approach the depot platform. At left is the stub-end track where the *Namekagon* coaches were stored overnight between runs. (Right) The conductor leans out the window of the way car to pick up orders as the helper powers past the depot and starts up the 1.43% grade of Hudson Hill. (Below) Near Sono, some 4.5 miles from the river, the fight's almost over. The helper could either cut off on the fly at Sono Junction or proceed another six miles to Roberts, depending on orders. The engine would then return to Hudson "against traffic" on the eastbound main, or it could cross over to the westbound track at Sono Junction and run light to Hudson To ease wear on the valve gear, the J-As were limited to 40 MPH when operating in reverse. All: *Lou Schmitz.*

(Above) Train 508, the *Viking*, with Class E No. 504 up front, loads mail and passengers at the Hudson depot in the mid-1950s. Twin Cities travelers headed to Ashland or destinations on the Bayfield line would transfer from Train 508 to the *Namekagon*, and continue north on the motor train. The St. Croix River drawbridge can be seen at the right. *M.P. McMahon.* (Below) In a grand display of smoke and steam, J-A No. 417 "gets its air" in front of the Hudson depot, prior to assisting a westbound time freight headed by a trio of EMD Geeps on October 27, 1955. The J-A may be going to St. Paul as it was unusual for helpers to be at the front of the train. *Stan Mailer.*

94

Train 7, a local passenger service, accelerates northwestward from Fairchild, Wisconsin, with new I-2 Class Pacific No. 374 up front on October 2, 1904. The I-2s featured clerestory cabs and Russian Iron boiler jackets. *J. Foster Adams.*

# 8.

# NEW POWER, NEW LINE, OLD LINE

The Omaha's need for larger passenger power brought five I-2 Class 4-6-2 Pacific-type locomotives in 1903. An additional twelve I-2s were subsequently delivered in 1907-1910. Engines 376-382 had Stephenson valve gear, while Nos. 383-387 used Walschaert gear. The Omaha chose to stand behind their design just as C&NW was introducing the heavier E Class 4-6-2 to its own system. The I-2s were next assigned to M&I Division trains to replace G-3 Atlantics and F-8 4-4-0s. In the same period, Omaha took delivery of I-1s until No. 363 was reached, then Nos. 222-225 and 101-106 completed the cumulation. In all, Omaha had eighteen I-1s with Walschaert gear, just before the K-1 and K-2 variation arrived in August 1911.

The first five K-1s displayed sophistication for their day. Each had the newly-perfected Schmidt Type "A" superheater, a new formula for boiler pressure (180 lbs. versus 200 lbs.), cylinder diameter (23" versus 21" for the I-1s), and a weight variation (8 tons more per engine) in favor of K-1s. They had a higher tractive effort and differed visually in having dry pipes. Even after superheating in the 1920s, the I-1s carried internal dry pipes. There were 26 K-1s in all.

The parallel development of K-2 4-6-2 Nos. 388-389 was related to the arrival of Northern Pacific's *North Coast Limited*. The pair were externally identical to the last batch of I-2s, except for the superheater and 5-1/2 ton weight difference. Elroy's newspaper reported the arrival of the new "monkey motion" engines (signifying power with external valve gear), which would prevail to the end of steam power. Nos. 388-389 were delivered on August 2, 1911 to serve on the NP train for several years.

The establishment of NP's *North Coast Limited* as a fixture for the Omaha and C&NW was a high point in 1911. Bearing numbers 421-422 in the timetables, the *Limited* made its first trip on Sunday, December 17, 1911, running over a virtually new speedway through nearly level Wisconsin. The NCL was billed as all-steel and electric lighted, with Pullman sleepers with drawing rooms and compartments, plus tourist sleepers and observation-buffet cars between Chicago and St. Paul. Train 421 stopped on signal at Kenosha, Racine and South Beaver Dam to receive passengers ticketed to Eau Claire and northerly points, as well as certain Chicago suburbs and stations south of Wyeville. Trains 405-406, the *North Western Limited*, were all-steel with like service, leaving Chicago three hours ahead of the NCL. During the USRA era in World War I, the NCL was replaced by C&NW's *North American* (still Trains 421-422). Such trains brightened the short, optimistic decade at Wyeville, its roundhouse available for the crack train's new E Class Pacifics and those of the Omaha.

Omaha's E Class speedsters eventually totalled 18, the final group arriving with few modifications in October 1916. They weighed 130 tons and replaced most of the I-2/K-2 Class on the Eastern Division mainline. The older power weighed 103 tons. It would be nearly 15 years before Omaha saw fit to design heavier passenger power.

Changes came fast on lines out of Spooner, as aging 4-4-0s were replaced by heavier power. In the winter of 1906, engine No. 73, a 66" drivered E-2 Class passenger favorite, was assigned to Train 65, the *Twilight Limited*. Due in Spring Brook at 5:23 PM, the old speedster sheared off its left main driver two miles north of town. All escaped the wreck without injury. Sister E-2 No. 70 relieved after running light from Spooner. Some of the last, small E-4 Class Ten-Wheelers (95-99 series) were recalled to St. Paul for reassignment. I-1 Pioneer No. 303 met with an accident in January 1907, due to broken rails in sub-zero temperature, a constant nightmare for crew and dispatcher alike.

Events along the C&NW and Omaha trans-Wisconsin mainline centered on a new route from Chicago and Milwaukee to the southern end of Omaha's territory. It began in 1909, and was named the Milwaukee, Sparta & North Western Railroad, extending from Lindwurm, northwest of Milwaukee, on the Wisconsin Division, to Sparta, at the west end of the Elroy-Sparta Cut-Off. The "New Line," or Adams Cut-Off, would be 169 miles long, plus a dogleg of 8.2 miles, to a junction with the Madison Line near West Allis, a total of 177.19 miles. Fifteen million dollars of bonds were sold, guaranteed by C&NW for the project.

Interest in an earlier state crossing from Princeton went as far back as 1884, and gained in financial circles by 1887. The first section was built in 1884 from Necedah to Necedah Junction (later Wyeville), actually a branch off the Omaha, but not operated by them. C&NW ran extra power and crews over the Omaha from Elroy to the Junction, as the 16 miles constituted C&NW's Princeton & Western Railway Company. The new mainline promised to cut many miles off the Chicago-St. Paul distance. In 1909, surveyors were reported working in the area north of Elroy, the town sensing ominously that great changes might come to its railroad population and economy. C&NW's old Madison Division stretched southward, following the Baraboo River Valley.

The Madison Division, as veterans often remarked years later, never allowed its trains enough straight and level track to "get a wheel on." By April 1910, the official count of broken drawbars, division wide, was 204. It came from the up and down character of the line north of the capital city. The year 1910 also marked an upsurge in traffic, and the new "Zulus" (Z Class heavy Consolidations) were hauling record loads. One engineer, A.W.

Foster, retiring off the division that year, mentioned that several times he had nearly 100 cars moving grudgingly over the C&NW to Elroy behind the infamous 2-8-0s. Arch rival Milwaukee Road was even testing a 2-6-6-2 Mallet around Tomah and its tunnel. Competition dictated a better railroad.

Newspapers in Adams County were reporting surveys in nearby towns along the proposed route during the winter of 1908-09. Wisconsin Central indicated interest in building to Friendship, which clouded C&NW's intent. Elroy, in turn, rightly worried that it would be bypassed by a level line north of the high ridges that encircled it. By summer, Necedah proved a rallying point, as surveyors located lines just south of the village and to Friendship. Marvin Hughitt met with James T. Clark, Omaha's Second VP aboard official cars arriving behind Train 501 from Chicago. Hughitt intended to look over Omaha's divisions in the spring of 1909. Surveys were completed west of Necedah Junction, but a route could not be found over the tunnel ridge save one parallel and just north of the Milwaukee's mainline. When announced in August 1908, it was revealed that the New Line might join the old at Baraboo, but the company intended to bypass that route in favor of flatland. It was the beginning of the end for Baraboo, a historic, old C&NW terminal. During the announcement, the name Wyeville surfaced to replace Necedah Junction.

Construction of a trans-Wisconsin air line would be a faster, shorter way to compete with Milwaukee Road for Chicago-Milwaukee-Twin Cities trade. The mainline, plus the Milwaukee

Belt Line, and the new switching yards along the city's outer edge, would reinforce C&NW competitiveness. The New Line would invite Milwaukee's industries to compete in Minnesota and Dakota and eliminate heavy trains on the Sparta Cut-Off and the Wisconsin River crossing at Merrimac. The Sparta Cut-Off, often called "over the hills" by Elroy railroaders, possessed mountainous topography. Survival for crews inside tunnels in earlier times was often challenging. (Your author made a memorable trip on C&NW's J-S Class No. 2380 over this line, through the suffocating tunnels, protected by a wartime gas mask.) In 1909, Elroy was awash in new power, and reportings of I-1s and I-2s arriving were frequent. On Sunday, February 14, I-2 Pacific Nos. 379-382 were brought in and set up for operation. On the 25th, I-1 Nos. 356 and 357 came off the C&NW, with No. 360 following later in the month. New M-1 0-6-0 No. 29 went to work in Elroy's upper yard, as F-6 0-6-0 switcher No. 27 worked around the big depot. Locomotive deliveries continued through May 1910.

In June 1911, Kuhn, Loeb & Company (New York) announced the sale of debentures, a $15,000,000 dollar issue of five percent gold bonds. They sold out quickly and $10,000,000 dollars was authorized for enlargement, extension and additional equipment.

Construction of the New Line followed the Bates & Rogers contract for concrete bridge sites. In 1910, the work went steadily across Adams County, avoiding town sites in favor of stations without problems. What became Adams was briefly South Friendship, a mile out of the community. C&NW held 1,200

In December 1911, Northern Pacific's *North Coast Limited* began operating via C&NW and the Omaha between Chicago and the Twin Cities. Omaha K-2 Pacifics 388 and 389 were delivered in August 1911 to power the premier train over their segment. The Chicago-bound Limited is shown hustling through Shennington, 2.2 miles east of Wyeville, on C&NW's Adams Cutoff. *Author's Collection.*

(Above) Wyeville in its heyday, looking southeast, with the Omaha double track mainline to the left, and the depot, tower and C&NW crossing in the distance. To the right is the power house and the 18 stall roundhouse. *Northern Photo Company.* (Below) A ground level view of Wyeville's roundhouse shortly after completion in 1911. Faced with over-expansion and imprudent planning, Wyeville's roundhouse was closed in 1924, while the Adams engine terminal emerged preeminent on the "New Line." *Ray W. Buhrmaster Collection.*

acres for expansion, allegedly acquired to prevent saloons from rising near its tracks. B&R moved from Necedah's Wisconsin River crossing to Grand Marsh in 1910, as other operators unloaded their tiny locomotives and dump cars at Packwaukee and Montello. Chief Engineer Leflinger's assistants set up shop in a former barber shop at Adams, awaiting better quarters. The great steel bridges at Buffalo Lake and the Wisconsin River at Necedah were spurred, both being major undertakings. Farther west, right-of-way settlement across Camp McCoy yielded extensive spurs into the camp's facilities. At South Beaver Dam, miles from the town site, a depot was located on the Heimler farm. In August, however, two trainmen died in accidents at Necedah, but the founding of Wyeville, the end of the main lap to the Omaha Road, was a high point in 1911.

Preparations for an 18 stall roundhouse and a 10 track, 700 car capacity yard continued at the joint Omaha-C&NW Wyeville site. Wyeville's depot opened in November 1911, just as NP's *North Coast Limited* came onto the road. Hardly a place for settling, Wyeville would prove fatal for Elroy and Baraboo, both short distances from the new town. The expected influx of workers to both Adams and Wyeville would be at the expense of the old towns. Farther east, in the new setting at Butler (near Milwaukee), C&NW planned a 60 stall roundhouse, a complete circle for the new, larger power expected. Beyond Wyeville, the main project was to bore another tunnel west of Tomah at Tunnel City. When completed, the New Line would be under the supervision of G.B. Vilas in Baraboo.

Conditions at Wyeville were always precarious, as C&NW had not settled on that town as a terminal for the New Line connections. Personnel were encouraged to move from Baraboo for the new jobs there. Later, the community was witness to the railroad strike of 1922, and a coal strike that same summer. Several strikers got in trouble for violence at Wyeville, and were charged, requiring bonds of $100 each. The affair involved hiring, or attempting to hire, non-union workers. C&NW placed an ad in the Tomah newspaper for machinists, boilermakers, blacksmiths and other railroad crafts to break the strike. The mails threatened to go to trucks due to poor service. On August 2, 1922, the railroad was sued for overpaying non-union personnel. They also provided food, clothing and housing in violation of the state railroad laws. In the summer of 1922, two Elroy-Winona trains were annulled to conserve coal (Trains 507-508). Allegedly, coal from Wales was enroute to the U.S. to fill the transport fuel gap.

C&NW President W.H. Finley reported in June 1923 that the road would invest in new equipment due to a shortage of cars and locomotives. Between 1916-1922, C&NW purchased 398 locomotives, 250 passenger cars and 14,353 freight cars at a cost of $45,636,039. The road had 2,434 locomotives, 2,439 passenger cars and 78,773 freight cars. Finley announced the additional equipment for 1923 would include 150 locomotives, 250 passenger cars and 7,951 freight cars, at an expenditure of $24,000,000.

One of the consequences of the new equipment was the closing of Baraboo's shop on June 1, 1924. This put sixty men out of work and was the first step toward removing division headquarters from the old location. This was followed on June 15 by the closure of Wyeville, certain to affect Omaha operations in the area. Wyeville's end furloughed seventy more men, with job assignments going to Adams. Two weeks before, rumors that Wyeville would be closed were ripe. The short notice was a hardship on many, their homes forfeited in the virtual loss of the community. One worker and his family packed up and sent their household goods to Deadwood, South Dakota, as he had landed the roundhouse foreman's job there. Other workers were able to find jobs at Adams, but many did not.

Meanwhile, the Omaha was engaged in finishing the new double-track between Wyeville and Merrillan. In 1911, another relo-

G-2 Class 4-6-0 No. 307 clips along with a westbound Limited near Menomonie Junction. The 69" drivered engine, one of three built by Schenectady in 1901, will have no trouble keeping the seven car train on schedule. All three G-2s were retired in 1929. *Lou and John Russell.*

138

Omaha received seven 81" drivered G-3 Class 4-4-2s in December 1905 and June 1906, following C&NW's development of their own D Class 4-4-2s. Engine No. 366 got its portrait taken at Fairchild on April 22, 1907, less than a year after delivery. *J. Foster Adams.*

cation was started to eliminate the grade and curve between Millston and Warrens. In March 1911, Omaha issued orders eliminating fast freight runs. They wanted to increase freight trains to "drag" proportions with one train doing the work of two. However, one drag required ninety minutes to run the twelve miles between Merrillan and Fairchild. Previously, it was made in thirty-five minutes. These new orders may also have been related to trackwork slow orders further south. Unhappy with deliveries, complaints came from old customers at Fairchild.

The partial arrival of heavy C&NW engines in Wisconsin came in 1909. C&NW's first E Class 4-6-2, No. 1507, arrived in Elroy, rolling its 75" drivers into town on the *North Western Limited,* at 1:05 AM on November 24, nudging aside the many D Class 4-4-2s. By this date, eight E Class engines were assigned to the Madison Division, but it was No. 1507 that made the first speedy trip up the Baraboo Valley. Five new Z Class 2-8-0s were assigned to the division, but were kept from Elroy by turntable troubles. More commonly known as a "Zulu" by Omaha and C&NW men, the Zs were rumbling along south from Baraboo to Janesville, stopping at the new coal chute at Monona Yard in Madison. At the same time, Class E Pacifics were being tested and broken in between Chicago and Janesville. With heavy traffic and a power shortage, C&NW pressed the fleet Es into freight service on round trips from Elroy to Baraboo, making daylight runs. In the fall of 1910, they went back on night passenger trains.

Heavy traffic in 1910 even had an assistant superintendent aboard a third yard engine at Elroy to wade through the conges-

tion. E.E. Nash of Eau Claire was in charge, remaining for several days in February. The condition of the cars after being subjected to the new locomotives was such that over 120 were "bad ordered" and awaiting heavy repairs. Most were of wood construction and fared badly when handled in 75 car trains behind C&NW "Zulus." Car damage wasn't the only problem with the big Consolidations. An increasing number of firemen were "resigning" or laying off, as the engines were difficult to fire, especially with poor coal and longer runs. Perhaps Omaha took a lesson from the parent's experience, for it purchased only two Z Class engines, in July 1913.

As though testing their new physical plant, in August 1909, C&NW ran a special consist of one baggage car, one coach and one Pullman from the Twin Cities to Chicago in seven hours, twenty-five minutes. Departing St. Paul behind Omaha 4-4-2 Class G-3 No. 369, the special was sponsored by the *Chicago American,* which later wrote about Engineer J.P. Smith, Fireman F.F. McManus and Omaha's Traveling Engineer M. J. Keating, who personally ran No. 369. The 195 mile trip down the Omaha was made in 197 minutes, as Keating had the high-drivered G-3 up to 100 MPH in certain locations on new roadbed. Five minutes were lost taking water at Eau Claire station, and three more at Merrillan to oil machinery. The Green Bay & Western delayed the train another minute, but soon the special was off again. Between Augusta and Fairchild, it took seven minutes to cover 9.3 miles, and between Valley Junction and Camp Douglas, 11.7 miles went under the 81" drivers in ten minutes. At Elroy, C&NW

4-4-2 Class D No. 1304 relieved Omaha No. 369. C&NW Engineer Chris Harrison and Fireman Henry Heind continued running as fast as the old Madison Division would allow. In the end, the 417 miles were covered in 445 minutes, including stops for coal and water, plus the engine change at Elroy. The dash was the last lap of the *Chicago American's* World Racers, young Chicago schoolboys engaged in a round-the-world trip, accomplished in forty-one days.

After 1903, when the Omaha completed its Black River Falls cut-off, forever isolating the old station from the mainline, one E.J. Vaudreuil petitioned the Railroad Commission of Wisconsin for a concession. He was promoting Vaudreuil, his town site just east of Black River Falls, and desired rail access to the new community. He proposed a 1.8 mile "spur" be built northerly from the Black River Falls station to the new town site on the new cut-off. The Black River Falls Advancement Association suspected collusion between the Omaha and Mr. Vaudreuil to create a new connection with the cut-off, allowing the Omaha to abandon the old high bridge and the sharply curved trackage from Black River Falls to Wright. The promoter succeeded in having his way and the Omaha proceeded to replace the old line in 1911-1912 with a Black River Falls to Vaudreuil segment.

In keeping with track improvements, the Sheppard-Wright section was double-tracked, and the Black River and Levis Creek bridges were widened in 1911. Controversy in Black River Falls raged all summer long, even as Vaudreuil unsuccessfully promoted his agricultural empire based at his equally static village. Later,

after the failure of his pea-canning industry, E.J. Vaudreuil fled to California. Still, the Omaha was determined to eliminate the excessive track at Black River Falls. This unhappy city, recently victim of a terrible flood, could only watch as the line was dismantled. The last train ran over the old iron bridge on Friday, November 3, 1911. On Saturday morning, a crew removed rails north of the bridge out to Wright. On Sunday, over one hundred men, probably released from mainline trackwork, gathered to remove the balance. The *Banner* speculated that fighting the Omaha on the issue was fruitless, even considering the bridge might be given to the city. Eighty-three years later, the bridge abutments in the city act as foundations for avant-garde housing. The line to Black River Falls, in its final form, commenced at Sheppard and ended at Vaudreuil (later, Levis).

Omaha Bulletin 426, issued January 4, 1912, covered the opening of Sheppard's interlocking plant, equipped with new standard three-position upper quadrant signals. Trains would be governed by rules related to the new signals, and would reduce speed to 10 MPH through the plant after January 6. Speed restrictions came off six weeks later. Usually, the Railroad Commission issued permits for interlocking plants after inspection, and the Omaha worked to complete all plants and have them inspected at one time. Thirty years later, in June 1942, the plant at Sheppard was dismantled in favor of hand-thrown switches. By then, westbound trains were beginning to run to Levis (formerly, Vaudreuil) and were backed into Black River Falls via Vaudreuil's controversial "spur."

(Above) The towerman at Sheppard operated the interlocking plant and the three position upper quadrant signals. (Right) Originally a siding built for Sheppard's mill, Sheppard became a junction when the Black River Falls cutoff was completed in 1903. The tower opened in 1912 to govern the south end of the cutoff and to control trains running into Vaudreuil. The tower was closed in 1942. Both: *State Historical Society of Wisconsin.*

(Above) The Black River Falls 1903 Cut-Off eliminated sharp curves, several grades and slow running through town. Here an Omaha I-1 powers a freight train across the new Black River bridge circa 1912. *Van Schaik photo, State Historical Society of Wisconsin.*

Valley Junction had three Milwaukee Road trains crossing the Omaha in regular movements each night during 1900. The depot operator was on Milwaukee's payroll, and his boss was G.H. Atkins, Superintendent at Babcock. Omaha men felt the Milwaukee employees had a better deal when the interlocking plant was installed in 1911-12. For awhile, controversy raged over a "non-employee" being allowed to work the levers when Milwaukee trains crossed through the plant, adding to the friction. Omaha, however, carried the depot on its books, billing Milwaukee for its portion of costs, around $28.50 per month. Operation was interrupted in September 1913, when the tower-man set signals against a westbound train. Its air failed and cars piled up at the scene. The Omaha petitioned to discontinue service by 1926, after the Milwaukee abandoned thirteen miles from Tomah to Norway the previous year, the tower was removed and sold locally. Valley Junction, a close neighbor of Wyeville, ceased to be a junction. The depot lingered into the Great Depression, and was finally dragged away to a nearby cranberry farm.

Improvements on the Omaha's mainline aimed for a safer, faster roadway, free of washouts or other problems. There had been a grim history of disasters due to the operation of many night passenger trains over the low level speedway. On August 8, 1912, Train 10, the *Atlantic Express*, plunged into the Little Lemonweir River, killing the engine crew, after a torrential rain took out the Omaha bridge just north of Hustler. Two years before, fast freight Train 87 clattered through Omaha's tunnel six

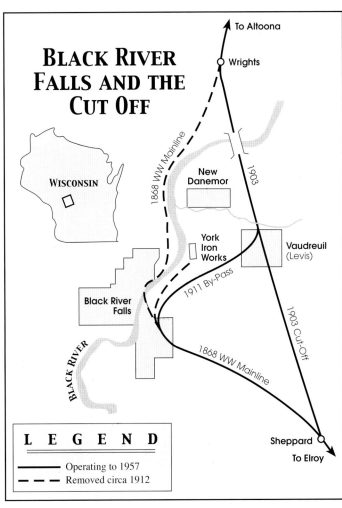

BLACK RIVER FALLS AND THE CUT OFF

WISCONSIN

To Altoona

Wrights

1868 WW Mainline

1903

New Danemor

York Iron Works

Vaudreuil (Levis)

Black River Falls

1911 By-Pass

1903 Cut-Off

BLACK RIVER

1868 WW Mainline

Sheppard

To Elroy

LEGEND

——— Operating to 1957
– – – Removed circa 1912

miles north of Elroy, only to derail four cars in the darkness, delaying local passenger Train 7 several hours at Elroy. A bright side of railroading came a few years before, on July 7, 1910, when a "Dan Patch" gas-electric car and trailer coach were coupled to the rear of Train 7, stopping at Fairchild for all to behold. The blue streamlined cars, en route to Minneapolis, were followed two years later by another such motor car, running under its own power. A new age had dawned.

Changes in passenger trains and accommodations grew steadily, and at the beginning of 1909, Trains 501-504 were to receive a combination parlor and cafe car in place of a full parlor car. Mail cars began to run through from Chicago to St. Paul on Trains 501-504, versus a return to Chicago from Elroy. It was no longer necessary to transfer mail between cars, but clerks did change at Elroy. Still another mail car went on Train 511 for a new Duluth connection, the car going Chicago-Eau Claire, with another car added from Eau Claire to St. Paul and return. C&NW was working to shorten mail service coast-to-coast, in concert with the Pennsylvania Railroad, intending to chop a day from the present schedules. It would be 95 hours, 35 minutes, from New York to Seattle.

ICC men discovered two vintage 1884 mail cars used on Elroy-Tracy runs and reported them to the Post Office department. Had they been coaches, the ICC people would have ordered them destroyed. As it was, the ancient mail cars exceeded by fifteen years the postal car age limit.

Elroy's depot received electric lights, with 200 candlepower, in August 1909, for its platforms above the joint station as well as inside the waiting rooms. In May of that year, Trains 501-504 became known as the *Twin City Express*, solid through trains from Chicago to Minneapolis. A new Chicago-Portland special had a third day arrival, and it featured electric lights throughout, Pullmans and al-la-carte dining service. It connected with steamships bound for Asia. At the same time, Omaha's new local, Train 14, ran from Elroy to the Twin Cities.

In 1909, Omaha's Elroy roundhouse required a large turntable to handle C&NW E and Z Class engines. A new pit was required to accommodate the 90 foot, 82,000 lb. table. On December 20, 1909, the old table was lifted out by a C&NW's steam wrecker, a difficult move in cold weather. For some time, the newer, larger power had been turned on a wye built for this purpose in the northern limits of the Omaha yard. All running repairs on locomotives were performed out-of-doors. Later, the new turntable was secured to its center bearing, and began a long term of service turning C&NW and Omaha engines. It was the last such installation at Elroy. Baraboo's turntable was removed and C&NW engines working from Baraboo to Winona were changed at Elroy instead. The company saw fit to further improve Elroy's enginehouse by making concrete floors in the south half of the house stalls, having rebuilt the north half the previous year. It looked as though the railroad would always be in Elroy.

New freight train service, connecting with Grand Trunk Western car ferries at Milwaukee, was inaugurated in April 1909. The object was to link the Michigan road with far west shipping points. The westbound train arrived in Elroy about 5:00 AM, and immediately left on the Omaha, arriving in St. Paul at 5:00 PM. There, transfers were made to Great Northern, Northern Pacific

or Soo Line (for Canadian Pacific). This service had been part of Train 583's work, but that train's schedule would not coincide.

In 1909-1910, a cold, merciless winter gripped Elroy, making operations difficult for man and machine. Locomotive engineers complained about safety screens below ashpans, installed to eliminate the fires clogging with snow, which choked off draft to fires, stalling engines. About January 13, 1910, Trains 513-518 were running only between Elroy and Madison due to bad weather. Few freights got through, although one train got as far as Lodi, north of Madison, and derailed, blocking both tracks. Elroy had two feet of snow and was running out of heating coal, the difference made up somewhat by local farmers supplying wood. Even the municipal steam plant (supplying water) had to use wood fuel in the emergency. Finally, the Omaha gave the city a car of coal until its shipment arrived. Nearby, Reedsburg was in total darkness after its plant shut down for lack of fuel. As it was, the January snows cost C&NW two million dollars. A derailment of Train 512, the *Duluth Limited*, in bad weather, had all but the last coach on the ties. The weather also caused all trains to be double-headed. On March 10, new E Class 4-6-2 No. 1509, shepherding Train 509 past the new interlocking tower on Elroy's south edge, went through a derail and onto the ties. The train was pulled back to Union Center and "wrong mained" northward. No. 1509 was picked up first, then the wrecking crew cleared part of a freight derailed at the depot on C&NW's (east) side of the depot. This was caused by a broken switch. Finally, on March 17, an inbound C&NW freight train, that included a car of wire cable, had a mishap. The big wire spool crashed through the box car door, crossed the street south of the depot and rolled some distance away. It took a wrecker to lift the load, which was bound for Butte, Montana, from Trenton, New Jersey. It was a close call!

In January's intense cold, Train 513 approached Baraboo, pulled by a freight engine. The train's steam was inadequate and coach stoves were lighted. One brakeman aboard found a quail nesting near the stove's kindling, evidently entering via the stove pipe to shelter from the cold.

The Omaha Road's usually frigid winters dictated certain rules governing tonnage ratings for locomotives. Trains were shortened in order to maintain steam pressure. Ratings were reduced ten percent between thirty degrees above zero and ten above, fifteen percent between ten above and ten below zero, and twenty-five percent at ten below. Thus, an I-1, running between Knapp and Eau Claire on flatland, would have only 1,150 tons in ten below zero weather, versus 1,500 tons in the summer months.

In the spring of 1910, an order of 36 all-steel passenger cars passed through Elroy to equip trains on the Eastern Division. Older wood cars, susceptible to fires, telescoping and worse, were being phased out. The new group was comprised of baggage, mail, parlor and dining cars, enough to outfit several main-line runs. Freight cars with steel underframes were forthcoming from Hudson Shops where 358 men were employed.

Much of the road's improvements came in expectation of more business, heavier trains, and a more competitive railroad. This required new power, which was manifested in a systemwide use of E, J, and Z Classes, ordered in large quantity. In 1912, the Omaha authorized the purchase of some $10,000,000 in equipment trusts, $6,000,000 of which were issued by year's end. The

(Left) Behind E Class 4-6-2 No. 506, a humble three-car Train 508, the *Viking*, exits the Omaha's one tunnel, located six miles north of Elroy, in the 1950s. The remote bore was abandoned in 1983. *Ken Kurn.*

(Below) The Altoona-Elroy wayfreight was a regular late steam assignment on the Omaha. After passing through the tunnel, the southbound train is rolling through the countryside, toward Elroy, behind J-A No. 421 on June 9, 1956. *Jim Scribbins.*

balance was held in C&NW's treasury, subject to use as needed. The purchase by C&NW of 249 "Zulu" 2-8-0s between 1909 and 1913 seemed a paradox. The purchase was made in conjunction with large 2-8-0s stabled elsewhere, at a time when investment in 2-8-2s might have been wiser. Omaha had just two examples of the heavy Consolidations, using them in switching, transfer or helper assignments.

Problems and mishaps continued as new and much larger power came to the system. In May 1910, Engineer Marquisee was bringing Train 4 to Elroy about 3:00 PM, rolling upgrade to the tunnel. The I-2 Class engine, No. 375, suffered a main rod failure. Without any more than splintering the tie ends, the train stopped unscathed. Train 4 made Elroy 1-1/2 hours late, brought in by a freight engine commandeered at Camp Douglas.

Even with occasional setbacks, Omaha's business in the fall of 1911 increased, at least at Fairchild. The *Observer* reported ten extras eastbound one day in October, while 31 loads were brought in off the Mondovi Branch. A new 200 ton coal chute was completed at Merrillan in time for the new engines, reputed to be able to haul seventy to ninety car trains. Operational headaches such as doubling a train into a siding for a meet would be solved with double-track. Changes in the Fairchild layout that year included Fairchild & North Eastern moving their depot to accommodate yard changes. Nathaniel Foster's F&NE extension was an answer to the petition of "a large number of farmers" interested in service along its forty-one mile Caryville route. But the towns of Augusta, Eleva, Strum and Osseo represented the opposite view, objecting to the draw-off of business. 1,135 carloads were gener-

ated in the sparse territory, plus a large quantity of carloads north of Fairchild. The Railroad Commission considered the final thirty miles east of Caryville poorly served, and public convenience and necessity required construction.

Omaha's operating revenues increased in fiscal 1913, but so did operating expenses. Wages also increased, but so did the amount of time worked. Maintenance-of-Way costs were $530,000. This covered re-ballasting of 33 miles of track, and replacement of 860 feet of bridging. Other expenses included a second track from Truax to Northline, thirty miles of which were placed in operation during October 1913. Block signals between Elroy and Wyeville, Merrillan and Eau Claire, and Northline to St. Paul were in operation by July 17, 1913. Another installation of thirty miles was completed later in the year, making the 194.57 miles of the Eastern Division under continuous block signal control. On October 30, Fairchild observed 28 trains passing through town from 7:00 AM to 6:00 PM, including gravel extras headed for Northline, from Wedge's Creek gravel pit on the Marshfield line. In that time, speedometers and electric headlights came to the Omaha, thanks to the Wisconsin legislature.

The Woodville area, while scenic, was the scene of several accidents. In 1910, I-1 Class No. 314 tangled with branch engine No. 98 just west of the original depot site, destroying the smaller Ten-Wheeler. On March 4, 1913, an extra west was ordered to meet Train 78 at Roberts, twelve miles away. The extra's crew headed into the siding and covered its headlight, but before the train stopped, it continued to drift toward the west switch. With Train 78 moving toward them in the darkness, the extra inadver-

At Elroy in the late 1940s, a pair of cabooses rest between assignments on way freights 21-22. Headend "way car" No. 6189 is accompanied by standard way car No. 6052, equipped with wood beam trucks and favored by crews for their excellent riding qualities. *Neil Torssell.*

144

Located 13.4 miles north of Elroy, Camp Douglas, Wisconsin, was built around the Omaha-Milwaukee Road junction. The depot, freight house and tower can be seen to the right in this southwesterly view from the 1890s. Milwaukee Road's line, in the foreground, was later double tracked. The crossing was the site of a major wreck in 1931. *Author's Collection.*

tently rolled onto the mainline. Train 78's Engineer, John Conway, had both legs broken in the pile-up.

Heavy grading was taking place between Wilson and Hersey, further reducing curves on the county line hill. On May 2, 1913, passenger Train 2 collided with an extra, killing Train 2's engineer and a baggageman, and severely injuring the fireman. The extra's crew had run to Baldwin for a meet with Train 2. Slowing for the east switch at Baldwin, the train ran nine car lengths beyond the switch. Train 2 was expected at 8:24 PM, but the extra had arrived at 8:11 PM. Unable to get in the clear, they chose to cut off the head end and run to the west, and return in a short while for the rear section of the train, but time worked against them. Without adequate flag protection, and using up 13 precious minutes, Train 2 was upon them at speed. Here was another reason for larger power, better brakes and electric headlights. Omaha's final construction in the Woodville-Baldwin area was an airline past Woodville's curves, giving the road a nearly straight grade through what had been a dangerous section.

Omaha's first J Class 2-8-2, No. 390, was delivered July 7, 1913, along with five others. Elroy's newspaper enthusiastically reported the passage of the two Omaha Zulus and J Class No. 399 on July 19. While C&NW used Zulus into town, Elroy hadn't observed a C&NW J Class on the Madison Division. The *Leader* said "this is a new class for this part of the country and is a monster... eight drivers and a trailer. All are superheated and have

the Baker valve gear... No wonder Omaha is doubling its bridge strength through here and laying heavier steel." Fairchild's paper stated the Js weighed 467,500 lbs., had 27"x 32" cylinders, air fire doors and power reverse, plus a coal pusher. They also rode on odd 61" drivers, now standard with C&NW's big engines.

In May 1913, Schenectady readied the first eight E Class 4-6-2s, soon to supplant Omaha's own design (I-2/K-2 Class) on heavy passenger runs. Nos. 500-507 were delivered and stored at St. Paul Shops, until the double-track program could be completed from Knapp to Northline in mid-October. Built a month before the freight power, the new Pacifics weighed 130 tons and were equipped with Baker valve gear, like the freight engines.

The problem of operating the new railroad fell upon men such as F.E. Nicholes. In June 1913, Nicholes wrote about installation of passing tracks at Wilson and Hersey, serving both directions on the new double-track. He wanted the eastbound passing track at Wilson completed by the fall so that Omaha's new, heavy power, handling 2,500 tons, could use another siding between Baldwin and Knapp. He claimed this fifteen mile section had heavy traffic at certain times of the day. The westbound Hersey installation allowed long drags coming up the hill in front of passenger trains to clear the summit and roll down to the siding. The Wilson siding would allow slower traffic to negotiate the line after passenger trains went down to Knapp.

At the junction of the old line into Woodville, another siding

145

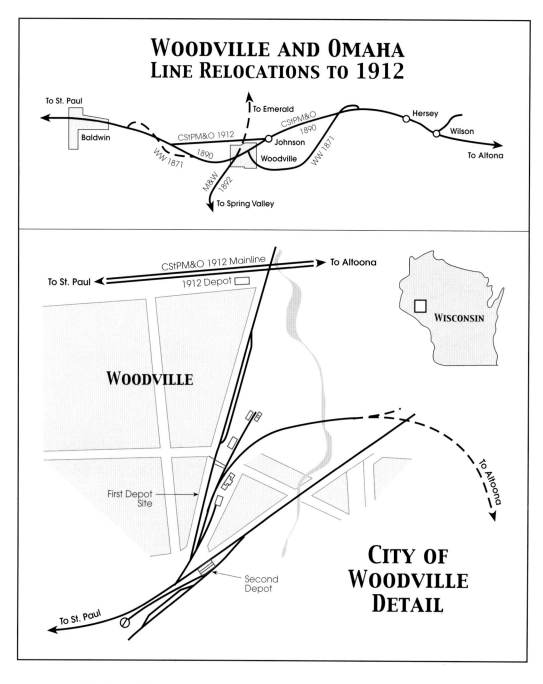

## WOODVILLE AND OMAHA LINE RELOCATIONS TO 1912

To St. Paul
Baldwin
CStPM&O 1912
WW 1871
1890
M&W 1892
To Spring Valley
To Emerald
Johnson
Woodville
CStPM&O 1890
WW 1871
Hersey
Wilson
To Altona

## CITY OF WOODVILLE DETAIL

CStPM&O 1912 Mainline
To St. Paul
1912 Depot
To Altoona

WOODVILLE

WISCONSIN

First Depot Site
To Altoona
Second Depot
To St. Paul

unpleasant. A gasoline engine was finally installed in the "express tower," a boon for Charlie Pope, the depot's agent. The original depot lingered on, serving as a freight house. Later, the building was leased to the Fred Cave American Legion Post No. 240.

In late 1915, Wilson agent Strasburg had his work cut out for him. He had to cover the arrival of Train 3 at 7:40 AM, then carry mail to and from the Post Office for Train 17. New hours had him on duty at 7:15 AM. Strasburg had a time getting the station "up to speed" as three stoves had to be lit to warm the depot, tickets had to be sold and baggage checked within ten minutes. It was too short a time, he testified, and to add the work for Train 3, especially the mail, was just too much. On December 31, 1915, passengers for Train 3 faced a cold, locked depot. He stressed that the new time was an injustice to him, personally and monetarily.

In 1928, Strasburg was still arguing his case! He worked 8:00 AM to 10:15 AM Sundays, covering another two trains, as well as dealing with Trains 108, 507

was proposed, holding fifteen cars. This would allow nightly freight Train 85 to eliminate a run down into old Woodville from the location ultimately called Johnson. Johnson would eventually hold Woodville and Spring Valley cars when there was stock or empties for the Spring Valley-Weston Line. Nicholes thought the Johnson addition would expedite handling the brachline's cars, but F. R. Pechin was not so convinced. He advised Nicholes to look into the matter further and consider any alternate less costly schemes. Pechin thought Wilson was too close to Knapp for the siding to be built. He had his reasons and was hard to convince.

Woodville ultimately received a second, newer depot alongside the new mainline fill, forty feet above the level of the village. This building required a stairway and a hand-operated elevator in a short towerlike building. Woodville's newspaper observed it took too long to raise baggage from the branchline to the mainline level, causing passengers to miss their trains. The stairs were slippery in winter, and "a cold wind from Duluth" made it all very

and 517, and their passengers. By the summer of 1942, the Wilson station had only a caretaker on Sundays, and after the cessation of Train 509's stop on July 5, 1942, no further trains were scheduled to stop at the station. New agent E.G. Grotenhuis would then be on duty 8:00 AM to 5:00 PM daily, except Sundays.

To present day, ghostly fills and cuts of two railroads are still evident along Highway 12 in the Woodville vicinity. Traces of the earthwork formerly within the village limits of Woodville are gone. The post-1913 mainline is nearly one-half mile from the old depot site, and the route to Emerald, abandoned in 1929, is barely discernible. Now, both depots are gone, but the foundation of the high-level depot is still in place. Woodville today has a modest collection of freight cars and railroad artifacts at the former site of the older depot, but little to suggest of the former presence of the Omaha, West Wisconsin Railway or the hard winters of railroading in St. Croix County.

(Above) Woodville, looking northeast circa 1900, with the second depot in the center and the line to Emerald on the left. The Spring Valley line was to the right, behind the cameraman.

(Left) Woodville's new 1912 depot boasted an elevator for handling mail and LCL freight.

(Below) The new depot and bridging for the 1912 Omaha line relocation can be seen in the distance in this northerly view of Woodville. The second depot is at the right. All: *Woodville Library.*

(Right) Elroy's 1899 roundhouse was a half circle in this 1910 era view. The "New Line" changed everything, and the 20 stall roundhouse was later reduced to a modest six stalls.

(Below) On August 15, 1948, Elroy's engine terminal was still a busy place with J-A No. 415 and E Class engines 502 and 501 in the roundhouse, and 4-6-2 Nos. 517 and 1611 (C&NW) on the adjacent ready track. Both: *Author's Collection.*

J-A No. 408 rides the Elroy turntable on July 7, 1955, just eleven months before retirement. *Stan Mailer.*

148

Elroy's cavernous depot and rail-road hotel was a social center at the turn-of-the-century. This is the C&NW (west) side of the depot. The Omaha held forth on the eastern side of the great wood building which included a rookery of offices and services. *Author's Collection.*

(Above) The Omaha day crew at Elroy switches a pair of coaches and a heavyweight diner left by Train 519, the *Dakota 400.* The cars will return to Chicago on 519's southbound counterpart, Train 518. Inaugurated on April 30, 1950 (replacing the *Minnesota 400*), the *Dakota 400* operated Chicago-Huron, South Dakota, via Elroy and the Sparta Cut Off. In 1955, the train began running via Wyeville, where it would have to back into the depot. *Neil Torssell.* (Below) Train 501, the *Viking,* has arrived at Elroy from Chicago and Madison. The train was brought into town by C&NW power, where it was replaced by Omaha Class E No. 514 for the trip to Eau Claire and the Twin Cities. The workhorse train, which ran very late with steam, made most of the stops, doing head-end business for the Chicago-Madison-Twin Cities route. *Don Kotz.*

149

(Above) Lending an air of urgency to the scene at Wyeville in 1947, Omaha Class E No. 516 leans hard into the mainline curve with a double-headed freight extra coming off the Adams Line. Omaha engines would take over for C&NW power at Adams, which was also a crew change point on the "Cut Off." At right, Train 418, the *Minnesota 400,* stands on the C&NW main, waiting for the 5:22 PM arrival of the *Twin Cities 400* from St. Paul. *William F. Armstrong.* (Below) Arriving from Winona, Train 418 rolls up to the Omaha mainline (now reduced to single track) at Wyeville tower, powered by C&NW streamlined 4-6-2 Class E-S No. 1617 on April 4, 1948. *Neal Torssell.*

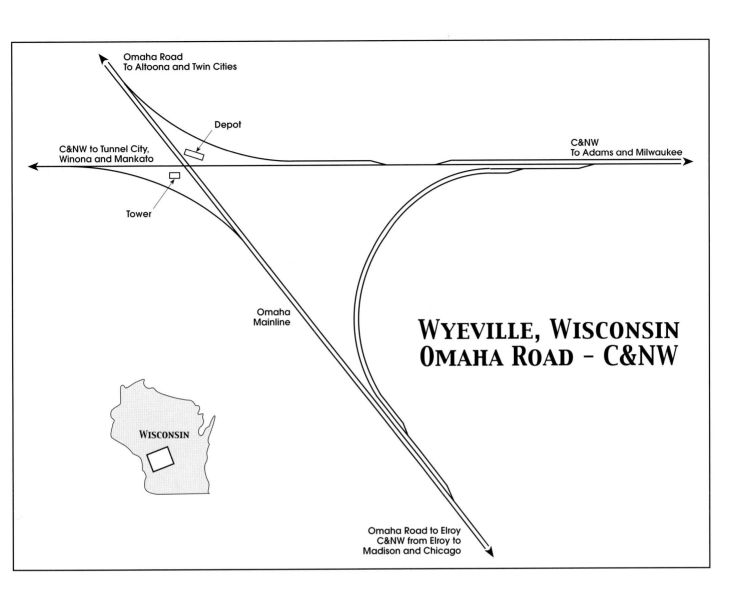

Omaha Road
To Altoona and Twin Cities

Depot

C&NW to Tunnel City,
Winona and Mankato

C&NW
To Adams and Milwaukee

Tower

Omaha
Mainline

# WYEVILLE, WISCONSIN
# OMAHA ROAD - C&NW

WISCONSIN

Omaha Road to Elroy
C&NW from Elroy to
Madison and Chicago

C&NW Class E-S 4-6-2 No. 1611 is on the point of the *Minnesota 400* at Wyeville tower in the late 1940s. The train has been turned and is ready to depart for the Mississippi Valley. The *Minnesota 400* was replaced on April 30, 1950 by the *Dakota 400*, which operated Chicago to Huron, South Dakota. *Don Kotz..*

(Above) An engine change at Adams in 1947 has Omaha E-3 No. 600 on the point of Train 403, the summer season *Mountaineer*, after replacing a C&NW 2900 series E-2 Pacific. The train is ready to depart for Wyeville and a trip over the Omaha to the Twin Cities, and ultimately, Vancouver, B.C., via Soo Line and Canadian Pacific. Omaha power frequented the Adams engine terminal, about 30 miles east of Wyeville, on C&NW's "New Line." *William F. Armstrong.* (Below) Fairchild, located 12.6 miles west of Merrillan, was the junction for the Mondovi branch, formerly the Fairchild & North Eastern. In May 1926, F-2 Class 4-6-0 No. 195 rests with the Mondovi local, having arrived ten minutes earlier, while E Class No. 507 holds the main with the *Viking*, Chicago-bound via Elroy and Madison. *State Historical Society of Wisconsin.*

(Above) Omaha Train 508 is braked along Merrillan's platform to stop just short of the Green Bay & Western diamond. Class E No. 516 leads an abbreviated consist this day, devoid of head-end cars.

(Left) Passengers prepare to board the train just after noon in 1940, while the conductor gives signals to Train 508's engineer. Both: *Earl Ruhland*.

Omaha received the 4-6-2 Pacific type wheel arrangement in May 1903, seven years before the parent road. This view, taken on December 16, 1905, depicts I-2 Class No. 373 with the original clerestory cab roof and small 5,400 gallon tender. *J. Foster Adams.*

(Above) Class I-2 Nos. 371-375 were built in 1903 with Player trailing trucks. All five engines were scrapped in 1937, surrendering their tenders to I-1 Class 4-6-0 Nos. 328-332. Thirty-one years old, No. 375 has spoked lead wheels at Minneapolis on September 10, 1934. (Below) I-2 No. 376 is shown at Minneapolis on June 21, 1933. I-2s 376-378 and 379-382 came from Alco in May 1907 and February 1909 with outside wheel bearing Cole trailing trucks, which were more flexible and stable than the Player type. Both: *Robert H. Graham*

154

Legend has it that the 1911 Schenectady K-2s, Nos. 388-389, were built to pull Northern Pacific's *North Coast Limited* over the Omaha. They weighed about 7,000 lbs. more than the I-2s, and had 23" cylinders versus the 21" cylinders of the I-2s. Years after that prestigious assignment, K-2 No. 388 was photographed at Minneapolis on July 17, 1932. *Robert H. Graham.*

(Above) Omaha's first E Class 4-6-2, No. 500, shows off its Boxpok center driver, coal pusher on the tender slope sheet, and the traditional Omaha brass, flat-topped "hooter" whistle. The manhole (aft of the steam dome) was used on engines 500-511. The 75" drivered 1913 Alco engine is ready for train 501, the *Viking*, at Elroy in 1951. It was retired in June 1953. (Below) Equipped with a "coffee can" style headlight, No. 516 illustrates the final order of the class, Nos. 512-517, at Elroy in October 1953. Both: *Stan Mailer.*

155

Omaha Class E-9 4-6-0 No. 176 is in charge of a stock train at Lake Wilson, Minnesota, on the Pipestone Line. The Ten-Wheeler was an 1891 Schenectady product that was retired in October 1928. The cars are "special feed and water" stock cars equipped with roof hatches for loading feed, plus water troughs located about mid-height in the car sides. *Lyle Larson Collection.*

# 9.

# WEST SIDE STORY

estern Division offices were transferred to St. James, Minnesota for the second time, on November 27, 1898. A new brick building housed the division officials, who presided over a roundhouse and sizable yard. The road had spent $165,000 on the engine terminal in 1890, but it now needed further enlargement for the new power just arriving. By May 1890, a 25 stall modern facility was raised, including smaller buildings. It took 250 carloads of stone, worked by a Mankato mason, just to ready the site for the brick construction. Water was piped in from a nearby lake. Back in the 1870s, contractor Frank Fowler had created the first roundhouse on the site.

The entire western lines of the North Western were awakening from the depression of the 1890s. Most of the area was dependent upon the wheat and flour business, and the arrangements made with the grain merchants underscored this. Many railroad policies were aligned with grain companies west of the Mississippi. Construction of elevators at various towns was decided on an advise and consent basis. While grain traffic was spotty, with peaks and valleys, Omaha's passenger trade was on the rise. In the 1880s, four trains handled the Minneapolis-Omaha trade. In the 1890s there were eight well-patronized Limiteds rushing across southwest Minnesota, with only Chicago Great Western in close competition by Century's end. By September 1902, connections between Minneapolis and Mitchell, South Dakota, were improved by the introduction of through service. This relieved mainline Trains 1-2 of local stops, St Paul to Worthington, restricting their halts to Merriam Junction, Mankato, St. James and Worthington. Additional overnight Twin Cities-Mitchell service was offered by Trains 15-16, due out of either terminal at 7:30 PM. The burden on Trains 1-2, in many areas, was such that it was seldom on time. Both trains often had up to three sleepers as well as coaches, some of which were transferred to the C&NW at Mankato. Des Moines cars were transferred at Lake Crystal. Head-end business to Worthington was considerable. By autumn 1902, business increased still further. Trains 1-2 were named, *Duluth, Twin Cities & Omaha Limited,* and the St. James depot received longer platforms as a result.

Still more activity came to the Omaha from a health spa aptly named Mudbaden. Located between Merriam and Jordan, Minnesota, the resort began in 1901, with mineral spring water and sulphurous mud touted as the route to health and happiness. The resort billed itself as the best in Minnesota for "supplementary treatments," able to administer to the nervous system and digestive organs. Mudbaden was just an hour's ride from the Twin Cities and was a stop for several trains.

In June 1902, Train 2, running late, approached Ashton, Iowa, at 50 MPH. In spite of heavier track east of St. James, the line into Iowa was less suited for making up time. The train derailed, the probable cause, a split switch. The engine and tender piled up near the depot, the baggage car splintered and several crewmen were badly injured. One mail clerk and the fireman died. A few days prior, a change in train scheduling put heavy sleepers and a buffet car just behind the headend cars. The St. James newspaper reasoned that if lighter cars had been up front, they would have been telescoped by the heavy cars usually carried in the rear, and loss of life might have been much higher.

The names for the western lines changed when the St. Paul & Sioux City Division was redesignated Minnesota & Iowa Division, and the Northern and Eastern Divisions were renamed after consolidation as the Wisconsin Division. In 1905, the Wisconsin Division was transferred to Eau Claire from St. Paul, with T.W. Kennedy as its Superintendent. T.B. Seeley was Chief Dispatcher at the time, E.E. Nash served as Assistant Superintendent, and S.G. Strickland was the General Superintendent.

In 1892, the Omaha developed a new yard engine, E-1 No. 10, with a similar trio arriving in March 1893. The depression slowed purchases and it was not until November 1897 that Omaha resumed buying switch engines. The E-1s also served as the prototype for the slightly heavier F-6 Class, at 55-1/2 tons versus 51 tons. These handsome little yard goats eventually numbered twelve in all, built in 1901, 1905 and 1907 respectively. Two Baldwin F-10s, weighing 55-1/2 tons, came in 1902, and were numbered 22-23. Nos. 270-272, 13-16, and 25-28 comprised the F-6s. At this time, many of the old 4-4-0s were being disposed of, and Omaha began to reuse their road numbers as new engines arrived. This was also common with C&NW. By 1909, when heavier switchers were needed, the road acquired its first Class M-1 (a C&NW letter symbol for 0-6-0s), and like the previous engines, these were equipped with Stephenson valve gear. The final group of M-1s, were delivered with Baker Valve Gear. Due to their cylinder diameter, the M-1s would have been Omaha's E-10 Class, but C&NW practice prevailed. A total of twenty M-1s were built between 1909 and 1913.

Years before, between 1886 and 1890, Omaha rebuilt at least six 4-4-0s into 0-4-0s. They were all Tauntons, natives of the west side. Other 4-4-0s were sold to various lumber railroads, and several went to the Fairchild & North Eastern Railway.

Mankato's industries were chiefly related to grain and stone cutting, and its quarried stone was found in many of the Omaha Road's bridges. In 1908, there were several firms, Fowler & Pay, McMullen's, T.W. Coughlin's and Widell's, busily producing car-

The long hill out of Mankato southward originally passed the tiny station of Minneopa Park, very different from today's mainline. In a rare scene from 1905, a passenger train leaves the depot. *State Historical Society of Wisconsin.*

loadings for the Omaha. Another major industry was Hubbard Milling Company, a landmark of the community in later years. Mankato Malt Company was also an Omaha customer. The nearby town of Kasota was the site of the old C&NW/Omaha transfer. It too enjoyed a stone industry with Breen & Babcock's Quarry, partially switched by the Omaha. A Hubbard & Palmer grain elevator was located there, plus a Peavey Elevator Company grainhouse and several cleaning houses. Switching activity involved C&NW, CM&StP and the Omaha. The story of the Western Division is one of agriculture and local produce with long distance cargoes going to Lake Superior destinations.

In 1922, the Kasota interchange between the C&NW and Omaha was active with traffic from the stone quarries. In February, the Omaha put on an additional switch engine at Mankato to assist in covering the work at Carney Cement Company and to do interchange work with C&NW. Carney resumed its quarry operations, and yard engines were unable to handle the assignment implicit with both town's industries.

By June 1, 1922, the situation had changed. A crew was assigned to switch both Kasota and Mankato. They began work at Mankato, switching industries on the old line east of town, working Carney's Quarry, and finally Kasota. To switch the interchange daily, Omaha would now discontinue accepting eastbound "dead" freight (non-time nonperishable traffic) to and from C&NW at Mankato, in favor of the interchange at Kasota. Several customers on the route produced sizable carloadings. Guarantee Sand Company had eight to twelve cars per day, Carney's Quarry did nine cars and the cement plant required up to twenty-five loads per day. Superintendent J.J. Prentice observed that Omaha's facilities at Mankato were a bit stretched with local business and the interchange traffic had to be split. His biggest problem was crew overtime, caused by the congestion in the yards. On occasion, trains were held outside the yard. This was sufficient reason to reopen Kasota's interchange.

Sioux City's list of railroad-served industries was substantial, led by the packing industry. The Cudahy, Swift and Armour firms received record loads of stock from surrounding grasslands from the 1880s onward. A cadre of 2,000 workers were engaged in the trade by 1910, many from eastern European nations, who settled in the "bottoms" of the Floyd River. The result was hundreds of carloads of meat for eastern and northern destinations for the five railroads serving the city. A product of the industry was the Sioux City Terminal Railroad Company, which operated a roster of switch engines beginning in 1907.

Over the years, several floods damaged industries and railroad facilities along the Floyd River. On June 8, 1953, a month after your author visited the road, a major flood destroyed the Sioux City Terminal Railroad, the stockyards, and took fourteen lives.

In season, the C&NW and Omaha lines in the Missouri Valley were host to heavy stock movements. Lines converged upon Sioux City and Omaha from connections with the eastern Dakotas. One line in particular ran southeast from Iroquois, South Dakota, to Sioux City, with connections at Hawarden, Iowa. This was a C&NW line, part of the Toledo & Northwestern construction. In 1910, C&NW built the Sioux City, Dakota & North Western Railway from Hawarden to Wren Junction near Hinton on the Illinois Central, to expedite traffic off the T&NW to the Sioux City area. C&NW had trackage rights over IC's mainline from Sioux City to Wren, going onto their own line at Wren, just north of the Great Northern crossing.

Western Division traffic at Sioux City warranted a large roundhouse, constructed in 1902 and enlarged to 38 stalls in 1910. Here, many of the small branchline engines were repaired. C&NW's Hawarden-bound power shared space with engines used between Sioux City and Council Bluffs, via Missouri Valley. One change was noted when Omaha's heavy J-3 Mikados were operated on C&NW Trains 17-18 between Sioux City and Omaha via California Junction and Blair, on the older west side line.

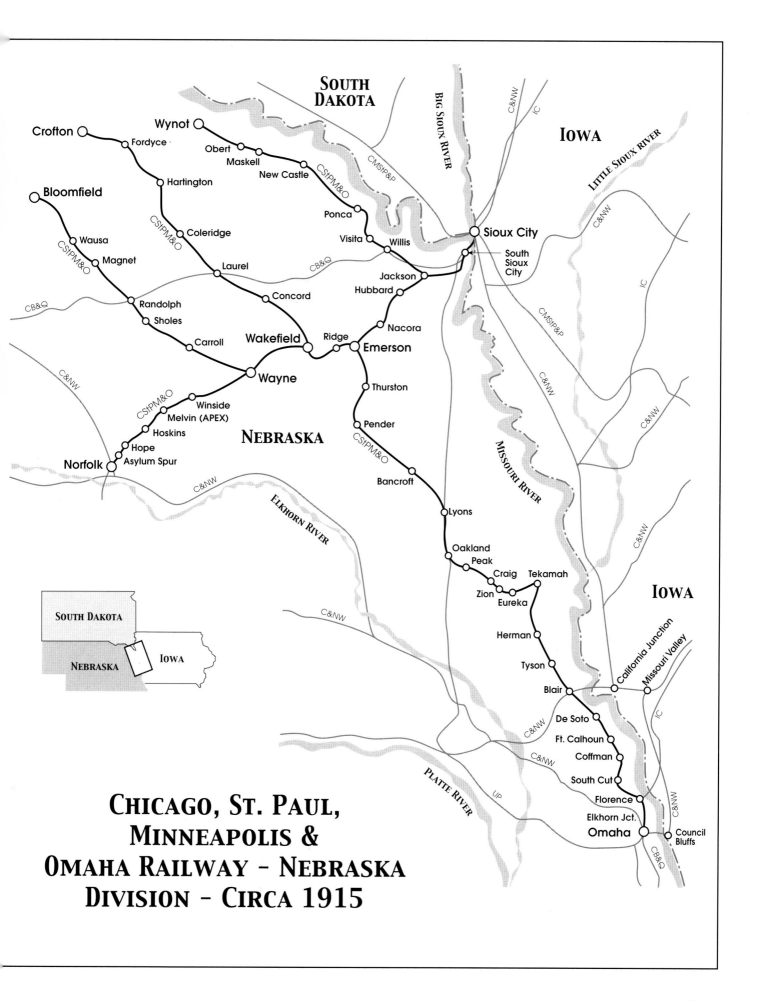

SOUTH DAKOTA

BIG SIOUX RIVER

C&NW

IC

IOWA

LITTLE SIOUX RIVER

C&NW

Crofton

Wynot

Fordyce

Obert

Maskell

New Castle

CStPM&O

CMStP&P

Bloomfield

Hartington

Wausa

CStPM&O

Coleridge

Magnet

Ponca

Sioux City

CStPM&O

Visita

Willis

C&NW

South Sioux City

CB&Q

Laurel

Concord

Jackson

CMStP&P

CB&Q

Randolph

Hubbard

Sholes

Nacora

Carroll

Wakefield

Ridge

Emerson

C&NW

Wayne

Thurston

CStPM&O

Winside

C&NW

Melvin (APEX)

Pender

Hoskins

NEBRASKA

C&NW

Hope

Norfolk

Asylum Spur

CStPM&O

Bancroft

C&NW

ELKHORN RIVER

Lyons

Oakland

Peak

MISSOURI RIVER

Craig

Tekamah

Zion

Eureka

IOWA

Herman

C&NW

Tyson

California Junction

C&NW

Missouri Valley

Blair

C&NW

De Soto

Ft. Calhoun

C&NW

Coffman

IC

South Cut

C&NW

Florence

PLATTE RIVER

UP

Elkhorn Jct.

Omaha

Council Bluffs

CB&Q

SOUTH DAKOTA

NEBRASKA

IOWA

# CHICAGO, ST. PAUL, MINNEAPOLIS & OMAHA RAILWAY – NEBRASKA DIVISION – CIRCA 1915

**Disaster at Bigelow:** On February 9, 1914, Train 2, the *Twin City Limited,* was involved in a spectacular accident. The train, powered by an I-2 Pacific, derailed near Bigelow, Minnesota (9.4 miles south of Worthington). *State Historical Society of Wisconsin.*

Several I-2 Class 4-6-2s were assigned to the Western Division. On November 5, 1914, hard luck I-2 No. 371, a victim of a wreck on the eastern side, was in trouble again. The engine was on Train 2, the *Twin Cities Limited,* rolling through a "14 below" night toward the Minnesota-Iowa border at Bigelow, Minnesota. Passing into Minnesota at 2:38 AM, Train 2 made Bigelow at 2:40 AM, eleven minutes late. At about 2:45 AM, the train derailed 2-1/2 miles east of Bigelow. No. 371 broke away from its train and stopped 1,650 feet beyond the point of derailment, its lead truck and one tender truck on the ties. Nearly every passenger car was on its side, with the exception of the head-end cars. Two fatalities, one Canadian passenger and one express messenger, plus seventeen injuries, were the result of a broken mainline rail. Counterpart Train 1 was delayed at Worthington while the wreck was cleared. One westbound passenger train, detouring over the Rock Island, derailed at Round Lake, and as the wreck occurred on a fill, cleanup work proved difficult.

In the winter of 1912, there was heavy snow around Sheldon, Iowa. The Omaha used five engines to ram drifts. On February 1, three mismatched "19 inch engines" and one 4-4-0 teamed to help an I-2 Class 4-6-2. Roadmaster Joseph Bruta made note of the matter, stating that when final payrolls for the month were tallied, it would illustrate the terrible weather that winter.

Record snows on February 23, 1917, completely filled the Springer Cut at Storden on the Currie Line, with a total depth of over 18 feet above the rails. However, Mr. J.J. O'Neill, later General Manager, claimed to have witnessed similar vertical measurements to 23 feet! On March 17, drifts between Worthington and Brewster were up to the cab roofs of stalled locomotives, and single engine consists arrived at Worthington with snow piled atop their boilers. To the east, the Spring Valley Line was buried under equally heavy snows.

In 1922, a measurement of railroad productivity was the tons-per-train-mile report. The old Nebraska Division had difficulty improving its record with power furnished by the Mechanical Department. The Division had a group of "20 inch engines" generally kept at Sioux City, ample power to handle business that fall. An interdivisional squabble arose when power was summoned

from Sioux City, but was then utilized by the Western Division. The Nebraska Division had to substitute lesser power, which could not handle the tonnage. They had to resort to double-heading or operating trains with fewer cars.

The Nebraska Division possessed a rough profile, which taxed Omaha's light power. Superintendent F.J. Taylor, stated that on October 26 he ordered an extra *Norfolk Turn* out of Sioux City with a "20 inch engine" and 600 tons. He was advised the roundhouse could furnish only No. 263, a high-wheeled "19 inch engine" capable of only 420 tons. G-2 Class No. 305, a larger Ten-Wheeler, recently shopped, was a candidate, but the Western Division had taken it away. The foreman offered Taylor another small engine to double-head with No. 263, but the pair was unequal to the larger 20 inch engine. E.C. Blundell brought the matter to General Superintendent F.R. Pechin, saying he was working to cut down overtime, increase his ton miles and generally utilize the older saturated steam power to the best advantage. Blundell stated his case to obtain the best available power, the G-1 Class, as it would be several years before I-1s would prevail on the Norfolk Line. As of 1922, the 20 inch 4-6-0 was the best for the Nebraska hills.

E.R. Gorman, Superintendent of Motive Power and Machines, received a letter from F.R. Pechin on the subject. The Nebraska Division had a total of fifty-nine engines assigned that year, but only forty-seven were in road service, Gorman explained that several 19 inch F-2 Class 4-6-0s, and two F-8 4-4-0s, were available, and No. 263 with an 18 inch Standard would handle as much as a 20 inch engine. That was hardly the point. The Nebraska Division needed engines capable of running off ton miles singularly. Blundell patiently responded to Pechin, pointing out the best engines shown in the assignment list. Engine No. 202 was far better than No. 193, although both were of the F-2 Class. No. 193 was not in condition to work, where the 202 was, and F-2 No. 212 was considered a first-class machine. On November 4, 1922, it was assigned to Oakland-Omaha wayfreight Trains 15-16. Blundell showed that two F-8s, Nos. 257 and 258, were of no use for freight duty, contrary to Gorman's claim.

Blundell's Nebraska Division had a large assignment of engines, all of the lightest variety. The G-1 4-6-0s could handle only a maximum of 575 tons on the mainline, and 595 tons on the Norfolk Line. The other divisions had what seemed to be the pick of power. The question of double-heading was brought up, but this raised costs and contributed to overtime, accounting for the Nebraska Division's increased expenses.

By the mid-1920s, as demand for time freight service grew, Omaha's fleet of newer, heavier power began to spill onto the Western Division. In 1926, eight J-3 Class heavy Mikados were ordered at a cost of $420,000, completing the heavy freight power purchases for Omaha. The new engines were designed to operate between the Twin Cities and Sioux City. General Manager Pechin announced the J-3 purchase on September 1, an order placed, not surprisingly, with American Locomotive Company. The road applied to the Interstate Commerce Commission for permission to issue an equipment trust certificate to finance the engines. At the same time, improvements were needed in order to handle the J-3s, and the St. James turntable was replaced by a 90 foot steel model from American

Bridge Company (three years before, an interesting cornfield meet occurred on the old table, when Train 2's I-2 Class 4-6-2 No. 377 crashed into K-1 No. 238 *on the table*). The passenger train made its erroneous way up the roundhouse lead, meeting the K-1 just as it left the table. The work went ahead feverishly to make the October 1 deadline, at an expenditure of $65,000.

The new power was such that St. James' newspaper carried a builder's photo of J-3 No. 437. *Railway Age* magazine carried a write-up in its June 26, 1926 issue, detailing the modified USRA engine, an improvement over the second group of J-2 Class. The J-3s weighed 10,000 pounds more and had Standard Type B stokers, Elesco Type SF exhaust injectors, cast steel Delta trailing trucks, and front-end American Multiple Throttles for their 200 pounds boiler pressure. A scant eight inches longer than the J-2 predecessor, they carried one Westinghouse pump on the front deck. After testing and inspection at Schenectady, they started west in three groups, the first leaving October 29th, the next November 3rd, and the last on November 8, 1926.

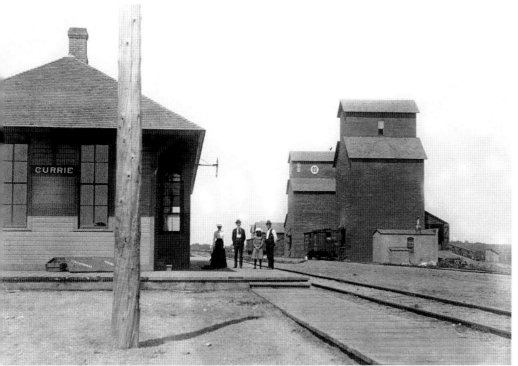

(Above) The 38.3 mile Currie Line was served by Train 62, which is shown at Dovray, Minnesota, 6.2 miles from the end of the branch. Omaha E-6 No. 134 was housed in a small engine-house at Bingham Lake, the branch's junction with the mainline.

(Left) This peaceful photo of Currie, circa 1902, has an interesting history. It was found in a Mexican pawnshop by a couple visiting from Riverside, California. Both: *Mrs. L. Gervais Collection.*

# WESTERN DIVISION

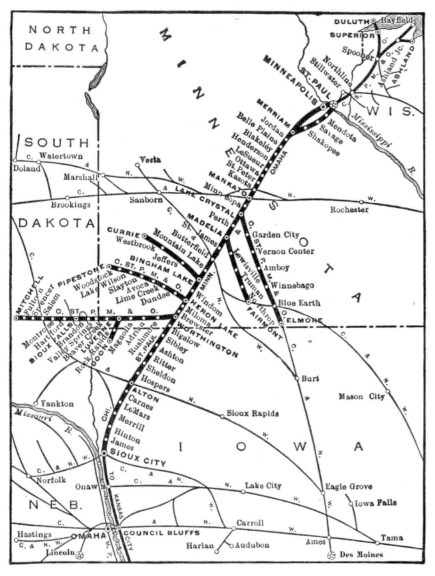

On November 9, the first assignment of a J-3 (the engine number was not recorded) came into St. James with 105 cars. On Monday, two more J-3's arrived with heavy trains. Expenses for improvements to operate the engines ran to $775,000. This included bridge rebuilding, passing track extensions, and work at Sioux City and St. James roundhouses. The last three engines were received on November 26, and at the onset, only ran as far as St. James. All were readied for the "opening" of the Sioux City-Worthington district, just being finished for their arrival. The St. James newspaper morbidly observed a number of St. James railroaders would be put out of work because fewer men were needed. A new 10th Street bridge would now take the J-3s, and new switcher No. 82. The J-3s were bringing in 75-100 car drags each day, but were still helped out of Mankato toward Lake Crystal, probably by an Omaha "Zulu" (Nos. 218-219).

The Western Division often suffered washouts on the flat prairie west of St. James and Worthington. Train 19, a freight with just 14 cars, left the rails and plunged into four feet of water on a dark September night. The accident occurred four miles southwest of Sheldon, Iowa, and three men were in the cab. Ole

Tiegum, the engineer, wound up with his foot pinned in the cab wreckage, his body submerged, except for his face. Ole's fireman and headend man escaped uninjured, but wondered about Tiegum. Soon enough they spotted Tiegum's face and he called out to them. Thirty minutes later, they had his foot free.

It was a night of washouts in northwestern Iowa which sluiced away into the Floyd River, taking out 400 feet of grade in a flash. Further down the Floyd, Illinois Central lost nearly two miles below LeMars, and Omaha Train 201 was trapped at the town, while Train 9 was marooned at Sheldon. During the washout, trains from St. Paul ran to Worthington and turned back.

In 1926, analysis of Omaha's freight traffic found that north-south movement was increasing in contrast to east-west. This new increase was answered with the J-3, while all other Mikados were committed to either the Eastern Division's Northern District (Nos. 390-408 inclusive), or the Eastern Division's Eastern District (Nos. 409-431 inclusive). Products were oil, gasoline, fruit and meat, items related to the new style of urban living, demanding a faster schedule for freight trains. The need for fast railroading brought the elimination of 382 grade crossings by November 1926 in the western region. Locally, Madelia enjoyed a shipment of 8,500 sheep in October 1926, in twenty-four double-deck stock cars. The week's total of inbound shipments amounted to fifty-eight cars.

The western line was steadily improving its operations, but throughout the balance of the "roaring 20s," a series of accidents plagued the road. In December 1926, a southbound light engine crawled cautiously through drifts and swirling snow in a merciless prairie storm. At 8:30 AM, the engine approached Northrup just as Train 8, the northbound Twin Cities passenger, eased out of the station. The two met head-on with the lead engine of the double-headed passenger train turning over into a ditch. Miraculously, injuries were few and the five Fairmont passengers and seven crew members were turned out into the cold.

In 1929, the practice of "Riding the Blinds" on Omaha passenger trains brought death to a Carleton, Minnesota, college student. Train 210, the *Twin City Express*, had seven cars and seventy-five passengers when it left the track while rounding a curve, then plowed for six hundred feet into a sandstone bluff. Earl Hanson, a summer student, was crushed between baggage car ends, while the engine crew sustained injuries when the engine slid on its side.

The Fairmont Line was one of the first assignments for Omaha's 1928 motor cars, Nos. 2000 and 2001. The units cost $45,000. Superintendent J.J. Prentice announced the inaugural in early June, to be used on Trains 7-8 with a crew of three. The two units were divided between the Worthington-Sioux City local Trains 13-14 and Trains 7-8. A trailing baggage car was assigned to Trains 13-14 and, later, to Trains 7-8, as the units had no postal sections. The 275-HP car ran from Minneapolis to Fairmont.

During June 1928, Omaha removed its old ice spurs at Lake Crystal, Minnesota. They proved to be a visibility hazard for new Highway 60, which ran between the lake and Omaha's mainline. With heavy traffic that year, the North Western looked forward to still greater demands systemwide, planning two new trains between the Twin Cities and Rapid City, South Dakota. Omaha Road rail improvement programs saw two 60 man gangs putting down 100 pound rail between Madelia and St. James, later extended to Heron Lake and Worthington. At Belle Plaine, Blakely, Le Sueur and Carney, sidings were extended to over a mile in length, to be ready by the August 1 grain rush.

Two Rotary Club specials rolled in from California, carrying members to the Minneapolis International Convention. They were all-Pullman, 12 car specials, handled by shining I-2 and K-2 Pacifics. A day or two later, a 100 foot landslide occurred opposite Henderson, Minnesota. A section foreman had noticed a crack in the roadbed and went for help. Returning, he was confronted with a large section now in the Minnesota River. Forces were gathered and the track was moved over onto solid ground and repaired, presenting only an hour's delay to traffic.

St. James, hosting the Watonwan County Fair in 1928, also hosted the C&NW's 60 piece touring band, which usually called Chicago's 40th Street Shops their home. The crowd pleasing band came in two special coaches at the rear of Train 209, the *Missouri River Limited*, all expenses covered by the railroad. The highlight of the season was St. James' Lutefisk Day on Friday, October 5, for which the great North Western band played.

A year later, C&NW adjusted their passenger service to compete with West Coast railroads and their connections with Chicago. Omaha Train 201, the *Gold Coast Limited*, stayed on the same schedule, but Trains 216-210 were changed to do local work from Sioux City to St. Paul. Train 210 had the Rochester sleeper, given to C&NW at Mankato, that served the Mayo Clinic trade. Train 202 took 210's place, becoming a fast, through train of sleepers. With roadway improvements, it was inevitable that the first E Class 4-6-2s were put to use on the west side, beginning with Trains 209-210 in June 1928. They were assuredly in use by December 1929, when engine Nos. 500, 502, 508, and 509 came west to run on Trains 209-202 and 201-210 respectively. Omaha engineers commented on the fine-riding qualities of the Es, as well as their ability to handle heavy trains.

While passenger service was bolstered, freight business was hardly lagging. Freight trains acquired names such as *Rob-Roy* (Train 20). Train 23 was the *Westerner*, Train 19 was the *Tex-O-*

The "Irish Guard" meets at the spa at Mudbaden, Minnesota, in May 1924. Officers present for a meeting of no small importance include J.J. Prentice, E.R. Gorman, J.D. Condit, W.H. Thorn, F.J. Anderson, J.J. O'Neill, J.E. McMahon and J.A. O'Brien. The Mudbaden Health Resort was 48 miles from Minneapolis on the St. Paul-Sioux City mainline. *State Historical Society of Wisconsin.*

*Kan* and Train 18 was the *Gopher*. A new fast freight schedule called for 31 hour Kansas City-Twin Cities service, earmarked for high-class perishable freight. The new service departed Sioux City at 4:07 PM and arrived in St. James, 146 miles away, at 9:15 PM. Refrigerator cars were iced at St. James, leaving town at 11:00 PM for early morning delivery. It required two new train crews at St. James.

In the early days of August 1929, just before the "great crash," Omaha's first twenty days were its biggest to date. The J-3s were busy with seventy-car grain trains rolling in from the southwestern territory, destined for the Great Lakes grain terminals at Superior and Duluth. In the road's first eight months, gross receipts equaled $2,655,002. For August, it was $2,840,742.

After the long night of the Great Depression set in, Omaha had its first grim accident with the big J-3s. Sibley, Iowa, operator Herman Wenick had orders to stop Train 20, proceeding eastward with forty-three cars in a blinding snowstorm. Passing through Ashton at reduced speed, Engineer Ed Bridewell and Fireman Ed Bloom strained to see ahead of their big engine and somehow did not pick up their orders at Sibley. On a sharp curve a mile-and-a-half beyond the town, they met Train 19 head-on, its forty car train smashing out of the storm, bright headlights useless in the white, choking swirl. The two J-3s were locked together, one smokebox jammed inside the other, cylinders sheared off by the impact, crewmen dead and injured, all at the mercy of steam, iron and cold. Engineer A.C. Peterson of Sioux City died on Train 19's J-3, along with his head-end brakeman, Gilbert Evans. Bridewell was badly injured, as was Bloom, who jumped with his brakeman. Wrecking crews the next day were unable to part the two Mikes, and pushed the "double engine" back to Sibley to cut them apart. Ed Bridewell had "wiped the clock" just before the collision, which lessened the impact, but he was caught as he jumped and badly injured. Neither engine left the track, while several freight cars caught fire, extinguished by Sibley's fire department. The glow was enough to summon Carl. R. Gray, Jr., E.R. Gorman and J.J. Prentice to the scene.

Omaha's 38 mile branchline to the headwaters of the Des Moines River at Currie, Minnesota, was completed in 1900. Both the Currie and the Pipestone Lines were agriculture-based operations, served in 1922 by a modest passenger and freight train.

A problem occurred at Currie on January 19, 1922, after the engine for Train 62 backed out of the two-stall enginehouse. A vital casting in the turntable broke, as the engine was being readied for the trip to Bingham Lake. Despite the cold, several men were able to jack the table back, allowing the engine to return to the shelter of the house. Bridge Foreman Johnson wired St. James for instructions. It was necessary to cancel the train, and combine two regular runs to Currie the next day. St. James dispatched engine No. 145, a Class E-6 4-4-0, to resume service. Trains into Currie over the next two days required extra crews to return their power to Bingham Lake at night, returning them in the right direction for the morning. The road felt that backing the regular power in cold weather on trains was dangerous. A temporary wye was considered, but in the end, the old Barronett table was brought down to Currie to be placed in service by spring.

Southeast of Currie, the Fairmont Line was the site of a bizarre incident during a June 1929 thunderstorm. Conductor Jack

Redmond was aboard his train, northbound from Fairmont, on a day filled with wind and rain. Redmond's crew worked their way through downed trees and phone lines, approaching Madelia, the junction with the mainline. Under a darkening sky, Redmond spotted a funnel-shaped cloud east of his train. Five minutes before they arrived in Madelia, the storm struck. The next thing Redmond noticed was a cut of eight stock cars rolling away from town, propelled by the wind. They chased them until a curve turned the cars broadside into the wind, where two cars were lifted off their trucks clear of the mainline. The others were safely switched onto a blind siding.

In Nebraska, beyond Sioux City and far from the daily run of the premier *"400"* passenger trains, rural branchlines slowed ominously in the late 1930s. The beginning of WWII in 1941 brought a spurt of activity, traced to gas-rationing. But by June 1942, Omaha had filed with the Nebraska State Railway Commission to discontinue daily, except Sunday, mixed trains to Crofton and Bloomfield. The railroad's plan was to substitute tri-weekly service, not unusual for the times. It had tried without success to obtain relief from substantial loss in previous hearings.

The Nebraska branches were connected to the outside world by Trains 9-10, the *Mondamin*, with Emerson being the key junction. Crofton was served by Trains 41-42 in 1934. Bloomfield was served by Trains 51-52. Both branches were worked from the terminal at Emerson. Centrally located, Emerson was also host to Sioux City-Norfolk passenger Trains 4-5. For a while, a motor train ran between Emerson and Norfolk. One of the dual-engine motor cars (Nos. 2002-2004) also worked between Emerson and Omaha as Trains 1-2, which continued into the 1940s.

As of mid-1935, I-1 Class 4-6-0s dominated the scene at Emerson, as the last F-9 and G-1 Class slide-valve Ten-Wheelers were taken away. The old engines were written off and scrapped after June 1, 1935. Still active were the three small, superheated 4-4-0s, Nos. 160, 136 and 144, used on Norfolk-Sioux City passenger runs. Emerson's sizable depot had a cafe supplying meals to employees and travelers. In August 1942, its contractors changed. That same month, the Railway Commission gave the Omaha (or "M&O," as Nebraskans called it) permission to discontinue Trains 4-5, the Norfolk accommodation. The case was heard in December 1941, but deferred until the effects of war could be examined in light of competition. In the end, mixed train and bus operations were the only alternative. Manpower and equipment could be better utilized elsewhere. Thus, Norfolk service ended September 3, 1942.

Railroading in Nebraska regularly suffered from washouts, and May and June of 1944 produced a rampage of water, cutting both the Crofton and Bloomfield lines, and also severing the Norfolk-Emerson route. The latter was out of service from May 11 to late June 1944. A bridge near Pender on the Emerson-Omaha route was badly damaged, and the Oakland-Tekamah sector was washed out. In early July, the rains returned, knocking out the northern half of the Crofton line once again. Reconstruction was effected by the U.S. Army Corps of Engineers.

Trains 9-10 were next to disappear from the Emerson area, the pair connecting Omaha with Sioux City. The end came in early June 1950, which also terminated true passenger service out of Omaha's Webster Street Station. Once again, mixed trains took up the post-war slack in passenger operations, as Trains 15-16 and 13-14 covered the old route north of Omaha. Thereafter, only mixed trains were available. Emerson, in turn, lost two more of its Omaha employees. Freight Handler E.C. Bramsen and Relief Operator Don Wagers joined engine service people leaving. Emerson became a bit quieter. In April 1956, the Omaha, nearing the end as a separate entity, ordered Crofton and Bloomfield trains to tie-up at Sioux City instead of Emerson. Only one man still lived in Emerson. Everyone else in the branch crew lived in Sioux City, commuting by auto. The change was expected to erase the roundhouse and coal chute work at Emerson, especially in the face of impending dieselization. It wasn't long before a Caterpillar tractor, with cable attached, pulled the coal chute over, salvagers extracting scrap iron and timbers. Thus, the steam era ended in Emerson, followed a few years later by abandonment.

Operations on the Sioux City-Norfolk Line, which included Crofton-Bloomfield service, was daily except Sundays. During World War II, it degenerated to three times a week. Until the early 1940s, Omaha handled transfers for Wyoming cattle brought in by C&NW and Union Pacific to Norfolk. It ended in the 1950s when highways were paved and trucks replaced the stock trains.

The Omaha shared the Norfolk terminal with UP. In later years, the Omaha and UP had daily passenger trains into the at the posh-sounding Norfolk Union Station, with UP operating a McKeen Motor Car until World War II.

C&NW's McKeen experience began at the same Nebraska town, when it borrowed UP car No. 16 for use between Norfolk and Bonesteel, a 60 day trial in early 1908. In most cases, Omaha used a turntable shared with UP 2-8-0s near the depot to ready its power for the return trip to Sioux City.

C&NW had a separate depot and a large yard several miles away at "South Norfolk." One stall in C&NW's Norfolk round-house was leased to the Omaha when power was required to lay over on the west end. C&NW used oil fuel exclusively at Norfolk and Omaha had to maintain a car of "lake coal," later buying UP coal. Often the latter was responsible for lineside fires due to the nature of UP's subbituminous fuel.

In early 1951, C&NW received six Fairbanks-Morse H16-66 road switchers, one of which was Omaha's No. 150. After a break-in period around Spooner, No. 150 became the primary power on the Norfolk Line. Lacking multiple unit capability, the engine received the nickname "The Lone Ranger." The unique six-axle F-M unit followed the lead of Baldwin for road switchers having lighter axle-loadings needed on branch lines. Anxious to dieselize and eliminate steam power in poor water country, railroads in the Dakotas turned to diesels as early as 1939.

The Omaha-Emerson district proved just as difficult to keep in place. Rampaging Logan Creek between Thurston and Pender laid waste to trackage several times. The new C&NW management elected to remove the damaged 4.7 miles (completed December 30, 1958), bowing to nature's rage. Lyons to Pender was removed in 1963. Previously, in the mid-1950s, the Wayne to Randolph mileage was abandoned, and finally, the northern 21 miles, from Randolph to Bloomfield, was retired in 1965.

I-1 No. 338 is shown at Fairmont, Minnesota, on May 22, 1934. The 28.2 mile Fairmont branch connected with the Omaha mainline at Madelia, 107 miles south of St. Paul. Fairmont was a junction with C&NW's Belle Plaine-Mason City line, which also connected with the Omaha at Blue Earth and Butterfield, Minnesota. The 1906 Alco product was retired in June 1953. *Charles T. Felstead.*

(Above) Mankato's depot looms behind F-8 No. 253, ready to leave with an afternoon local.The 73" drivered F-8 will have an easy time of it after climbing the low grade to Lake Crystal.

(Right)   Omaha E-4 Ten-Wheeler No. 96 switches cars at Mankato in the 1920s. The 1885 engine was retired in 1927.

(Below) In the 1920s, Mankato's eight stall roundhouse was home for small power such as No. 135, an 1887 E-6 scrapped in 1927. All: *John Teskey Collection.*

(Above) Several E-4 4-6-0s were assigned to yard duty at Mankato. No. 99, an 1885 Schenectady engine, was retired in December 1927. (Below) Before 1920, many passenger miles were run off behind big 4-4-0s, like F-8 No. 260 preparing for a noon departure to the Twin Cities. The Eight-Wheeler came from Schenectady in 1898 and lasted in service until May 1935. Both: *John Taskey Collection.*

(Above) Omaha "switcher Ten-Wheeler" No. 247 was the lone example of the F-4 Class. Originally built in 1891 as an F-1, the engine was rebuilt to F-4 in 1895 and finally retired in 1929. No. 247 is shown at Mankato in the company of a C&NW E-1, the latter on a westbound passenger train.

(Right) Omaha I-1 No. 329, assigned to an extra movement, awaits clearance in Mankato's yard.

(Below) In 1925, Class I-1 No. 315 crosses near the Mankato interlocking tower and grain elevator, as a Ford "tin lizzie" awaits passage. Mankato was a busy C&NW and Omaha junction. C&NW trackage is on the left. All: *John Taskey Collection.*

(Above) The Mankato depot switcher on June 14, 1950, was Baldwin VO-1000 No. 87, in black paint with yellow and green stripes. Omaha acquired four 660 HP Baldwins and five of the 1000 HP units in 1944-1945 and 1949. The early Baldwin carbody had "angled" radiator grills and rounded sheet metal along the steps ahead of the cab. *Don Christensen.* (Below) After departing Mankato Union Station, a pair of Omaha Fairbanks-Morse units step through the switch points at the Mankato interlocking tower with eastbound Train 518, the *Dakota 400,* heading for Chicago via Winona, Wyeville, Madison and Beloit in 1950. *Ken L. Zurn.*

(Above) In 1910, there's a nice crowd waiting for the Omaha local at Slayton, Minnesota, located about halfway on the 55 mile long Pipestone branch.

(Right) Heron Lake, 18.4 miles northeast of Worthington on the St. Paul mainline, was the junction for the Pipestone Line. Here, Omaha F-8 No. 259 has stopped at the depot with Train 6 sometime around WWI. Both: *Author's Collection.*

(Below) Action at Heron Lake has the Pipestone mixed train arriving on October 21, 1959, as photographed from the cab of the northbound *North American*, which was discontinued a few days later. *William F. Armstrong.*

Blue Earth, Minnesota, was a junction with C&NW's Fox Lake-Mason City-Belle Plaine line. C&NW 4-4-0 No. 522 (at left) will head southeast toward Mason City, while the Omaha local will depart for Elmore behind E-6 No. 178. *Author's Collection.*

(Left) The Blue Earth depot in 1950, with the original Omaha depot at the far left. Blue Earth was just under ten miles from the end of the Elmore Line. William *F. Armstrong.*

(Below) The border town of Elmore, Minnesota, was the junction for Omaha's 43.3 mile branch from Lake Crystal and C&NW's line to Ames and Des Moines, Iowa. This circa 1900 view shows a three car train ready to leave for Lake Crystal, the mainline junction. *State Historical Society of Wisconsin.*

(Above) Worthington, near the southern Minnesota boarder on the St. Paul-Sioux City mainline, also served the Sioux Falls-Mitchell branch line. The imposing depot, shown after the turn-of-the-century, sported a domed East Indian decoration on the roof. *Nobles County Historical Society*.

(Left) Train 3, with F-8 Class No. 275 up front, stops at Worthington, Minnesota, the depot platform heavy with headend and mail shipments. *Worthington Library*.

On May 1, 1934, Union Pacific *Streamliner* M-10000, the first of UP's grand fleet, made a stop at Worthington while on tour of the country, attracting a large crowd. People were invited aboard for a short ride to St. James, after which the train visited the Twin Cities. *State Historical Society of Wisconsin*.

(Above) This quiet scene of I-1 No. 322 at Worthington's six-stall roundhouse was taken in the early 1950s. The structure served engines for Omaha's Sioux Falls-Mitchell line. (Below) Paired C&NW E7 units accelerate Train 203, the *North American*, out of Worthington at 2:40 PM with several yellow and green heavyweight headend cars in the consist. Sioux City is 91 miles south, after which the train will take C&NW to Council Bluffs, via California Junction and Missouri Valley, with an 8:20 PM arrival in Omaha. Both: *William F. Armstrong.*

(Above) Omaha passenger diesels arrive at St. James, Minnesota, at 12:55 PM on June 6, 1947, with Train 203, the *North American*. Ahead is a seven stop, 57 mile run to Worthington. The units were placed in service prior to the application of stainless steel nose medallions, and this could be their first revenue trip. Omaha's four Fairbanks-Morse "Erie-Builts" came in May 1947 and operated over the entire C&NW system. *Don Christensen.* (Below) C&NW power is in charge of the *North American*, which is ready to leave Sheldon, Iowa, in May 1952 for a 5:15 PM arrival at Sioux City, 57.2 miles to the south. The depot, at right, was a joint operation with the Milwaukee Road. *Don L. Hofsommer.*

(Above) On November 1, 1952, M-3 No. 83 is on the turntable lead at Sioux Falls, South Dakota, where the Omaha maintained an eight stall roundhouse. Sioux Falls, 62 miles west of Worthington on Omaha's 134 mile line to Mitchell, South Dakota, was home for some "post-USRA" 0-6-0s. M-3 engines 83-86 were built in January 1921 by Alco-Richmond with M-2 sized cabs and tenders. *Norman Priebe.* (Below) Crossing the Big Sioux River, helper engine No. 86 is shoving hard behind the caboose of a heavy freight train at Sioux Falls in 1952. *Marvin Nielsen.*

Mitchell, South Dakota, was the end of the Omaha's westward expansion ambitions. The town's name came from banker Alexander Mitchell who captained Omaha's competitor, Milwaukee Road, in its early years. Agriculture and settlement in the area was marginal. *State Historical Society of Wisconsin.*

(Above) Passenger operations on the 133.9 mile Worthington-Sioux Falls-Mitchell line included Train 81, which was dominated by the last of the Omaha's big 600 HP motor cars. On November 1, 1952, No. 2002 brings the westbound train into Sioux Falls with a baggage car and Limousine Coach No. 2000, released from the *Namekagon.* motor train. *Norman Priebe.*

(Right) Motor car No. 2002 leads Train 80 across South Duluth Avenue as it arrives in Sioux Falls from Mitchell at 10:57 AM on August 17, 1950. After a 20 minute lunch stop, the train will head off to Worthington, Minnesota. *Marvin Nielsen.*

I-1 No. 345 is heading off to work in Sioux Falls on November 1, 1952. By this date, engines with Stephenson valve gear were rare and the 1906 Ten-Wheeler will be in service for less than two years. *Norman Priebe.*

(Above) Train 81 is at the Illinois Central diamond in Sioux Falls with Class I-2 No. 383 on the point and a baggage car and coach trailing. The 1910 Alco 4-6-2, one of few to have a steel pilot, was retired in June 1953. (Below) After departing from Mitchell at 9:15 AM, Train 80 is about three miles from Sioux Falls and an 11:30 AM arrival. Ahead lies a 61 mile, eight stop trip to Worthington and a connection with Train 204, the *North American*. Power this day is I-1 4-6-0 No. 224, at home in the higher role of passenger work. Both: *Marvin Nielson.*

# THE BONNIE DOON

Doon, Iowa, situated in rolling country along the Rock River in Lyons County, had a population recently of 437. Doon came into existence in 1868, its name the result of explorer-entrepreneur L.F. Knight's inclination to recite poet Robert Burns' work on the spot: "Ye banks and braes O' Bonnie Doon. . . rolled gently out from the hills above the Rock, and another American small town was born." There was also a large hotel named *The Bonnie Doon* later in its history, adding dimension to the legend.

Dutch settlers embraced the county, and in 1879, the Worthington & Sioux Falls Railroad Company of Iowa came to town, intending to pass through to Sioux City, if possible. It didn't, since funds were not available. Doon was the end, with a modest depot, a single-stall enginehouse, and a very basic track layout. Built close to the Rock River for much of its distance, the Bonnie Doon branch suffered washouts as early as 1881. It was still believed then that Sioux City would be reached by the branch

road. If extended six miles south to Rock Valley, locals could have access to Sioux City markets via Milwaukee Road and Sheldon. Doonites were closer to St. Paul in a way. Locals met to promote a petition to grant lands for a Doon-Sioux City extension, and to obtain unearned land from 85,000 acres in northwest Iowa. The land, as it was, centered a debate between Milwaukee Road and the Sioux City & St. Paul faction. Still, the branch was not extended. Somehow, 85,000 acres shrank to 20,000 acres and thoughts of expansion ended with the creation of the Omaha Road.

The Bonnie Doon did a modest, mixed train business, eventually hemmed in by construction of the Sioux City & Northern, connecting GN's Sioux Falls branch with Sioux City. GN's entry eclipsed any further ambitions for the Doon Line. In 1903, several families migrated from Doon to Birchwood, Wisconsin, their belongings going by Omaha Road all the way to the new land in north Wisconsin. Regular passenger service (under Trains

98-99) tied up at Doon, run by men with long seniority. In the winter of 1921-22, Alice Whealan, her father and brother, were aboard the train in a derailment. Her father was a brakeman, and they were bound for St. Paul to spend Christmas with relatives. The engine, a 4-4-0, passed over a soft spot, and the entire five car train fell between spread rails. Alice remembered the coach "wracking back-and-forth" and her father telling his children to sit still.

The Doon branch rolled to a less-than-quiet end in 1933. That end was opposed by elevator interests, unmindful of financial losses to the railroad as patronage went to new highways and the GN. The ICC abandonment petition was filed in January, citing "continuous source of loss." Until 1918, there had been exceptionally worthwhile business, perhaps making two runs per day, hauling 18 stock cars daily in season. The five man crew was now down to three, which was more than adequate.

During the 1920s, Omaha officials

Early power for the Doon train, this Eight-Wheeler was built for Omaha & North Western in 1876, and had five different names and numbers on its side before becoming Omaha No. 249. It was finally retired in 1898. *State Historical Society of Wisconsin.*

talked at meetings about losses, proving that branch business had dried up. A hearing in June 1933 cited a $50,000 loss to the railroad. Locals squabbled, but abandonment was set for October. Train 99 rolled into Doon on the afternoon of October 23, and Train 98 left at 4:30 PM, ending service. The next objective was to remove the track before the winter freeze. Doon had been served for fifty-four years, and was now the third abandonment in company history.

But it was not the end. Continental Construction Company, Chicago, had the track removal contract, and the following Sunday, a work extra arrived with the equipment. Locals were hired, and a locomotive and flat cars were furnished by the Omaha. The work went swiftly with 25 men working two ten hour shifts. Any business in Rock Rapids was handed over to Illinois Central and Rock Island, but on November 11, Omaha had been restrained from removing trackage north of Ash Creek, on the Iowa-Minnesota border. A grain company insisted on service, stalling the removal process. Service to Ash Creek continued until January 28, 1934, due to Minnesota's sole jurisdiction over the stub. Nearly a year later, on September 28, 1934, the last train went to Ash Creek to take away three carloads of grain. Still, the removal was postponed until the spring of 1935, even though the Ash Creek businessmen fought it as far as Washington, D.C.

The Doon people moved away. Conductor Van Valkenburg went to Pipestone, the engine crew went on to yard engine duty at Worthington. Another employee went to Le Mars, while Station Agent W.J. Ross, Doon's man for 17 years, was posted to Lake Wilson. The final piece of the line at Luverne today serves agribusiness, its end pointing southward toward the Iowa village, mindful of a small railroad and Robert Burns.

(Above) In 1927, a group of young girls, friends of the photographer Frances Keegan, posed on the rear platform of the mixed train at Doon.

(Right) In December 1921, the Doon train ran into trouble south of Rock Rapids. A rider, young Alice Whealan, provided the photo and described the accident, which was later determined to have been caused by the engine spreading the rails, dropping the five cars on the ties. The branchline was abandoned in 1934. Both: *Author's Collection.*

(Above) The Sioux City Shops were nearing completion when this photo was made in 1902. To the left is the new 15 stall roundhouse, the low-pitched roof design common around the turn-of-the-century. Just right of the smoke stack is the power house, in front of which is construction for the water tank. At far right is the new locomotive/machine shop, with a paint shop on the back side. The roundhouse was expanded to a full circle by 1910, with 23 stalls added in two sections. *State Historical Society of Wisconsin.* (Below) This 1920s high angle view of Sioux City's 38 stall brick roundhouse shows several stored engines in the foreground, including Omaha G-1 4-6-0 No. 295 (partially obscured), E-6 4-4-0 No. 146, C&NW Class D 4-4-2 No. 1030, and Omaha G-2 4-6-0 No. 306. *Woodworth Commercial Studio.*

(Above) Omaha 4-6-0 No. 304, one of the pioneer Class I-1s from Schenectady in 1901, is spotted at Sioux City on May 25, 1934. Behind the tender is the power house. Many of the 304's details are retained from its original appearance, while the shop forces at Sioux City asserted some independence by using gray graphite paint for the smokebox and firebox. The engine was retired in late 1946. *Robert H. Graham.*
(Below) In 1949-1950, Omaha received 12 EMD F7 cab units. The 1500 HP diesels originally ran in matched pairs, but were eventually operated in mixed sets throughout the C&NW system. Nearly new F7s 6504-C and 6504-A were at Sioux City on June 14, 1950. *Don Christensen.*

(Above) At Sioux City's joint Illinois Central-Omaha depot, M-2 No. 46 has spotted a tank car at the water column to be filled for weed spray service on June 24, 1948. Omaha's nine M-2 Class switchers came from Alco in 1917 and were just like the parent road's M-2s. No. 46 was retired in June 1956. *Don Christensen.* (Below) M-1 No. 31 and a mail car stand at the Sioux City depot on August 22, 1940. The 1909 Alco engine was retired in March 1945. All but three of the 20 member class were off the roster by mid-1947. *John Boose.*

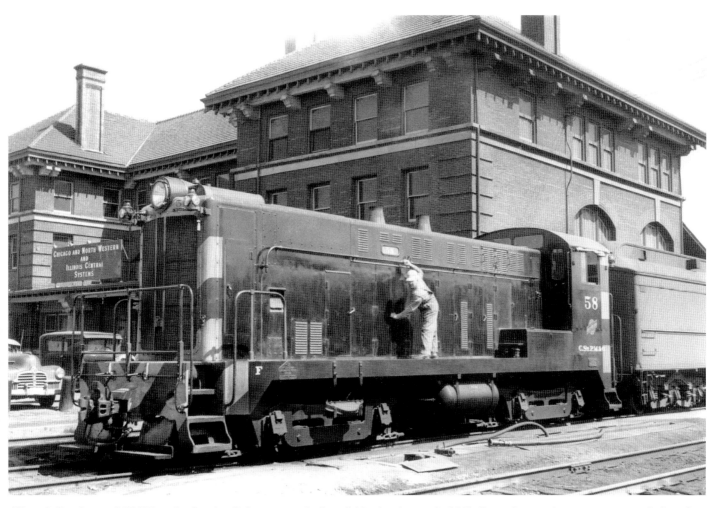

(Above) Omaha and C&NW early diesel switchers came in the all-black scheme. In 1948, the yellow and green passenger train colors became the system standard for new diesel locomotives and the older units got yellow and green safety stripes on the ends. Over time, the black engines got repainted, but on April 5, 1950, Baldwin model VO-660 No. 58 displays the interim scheme at the Sioux City depot. The 1945 built engine is setup for road service with marker lamps on both ends. *Don Christensen.* (Below) By the late 1940s, diesels had taken over a number of mainline steam assignments and C&NW units were common on the Twin Cities-Council Bluffs-Omaha passenger trains. Paired C&NW E7s 5012-A and 5012-B have arrived at Sioux City with the *North American* on May 14, 1948. *W.C. Whittaker.*

(Above) Class M-1 No. 31 is posed in Sioux City's industrial area in 1938. The Omaha adopted C&NW 's standard locomotive classification letters by February 1909, when its first M-1 0-6-0s arrived from Alco. Virtually the same as the parent road, Nos. 29-31 were Omaha's first piston-valve switchers. They had Stephenson valve gear and cylinder saddles arranged in a "semi-slant" fashion. (Below) This interesting view, featuring M-1 No. 32's 5,500 gallon/8 ton tender, was an accident claim photo taken at Sioux City. Both: *Woodworth Commercial Studio.*

(Above) Sioux City's sprawling stock yards, as seen in this 1940s view, covered 1,500 acres. The giant facility was served by the Omaha, C&NW, Milwaukee Road, Great Northern, Illinois Central, Sioux City Terminal Railway, and Chicago, Burlington & Quincy. The train in the fore-ground is on C&NW trackage. The large buildings to the right housed the Livestock Exchange commission. *C&NW Ry.* (Below) Omaha Class H-2 No. 228, its ancient headlight still operational, is in yard duty at Sioux City not long before it was retired in 1939. After the eight M-5 0-8-0s came in 1928, the remaining 2-8-0 transfer engines finished out their careers on the Western Division. *Holman F. Braden.*

The final development in Omaha's freight power came in November 1926, when eight "improved USRA" Mikes arrived on the Western Division. The Schenectady-built engines had cast-steel Delta trailing trucks, Standard type "B" stokers, front end throttles, and carried air pumps on the pilot deck. Nos. 432-435 had thermic syphons and 270 square feet of heating surface, while Nos. 436-439 lacked syphons, but had 280 square feet of heating surface. Tractive effort was 63,000 lbs. (Above) J-3 No. 434 brings its train into Sioux City on June 14, 1950. The left side is littered with plumbing for the Elesco exhaust steam injector carried low on the front firebox corner. *Don Christensen.* (Below) The engineer's side of No. 432 is displayed in a July 1953 photo of the 63" drivered engine. It was retired in August 1954. *Ken L. Zurn.*

This excellent front end view of J-3 No. 432 was taken at Sioux City around 1936. *Woodworth Commercial Studio.*

(Above) Still in good working condition at Sioux City in 1950, K-1 No. 261 was built by Alco in March 1913, part of Omaha's last group of ten 4-6-0s. It was retired in June 1956. *Don Christensen.* (Below) M-3 No. 86 sports a graphite smokebox and firebox at the Sioux City coal chute on May 25, 1934. Delivered by Alco-Richmond in January 1921, Class M-3 Nos. 83-86 were a modified version of the USRA design M-3s. They were slightly heavier, with larger M-2 size cabs and smaller M-2 tenders. *Robert H. Graham.*

(Above) Fourteen month old Baldwin VO-660 No. 71, at Sioux City on May 31, 1950, displays its original yellow and green paint scheme with end safety stripes. *Route of The Streamliners* promotional lettering, with *Route of The "400"* opposite, followed parent C&NW practice, even though the Union Pacific-C&NW *Overland Route* "Streamliners" didn't operate over the Omaha. *Don Christiensen.*

(Above) Omaha's lone Whitcomb diesel switcher came in June 1943 in an all black scheme. It's pictured at Sioux City on June 7, 1948, shortly after receiving yellow and green safety stripes. (Below) Another black locomotive with safety stripes applied in 1948 was Alco S-2 No. 90. Delivered in October 1940, the 1,000 HP diesel switcher is between assignments at Sioux City on June 24, 1948. Both: *Don Christiensen.*

(Above) Omaha I-1 No. 222 is ready for assignment at Omaha on April 22, 1951, with a full load of "lake coal" in its 15 ton/7,500 gallon tender. The "Three Duces" was delivered in April 1910 by Alco and was retired in June of 1956. *Jim Scribbins.*

(Right) Old timer E-1 No. 267, renumbered from 270, is shown near the roundhouse at Omaha on June 2, 1922. Four E-1s were built in 1893 by Schenectady. They were retired in 1929-1931. *Author's Collection.*

(Below) Schenectady built M-1 No. 18 was at Omaha on September 26, 1939. It was retired in June 1956. *F.G. Karl.*

(Above) Omaha's overnight Train 201, the *Nightingale*, is completing its trip from St. Paul to Omaha on April 22, 1951. Twin C&NW E7s head a sizable head-end consist near the Council Bluffs roundhouse. (Below) On the same day, Train 204, the *North American*, is ready for departure at Council Bluffs. The train is headed for Sioux City and St. Paul via C&NW 's line through Missouri Valley and California Junction. After the *Nightingale* and *North American* were dieselized in the late 1940s, C&NW power was a common sight on the Omaha's Twin Cities-Council Bluffs-Omaha trains. Both: *Jim Scribbins*.

(Above) The official portrait of Omaha motor car No. 2002 was taken on July 29, 1929, at the Pullman plant in Chicago. *Author's Collection.*

(Above) Omaha's "West Side" passenger train was the *Mondamin,* which operated from the 1885 Webster Street station in Omaha to Sioux City, Iowa, via Emerson, Nebraska. For years, one of the 600 HP dual-engined gas-electrics handled the train, as seen in this view of motor car No. 2002 ready to depart with north-bound Train 210 circa 1939. *Bernard Corbin; Lou Schmitz Collection.*

(Right) Steam power was employed on the *Mondamin* during WWII, and whenever the three car capacity of the gas electrics was exceeded. In August 1949, Train 210 is in charge of K-2 Pacific No. 389. *Lou Schmitz.*

(Above) G-3 Atlantic No. 364 takes on water at Emerson, Nebraska, on August 22, 1940. Emerson, 29.1 miles from Sioux City, Iowa, was the junction for the 46.3 mile Norfolk Line and the West Side's mainline from Sioux City to Omaha, Nebraska. *John Boose.* (Below) In 1937, I-2 No. 381 pauses at Emerson at 5:30 PM to load passengers and mail on Train 5. The train will depart for Norfolk with a 7:10 PM arrival at Union Station. Additional stops will be made at Norfolk 7th Street depot and C&NW's South Norfolk depot. The I-2 Class engines were probably the heaviest power used on Trains 4-5, which normally consisted of a mail car, a full baggage and a single coach. *Holman F. Braden.*

On September 15, 1906, E-6 No. 141 stands in water at Ponca, Nebraska, as a rowboat takes off passengers. The Omaha extended the old Covington, Columbus & Black Hills line to Newcastle in 1893, then to Wynot in 1907. The Missouri River flood plain played havoc with the 45 mile line, which became a marginal operation, finally abandoned in 1933. *State Historical Society of Wisconsin.*

(Right) E-8 Class No. 164 is at Bloomfield, Nebraska, with a two car passenger train on September 6, 1906. Behind the coach is a baggage-coach combine. The 91 mile Bloomfield Line was abandoned in the 1960s. *Bernard Corbin Collection.*

(Below) Class F-2 4-6-0 No. 192 is having difficulties. With its tank water critically low, shovelers fill the tender. The engine was marooned near Wausa, Nebraska, on the Bloomfield branch line. *State Historical Society of Wisconsin.*

(Left) Winside, Nebraska, looking west circa 1947, was near the half way point on the Norfolk Line. Small towns like this had precious little business to offer and could not save countless Midwest branches from abandonment. *W.M. Lenzen.*

(Below) Dieselization came to the Norfolk Line with the introduction of Fairbanks-Morse road switchers. Pioneer No. 150, shown picking up orders at Winside in the summer of 1951, ran off many miles and many seasons on the Omaha's Western Division. *Ken Brovald.*

(Above) Winside enjoyed the Omaha's Norfolk train only occasionally. In the fall of 1947, I-1 No. 101 eased up to the station. The engine was later renumbered to 364, making room for diesels on the locomotive roster. *W.M. Lenzen.*

(Below) F-M H16-66 No. 150 was intended to operate long end forward. Delivered in early 1951, it lacked Multiple-Unit capability and was nicknamed "The Lone Ranger" by locals. The unit is switching cars at Sioux City in mid-1951. *Woodworth Commercial Studio.*

Just west of Emerson, K-1 No. 183 eases along the 46.3 mile Emerson-Norfolk Line, with a short westbound freight train on March 24, 1956. The engine has just over two months of service left before being retired in June. *Lou Schmitz.*

(Above) In 1937, E-6 No. 144 occupies the street crossing east of Norfolk Union Depot, which Omaha shared with Union Pacific. Civil engineer Holman Braden often shot photos of the Norfolk passenger train on his way to work.

(Right) No. 144 is exerting all its tractive effort to reach Apex, Nebraska, the scenic high point on the Norfolk Line. Train 4 utilized the three superheated 4-4-0s rebuilt in the 1920s, Nos. 136, 160 and 144. Both: *Holman F. Braden.*

(Above) Train 4 has G-3 Atlantic No. 369 for power at the Norfolk depot in 1937. Omaha passenger engines utilized one stall rented from C&NW at their South Norfolk roundhouse. Also maintained was one car of eastern "lake coal" for Omaha's use. Their power was the only coal-fired equipment at the C&NW facility, as C&NW was all oil-burning west of the Missouri River. The 81" drivered 4-4-2 was retired in 1946. (Below) E-6 No. 144, with Train 4's standard three car consist, after departing C&NW's South Norfolk depot in summer 1937. The 63" drivered 1887 Schenectady engine was rebuilt with a new boiler in 1925 and remained in service until 1940. Both: *Holman F. Braden.*

(Above) I-1 No. 102 is in charge of Extra 102 East at Norfolk in 1937. Part of the last group of I-1s delivered in 1910, the engine was in service until June 1956. Stock extras regularly passed through Norfolk prior to 1940. Many were transferred from the "Elkhorn," the old C&NW subsidiary Fremont, Elkhorn & Missouri Valley, which met the Omaha at South Norfolk. Others were made up in the joint Union Pacific-Omaha yards. Often double-headed on the Omaha by I-1 combinations, photographer Braden noted that the traffic disappeared when the parallel highway was paved to allow trucks. (Below) At Wayne, Nebraska, a stock extra led by double headed I-1 Nos. 311 and 324 prepares to depart for Emerson and Sioux City in 1937. Wayne was the Norfolk Line's junction with the Bloomfield branch. Both: *Holman F. Braden.*

(Above) I-1 No. 321 departs Uptown Yard in Norfolk with stock Extra 321 East in 1937. The 1903 engine was retired in 1945. *Holman F. Braden.*

(Above) Engineers of a double headed stock extra pay close attention while making a back up move just off the Elkhorn River bridge at Norfolk in 1937. Delivered in 1901, No. 302 was the oldest of the I-1s, while No. 312 came the following year. The pair were retired in 1945. (Below) At Norfolk, double headed I-1 Nos. 331 and 302 are crossing the Elkhorn River with Extra 331 East in 1937. Both: *Holman F. Braden.*

At Milepost 82, Class E-3 No. 600 splits the signals with Train 515, the *Victory*, heading toward the Twin Cities in a classic Wisconsin winter scene just west of Truax. *M.P. McMahon.*

# 10.
# GRAY MATTER

General Manager A.W. Trenholm was appointed by the United States Railroad Administration (during WWI) to manage several small properties, some related to the Omaha, including the Minneapolis Eastern, Minnesota Transfer, St. Paul Bridge & Terminal, and St. Paul Union Depot Company. It was a time of the Omaha Road's best showing, and James Truman Clark became the company's President until he passed away in 1922, after forty-eight years of service. Clark, who was a cousin of Marvin Highitt, C&NW's President Emeritus and recently made Board Chairman, was replaced by W.H. Finley. In 1920, Harry E. Barlow, a University of Minnesota graduate, became Chief Engineer, and Eugene R. Gorman, who began his railway service in 1901 on the Arpin-owned Chippewa Valley & Northern, at Bruce, Wisconsin, became Assistant Superintendent of Omaha's Eastern Division.

Another officer with a long Omaha career was Frank R. Pechin, who became the General Manager in 1925. Pechin had quite an active and exciting life. Years before, in the 1880s, he was an adventurer, working North Western trains into Deadwood, South Dakota, making the acquaintance of Deadwood Dick and other notable westerners. Pechin hailed from Pennsylvania and was an accomplished boxer. He came to the Omaha from C&NW and rounded out his career in December 1929 at age seventy. Edward L. Pardee began in 1896, and became General Passenger Agent in February 1928. John M. Ryan, from Hudson, rose in the car shops to Assistant Master Car Builder in January 1929, and succeeded the Master, W.H. Thorn, who retired in October 1933. It was Ryan who supervised the *Namekagon* motor train project (see Chapter 14).

After serving the Omaha less than three years, President Finley resigned because of ill health, and Fred W. Sargent, Vice President and General Counsel, was elected to succeed him. In June 1935, Marvin Hughitt, who was Chairman of the Board of both C&NW and the Omaha Road, resigned. That same year Frank Pechin took over operation and maintenance management. One of the changes brought about was the merger of the Eastern and Northern Divisions.

After being appointed Vice President of Operation and Maintenance in July 1929, Pechin served a few months, then retired at the end of 1929. It was then that Carl R. Gray, Jr., was appointed General Manager. On January 1, 1930, Gray was also given the position of Vice President and General Manager.

Carl Raymond Gray, Jr., at one time worked away from railroading, but was not successful. Fate decreed he was to follow his father into the field. Carl R. Gray, Senior, an Arkansan by birth (1867), left the University of Arkansas and entered railway service for the St. Louis & San Francisco in 1883. Gray Sr., rose to Senior Vice President in 1911, the year his son entered railway work. Both worked for the Spokane, Portland & Seattle and Oregon Electric Railways in Portland, Oregon. His father moved on to become president of Great Northern in 1920. Prior to his first job on the OE, the younger Carl graduated from the University of Illinois with a BA in Railway Administration. After 1915, he was involved in engineering for a coal company, then a slate

Carl R. Gray Jr., came from a railroad family and joined the Omaha in 1929. After serving in World War II, he rejoined the road and was responsible for many of its postwar improvements. *State Historical Society of Wisconsin.*

(Above) Omaha Class E-3 No. 600 was just eight months old when photographed in July 1931. Ostensibly built for the *North Western Limited,* Nos. 600-602 were delivered by Alco in late 1930. Stories circulated that the 600s should have been 4-6-4s, but it was not to be. Omaha officials wanted an engine capable of fitting the 90 foot turntables on the Eastern Division. The two-wheel Delta trailing truck carried 65,000 lbs., considered by many as being too heavy for a two-wheel truck. *Robert H. Graham.* (Below) A rare view shows all three 600 series engines together with their original 14,000 gallon tenders positioned in numerical sequence. In 1933, the tenders were rebuilt for greater water capacity. *M.D. McCarter Collection.*

firm, before entering the army in 1917. His army career was impressive. He rose to Lt. Colonel of Traffic and Transportation, moving finally to Washington, D.C., to assist General Stagg, the director of Purchase, Storage and Traffic.

Gray was General Superintendent of Montgomery Ward & Company for two years, then their General Manager until 1922. He next joined City Ice Company, continuing with that firm until 1925. After another two years with Central Manufacturing Bank, Chicago, C&NW's President Fred Sargent prevailed upon him to return to railroading. He became manager of the Industrial Department for C&NW and CStPM&O, at Chicago, July 1, 1929. On January 1, 1930, he became General Manager of the Omaha in St. Paul. Throughout the post-World War I period, Gray remained affiliated with the Army Engineer's Reserve, setting a course for future endeavors. Gray remained GM until August 1, 1937, then was elected Executive Vice President, serving until May 15, 1942, when he was called to active duty. Previously, in February 1939, he was assigned as General Manager of Military Railroad Service, and rose to the rank of Major General by war's end. Gray was elected VP of the C&NW system on May 1, 1946.

In 1930, as General Manager, Gray outlined an improvement plan for the Omaha. Addressing the Hudson Commercial Club, he related his intention to reballast the Omaha mainline and install 100 pound rail for sixty miles. The ballast program would cover 125 miles, and the total cost of the track program would be ten million dollars. It was Gray's intention to put the road on a competing basis with Chicago Great Western, which was receiving its heavy Texas type 2-10-4s for general freight service. By early 1930, Omaha was reballasting forty-two miles of Western Division track between Mankato and Mendota, employing a gang

of 130 men and 92,000 cubic yards of gravel. Another section near Windom was good for 10.5 miles of new ballast. The aim was to have fifty-three miles done by October. The track was raised eight inches between Mankato and Ottawa, and six inches from Merriam to Mendota. The St. James-Lake Crystal section was ballasted earlier, with some 80,000 ties distributed from Mankato to St. James.

One of the innovations by the Omaha was a new train called the *Nightingale*. Announced by Passenger Traffic Manager E.L. Pardee, Trains 201-202 began operating January 15, 1930, with "luxurious Pullman lounge cars," leaving Minneapolis at 7:50 PM and St. Paul at 8:35 PM, and arriving in Omaha at 7:32 AM. Train 202 left Omaha at 9:45 PM, arriving in St. Paul at 8:15 AM and Minneapolis at 8:55 AM. The *Nightingale* also featured a fine dining-lounge car, designed by C&NW engineers, with a three-section ladies lounge, a dining section and main lounge. It had deep pile carpet with ten blue and green leather chairs in the ladies section. Between meals, the diner became a library. The kitchen was available for buffet service with electric lights and ample smoking compartments.

As new trains and new schedules can bring the unexpected, so it was with the *Nightingale*. In its first month, Train 201 collided with a Scott County snowplow trying to beat the train to a crossing at Blakeley, Minnesota. Delay was three hours, but damage was moderate. The *Nightingale* prevailed and the snowplow was demolished.

Improvements on Omaha's Eastern Division were ready by summer 1928, as a new passenger train, the *North Western Limited*, was completed at The Pullman Company's Illinois plant. The cars were considered to be most luxurious, and would enter

A serious wreck occurred at Camp Douglas on February 28, 1931, involving two-year old E-3 No. 601 and a Milwaukee Road train powered by 4-6-4 No. 6409, also fairly new. Both engines were out of commission for several months. *Author's Collection.*

service in late August. The new entry into Chicago-Twin Cities service cost one million dollars according to news dispatches released by C&NW President Fred W. Sargent. The observation-solarium was said to let in healthful ultraviolet rays. The *North Western Limited* (Trains 405-406) went on display in St. Paul just before service was inaugurated, and included a six-room solarium observation car, an eight section-one drawing room-two compartment sleeper, several fourteen section sleepers, a radio-equipped club lounge, a breakfast diner, and coaches. The train was equipped with roller bearings and Majestic radios (also available to patrons of the *Viking, Duluth-Superior Limited,* and *Chicago Limited*). Train 405 connected at Altoona with Train 503 to Duluth, offering a fourteen-section sleeper to the Twin Ports. Train 406 added a diner at 5:00 AM in Milwaukee for the Chicago lap.

Business on the Ellsworth branch included stock in season, and in the town of Beldenville, the railroad commission ordered stockpens built. It was 1917, and World War I was affecting prices. Early that year, 255 cars of stock were loaded at Ellsworth, and Beldenville wanted part of the business. By the summer of 1918, they had a facility. In 1927, the crop was cabbage, and cars were iced at River Falls, courtesy of Kinnickinnic Ice Company. The Great Depression brought other problems to Beldenville. The cabbage shipping season was four weeks in fall, the sole reason for an agency there, and the Omaha lost $2,935 on the facility. Beldenville, an unincorporated village, was home to twenty-one families, just 3-1/2 miles from Ellsworth.

Discontinuance of the Ellsworth passenger service allowed removing Beldenville's agency in 1935, one of countless tiny stations rendered obsolete by the hard times of the 1930s. Stillwater-Ellsworth service utilized the same equipment, in most cases, concentrating on delivery of passengers to Hudson for mainline trains. With highways improving, Omaha passenger service was under heavy attack. When the first two gas-electrics were ordered (Nos. 2000-2001), some interest arose in assigning them to Ellsworth-Stillwater runs, but losses mounted too quickly. In August 1929, the Omaha petitioned to remove Trains 625-628, leaving mixed Trains 626-627 to share riders with buses. As if to hurry the coming decision, seventy year old Conductor G.W. Fowler retired off Trains 625-628 with forty-seven years of Omaha service behind him. Fowler, born at Elroy in 1882, entered road service in October 1890.

At a hearing in Ellsworth, on September 20, 1929, Omaha agreed to operate a morning and evening train, December 15 to April 15, or later if weather was bad. Trucks would be provided for mail in summer. Auditor Busch stated losses of $1,000 per month, with ridership at about four passengers per day. Losses continued, even as "Black Tuesday" drew the nation into further distress, and another hearing was scheduled for the following October. Total branch loss to year's end was $56,000. The mail service went to star route trucks, and the abandonment petition was granted October 16, 1930.

The fateful summer of 1929 introduced four powerful gas-electric cars to Omaha passenger schedules. The latest in the new technology of internal combustion motive power, Nos. 2002-2005, featured mail, baggage and passenger spaces of varied lengths. The Spooner area was chosen to try several motor cars

and one was introduced on the old North Wisconsin as Trains 62-361 and 364-63 between Minneapolis, Spooner and Ashland. New Richmond's newspaper was less than kind in detailing motor car 2003's tardiness on July 30, 1929, also claiming No. 2003 to have an unimpressive whistle. The two oil-burning engines were referred to as diesels, but the impact just before the Great Depression was substantial. The big 600 HP units hauled a baggage-mail car and a regular coach. It was the wellspring of the *Namekagon* a decade before the colorful motor train was placed in service.

During 1929, mainline motive power needs were examined in light of speed increases and weights of Eastern Division trains. On May 11, 1929, letters of inquiry went out to locomotive designer William E. Woodard of Lima Locomotive Works, as well as Baldwin and Alco. Omaha was looking for a super Pacific type to operate on the Elroy-Twin Cities route.

Woodard's answer to what seemed impossible conditions was to recommend a 4-6-4 type. His contention was that the new power would be better as a Hudson. Woodard was sure added weight could not be tailored to a 4-6-2 design as the Omaha wanted. The 67'1" engine and tender wheelbase for the E Class 500s allowed them to easily fit the turntables then in use. If the proposed new power was much longer, it would require turntable changes. J. E. Dixon of the Omaha had discussions with Lima, still referring to the engines as Pacific types. Attention was paid to the estimated weights on the two-wheeled trailing truck, some 70,000 pounds resting on two 9x17 inch journals. The meticulous questioning continued as to weights, measures and costs involved, which included exploration of a one-piece and a two-piece engine bed, an important feature giving the larger power greater rigidity. Omaha was sure of their needs, and continued to hold out for the two-wheel trailer truck, which would incorporate a booster. Omaha reiterated their need for a length not to exceed seventy-five feet, and a total weight of 354,000 pounds, with 200,000 to 210,000 pounds on drivers. Omaha finally got what it wanted from American Locomotive Company in the form of three E-3 Class super-Pacifics built in late 1930.

The E-3s were practically the last Pacific types built for an American railroad. They were apparently just sufficient to cover tight scheduling of Trains 405-406, the *North Western Limited*. Engines 600 and 601 arrived in St. Paul on November 3, 1930, but No. 602 was held up for another month.

Normal procedure in the steam age was to send a messenger with a new locomotive to oversee and administer to its in-transit requirements. In the 602's case, Arthur Willett, a seasoned traveler native to Wisconsin, rode the cab 1,222 miles to St. Paul. Willett delivered the mighty E-3s, which cost over $300,000, spending eight days on the road, but this was routine, as he had been delivering locomotives for Alco for twenty-five years. He traveled the world over, setting up new power as far off as China.

The E-3s were quite different from any North Western power to date and reflected trends dictated by factory practice. They drew on technology found in several 4-6-4 designs, notably New York Central's, and even rival Milwaukee Road's big F-6 Class Hudsons. Both employed outside-frame pony trucks, as did C&NW's H Class 4-8-4s. The E-3s were equipped with American multiple throttles, Baker valve gear, Standard type "BK" stokers,

Franklin boosters (which contributed 13,100 pounds tractive effort), two Westinghouse cross-compound air pumps on the pilot deck, 75" drivers, a grate area of 70.3 square feet, thermic syphons, low water alarms and, originally, one Sellers exhaust steam injector. What Omaha got was a massive modern Pacific that filled its needs. Overall length exceeded 87 feet over couplers, the entire engine fitting the turntables with some overhang. The 12 wheel welded tender was only seven feet longer than that of the Class Es, but the E-3s carried 14,000 gallons of water and 16 tons of coal, versus 8,275 gallons and 15 tons for the smaller engines. Starting effort was nearly twice that of a class E: 64,600 pounds versus 36,700 pounds. Several years into their careers, the E-3 tender water capacity was enlarged to 16,400 gallons. After World War II, roller bearings were applied.

In the 1940s, several unusual and original ideas were applied to the 600s, including two-position Tyler exhaust nozzles in the smokeboxes. Operated by an external cylinder similar to a small power reverse unit, the characteristics of the engine exhaust could be changed to improve draft. Another innovation was the removal of the steam dome in favor of a collector pipe, similar to Canadian Pacific practice. No. 601 also received a full set of Boxpok

drivers, while boosters on all three disappeared due to maintenance problems. One of the more remarkable engines in the Midwest, the E-3s routinely operated as far east as Milwaukee's Lake Front station, while C&NW's oil burning 2900s ranged as far west as the Twin Cities with the new, high speed "400" trains operating Chicago-Twin Cities via Milwaukee.

Engine 601 suffered damage in a momentous collision at Camp Douglas, Wisconsin, at the crossing of Milwaukee Road's mainline. On February 28, 1931, No. 601 was in charge of Train 515, the *Victory*, consisting of three express cars, two mail cars, two deadhead sleeping cars, a combination car, five sleeping cars and a lounge car. The Omaha train was crossing the diamonds when it was struck by Milwaukee Road Train 16, the eastbound thirteen car *Olympian*. The Milwaukee train was required to stop at the crossing, but engineer James Taylor misjudged the speed of his big Hudson, No. 6409, and upon reaching the stockyards about 1,700 feet from the crossing, made a full emergency application of the brakes. It was all too late, however, and he plowed into the Omaha train at an estimated speed of 35 MPH.

Taylor's fireman, Albert Woods, was killed, as engine 6409 careened to a halt beyond the depot. Omaha's engine was

In a classic winter scene, E-3 No. 602 charges under a wooden overhead bridge with the eastbound *Viking* in the mid-1950s. The consist includes express and mail cars and a couple of coaches. The Omaha Road operated right-handed on double track territory. *M.P. McMahon.*

wrenched off the rails to rest at right angles to the road's mainline. The first car was completely demolished and six trainmen and eleven passengers were injured. Three of Train 515's cars were derailed. The investigation found that Taylor had nullified the Automatic Train Control by use of the acknowledgment lever, which might have averted the collision. This was done at a point 5,659 feet west of the crossing, enough space to bring Train 16 down from its 78 MPH speed.

Omaha's No. 601 was out of commission for some time. Returned to St. Paul Shops, the engine had a gaping hole in the tender, and extensive damage elsewhere. Its frame was sprung, a condition discovered years later. Milwaukee No. 6409 came out of the shop with distinctive features, resembling the later F-6a.

Operation of the 600s yielded problems with their temperamental Sellers injectors, producing delays. Some years later, these units were replaced with Elesco steam injectors, but not without incident. Arriving at Mankato, a 600 equipped with the new device dropped its water load, showering passengers with hot water and mud. This was during the period of Western Division operations for the 600s, on Trains 201-202. A 600 could run from St. Paul to Mankato before taking water and make St. James on a load of coal, gliding along on roller bearings with 14 cars behind the drawbar. Finally, in the early 1950s, the 600s worked freight assignments, prior to dieselization.

When the 600s were equipped with roller bearings, the installation included sighting with a surveyor's transit to run a line down the center of the mainframe. The line ran from the cylinders to the drawbar pin hole, successfully done in the case of 600 and 602. In 601's case, the frame was discovered to be 2-1/2 inches out of line at the rear due to the Camp Douglas accident in 1931. For several years after the collision, the 601 ran off considerable miles, "out of tram."

Omaha's experience with boosters was evidently not a happy one, and the 600s lost their original boosters in the 1940s, due to maintenance costs. Engines 508 and 509 were also equipped with trailing truck boosters, which were removed after eight years.

For Omaha, 1930 ended in a net deficit and the grim results came soon enough for small stations, the rural core of railroad service. On the Eastern Division, stations like Hersey, Millston, Tramway and Trego were examined and found to be too expensive. Hersey was two miles from Wilson and Woodville was four miles west. Only 18 carloads arrived there in 1930. At Millston, caretaker status for the station was applied for, but denied, since the railroad commission considered the business adequate. With Warrens at eight miles and Black River Falls at twelve, the produce grown locally required an agent. At tiny Tramway, a 940 foot work spur, built in 1888 and unused since 1913, was scheduled for removal, the commission agreeing. The interlocking plant at Trego, barely 20 years old, was recommended for closure in 1933. This meant layoffs for the two levermen.

A three car Train 508, the *Viking*, speeds along between Hudson and St. Paul in the 1950s with E-3 No. 600 up front. Photographer Pat McMahon's father was an Omaha railroader and young Pat nearly followed suit, but settled for an art career instead. *M.P. McMahon.*

(Above) Heavy Pacific No. 601 poses at Minneapolis in July 1954. Roller bearings and Boxpok drivers are evident, together with the removal of the steam dome and substitution of the perforated collector pipe. With front end throttles in use, the dome was not needed. Also shown is the extended stack, new boiler front, Mars light, and extensive lube lines, fed by the mechanical lubricator. *W. Krawiec.* (Below) The engineer's side of 601 is displayed at St. Paul in June 1952. The pilot mounted air pumps and protective shields can be seen nicely. *Bruce Black.*

After the fiasco of Wyeville and its closing, Adams became the east end of Omaha operations, with C&NW crews running to Altoona to balance miles of Omaha men going to Adams. In the fall of 1930, Adams employed 335 C&NW men. By December, an aid organization headed by Carl R. Gray Jr., which included other Omaha men, distributed food, fuel and clothing to the unemployed. In addition, Adams stipulated that any municipal shipments must go via Omaha and C&NW. In January 1931, switch jobs were increased at Adams over Butler, especially in the case of southern Minnesota and South Dakota tonnage.

Omaha's loss of revenues systemwide dictated a necessity for economizing. No dividends had been paid on its common stock since 1923, and the rate of dividend on its preferred shares was reduced from seven to five percent, paying none since 1927. The heavy losses of the last two months of 1929 were attributed to traffic decline. At this point, C&NW owned ninety-three percent of the Omaha Road's capital stock. The need to correct the road's drift was apparent: Omaha lost over one million dollars in 1930, as earnings failed to meet fixed charges.

More significant cuts in service came in 1931. Livestock and way freight shipments declined, passing inevitably to motor carriers. Lake Wilson's newspaper was chagrined with the loss, condemning the regional railroads for not modernizing and competing. Omaha had volunteers among its regular railroaders who met with farmers face-to-face. J.J. Prentice, faced with departmental reductions, went out to the branch lines and coaxed back business

Stillwater, Minnesota, in July 1936, still had passenger service over the Omaha to Hudson. Mixed Trains 600-607, running the six miles to the mainline, would soon disappear. In the distance, the one-car express stands at Stillwater's depot. Northern Pacific's enginehouse is in the mid-foreground. *Minnesota Historical Society.*

from trucks. For passengers, Omaha lowered fares between Heron Lake and the Twin Cities. Tickets to major area cities were going for three-fifths of the original one-way fares.

St. James, which once enjoyed twelve passenger trains a day, was now reduced to eight. Trains 203-204 took the mail once assigned to Minneapolis-Sioux City Trains 5-6. The Black Hills-Mankato connection with Train 10 was also threatened with extinction. One of two runs was cut off the Pipestone branch, yet on June 5, 1930, several specials were run for Land O' Lakes Creameries. Some 2,000 people rode to that firm's "Butter Building" in Minneapolis, requiring three Omaha trains and two Minneapolis & St. Louis trains, passing through St. James.

In the midst of the Depression, Omaha found time to celebrate fifty years of service to its territory. The high point was to be a series of reenactments of the West Wisconsin's first meeting at Hudson. It was planned and promoted by Carl R. Gray Jr., and would involve several railroad departments and Hudson's Mayor J.W. McGilvran. The show was to include C&NW's *Pioneer* and possibly a "big H locomotive."

Duplicates of old equipment would be brought to Hudson, or created at Hudson Shops, under Master Car Builder W.H. Thorn. Carl Gray Jr., was actually emulating his father's similar work on the Union Pacific at the time, complete with period costumes, re-unions and new enthusiasm to combat the Depression. All spring, city and railroad prepared for the June 6 date, and four cars were chosen for cleanup. Power selected for the old train was 4-4-0 No. 136, equipped with a fake balloon stack.

The stars of the show were an E-3 Class Pacific and the *North Western Limited*, to be parked alongside Hudson's freight house with the antique train. These actions did help morale, and St. Paul

Shops went to a five day week from four days for a time. It happened that locomotive repair work was being centered in St. Paul, while small power was steadily being phased out. Extra hours at the Hudson Shops helped families there, too.

A month before the great day, Hudson's newspaper promised a "million dollar train" would be available to visitors. At 9:30 AM, an extra would run to the old land office on the Willow River's north shore, and Omaha vets of the "*400*" would disembark for the festivities. "Movietone" newsreels were made, and radio KSTP, St. Paul, would carry the event live. Officials of the Omaha arrived from the east, including President Fred Sargent, C.W. Nash from Kenosha, Arthur S. Pierce of New York and several Chicago board members. One Hudson business displayed a link-and-pin coupler prominently in their store window.

Omaha found that it could eke out modest improvements in the spring of 1931. In the west, the 100 lb. rail program continued around St. James, employing 182 men. Two years later, 1933's first extra train moved out of St. James in May, followed by others moving grain and livestock. April had shown a six percent increase in ton miles, yet the times showed few white flag extras. St. James' switch crew worked several days that month, a noteworthy event. More encouraging, 17 more men were put to work, some getting their first check since November 1932. At Kasota, the quarry received orders for material destined for the new St. Paul Post Office, which meant an extra switch engine on duty. Another extra went on the Elmore Line. Still, everyone looked toward revival in desperate times.

The end for the extension of the former Covington narrow gauge to Wynot, Nebraska, came in 1933. Omaha extended this line in standard gauge from Ponca to Newcastle in 1893, and from Newcastle to Wynot in 1907. While once considered productive, competition from trucks finished the branch. The abandonment entailed 44.9 miles.

The end of the Nebraska Division as a separate unit came on May 17, 1933, when it was consolidated with the Western Division. On October 1, 1933, the entire railroad was divided into six districts: First and Second Districts comprised the old Eastern Division; the Third was the old Twin Cities Terminal Division; the Fourth, Fifth and Six Districts made up the old Western Division. Joe Prentice became "Super" of the entire west end of the

Omaha Road, and the old Omaha city office was discontinued. It was 619 miles plus 265 miles of the old Nebraska Division. A year before, the Assistant Superintendent moved to Mankato, but now he was to return to St. James.

Washouts, the terror of Missouri Valley railroads, raged north of Mankato in May 1933. It was the worst in 30 years, and the mainline was covered with mud slides and was torn apart in fifteen places. Train 209 was halted at Le Sueur and had to back to Merriam. After running over the M&StL to Waseca, the train entered Mankato on C&NW trackage, then on to St. James, five hours late. Train 203 arrived via the same route, two hours late, after a freight derailed and tied up the mainline.

A second major storm struck the railroad with semi-comic results in June. A 75,000 bushel bin type elevator at Butterfield was felled by violent winds, collapsing onto the Omaha's main-

(Above left) Eau Claire Tower covered the Milwaukee Road trackage (and Soo Line trackage rights) over the Omaha mainline east of the latter's depot. Through efforts of several Eau Claire railroad veterans, the tower was moved to a local park for restoration. *Author's Collection.* (Above right) Toward the end of steam, Omaha's "West Side Job," utilizing K-1 Class No. 230, proceeds through the Eau Claire Tower plant, headed for Altoona in early 1956. *Robert Larson.* (Below) Omaha's Train 104 is twenty cars long this spring day in 1956, and I-1 No. 357 is about to clump over the Soo Line at the Tower. The photographer indicated this was the last of steam at Eau Claire. *Robert Larson.*

209

line. Two miles away, at Mountain Lake, two empty cars, a box and a tank car, were propelled by the same gale to Butterfield where they collided with the rear of time freight Train 20. To make matters worse, the felled elevator rolled west for 150 feet when it hit Train 20's locomotive! Fortunately, the big J-3 Class 2-8-2 suffered little damage. Also at Butterfield, at the C&NW interchange, three box cars were blown over. Such were the hazards of railroading in the flatlands in the 1930s.

In late 1933, despair over stock prices among Iowa farmers brought about a small war. Outside Sioux City, Train 19 was fired upon and engineer Roy Newman had to keep low in the cab, claiming an estimated 500 armed men were swarming about the city. Elsewhere, angry farmers overwhelmed a stock train and threatened to release the animals. Near Wren Junction, a Great Northern bridge was set on fire, causing trains to be detoured over Illinois Central into Sioux City. Other bridges were burned before stock prices were settled and peace returned to the Floyd Valley.

One bright sign of better times was Union Pacific's new streamlined train, M-10000. Finished in February 1934, the three-car yellow and brown train was displayed along Omaha's Western Division. The train, produced by Pullman-Standard, employed an aluminum superstructure powered by a Winton 600 HP distillate engine. It made display stops at Sioux City, Worthington, St. James, Mankato and the Twin Cities in May 1934. That same year, CB&Q and Milwaukee Road launched their high-speed streamlined trains in Chicago-Twin Cities service. C&NW also began work on its famous *"400"* name trains. Entering the competition on January 2, 1935, a bitter cold after-

noon, Train 401 raced over Omaha's Eastern Division in good time. Power was specially rebuilt C&NW No. 2902, a Class E-2A oil burning Pacific, capable of 100 MPH speeds.

The *"400"* that day handled a five car train making only five stops, one being Eau Claire. Departure time was mid-afternoon, allowing businessmen to board after completing a regular business day. Arrival was 11:00 PM and 10:30 PM, with Trains 400 and 401 meeting at Adams, 209 miles from Chicago. One drawback was that Adams, located in the midst of 100 miles of straight track, made for tight operation. Penstocks were located at Adams to allow both *"400"* trains to take water without cutting off the engines. The trains were successful enough to require more coaches and carried almost 10,000 passengers in standard-weight, rebuilt cars, a frugal departure from C&NW's rivals. Use of North Western power over the Omaha occurred frequently after this, and Omaha's three big 600s were seen daily in Milwaukee. In time, C&NW Class H 4-8-4s were used for a decade in heavy freight service to Altoona, and power exchanges were evident during the Second World War.

Another turn of events came for Hudson Hill's difficult operations. With a specific rule in place governing freights between Northline and St. Paul in 1935, discussions raged over the retainer rule modifications, since delays were getting out of hand. Cars carrying over 50 tons required retainers to be set. The tonnage of eight of 26 trains was over 2,000 tons westbound, and each made a helper stop at Knapp. Safety prevailed, however.

Motive power on the plodding freights continued to be J or J-2 Class Mikes, with one of the two 2-10-2s on the rear end in

In zero degree weather, E-3 No. 601 makes time with Train 508, the eastbound *Viking*, heavily laden with express reefers and head end cars, on Christmas Eve day in 1952. The big 4-6-2 Pacific was in service until June 1956. *M.P. McMahon.*

In 1955, the children of Ellsworth were treated to the last ride out of town on the Omaha. Featured was the Limousine Coach, from the *Namekagon* motor train, recently retired from service on the Worthington-Sioux Falls line. *Harold Van Horn.*

Hudson helper service. Helpers also operated westbound from Altoona to Hersey, but in most cases, the first time brakes were used was when the train stopped at Hersey to cut off the helper. Motive Power Superintendent Gorman was against the practice in 1935, especially in the face of *"400"* passenger train operations.

Caroline Tower once guarded the triple crossing of the Milwaukee Road, C&NW's old Winona & St. Peter line, and the Omaha just south of Kasota, Minnesota. The site witnessed many 19th Century transfers between the three roads, but in 1937 it was scheduled for removal as modern signaling made it obsolete. At one time, there was the nucleus of another village with a general store and small depot. By end of summer 1937, C&NW's original Winona line was removed, leaving only the Milwaukee's branch crossing the Omaha. Caroline, named for a distant daughter of the landowner, would soon pass from Omaha's directory.

Overlooked during the 1920s, was a need for a modern, medium sized freight engine on the C&NW. While the 1923 batch of J Class engines were an improvement over the original, they still retained their 61" drivers. Most 2-8-2s, including Omaha's J-2s and J-3s, rode on 63 or 64 inch drive wheels, and it made quite a difference. Ten years after the last Js arrived, there was a need to create a fast freight engine for C&NW and Omaha secondary lines. The answer for the two roads was the J-A.

The Omaha began its J-A program with Nos. 409 and 413 in August 1937, and by early 1938, Nos. 411, 412 and 415 were completed. The engines featured 64 inch Boxpok drivers, increased boiler pressure (to 200 pounds), a new superheater yielding 20% more efficiency, BK stokers, Elesco exhaust steam injectors, Alemite valve gear fittings, plus mechanical lubricators for valves, cylinders, air pumps and the stoker engine. The tenders were lengthened nearly six feet to carry 11,000 gallons of water, an increase of 2,725 gallons. They carried 15 tons of coal.

Compared with the J-2, the new J-As could develop 62,000 lbs. of tractive effort versus the J-2's 63,000 lbs. They were able to handle 95% of the J-2's tonnage and their use was unrestricted on most of the system. C&NW rebuilt some 38 of their J Class to

J-As, while Omaha converted 24. The J-As dramatically boosted performance of both roads' time freights. By 1948, the J-As were the rule on secondary mainline runs, the "straight J" an exception. All over the North Western, where time freights were carded, the J-A improved service. At important junctions like Mankato and Wyeville, C&NW J-As brought connecting tonnage and delivered it to waiting Omaha J-A powered freights.

At the same time, C&NW prepared the Adams Cutoff to take even heavier power: the Class H 4-8-4s. They were the road's largest engines, weighing 409 tons with tender, and had the distinction of being delivered by Baldwin just as "Black Tuesday" brought the roaring twenties to a halt in mid-October 1929.

The H Class came to Wisconsin after April 1, 1938, to work heavy freight schedules in competition with equally large 4-8-4s of the Burlington and Milwaukee Road. The H's dominated fast freight Trains 483-484 and 479-490, their assignments stretching from Proviso to Altoona. West of Altoona yard, Omaha J-A and J-2 Mikes prevailed due to mainline bridge and curve restrictions which precluded the use of the big 4-8-4s. The H's were too long for Altoona's 90 foot turntable and were turned on a wye east of the roundhouse.

An H Class engine could take 4,500 to 4,800 tons over the 110 mile stretch between Adams and Altoona in less than two hours, sometimes taking water at Wyeville. The district was a speedway, and one veteran of fast railroading remembered trips in one hour and 50 minutes! This part of the mainline was notable for passenger train speeds over 100 MPH, especially in the case of passenger Trains 400-401. Speed restrictions included Black River Bridge and a 45 MPH slow order over the Green Bay & Western crossing at Merrillan.

The big engines were modernized piecemeal, and after the war, it was decided to rebuild the class to eliminate several problems, and the H-1 Class was born. With new road diesels arriving on the property, many H-1s lived just long enough to consume their new flues in four year's time. The H-1s were gone from the Wisconsin scene beyond Milwaukee by the spring of 1949.

(Above) Omaha Class J No. 395, one of eight engines (out of 32) not rebuilt to J-A, is shown at St. Paul on September 9, 1947. *J. Westphal.* After improving the J Class in the mid-thirties, Omaha embarked upon a rebuilding program at St. Paul Shops, with Nos. 409 and 413 completed in September 1937. The work included raising boiler pressure to 200 lbs., an improved superheater, 64" Boxpok drivers (an increase of 3"), BK stokers, Elesco exhaust steam injectors, and mechanical lubrication for valves, cylinders, air pump and stoker engine. Rebuilt J-A engines could handle 95% of the heavier Class J-2's tonnage. (Below) J-A No. 413 is posed at Altoona on October 18, 1952. *Stan Mailer.*

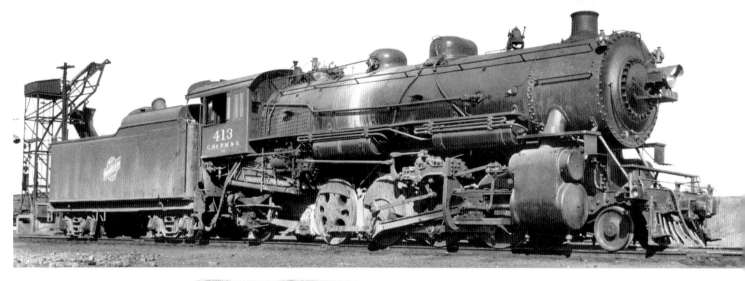

An overhead view of J-A No. 417 at Altoona displays the lengthened tender the Omaha J-A rebuilds received. The water capacity was increased to 11,000 gallons with 13 tons of coal. *A. Robert Johnson.*

(Above) In 1950, J-A No. 400 rolls a freight northward near Bloomer, on the Altoona-Spooner line. In the latter days of steam, several J-As received Mars lights, probably for extra passenger duty during the Korean War. *M.P. McMahon.* (Below) J-A No. 417 rolls through pastoral farmland near Humbird, Wisconsin, on June 9, 1956. *Jim Scribbins.*

(Above) J-2 No. 430 has an oil train in tow as it storms past Menomonie Junction toward the high country on February 13, 1953. Between Altoona and the Twin Cities, Omaha J-A and J-2 2-8-2s ruled mainline tonnage as bridge and curve restrictions prevented C&NW's heavy Class H 4-8-4s from operating west of Altoona yard. Class J-2 Nos. 426-431 were "USRA copies" built by Alco in 1921 that sported better headroom in their cabs, a request made by crewmembers who frequently came in contact with roofs. *M.P. McMahon.* (Below) A gathering at Atoona has C&NW Class H No. 3014 flanked by Omaha J-As 418 and 405 while waiting for fire cleaning at the ash pit. *A. Robert Johnson.*

(Above) For over a decade, C&NW's great H-Class worked heavy tonnage between Wyeville and Altoona on the Omaha. Train 490, 100 cars long, is at Altoona on September 22, 1945. Without delays, the 3034 will be in Adams on the "New Line" within two hours. *A. Robert Johnson.*

(Above) C&NW received 35 mammoth Class H 4-8-4 Northerns from Baldwin in 1929. The fireman's side of No. 3014 is shown at Altoona on March 17, 1945. *A. Robert Johnson.* (Below) On July 1, 1938, C&NW 4-8-4 No. 3032 stands on the westbound main at Millston, Wisconsin, 17.8 miles northwest of Wyeville. This section was double-tracked by the Omaha in 1911. C&NW's Class H engines were too heavy for most lines in Wisconsin, but they did power Chicago-Twin Cities time freights via the Adams Cutoff and the Omaha as far west as Altoona. *Roy Peterson.*

(Above) I-1 No. 344, equipped with a flanger plow, pauses with a way freight at Baldwin on the "Mountain Division" to work local cars in the early 1950s. By the winter of 1953, most of Omaha's last Stephenson-geared I-1s were headed for the Duluth scrapyards, and No. 344 was no exception, being retired in November 1953. (Below) I-1 No. 333 idles at Shawtown. The "West Side Job" once worked the Shawtown Subdivision, a steeply graded line curving down to the Chippewa River, which served storied lumber mills on Eau Claire's south side. The 1905 Stephenson valve gear engine was retired in 1952. Both: *M.P. McMahon.*

(Above) Omaha F-2 Class No. 202 pauses at the Menomonie depot in July 1932. Trains 32-33 connected the college town with Menomonie Junction, three miles north on the mainliine. The ancient Ten-Wheeler came from Schenectady in 1893, got rebuilt in 1924 and was finally retired in August 1936. The round barn was a patented local product. *George Harris.* (Below) K-1 4-6-0 No. 203, with a footboard pilot, rests for the weekend at Menomonie in 1950. The 1913 engine was in service until December 1956. *M.P. McMahon.*

(Above) Historic Chippewa River: J-2 No. 431 rumbles across the "new" Chippewa River bridge in Eau Claire, bound for the Twin Cities. The span was finished in 1912 and is located further upstream from the original bridge. (Below) Near the end of steam, M-3 No. 77 heads into the roundhouse at Altoona to remove J-A No. 411, condemned to scrap. It's October 19, 1955, and steam will flicker and die out in the next eight months. Both: *A. Robert Johnson.*

(Above) For many years, I-1s were used as switch engines in and around Eau Claire. Here, No. 327 works a cut of cars eastward toward the city's depot. The locomotive's small tender prevented extensive use of the aging I-1 on Eastern Division way-freights. (Below) Mainline dieselization of the Eastern Division brought "covered wagons," then GP7s in multiple, to cover freights such as eastbound Train 490. By November 1953, even the EMD "Geeps" were grimy, but Train 508 was still steam powered. Here, E Class No. 512 gallops out of Altoona with the Viking on its way to Chicago via Wyeville and Madison. Both: *A. Robert Johnson.*

# SMALL POWER

The Omaha and C&NW were not known for experimentation or re-design of existing locomotives. There was a time in the 1920s, however, when both companies needed economical branchline and passenger power. Because of dwindling profits, necessity mothered invention of rebuilds just before the introduction of the gas-electrics. While the North Western launched a massive campaign to superheat its vital R-1 Class, it also designed new boilers for S Class 4-6-0 survivors and a handful of Class C-5 4-4-0s. The Omaha followed suit, fitting new boilers to about 22 of the original F-2s of 1890-92 (Schenectady), and three of its eligible 4-4-0s, probably using identical boiler designs.

The three 4-4-0s, E-6 Class Nos. 136 and 144, and E-8 No. 160, were superheated in 1931. Both the Ten-Wheelers and the 4-4-0s received extended wagontop boilers, the 4-4-0s from necessity taking 8 inch piston valves for superheated steam. They went to work on various lines, notably the *Bayfield Scoot* between Ashland and Bayfield. In the 1930s, they served Norfolk, Nebraska, Trains 4 and 5, and also the latter day *Fisherman* trains to Drummond. The "little giants" were fairly successful on two and three-car light passenger runs. The 4-4-0s were also useful in winter too, since the gas-electrics were hard pressed to provide steam heat.

Elsewhere, the Omaha operated its last "normal" small 4-4-0s, a few working the Doon branch. Nos. 161 and 171, went to the deadline in May 1933. In the lean, early days of the Depression, Omaha superheated four of the larger F-8 Class 4-4-0s, Nos. 257-259 and 276, for work on light passenger runs. The first three were completed by October 1931 and No. 276

followed in December 1932. With a drastic reduction in passenger business, the superheated F-8s were a sensible addition. Therefore, the seven 4-4-0s were the only slide-valve saturated steam power to be modernized. Superheating of the larger power, including all I-1 4-6-0s, I-2 4-6-2s, G-3 4-4-2s and even the plodding J-1 2-10-2s was completed by 1930.

Several classes of smaller power were disposed of in the mid-1930s, most notably the F-9/G-1 4-6-0s (all non-superheated), F-8 4-4-0s, all F-2 4-6-0s and a few 0-6-0 switchers. What remained for secondary assignments were the now universal I-1 and K-1 4-6-0s.

Engine 152, an 1888 D-11 0-6-0, was sold to Hamm's Brewery in 1908. Returned in 1916, the outcast was earmarked to become another St. Paul shop "goat," one of several to receive the number X-0. This was followed by No. 2151, alias X-199900, formerly M-1 Class No. 1, the last of the little tank engines to work at the shops.

In 1937, the Omaha retired its first I-2 Class 4-6-2s, the noteworthy pioneer 1903 vintage Schenectady engines, which worked heavy trains on the Eastern

Division, and were last assigned to Trains 201-204 on the Western Division. Authority to dispose of the I-2s came as No. 371 was in St. Paul Shops, where it was summarily scrapped. The work was subsequently given to C&NW E Class engines equipped with Automatic Train Stop for operation on C&NW's Missouri Valley-Omaha mainline.

The Omaha began servicing diesels at Minneapolis after the 1939 delivery of four C&NW EMC E3 passenger diesels for the streamlined *"400."* A year later, the Omaha selected three different yard engines to start dieselization. By June 1944, EMC SW1 No. 55 was active at Hudson. The 600 HP all-black pioneer did well on the sharp curves associated with the car shop's blacksmith and ice-house spurs, besting little F-6 0-6-0 No. 15 in its last days.

To utilize the diesel's 24 hour availability, traveling engineer Erickson participated in a test with Trains 626-627, the *Ellsworth Mixed*. It was reported that diesel No. 55 handled seven loads and one empty (526 tons) upgrade from Hudson's depot, over the first four miles at 8 MPH. Running easily on the Glover

(Above) E-8 Class No. 160 was one of three 4-4-0s rebuilt with new boilers and superheated in 1925-1926. Shown at Norfolk, Nebraska, in 1937, the 1888 engine was retired in 1940. *Holman F. Bradon.*

flats, the next three miles were covered at 12 MPH. Finally, the train loped into River Falls at 12 MPH. Officials on-board concluded the SW1 would be rated at 600 tons for the grade up out of Hudson. Erickson stated that No. 55 went to Ellsworth from River Falls at an average speed of 15 MPH, taking the curves nicely. Here was the wave of the future.

In May 1946, one of two yard assignments utilizing No. 55 was annulled, and the way was clear to put the unit on the Stillwater mixed, as the schedules allowed the use of the same equipment as the Ellsworth train. The yard duty was made for a time at 7:30 PM, allowing No. 55 to work branch trains and still be available for shop switching. On May 11, 1946, I-1 No. 351 was released at Hudson upon arrival of Train 616, temporarily dieselizing the two assignments.

A decade later, a combination coach-baggage car was still trailing the Ellsworth run, ultimately running at night. Still later, as the two branches east of Woodville declined, No. 55 was used until abandonment came to the Spring Valley and Ellsworth branches. Mixed trains regularly made connections with Train 508 at Hudson, with John Hellseth, the second oldest man on the division, as conductor. This job ended, along with the tri-weekly operation in December 1963.

(Above) Shop engine No. X-0 (2nd) was built in 1888 as Class D-11 No. 152. After a stint with Hamm Brewing Company, the Omaha got it back and rebuilt it into a "tank" engine for shop transfer service. It's shown at St. Paul Shops on June 1, 1939. *Robert H. Graham.*

(Above) The last St. Paul shop goat was photographed on November 25, 1955. Formerly Class M-1 No. 1, it was rebuilt to 0-6-0T engine No. 2151 in 1947, and then renumbered to X199900 in 1955. *Robert Guhr.*

(Left) Famous Fifty-Five was part of Omaha's initial thrust into dieselization, coming from Electro-Motive Corporation on October 26, 1940. Shown at East St. Paul on June 13, 1957, No. 55 was a Hudson fixture most of its life, regularly working mixed trains on the Ellsworth, Stillwater and Spring Valley branches. The all-black diesel received yellow and green safety stripes in 1948, and a Mars warning light atop its front hood. *Robert Larson.*

In October 1955, engine No. 184, a K-1 Class 4-6-0, gets ready to depart Park Falls. Several railfans are present for the line's last autumn in steam. *Jim Scribbins.*

# 11.

# TO PARK FALLS

The Omaha's Park Falls extension began as a combination settlement line and new wood supplier to the Eau Claire - Chippewa Falls - Rice Lake mills. Initial construction of subsidiary Chippewa Falls & Northeastern Railway Company was just twelve miles of branchline from Chippewa Valley Junction (Tuscobia) to Birchwood, and was opened for operation on November 20, 1901. The CF&NE helped Omaha offset pineland exhaustion in the north country by ushering in new pulpwood and veneer operations. Several mills also managed to cut a small share of dimensional lumber. The line opened the upper reaches of the Chippewa Valley to railroad logging in parts of Sawyer and western Price County. CF&NE, however, was not completed the full 75 miles to Park Falls until early 1914. In 1900, the old Wisconsin lumber firm of Knapp, Stout & Company of Menomonie and Rice Lake dissolved, and its land opened for settlement by the new north's hardiest arrivals.

Knapp, Stout & Company logged the region from the days of river drives and oxen power, its beginnings tied to an 1853 partnership. Their interests reached up the Red Cedar River from Menomonie to Prairie Farm and Rice Lake, finally ending in the Birchwood area, leaving behind old company farmland and countless stumps. KS&Co, in its time, dealt with big timber speculators such as Cadwallader C. Washburn, Ezra Cornell and Philetus Sawyer. Another legacy was the Wisconsin Land Company, the appointed vendor of the cutover. KS&Co presence in Rice Lake dates to 1868, with holdings northeasterly in following years. Its founding fathers were John H. Knapp, Henry L. Stout, William L. Wilson and Andrew Tainter, who left their names in Omaha's geography. Disposal of the lumber company's lands and the era of the paper mill coincided with Omaha's arrival in Birchwood in 1901.

The Omaha's contractor for the first 40 miles was Winston Brothers of St. Paul, who began in May 1901. First surveys went out from both Rice Lake and Haugen toward lands of Arpin Hardwood Veneer Company, east of Rice Lake. Already the Wisconsin Land company was engaged in enticing hardy families to the cutover, and to induce railroads to follow. A prize was offered to the first railway to build to Birch Lake Dam (later, Birchwood). It was expected the Omaha would win, but there was competition.

Rice Lake & Northern Railway Company, soon to be Soo Line property in 1904, struck out for the same Birch Lake Dam location in 1901. The land company had 50,000 acres available east of the dam, and the two-railroad race was much in its interest. RL&N ultimately reached Reserve, north of Birchwood, and

trackside editors had it extended as far north as Ashland County. One of RL&N's officers was George M. Huss of Western Springs, Illinois, a land speculator and promoter with holdings north of Birchwood. Newspapers were certain cattle grazing would prevail where Knapp, Stout & Company supply farms once flourished, and that nearby sparkling lakes would attract vacationers. While Birchwood girded itself for great land sales, Winston Brothers opened nine grading camps along the Omaha's route. The contractor fielded 350 men with 100 teams in the summer of 1901.

RL&N reached Birchwood first, completing their Rice Lake-Birchwood lap a month ahead of the Omaha. On October 14th and 15th, special trains were run to the town lot sale at a rate of $1.40 per round trip. Within the year, reports about Birchwood's fishing and hunting circulated, and Birchwood was deemed a vacationland, the first along the new railroad.

Descendants of the Stout family established vacation homes on nearby Red Cedar Lake, as had others connected with the land company. At Narrows, two miles west of Birchwood, a small station was erected for Harry L. Stout's convenience, his retreat located on an island. A motor launch dock was built alongside the high railroad trestles, which allowed for visits of special friends alighting from private cars. The rolling palaces would be spotted on a short siding at the small station. Both lines had wood bridges over the deep waterway at Narrows, as the RL&N paralleled the Omaha into Birchwood. It then crossed over the Omaha on Birchwood's east side and proceeded north to Reserve.

The halting of Omaha's eastward construction was due in part to difficult and time consuming earth moving and trestle building, in addition to major sinkholes that had to be crossed near Park Falls. The track reached Radisson in 1902 (34.6 miles); Winter in 1904 (45.5 miles); Draper in 1906 (55.7 miles); Kennedy in 1908 (64.7 miles) and Kaiser in 1910 (69.7 miles). Part of the problem, however, was an economic down-turn in 1907-08. The importance of these small stations was magnified by logging railroads built off into timber tracts and, in some instances, sawmills.

Just east of Birchwood, Arpin Hardwood Lumber Company had logging operations in the Yarnell-Woodale area. Arpin's own Chippewa Valley & Northern Railroad, a 28 mile logging line, ran to within a mile of Yarnell, but didn't connect with the Omaha. Arpin's mill was located at Atlanta, nowadays an empty location at CV&N's south end, near Bruce. Atlanta's mill burned about 1918 and CV&N expired. Other Arpin loading sites were Crooked Rapids, east of Radisson, and Ojibwa (mile 40.2). The Arpin brothers started logging on the Yellow River and left their name on a townsite northwest of Wisconsin Rapids in 1890.

At Winter, in 1906, the John H. Kaiser Lumber Company

# 1901 – NEW LANDS, LOGS AND LINES

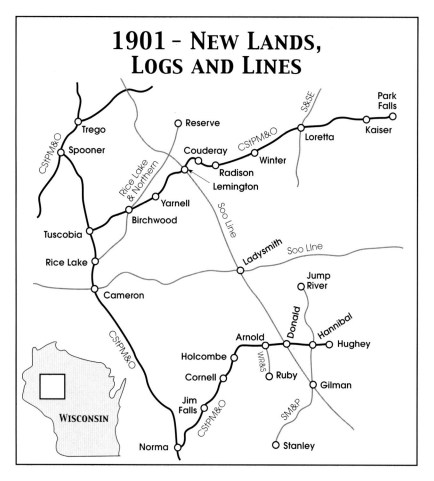

Kennedy was the Omaha's east end for two years, but permanent settlement was not its lot. Afterwards, it just melted away, with most of its buildings dismantled by 1940. Delco, more of a business outpost, was moved by its owners 2-1/2 miles west. Delco established a post office in 1927 and continued to deal in logs until 1933. One of its spurs reached toward Glidden, in southern Ashland County. Delco's work focused on peeling logs, the bark directed to tanneries and the logs to Eau Claire. The Dells Pulp & Paper Company organized the New Dells Lumber Company to run the show at Delco. The siding lasted until 1955.

Park Falls' newspaper reported steadily on construction eastward for years, including excavation problems. While promising logging opened west of town, George H. Atwood persuaded his more famous business partner to acquire 53,807 acres of timberland, from the Wisconsin Central for $243,000. The partner was Frederick Weyerhaeuser. Their Atwood Lumber & Manufacturing Company was incorporated in June 1907 and influenced Omaha's action. In turn, WC published higher rates systemwide, and it worked to pull Omaha into Park Falls in competition for the four mills' business.

The Atwood mill proved a disappointment to its owners. The timber supply was inferior, and a fire reduced the prospective bounty. Atwood had completed work at their Willow River, Minnesota, mill about the time Weyerhaeuser closed its Lake Nebagamon, Wisconsin, operation. Their combination at Park Falls brought from both old sites men and materials to create the last great Weyerhaeuser sawmill in Wisconsin. The Nebagamon machinery came to Park Falls in 30 carloads. The Atwood mill operated as such from 1907 to 1913, but was finally sold to Edward Hines on February 19, 1913, for $700,000. In its time, the Atwood mill had a 15 mile railroad south of Park Falls and west of the Flambeau, but it did not connect with the Omaha other than at the Park Falls millsite. Lakes (mile 69.7) had a sawmill in operation before the railroad came. When train service opened to the settlement, it arrived at a modest depot fashioned from a box car. Lakes served prime customer Blackwell & Kaiser Lumber Company, with A.E. Kaiser being a prominent Park Falls businessman since the 1880s. Shortly, the newly platted townsite became Kaiser, which acclaimed its new name by registering minus 36 degrees that winter.

A Park Falls newsman who drove five miles out to track's end at Kaiser, pronounced it "difficult country." The branch's Butternut Creek Bridge was 400 feet long and 30 feet high, with over 200 oak piles. Just east of the bridge, a big cut measured 300 feet long and 17 feet deep. Balch Construction Company used a steam shovel to move earth, with dinky tank engines and Koppel dump cars serving the belching Bucyrus shovel. The last spike was scheduled no later than July 1, 1911.

The Kaiser outpost remained the closest point to Park Falls for nearly two years. Some work was completed in 1912. Omaha's survey crew went over the route in a final check in mid-1913. In July, another steam shovel was reported working for new con-

began its operations. Later, Bissell Lumber Company (1928-34) used its old grades. A line from Rice Lake Lumber Company went north to Blaisdell Lake, about 9 miles, and helped feed logs to Rice Lake's big mill. The most extensive and ambitious activity on the entire branch was at Loretta (mile 54.7) and the crossing of Superior & South Eastern Railway. S&SE began at Grand View on Omaha's Ashland-Bayfield Line, reaching 25 miles southward to Atkins Lake by 1906. Owner Willow River Lumber Company, of New Richmond, sold logs locally and also made sales to Michigan furniture manufacturers. Willow River sold out to Edward Hines in 1922, and the Chicagoan abandoned 11 miles out of Grand View, while building a new line north from Loretta in 1921-22. This phase of S&SE operations continued until 1933. Another facet of Hines' large operations, the Hines Hardwood and Hemlock Company, was created from the older Rice Lake Lumber Company. The Loretta mill was of considerable size and named for Edward Hines' sister Loretta Clubine. Still another vest for Hines' suit was the E. Hines Farmland Company, another settlement company bent on selling logged-off lands.

The long-awaited push to Park Falls came in bits. In June 1908, a 20 mile contract was made to a point initially called Lakes, only five miles west of Park Falls. Among the new locations were Kennedy and Delco, platted in 1908 on old Cornell lands. Sold first to Sage Land Company, the land then went to Dells Pulp & Paper Company, the leading Eau Claire papermaking firm. Delco Spur connected several logging lines to the Omaha. They ran to seven logging camps north of Kennedy. There was a functional depot (a box car body), which forwarded the lumber company's countless carloads westward. The cut included hemlock, birch, maple, basswood and some pine.

Competitors Omaha and Soo Line (which controlled Rice Lake & Northern) built toward Birchwood. The two lines paralleled each other over the "Narrows" of Red Cedar Lake. This tiny Omaha station was built by request of Harry L. Stout, and the stub track often held private cars of his prominent friends. Stout, a descendant of Wisconsin's legendary Knapp, Stout & Company, owned vacation land nearby. *Larry Easton Collection.*

(Above) Winter, at milepost 45.5 on the Park Falls line, was reached in 1904, where local passengers pose for a photographer named Smith. (Left) A pair of 4-4-0s arrive on a caboose hop at Yarnell, milepost 21. Engine No. 122 is an 1883 Rhode Island E-5 Class, while No. 55, behind, is an 1881 Baldwin D-5, sturdy power for daily log trains off the new road. Both: *Author's Collection.*

# Superior & South Eastern Railway

## Grand View - Clam Lake - Loretta

Shortly after the Omaha built through the White River Valley in Ashland County (in 1883), Minneapolitan Wesley Neill and associate Charles H. Pratt formed the Neill & Pratt Lumber Company. Their mill site was located at Pratt, near Grand View, 23 miles south of Ashland. Grand View displayed an excellent panorama of the White River Valley. The Neill & Pratt operation eventually gave way to John E. Glover's Willow River Lumber Company, originators of the Superior & South Eastern Railway, which built east and south into Glover's tracts beginning in 1903. The line spanned 25.17 miles, eventually reaching Clam Lake and Lake Namekagon. S&SE delivered its logs to the Omaha at Grand View and had a three-stall enginehouse located on the original Neill & Pratt mill site. Willow River's mill (and John Glover's home) were located at New Richmond,

125 miles south. Thus, Willow River was a good Omaha customer between 1900 and 1920.

Willow River Lumber Company sold out to Park Falls Lumber Company in 1920, one of many finally acquired by Edward Hines Lumber Company. Hines became a major lumber producer in the Omaha's territory after acquiring several older Wisconsin mills.

Loretta (named for Loretta Hines Clubine, Mr. Hines' sister) was a new company milltown located on Omaha's Park Falls Line, 20.2 miles west of the line's namesake town. With modern amenities for 600 loggers, S&SE and Loretta were planned for 20 years' logging, a prophesy nearly fulfilled. In 1922, S&SE was abandoned out of Grand View, and built from Loretta north to Clam Lake, thus turning the operation completely around. By 1925, Park Falls Lumber Company had

become Edward Hines Hemlock & Hardwood Company.

Superior & South Eastern finally had a fling at common carrier status, after filing application on November 4, 1927, to retain earnings from a 22 mile line south from Loretta, built in the interests of Hines Hemlock & Hardwood Company and the Hines Farmland Company. 8,600 people now lived in Sawyer County, and the farmland company proposed to develop the 160 square miles adjacent to the S&SE. A trackage rights agreement was arranged to furnish the common carrier condition aiding the hoped-for agribusiness. After the Great Depression, the S&SE and Loretta were forfeited. The railroad was abandoned in 1933-37, and the equipment scrapped at Loretta. The Hines company continued to log their land by motor truck, transferring the logs at convenient Omaha sidings.

The Superior & South Eastern met the Omaha at Grand View, on the Bayfield Line, and later at Loretta, milepost 54.7 on the Park Falls Line. The road acquired a unique stable of motive power including a couple of Lima-built rod engines and a few Shays, plus this 59 ton Mogul built by Davenport Locomotive Works, pictured along with crew members and Way Car No. 1. *H. Peddle Collection.*

tractor Palmer & Young of Minneapolis. A stream of officials from St. Paul, including Vice President J.T. Clark, came to advise and inspect in September, and pressure was applied to the extent that a second shift, working nights under electric lights, was put on the sink holes. Crews working from both ends were deployed to conquer four bad spots of great size, one of which was 600 feet long with water 15 feet deep. Pile driving and steam shoveling continued in a jungle-like scene into the fall. Lyman Town, just west of Park Falls, included another deep, long cut which required work by its own steam shovel. By November, steel was laid to Smith Creek, several miles out, and all hoped for completion by December.

Park Falls had expected the new railroad for a decade, and finally, in December 1913, the Omaha eased into the milltown. Passenger service was discussed, yet one final glitch was the marshy ground, which meant the new depot lacked a basement. Similar problems faced the construction of a two-stall enginehouse. Nonetheless, train service began just as contractor George J. Grant finished off the Omaha's buildings on April 1, 1914, with the westbound train leaving at 7:00 AM. At Park Falls, the flow of logs would continue unabated until the branch's demise. Now the city on the Flambeau River claimed two depots in use. The Omaha's depot, with its Flint brick platform, was serviceable for the next 50 years.

In 1911, Park Falls had about 2,000 residents and, by 1914, an impressive array of mills. Flambeau Paper Company, which remains in operation, evolved from the energetic pursuits of Neenah's Henry Sherry, who bought land around the waterfall on the Flambeau River in 1885. Sherry had several timber operations in Central Wisconsin before his move to the north country. By 1889, toward the close of pine logging in the old Wisconsin Central and Cornell lands, Sherry opened his first pulp mill in Park Falls and was responsible for the formation of Park Falls Lumber Company in the early 1890s. The paper company rose from Sherry's Park Falls Paper & Pulp Company, a parallel operation. With the 1890s depression pressing Sherry's varied operations, it was necessary to reorganize and, in 1899, Flambeau Paper Company rose beside the river.

Another prominent mill was Roddis Lumber & Veneer Company, just northeast of the Flambeau mill and another midstate immigrant. Roddis had its original plant in Marshfield, coming north in 1903. RL&VCo could cut 60,000,000 board feet per year, running its own railroad which grew to over 50 miles by 1938. Roddis lands were east of the river and, for a while, the road was a common carrier.

Both Omaha and parent C&NW made a business out of leasing rail to loggers in Wisconsin. An agreement was made in late 1914 to supply Atwood with 65 pound used rail for locations between Radisson and Park Falls. Yarnell received four switches and 1-1/2 miles of 65 pound steel and Summer Spur (near Winter), another 1-1/2 miles. In late 1915, Park Falls Lumber Company was planning a mainline south from Draper, just east of Loretta, utilizing leased rail.

The Arpin Company became involved with the Omaha in a rate case dated June 30, 1910. An extensive fire damaged trees in 1909 near the Omaha's line, and Arpin required a fast cutting operation to salvage the wood. Arpin's own Chippewa Valley &

Northern could not be extended quickly enough to transport the logs from the burn. The timber was instead cut and hauled to Radisson, which subjected the timber to a higher Omaha freight rate of five cents per hundred weight. The logs had to travel a roundabout way to arrive at Atlanta's Arpin mill. Evidently, Omaha's larger charge between Radisson and Birchwood took advantage of the difficulty. Arpin appealed, stating that Soo Line's rate between Birchwood and Bruce (via Rice Lake and Cameron) was 45 miles at $6 per car, against 22 miles at a higher Omaha rate. Soo Line took into account the "two-way haul," which seemed to prevail on logs and lumber. Hauling logs to a mill and finished lumber away from the same site allowed a lower rate, but 2/3 of the logs were hemlock for Arpin, with a balance in basswood and birch. The average carload was only 12,000 pounds and Omaha netted about 375 carloads. In the case of hemlock, the commission found that the Omaha was using an excessive rate, as the entire carload was worth only $32. The rate was reduced and a refund issued.

In November 1913, Robert H. Pritchard was the agent at Brill (mile 4.8). Pritchard was also a local merchant who met all trains, sold tickets and cared for the tiny two-room depot. He liked to work out of his store, which also acted as a railroad office.

Pritchard's methods were assailed by a Chicagoan who took the Omaha to task for damage sustained by a paint can, which traveled as Less-Than-Car-Load. These shipments had to be pre-paid and were billed to either Rice Lake or Birchwood; tiny Brill was not so endowed. The Chicagoan's paint can was the focus of the railroad commission's hearing on November 7. The Chicagoan claimed service was inadequate even for processing a damage claim. Pritchard's friends, well-satisfied with his services, rose to his support and confirmed that conditions were adequate, especially for a new railroad. Pritchard continued to serve the seven-building town in his informal way.

Superintendent C.D. Stockwell had problems with Omaha passenger service on the Park Falls Line. He noted a good many passengers arriving in Park Falls did so via the Soo Line from Chicago, declining Omaha/C&NW service to Rice Lake and easterly on the new branch. He recommended the regular Rice Lake to Park Falls trains in 1914 be scheduled in the morning to compete. He had in mind a connection with Train 98, the westbound *Twilight Limited*. Omaha found itself a full 24 hours behind Soo Line service to Park Falls, having at first a mixed train competing with full-passenger trains. Company officials were certain Omaha could acquire more business.

The nearby Rice Lake Commercial Club agreed. Among others, Orrin H. Ingram Jr., held a club membership. As the son of the pioneer lumber baron, he had a summer home nearby. Ingram and others considered Omaha's Park Falls passenger accommodation largely a joking matter. The Commercial Club concluded Train 242 should leave Rice Lake upon arrival of the premier morning express, Train 96, operating Eau Claire-Duluth. During the summer of 1915, Train 244 left Rice Lake at 8:30 AM, then put in up to 9-1/2 hours traveling to Park Falls.

Stockwell also suggested making a connection at Tuscobia with eastbound Train 91, the *Day Express*, which would transfer its summer-only passengers at the tiny junction station. Mixed Trains 243-244 employed a coach and a combination car, but the full coach was removed in 1915. Consensus among Park Falls patrons was that summer freight operations could be cut to three days per week. Most of the logs moved in the winter, allowing the Omaha to concentrate on the passenger business in summer.

Park Falls Lumber Company's (later Hines) W.B. Clubine agreed. Clubine's company was cited as being able to do their own switching, part of which the Omaha had performed with its initial mixed train. Omaha then introduced extras, such as the *New Dells Log Train*, which would run through and handle loads from Park Falls. The business in the fall and winter was filled with the needs of smaller contract loggers, for whom the number of flat cars was inadequate. The limited flat car supply required prompt movement to and from destinations, an absorbing game in the early days of the Park Falls Line.

Another problem was the lone passenger out of Lemington, a station on a very heavy grade. In November of 1918, Mr. Pechin wrote to Stockwell about Train 243, its scheduled stop and the resultant delays. The Lemingtonite rode only to Birchwood (a 12 cent fare), but considerable effort was expended starting a heavy train on the Lemington Hill. When filled out, Train 243 often had to back up about one-half mile, its overtaxed 4-4-0 requiring extra space to make a run for the hill. With some subtle encouragement, Lemington's lone rider soon made other arrangements.

A year previously, Omaha was required to build an interchange at Lemington with Soo Line's newer (1909) Owen-Duluth line. Several logging firms wanted to transfer carloads to the competing Soo from Omaha's sidings. The originating carrier understandably opposed the commission's ruling, as it stood to lose ton-miles. The Park Falls Line passed 26 feet above the Soo, and the new interchange would cost around $30,000. The commission order required Soo to bear 75% of costs, and Omaha the balance. Menasha Woodenware, Fountain-Campbell, Menasha Paper Company, and Arpin Veneer were interested in moving logs 25 miles south to Ladysmith, the center of their operations. The transfer would cut one day's time plus 43 miles from the movement. The Omaha's underlying problem was rate arrangement for the offered traffic. Soo Line had a low cost answer, while Omaha kept to a lumber rate.

Still another party joined the demand for the Lemington interchange, adding interest in restoring Wooddale after Ahnapee Seating & Veneer Company's need lapsed and the siding was removed. Omaha didn't want another station between Birchwood and Lemington, but events conspired in 1918 to create a Wooddale siding, complete with box car station. The company began to rebuild Wooddale, but was halted by the United States Railroad Administration. Omaha settled with its tormentors, and continued to make the Lemington stop for mixed Trains 243-244. With but two stores at Lemington, business wasn't heavy.

Wisconsin Colonization Company was still active at trackside, offering the old Arpin lands to settlers. 8,500 acres were available on the old Chippewa Valley & Northern, north of Bruce. WCCo offered its leading agrarians a $30 prize for the largest cleared farm. Radissonian Tom Kidrowski won, Omaha's Industrial Commissioner serving as a judge.

Park Falls' passenger service remained adequate from 1914 through 1926, when the mixed train and the day passenger local ruled the timetable. In late October 1926, Omaha published a notice to discontinue the day run in favor of mixed-only accommodation. New Train 245 was scheduled to leave Rice Lake at 9:00 AM and arrive at Park Falls at 5:15 PM. The mail would be covered by an RPO clerk as far east as Couderay, with closed pouch delivery prevailing for the remaining miles to Park Falls. A hearing was held November 5, 1926, which disclosed that Trains 241-242, inaugurated in 1914, were no longer covering expenses. In 1918, during USRA days, the trains were removed for fuel economy reasons, but Rice Lake's businessmen opposed the wartime measure, citing the loss an inconvenience. The railroad commission directed resumption by January 1918, noting that business could be transacted in Park Falls from Rice Lake in a single day, a weighty consideration. Aroused in 1917, Rice Lakers alleged a great inconvenience was again confronting them.

The commission observed the territory was largely in cutover land, but some thriving communities and lake resorts were developed on line. Hospitals were found only at Rice Lake and Park Falls, and serious injuries would face a mixed train ride to medical aid. The commission found for continuation of service, suggesting the use of gas-motor propelled equipment, where 40 cent train-mile costs were promised over 50 cent steam train-miles. Further hearings followed Omaha's application for discontinuance in the spring of 1927, showed earnings of only $8,000 for the summer of 1927.

The call for gas-electrics didn't go unheeded on the Omaha. Parent C&NW was well into this program by 1927, forswearing a substantial investment in reboilered 4-4-0s and 4-6-0s created for similar work in the early 1920s. The North Western first acquired St. Louis, and finally Pullman-built doodlebugs, which edged out more expensive ways of handling mail and express, the real money-maker for branchlines. Omaha would finally field a small fleet of high-horsepower gas-electrics.

General Superintendent F.R. Pechin directed his Eastern Division staffers to report their findings for the ideal gas-electric to be used in the north country, and what the carbody design would have to be. Pechin observed the company was considering gas-electrics for Trains 7-8 between Omaha and Emerson, Nebraska, plus Ashland-Bayfield use, and also for the Park Falls Line. Discussions previously had considered a motor car from April to November on the Park Falls Line, with proper mail-bag-gage-passenger space. November to April would necessitate a heavier steam train, while the reverse was true for the Ashland-Bayfield run. Bayfield had heavy fish shipments by express in the summer, requiring a trailer for the motor car, or steam substitution. H.P. Congdon noted the Northern Pacific Brill-built car No. B-17 was operating between Duluth and Ashland, and considered it ideal. The final solution would not include a Brill entry, but one considerably more powerful.

Omaha continued their gas-electric study, which included prospective operations on the Ellsworth and Stillwater branches on the Eastern Division. On May 30, 1928, Pullman delivered two 275 HP cars. They were 52 ton designs without Railway Post Office space, which had dissimilar floor plans, thus setting a trend for future cars. By delivery time, Omaha had brought mixed train service to the Ellsworth line and eliminated the need for a doodlebug. One of the new cars (Nos. 2000-2001) began regular operation from Minneapolis to Fairmont, Minnesota, while the near

(Above) The end of track at Park Falls is shown with the depot at left behind the box cars. Also shown is the two stall enginehouse. Service to Park Falls began April 1, 1914. *Author's Collection.* (Left) The line reached Kaiser at mile 69.7 in 1910. The John H. Kaiser Lumber Company started operations there in 1906. The "portable depot" was probably an old box car body, or a specially built unit, capable of shipment on a flat car. Local pick-up-and-delivery service was provided by a 2 HP snow buggy. *Price County Historical Society.* (Below) Radisson was MP 34.6 on the branch. In its early days, the mixed train stopped for straw-hatted drummers or land speculators after the road reached the town in 1902. The name came from an early French explorer of Wisconsin. *Author's Collection.*

twin was put on between Worthington, Minnesota, and Mitchell, South Dakota. The Mitchell car was tested a few days earlier between Worthington and Sioux City. In both western operations, trailer cars were used.

Two years later, on August 1, 1929, and just weeks before the Great Depression changed everything, a new 600 HP gas-electric made a special test trip from Hudson to Spooner. It was No. 2004, a burly 92 ton dual-engined, four-traction motor machine drawing two coaches. Omaha had expected its cars to be operational by this date, but it took much longer. No. 2004 went into Park Falls service the second week of August, with Engineer Thomas Shudi. Park Falls was certain that the steam train was history, but it was not so.

Conditions in December 1932 would bring the end of pure passenger service on the line. The lumber trade was dormant, with no prospect of revival for the time being. Hearings were again held in Rice Lake and Radisson into early 1933, establishing losses for Trains 243-244. The commission showed that gas-electrics reduced costs, but didn't bring in enough revenue. Logging lines were quickly folding and their Shays were cut up on weedy sidings. Omaha hoped passengers would return with prosperity, but gross earnings of 1932 were one-quarter of the 1929 figure. The Commission granted the discontinuance, scheduled for May 1, 1933.

Branch way freights 245-246 finally became the one and only Park Falls conveyance, a tri-weekly affair. Mail handling continued, linked with mainline Train 503 at Rice Lake, but only one clerk worked as far east as Winter. It was something of a concession to good customers, such as Park Falls Lumber Company which was an asset in Omaha's solicitation of business.

Despite their competition at Park Falls, Soo Line and Omaha considered joint terminal facilities. Omaha admitted to the lack of electric lights in its depot, plus inferior engine service equipment, and the Omaha used a quaint and dangerous air operated coaling station for its I-1 and K-1 4-6-0s, which lasted until the end. The Omaha handled its "lake coal" (eastern bituminous brought to Superior by lakers) in manually tripped buckets. Economics also dictated the use of Spooner as the western terminal where the combination car could be serviced or changed. Mileage expanded to 104.7 miles, but despite the greater distance, the Omaha netted only 118 carloads per month.

Back in the winter of 1927, the complex details of the branch's workload showed a series of log extras, responsible for placing carloads of logs on Hines' landings at Park Falls. The first went to work in the evening, often with power from the mixed train. One extra crew started from Spooner on Mondays, while another would leave the Rice Lake terminal, running ahead of Train 245, to turn at Loretta and pick-up loaded log cars. There were often cars billed at remote places like Crooked Rapids and Delco. A feeder was an Altoona-Rice Lake extra that brought empties back to the woods.

A "First Extra" left at 7:00 AM from Park Falls, taking empties to Loretta, Crooked Rapids and Couderay, picking up loads at each location. The extra usually worked only one train, but if tonnage dictated, it had to "double Yarnell," a westbound one-percent grade three miles long. The Couderay station put out the orders for such activity. The extra tied-up at Rice Lake.

A "Second Extra" went out at 5:30 PM, with up to 27 empty flats, to Loretta and Crooked Rapids, taking loads from Oveland Spur for Birchwood. If the extra was short, it filled out with Rice Lake logs, again doubling from Couderay, and set out empties at Loretta. Crooked Rapids empties took precedence over Loretta's requirements. Just after 7:30 PM, the "Third Extra" drew an available engine and its long line of empties, and headed for Lemay's Spur. They were to turn there and take all loads and spot empties, leaving Rice Lake logs for the morning extra from Park Falls, and take in the Park Falls log loads. After setting out its loads on lumber company trackage, the third train crew tied-up. Still another pair of extras worked eastward from Rice Lake (the first started from Spooner on Monday mornings) taking Hines' flat cars to Crooked Rapids, whatever the mixed train left behind. In this intricate way, each logging operation was supplied daily with empty flats, their finished loads taken away from busy log jammers and creeping Shay-geared woods engines. It was nearly always 30 loads in motion toward either end of the line, or to Algoma Plywood & Veneer Company at Birchwood. Finally, the woods were no longer producing a return and began to decline by the late 1920s.

The two stall enginehouse at Park Falls held its branch power for all-too-short periods. Shopmen were hard-pressed to attend the big Ten-Wheelers in the short time at the eastern terminal, a concern to many. Spooner's trainmaster decreed the use of incoming power for part of the switch assignment, including extras and prospective relief. Crew assignment was another thorny issue, as few would stick to the extras because of remote layovers. The oldest extra conductor had to take the run according to rules, but experience showed that such men would lay off after a few days on duty. It was suggested that Rice Lake trains might better work out of Spooner, where more men were available. By March 1929, four of the extras were annulled for the summer, closing out the high-level of activity.

The two Hines mills were glutted with logs and unsold lumber in the Fall of 1932, as the Great Depression reached the forests. Without movement of wood, Hines faced default, and appealed for a better rate for access to Soo Line points. It was denied. While Hines had its problems, Omaha lost four unusual old box cars called "hog fuel cars." These were 11000-series cars with special ports for sawdust loading, a fuel for sawmill boilers. Leased to Hines at Loretta, and interchanged to Superior & South Eastern in late 1930, the quartet was lost to Omaha's car inventory. The matter was settled when they were found stored at Loretta well into 1933. Slow accounting finally had the cars sold to Hines for $150 each in mid-1936.

Log trains rolled occasionally throughout the 1930s, with but one extra crew assigned. Power would be the daily mixed train candidate, invariably an I-1 or K-1. This extra would take Hines' flat cars (actually leased from Omaha) from Park Falls to Loretta and Winter. In March 1940, the lease fleet was down to 50 cars, but, a year later, Hines needed 75 steel underframe flats to be supplied at the rate of 10 per day. Sent to Loretta for fitting of bunks and poles, the cars were invariably delivered late, some because of a September washout on the Ashland and Park Falls Lines. Others were busy with war work on the C&NW. By September, Hines had received only ten cars, but expected to log off some 25

(Above) Class F-2 4-6-0 No. 205 delivers a heavy train of logs to the mill at Couderay. *Author's Collection.* (Below) I-1 No. 316 has brought in a wrecker to cleanup a spill of log flats near Winter. Logs flowed off-and-on the branch at Couderay, 30 miles from Tuscobia, along the Couderay River. Today, no trace of Couderay's mill exists. *William O'Gara Collection.*

# Loggers and Industry Along the
# Park Falls Line

(Above) Henry Sherry's Flambeau Paper Company, shown in 1925, is still in operation along its namesake river in Park Falls. Sherry's pioneer operation dated from 1885. (Right) Sherry ran several Shay engines, including one of considerable age. This Shay is at Park Falls circa 1900. Both: *Price County Historical Society.*

(Below) J.H. Kaiser Lumber Company operated several Shays over spurs off the Omaha. Engine No. 1 is pictured at the town of Winter in 1909 with flat cars leased from the Omaha, a practice that continued throughout World War II. *Minnesota Historical Society.*

(Above) Roddis Lumber & Veneer Company was located northeast of the Flambeau mill at Park Falls. (Left) Roddis had its own extensive logging line with several small rod engines, including the low-drivered 2-6-2 No. 7, depicted in camp near Park Falls. (Below) Beginning in 1907, Atwood Manufacturing Company operated into 1913, when it was sold to Edward Hines. All: *Price County Historical Society*.

million board feet in 1941, to be loaded at Winter and Loretta. Hines increased their order to 125 cars to compensate. The 1942 requirements for Ojibwa, Winter, Loretta and Oveland Spur were 90 cars, a figure Omaha could not fulfill. Hines had to settle for 65 cars. Meanwhile, Algoma Plywood & Veneer Company at Birchwood reopened under local management, and would need log flats, too.

E.R. Gorman, Superintendent of Motive Power and Machines, wanted to eliminate saturated steam locomotives on his railroad, as did the C&NW. Gorman regularly assigned a "19 inch" switch engine to Rice Lake, an F-6 Class 0-6-0, to work the Hines mill. In 1936-38, Rice Lake hosted engine Nos. 14, 24 and 26 alternately, but Gorman's office wanted to substitute Park Falls road power. Power for Trains 245-246 was stabled in the mill town, idling for up to 15 hours, if on time. There was seldom a full eight hours workload for the 19 incher, but I-1 use would require track changes at the Rice Lake Hines mill, which, in turn, was a Soo Line responsibility. Gorman had five I-1/K-1s altered with footboards and backup headlights, and also had a 4-6-0 put on Trains 103-104, another Rice Lake termination. The use of road engines in yard service would cost an additional $10 per month in wages. One I-1 remained with its snow flanger intact, thereby being an inflexible non-switcher. The work was completed on December 15, 1939, just days before the January 1, 1940 deadline for saturated engines. All of the 4-6-0s were the newest, equipped with Walschaerts valve gear.

The arrangement was altered in September 1941, when the Operating Department requested J Class 2-8-2s for the Altoona-Rice Lake run, as train weight figures were reaching over 2,000 tons. Pressure was on to increase this amount, which stretched the I-1s to the limit. But the Altoona connection was the way Rice Lake power was routed for inspections, which compromised the plan. In the end, and for a while, the Js were withdrawn.

In 1937, Omaha cancelled a contract nearly as old as the Park Falls Line. Hines had signed a lease with Omaha for "track metal" in 1913, which was converted to a sale in 1929. Omaha chose to recover the value more completely. As the spurs with old Omaha rail were pulled out in the face of depression, north country logging went over to trucks, which continued to use the now-abandoned spur right-of-way. In the spring of 1938, however, signs of renewed passenger trade brought two wood smoker coaches out of storage, Nos. 73 and 84. They were cleaned up and brought to Rice Lake, but only car 73 was used, trailing behind the usual combination car, which lasted into the 1950s.

In wartime years, the Rice Lake terminal was vacated and Spooner became the home of Trains 245-246, which established the final form of service to Park Falls. Some of us had a chance to sample the nature of the rustic train, such as a short ride to Tuscobia from Spooner in the summer of 1953. In October 1955, five Milwaukee railfans rode the line, arriving via Soo Line on a frosty north country day. In both cases, long before regulations would prevent it, such a ride could be sampled via the express compartment. There was a reasonably clean I-1 leading a modest dozen freight cars and combine No. 443, which dispensed necessities to the appreciation of locals. It would soon end, but not before the first diesels supplanted the Ten-Wheelers, which fell like the leaves of the final autumn along the upper Chippewa. I-1 No. 102 made the circuit on April 11, 1956, then SW8 diesel No. 127 served for two months. EMD Geeps finally took over until the end on August 1, 1965.

An unusual day at Birchwood has I-2 Class 4-6-2 No. 387 rolling a lengthy passenger train on the Park Falls branch in the 1930s. The "extra" is possibly a vacation special or a CCC train of summer workers. *Sawyer County Historical Society.*

(Above) The humble junction with the Eau Claire-Twin Ports mainline was at Tuscobia, 19.7 miles south of Spooner. On November 25, 1955, I-1 No. 361 trundles across Highway 53 enroute to Park Falls, leaving the mainline to the left. *Marvin Nielson.* (Below) The steam era ended for the Park Falls Line on May 4, 1956, when the first diesel arrived to take over the mixed train. Omaha SW8 No. 127, an 800 HP EMD diesel, heads up the ten car local at Park Falls, with the combine bringing up the markers. *William F. Armstrong.*

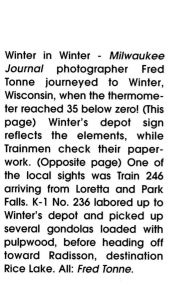

Winter in Winter - *Milwaukee Journal* photographer Fred Tonne journeyed to Winter, Wisconsin, when the thermometer reached 35 below zero! (This page) Winter's depot sign reflects the elements, while Trainmen check their paperwork. (Opposite page) One of the local sights was Train 246 arriving from Loretta and Park Falls. K-1 No. 236 labored up to Winter's depot and picked up several gondolas loaded with pulpwood, before heading off toward Radisson, destination Rice Lake. All: *Fred Tonne.*

Photographer Jim Scribbins and several other railfans were on hand to record the final autumn of steam on the Park Falls Line. (Above) On October 9, 1955, K-1 No. 184 makes up mixed Train 246 at Park Falls. (Right) The train pauses for business at Radisson, the mid-point on the branch. The depot's wooden platforms are gone, but otherwise, things haven't changed much from early times. (Below) The Ten-Wheeler does some switching at Brill, 4.8 miles from Tuscobia, the junction with the mainline. All: *Jim Scribbons.*

(Above) K-1 No. 184 gets its 7,500 gallon tender filled from the water tank at Couderay, about a mile west of Radisson. (Below) The tie-up for branch power at Spooner has K-1 No. 204, just in from Hudson, ahead of No. 184, power off Train 246. The two K-1s came from Alco in 1913, part of Omaha's last group of ten 4-6-0s delivered. The pair were retired in June 1956. Both: *Jim Scribbins*.

Omaha's Spring Valley branch began as the Woodville & Southern Railway, a faltering logger's shortline in the late 1880s. Junction with the Omaha was at Woodville, soon to be the site of extensive track relocations for the Omaha. W&S started with five miles of line to Wildwood, south of Woodville. By 1892, W&S became the Minnesota & Wisconsin Railway Company and built another ten miles north to Emerald, on Wisconsin Central's mainline..*Author's Collection.*

# 12.

# THE WESTON LINE: SPRING VALLEY AND EMERALD

The Omaha's Weston Line, which later by dint of natural catastrophes became the Spring Valley Line, began as a tramway in 1883 in the heyday of logging in St. Croix County. Several timber operators, including E.S. Austin, logged in the high country just west of adjacent Dunn County. Austin's St. Croix Land & Lumber Company employed at least one Shay locomotive, his mill located in Hersey on the Omaha mainline. He also considered other timber sites south of the Omaha, in the Eau Galle and Burkhardt valleys near present day Spring Valley. A neighboring logging road was the Cady Mills Railroad of D.C. Davis & Sons, which also stabled several Shays. Davis began in 1885, at the same time Austin founded his new milltown, appropriately named Wildwood, five miles south of Woodville. Austin's road evolved in the late 1880s into the Woodville & Southern Railway Company, in operation when iron ore was discovered nearby.

The find began with a location near Wilson, close to the Omaha's Eastern Division majestic climb to the county line. The iron field attracted investors, including Minnesota's Senator Dwight M. Sabin, also a Stillwater industrialist. Eau Claire's press claimed the mines were substantial enough to win an Omaha spur. The "Knapp Range" was reported to ship 30 to 70 tons of iron ore daily, at first, over the Omaha to the York Iron Furnace at Black River Falls.

The Woodville & Southern Railway was incorporated October 11, 1889, with five miles of shortline from Woodville to Wildwood. Another three miles led to an iron deposit near County Line, 2.9 miles north of Spring Valley. W&S struggled with little success until April 25, 1892, when Sabin, H.C. Truesdale and others acquired the roller coaster shortline, recapitalizing and renaming it Minnesota & Wisconsin Railway Company. W&S had surveyed and built a line ten miles northward from Woodville to Emerald, which was operational by early 1893. Its principle online customer was the Fleming sawmill just south of the Wisconsin Central connection in Emerald. The new extension opened a direct route to Milwaukee for the expected ore destined for Bay View Furnace on Jones Island. The new M&W installed an interlocking at Woodville in 1892 to cross Omaha's original mainline during the years of the old mainline location. M&W had at least two engines, both 4-4-0s, Nos. 4 and 5. Number 4 was ex-Northern Pacific built in 1872. No. 5 was a Mason product.

In 1890, lumbering in St. Croix County was waning, and with its demise, E.S. Austin left the scene. His village of Wildwood died out in 1897. Spring Valley blossomed around the new Eagle Iron Company furnace, the roaring, vibrant brainchild of Chicagoan S. Frank Eagle, who expended $150,000 on the project. Eagle's operation had a capacity of 100 tons of pig iron daily and employed several hundred men. The company claimed sever-

al surface pits located in a narrow glen just west of Spring Valley, and the railroad brought ore loads down a dangerous three mile 2.32 percent grade to the new furnace. The Omaha chose to acquire M&W in light of the new furnace.

M&W suffered foreclosure July 15, 1896, to the St. Paul Title Insurance Company and, on December 1, 1896, the road was conveyed to the last of the shortline companies, Minnesota & Wisconsin Railroad Company. The Omaha purchased the final form on June 7, 1902, after operating the road the previous year., thus accruing 20.08 miles, Emerald to Spring Valley.

The Omaha encountered some unusual problems in acquiring the steeply-graded M&W, which cost $450,000. Unfortunately, Spring Valley's furnace was seldom in operation in the lean 1890s. Chippewa Falls' press considered the shortline well off and still profitable despite spotty iron production. Its chief product in the spring of 1901 was considerable slag ballast directed toward Omaha maintenance work.

M&W had six dilapidated ore cars, little more than wood gondolas, in need of repair. Superintendent W.C. Winter ordered the units renovated as he had no substitutes, and they went off to Hudson in pairs. At first the authorities didn't want them lettered for Omaha as M&W was not formally integrated. In time, all received automatic couplers with updated air brake equipment and on-roster qualifications.

An arrangement was made to move Spring Valley slag at 13.8 cents per ton for use as branchline ballast. M&W used nine special brick-topped flat cars, devoid of paint and lettering, that could withstand the scorching loads. They were only 20 ton capacity, requiring quick turnaround. Finally, Omaha's own Rodger ballast cars were used, the slag heaved over by "sons of toil" at $1.75 per day. The slag scene included below-zero shoveling, while cars caught fire and frozen fire hoses burst.

Construction to Weston was at the behest of Eau Claire lumberman William J. Starr, owner of 14,000 acres of Eau Galle regional timberland. The only practical way into Starr's holdings was via the Spring Valley-Elmwood route, susceptible to frequent washouts along a seven mile canyon-like stretch. At the same time, Green Bay & St. Paul Railroad, brainchild of Green Bay & Western, surveyed a link toward St. Paul, probably entering the same narrow valley. For W. J. Starr, however, his hardwood required an outlet and he prevailed upon the Omaha, which received an operating headache with the extension. Locals had it also extended southward to Durand on the Chippewa, but Weston was the end until April 1934.

Weston was reached by the Omaha in mid-1902, after pausing at Comfort the previous winter. Both were loading sites for logs and candidates for further settlement. The first year's service was marred by the departure of the Weston train, which left a patron on the Spring Valley platform. It was necessary return 16 miles for the lone passenger or face the state railroad commission.

In its last days, M&W struggled with the hand-me-down equipment, especially the two engines that faced the steep hills out of the Eau Galle. The car roster of ten flats, six ore cars, one caboose and a combination car were added to the Omaha lists. Master Car Builder J.W. Muncy chose to renumber the combination car to 419 after it was equipped with automatic couplers. It was then cautiously restricted to branchline duty. A.W. Trenholm also authorized the M&W engines to receive Nos. 203-204, but only after the link-pin couplers were replaced.

Branchline operation required some fine-tuning in 1903. Several stations were relocated to favor level spots between the short, steep ramp-like knobs on the line. Doubling sidings, the mark of a true 4-4-0 powered branch, were altered to provide better station halts for the daily mixed trains. Brookville and Wildwood spurs were abandoned in favor of a level doubling siding a half-mile south. Previous to this, trains had to back up nearly 1-1/2 miles to overcome the southbound hill, a grade of well over one percent near Brookville.

Dangerous conditions were soon to bring on a grim accident that year. A regular northbound mixed train stalled near County Line. The last three cars had to be cut off, including the combine. While the head end was taken to safety, the air leaked off the rear

end which rolled back down the steep hill toward Spring Valley. Leading the runaway, the combine bore the brunt of a collision with a standing work extra, killing one and injuring four.

Omaha's roadmaster removed Wildwood spur and moved the materials one-third mile north. The new Wildwood siding held just eight cars and was barely 350 feet long. A platform was installed 2,000 feet south of the old County Line station. It was an informal time that served the occasional rural passenger of the daily mixed. Wildwood, County Line and Brookville survived until WWI, then vanished. Some agriculture was served in the area, especially around Wildwood, in an era of sugar beet production. After the runaway accident, a new County Line siding allowed the mixed train to stop its combination car in relative safety, 200 feet from the hill's crown. It continued as a doubling spur until larger engines ended the practice.

The iron furnace property was reorganized as Spring Valley Iron & Ore Company by 1901, but its fortunes were minimal. Omaha officials were concerned about slag production. Emulating C&NW, Omaha utilized self-clearing gondolas with drop bottom doors, that had been employed at a North Chicago rolling mill, an innovation over hand-spread methods. Ballast accounted for the majority of Spring Valley carloadings.

Omaha spent considerable time trying to get the iron company to remove its ore washer plant bins, which leaned ever closer to fouling the branchline. Line relocation was impractical since the trackage was in a cut feeding into a reverse curve. As it stood, coach steps ran too close to rocky outcrops even after sectionmen had thrown the ties out to the maximum. M&W's extension to the furnace was initially an industrial spur, and the original iron company wasn't concerned with standard railroad practice. Still, the bins continued to sag for years, while the none-too-prosperous iron firm refused to placate the railroad. By 1909, no one was present at the works to decide the decaying wash plant's fate. Owner, Frederick H. Foote, by then a Sarasota, Florida, resident, continued to hold the Omaha at bay, stating that washer removal would cripple his investment. Roadmaster E.C. Blundell was highly concerned, and finally, by 1917, the obstruction was removed.

(Above) Early hardwood logging activity by Starr Lumber Company utilizing Omaha flat cars at Weston (note the depot in background). *Mrs. Loretta Brown.*

(Right) In 1902, the Omaha built to Weston, 26.5 miles southwest of Woodville, to load hardwood timber and to create a townsite. Most of the settlement burned in 1921 and the railroad abandoned the line in 1934. *Author's Collection.*

(Above) Iron ore was a prime target for the Stillwater-based investors of the fledgling Minnesota & Wisconsin Railway. A promising customer was the Spring Valley Iron & Ore Company, located in the village of Spring Valley, 10.4 miles south of Woodville. The furnace had spotty success in the 1890s.

(Left) The ore washing plant bins later decayed, threatening the branchline before being removed in 1917. Both: *Doug Blegan Collection.*

Omaha's D-5 Class 4-4-0 No. 58 pauses in front of the iron works with special slag cars alongside the furnace. The rectangular tower still survives. *William O'Gara Collection.*

243

In 1907, Omaha turned its attention to Wildwood when a complaint reached the railroad commission regarding service. Some 36 residents in the adjacent territory stressed that trains were usually late and station facilities were nearly nonexistent. The eight passenger trains per day were well patronized by locals, and all pressed for a suitable depot midway between Woodville and Spring Valley. By the eve of World War I, Wildwood arose briefly as a livestock shipper, recording 63 outbound cars in 1916. It had a small depot and platform plus a siding, but it still had 1.7 percent grades in either direction. Worse, northbound trains worked into a 2.92 percent hill shortly after. Such heady business activity required a stock pen, but in 1934, Wildwood's idle station was surplus and sold off. The agent was asked about facilities at the lonely place and replied nothing was left, and no one would ever know there had ever been a place called Wildwood.

William Starr's mill continued to operate at Weston until its closing in 1910, but initial business was heavy enough for Starr to request another siding to his property. Local agent W.E. Boe had but one customer, and Starr was accommodated. Starr's cord and slabwood by-products sought markets in larger towns for fuel and were shipped out of Weston in quantity. Starr's cuttings reached as far as Rock Spur, mid-point on the Elmwood-Spring Valley section, but this ended all too soon.

Telegraphers at Weston received $77.50 per month after December 15, 1907, with hours from 6:00 AM to 4:00 PM, a 13 hour day. Worse, when mixed Train 33 arrived between 8:45 and 9:15 PM, it was still the responsibility of the agent until excused by the train dispatcher. He did, however, have Sunday off.

Weston's rise as a terminal required a single stall enginehouse, turntable, coach washing facilities and extra trackage. Secondhand materials were used for improvements as costs grew excessive. An ashpit built of 56 and 65 pound rail and old "I-beams" was cancelled in favor of scrap iron plates. The enginehouse was 82 feet long and originally had a 56 foot wood turntable. It was eventually replaced by an iron American Bridge Company table. On January 21, 1917, an enginehouse fire wiped out the building

and severely damaged E-4 Class 4-6-0 No. 95. Superintendent Pechin instructed the engineering staff to take down the unused New Richmond enginehouse, and reconstruct it at Weston.

Mainline changes were also made at Woodville. The junction town received a 56 foot turntable, one of two New Jersey Steel & Iron Company tables in the company's inventory. It was located southwest of the old wooden depot, now cut off from the mainline. Emerald-bound movements no longer crossed a busy mainline, but edged through switchwork, which replaced the diamond of M&W days. Mixed Trains 32-33 trotted off northward to Emerald Monday-Wednesday-Friday by 7:30 AM, returning from the Soo Line connection by 8:25 AM. In the 1920s, Trains 32-33 were actually an extension of Train 30, which left Weston at 4:40 AM, one of three northbound off the branch. Trains 35-36 turned at Spring Valley and headed back to Woodville.

Weston's luck gave out with a fire in the summer of 1920, which hastened a downturn in traffic. The fire deprived Omaha crews of acceptable living quarters. Both railroad and town people requested schedule changes, which would tie-up crews in more cosmopolitan Elmwood. The noon train would make a Weston turn from Elmwood to accommodate sparse trade. The people at Elmwood contributed 80 signatures, but, as it was, Train 30 averaged less than one passenger per day, sometimes going for weeks without any passengers at all, handling only the mail pouch. Conductor Keyser and his brakeman lived at Spring Valley, but slept in the combine at Weston overnight to be up at 4:40 AM. They idled over Sundays in the same fashion.

Throughout the 1920s, Elmwood worked to secure the railroad's terminal. Free land was offered and highway improvements had enhanced the region. Pechin explained, by letter, the difficulties and costs hidden in the move. Cited was the $14,700 cost of moving a turntable from Omaha to Oakland, Nebraska. He deemed it prohibitively expensive. It was also shown that very little traffic was coming from Weston.

The end for the Emerald Line came in the fall of 1929. The state railroad commission announced a hearing would not be held

Destruction by flash floods was frequent at Spring Valley. The April 1934 waters snipped off the Weston segment. This 1942 view at Spring Valley shows run-off damage that cut the line at the town's south end. *Doug Blegan Collection.*

since there were no objections to abandonment. The 9.59 mile line had Monday-only service, which soon ended without much fanfare. Gone with it was the dream of the Prairie Farm & South Western, graded in the teens toward an Omaha connection at Emerald. Its vacant embankment remains in pastureland north of Emerald to this day. PF&SW would have utilized miles of the old Glenwood Manufacturing Company logging line, owner of old West Wisconsin 4-4-0 No. 11.

In the wake of the Great Depression, Omaha chose to end service to Weston. Hearings were requested to discontinue Trains 30-31, while Spring Valley's old charcoal kilns, unused and still on Omaha land in 1925, were now dangerous ruins. Leftover slag remained on the property and Omaha had to remove the waste material. Tracks were finally removed decades after the last iron went out of Spring Valley.

Closure of Weston station came after the railroad commission was petitioned in the fall of 1931, the hearing held at Weston on September 24. Trains 33-34 still ran, but the village's sole industry, lumber, was all but gone. The 1929 earnings were $6,000, falling to $3,600 in 1930. Locals realized the railroad's plight and settled for a depot custodian in lieu of an agent, selected from the train crew. The future of the branch looked bleak.

Heavy rains followed 1934's Easter snowstorm, bringing raging streams in western Wisconsin. Two miles south of Elmwood, the rains took out Bridge E-115, severing the line and settling the future of Weston's terminal. Replacement cost was $7,500. 9.2 miles of track were removed, while the 1934 public timetable only deleted the scheduled arrival times at Comfort and Weston. Earnings by 1934 dropped to half of 1929's, and the traffic department saw no objections to abandonment. Ironically, Weston's W.E. Boe, entrepreneur and former Omaha agent, had a carload ready for Minnesota and inquired about service resumption. Boe and others were kept in suspense until the branch abandonment application was received May 9, 1934. The end of track would thereafter be 800 feet beyond Elmwood's final switch. Omaha's survey of business uncovered that only three cars moved into Weston in 1934.

There were several bids to remove the line, plus one isolated gondola at each station. Escanaba's Harry P. Bourke, a colorful remover of many north country railroads, wanted to combine the Weston abandonment with his Stanley, Merrill & Phillips contract in August 1935. Locals also bid, but Foley Brothers of Minneapolis signed to remove the Weston segment, including all buildings, in the spring of 1935. President Carl R. Gray Jr., suggested 4-4-0 No. 136 be used over a temporary bridge, as the engine weighed only 45 tons. The E-6 would not exceed 5 MPH on the structure. Nothing on line was to be left behind. Surplus ties went to Worthington, Minnesota, while the turntable was billed to Altoona via condemned flat cars. Foley Brothers was billed for 91,600 pounds of coal for No. 136, as it was operated for them. The engine was run out of East St. Paul to Elmwood on April 25, 1935, returning May 13, by double-heading with Train 34, the regular Elmwood mixed.

The Eau Galle's runoff continued to damage the line to Elmwood every few years. On September 17, 1942, a flash flood tore out most of the trackage between Elmwood and Spring Valley, and Omaha petitioned for the line's abandonment. Previously, there had been a survey for a new flood-free route to Elmwood, but due to high cost, it was never built. Several improvements had been scheduled for Elmwood, but these were cancelled by the fearsome waters.

After several bouts with floodwaters, the Spring Valley Line settled into a wary coexistence with the Eau Galle River. Business was more modest now than with iron or lumber, typical of Wisconsin small towns. The U.S. Army Corps of Engineers created a large dam to control the damage after the 1942 flood, but too late to save the Elmwood section. Power on the mixed trains graduated from F-2 Class 4-6-0s to I-1s and K-1s, which began to show up after 1931. Mixed train service continued as Trains 33-34, although operations began at Menomonie as Trains 32-33 and returned as Trains 34-35. Dieselization began in the 1950s, with SW1 No. 55, the pioneer of the Ellsworth Line. Spring Valley service ended in October 1965, with an aging GP9 as power.

Engine 58 anchors a pile driver for rebuilding work on bridge No. 18. Due to flash floods in the narrow canyon below Spring Valley, this type of work was frequently required. *State Historical Society of Wisconsin.*

(Above) Elmwood was just seven miles from Spring Valley and 17.4 miles from Woodville. The depot is shown in 1908. *Author's Collection.*

(Right) Power on the Weston Line prior to World War I was often E-4 Class 4-6-0 No. 95. On January 21, 1917, the engine sustained fire damage when the single-stall enginehouse at Weston burned. The 1885 Schenectady product was rebuilt and ran ten more years before being scrapped in 1927. *Author's Collection.*

(Below) Stock day at Elmwood brings out engine No. 95 around 1922, a few years after rebuilding. *Lou and John Russell.*

(Above) Business at Elmwood came from agricultural areas nearby. There was also livestock in season to fill Omaha's stock cars. *Lou and John Russell.* (Below) Weston branch power at one time included E-6 4-4-0 No. 128, shown at the south edge of Woodville in the summer of 1922. Photographer Adams was en route from Fairchild to the Pacific Northwest and had several minutes in between trains to take pictures. Train 507 arrived five minutes before branchline Train 35 departed. The 1886 Schenectady product was sold to Fairchild & North Eastern in December 1927, a road built by Adam's relative, Nathaniel C. Foster. *J. Foster Adams.*

This scene from the early 1950s has K-1 4-6-0 No. 203 switching at
Cornell on the Hannibal branch. The depot is in the background.
*A. Robert Johnson.*

# 13.

# TO HANNIBAL AND HUGHEY

From Wisconsin's rural Chippewa and Taylor Counties, a substantial railroad fill is traceable east of the Chippewa River town of Holcombe. The surrounding land is flat and desolate, with scarcely any serious agriculture. At the fill's end, on the bank of the Yellow River, lies Hughey, only a location today, devoid of structures and 48 lonely miles from Chippewa Falls. Hannibal is four miles to Hughey's west, a decaying village, but once host to two railroads in search of suitable hardwood.

In 1890, the Chippewa Valley log shed produced nearly a quarter of Wisconsin's pine, but it was near the end of softwood production. Much of the land was barren cutover by the end of the century, its owners gearing up for sales to north country newcomers. Knapp, Stout & Company, for example, fielded a land-selling arm, which disposed of surplus acres in nearby Barron County. Keen on selling its lands, Chippewa Valley Colonization Company canvassed for desirable citizens to take the available turf. North Wisconsin was billed as "rich in lands fit to make any settler an independent, respectable yeoman."

Railroads returned briefly to the once-exalted role of the "Great Civilizer." At the time, the Omaha was allegedly opening up 400,000 acres, much of it at $15-$30 per acre. In that time, Chippewa speculator S.C.F. Cobban sold nearly 600 acres in the town of Anson to a Madisonian. Land sold well for several years in the Chippewa Valley at the time of the new settlement lines. The development of the Jim Falls and Brunet Falls townsites would bring industrial possibilities to the district.

Omaha's construction company, the Eau Claire, Chippewa Falls & Northeastern Railway, was incorporated January 15, 1902, to build to Little Falls (later, Holcombe), on the Chippewa River, 26 miles to the northeast. Officers were W.A. Scott, President, James T. Clark, Vice-President, plus others of the Omaha's staff. Capital stock was $50,000, with $35,000 issued to the Omaha Road as a partial payment for construction advances, cancelled upon sale to the Omaha.

Eau Claire attorney T.F. Frawley headed a land company to work closely with ECCF&NE during right-of-way acquisition. Surveys were made along both banks of the Chippewa River to Cornell as quietly as possible, but soon local newspapers were speculating on its destination. Rib Lake, Ladysmith and even Lake Superior points were serious contenders for the line's end. Frawley had his own ambitions to reach the Yellow River. His firm was one of many hustling to sell land in advance of the new railroad. By spring 1902, Dells Pulp & Paper Company purchased the Jim Falls water power site, unveiling the railroad's purpose. It would serve and be served by new dams, which would power

wood product manufacturing and bring hydro-electric power to the region.

The background for railroad advancement up the Chippewa River traces to lands owned by Cornell University, Ithaca, New York. Forty-five years before ECCF&NE, Ezra Cornell planned a 2,000 acre townsite at Brunet Falls, during the heyday of townsite speculation. By 1902, Cornell University saw fit to sell its Wisconsin landholdings, and Eau Claire interests incorporated Cornell Land & Power Company to acquire the site. CL&P sent a representative to Ithaca ahead of competitors to close the sale. In time, negotiations for the Jim Falls location bowed to the founding of Brunet Falls Manufacturing Company, 11 miles upstream.

Grading for the ECCF&NE began in the spring of 1902, and followed the eastern bank to Cornell. It was observed a more specific destination would be a junction with the Wisconsin Central, four miles north of Medford. When completed to Hughey, Yellow River Lumber Company's landing on the Yellow River, and after a line change in January 1917, the branch measured 48 miles. Beyond the Hughey log landing, right-of-way was acquired for 18.3 miles, "bought and held, but (with) no track ever laid." The region east of the Yellow River was swampy lowland, posing difficulties for contractor Winston Brothers of St. Paul. Visible today, the near-used route would have met WC near Whittlesey, possibly to compete for logs in the latter's territory.

Tracklaying in summer 1902 was an all-out affair, with 2,000 men arriving from Chicago and Duluth. Then, as now, the land northeast of Cornell was only beginning to be occupied. Southward, the first hamlets, Cobban, Anson, Jim Falls and Brunet came into being. The Winston Brothers crew finished grading by August without a bridge over the Yellow River. Soon enough, Yellow River Lumber Company operators at Hughey began to round up logs with a sternwheeler above the present site of Miller Dam. While the first rails went down, immigrants came to the sawmill towns east of Holcombe. Today, these short-lived towns no longer exist.

The ECCF&NE's first autumn brought trouble to the original bridge at Anson, five miles out of Chippewa Falls. Heavy rains caused a log jam, damaging the new structure. At the same time, D.R. Davis of Jim Falls speculation offered a premium to the first couple married there, as lots were selling briskly. The Omaha fielded its first excursion to Jim Falls on a Sunday afternoon in mid-October. About one thousand rode to the Falls, where the day's entertainment was open bidding on Davis' lands. The ECCF&NE was completed to Hughey in 1903, considered a temporary end for the new line. During the previous winter, local businessmen met with Omaha's J.T. Clark in St. Paul over the requested Ladysmith extension, which would have left the new road at recently renamed Holcombe. Rails to Sillhawn (later, Arnold), 33 miles into the new country, were spiked in August after heavy rains and rail shortages delayed progress. A revival of interest in crossing the Yellow River brought about a plan for a 400 foot bridge. The promise included materials to be in place by fall. Expenditures to date totalled $50,000 for surveying and grading. It was recorded that Medford was not interested in Omaha service, possibly the voice of Wisconsin Central interests.

The building of ECCF&NE constituted a race with shortline logger/common carrier, Stanley, Merrill & Phillips Railway, a protege of the big North Western Lumber Company operation at Stanley, east of Chippewa Falls on the Wisconsin Central mainline. NWLCo began in 1873, with a large mill just south of Eau Claire on the Chippewa River, developed from Porter & Moon's mill (Porter's Mills). D.R. Moon, G.E. Porter and S.T. McKnight of NWLCo were affiliated with Weyerhauser's "down-river" millmen. The town of Stanley was platted in 1881, with a large stand of timber stretching northward for 40 miles, some of which was purchased from Cornell University. It was into this same stand that ECCF&NE built in 1903, in a dead heat with the Stanley shortline. SM&P was chartered August 19, 1893, aiming for Merrill and Phillips with 150 miles of projected track.

After this lofty aim, SM&P's goal was more modest. An inevitable crossing of SM&P and ECCF&NE materialized at Hannibal, a 19th century lumber distribution center named for the Missouri town on the Mississippi River. McKnight and other officers also staffed the SM&P, shortly reorganizing the 30 mile line to common carrier status. The two roads, along with John S. Owen Lumber Company, of Owen, Wisconsin, made an agreement regarding joint depot maintenance at Hannibal, which continued to the end of the SM&P. Owen, SM&P and Omaha log trains operated on common trackage, especially along the Yellow River. SM&P ultimately reached Jump River in 1906, possessing 48.97 miles of mainline laid with 60 pound rail.

SM&P had eight locomotives and over time averaged two passenger cars, most of which came from Hicks Locomotive & Car Works of Chicago. The new depot at Hannibal, an Omaha design, conducted an impressive passenger trade whose questionable highlight came with SM&P's short-lived Fairbanks-Morse-Sheffield Model 24 gasoline motor car. This economic solution to light patronage succumbed to an engine fire within two years of inauguration. Before North Western Lumber Company sawed its last log at Stanley on September 14, 1920, SM&P had operated under United States Railroad Administration control, sustaining losses for the year 1918. SM&P petitioned for abandonment on August 8, 1924, after several years of dormancy. Further operations were requested by the John S. Owen Lumber Company and this was done via a contract with Soo Line, which operated the line from Gilman to Jump River (Walrath). The Stanley-Gilman section was removed concurrently. Soo Line averaged 29 log loads per trip in the mid-1920s, making two or three trips weekly by the 1930s, turning cars over to Owen-bound way freights at Gilman. After April 16, 1933, when Soo Line's ten year lease expired, SM&P collected rust. Track was removed in the fall of 1934 by contractor H.P. Bourke of Escanaba, Michigan.

Arnold, formerly Omaha's Sillhawn station, took its name

from the N.H. Deuel family. Deuel suggested his son's name and Arnold was so renamed. A modest settlement with a small sawmill, Arnold achieved fame as the junction with Wisconsin, Ruby & Southern, which ran from the mill site to the Hawn Lumber Company at Ruby between 1905-1915. The lumber company owners included Messers Sill and Hawn, hence the original pre-Deuel name. The lumber company, in turn, was named for Ruby Hawn, a daughter of the owner. Arnold station survived until 1982, finally succumbing to fire.

Six miles east of Arnold, the nearly abandoned settlement of Donald marks the site of the former Fountain-Campbell Lumber Company mill, the source of carloadings for both Wisconsin Central (Soo Line by 1909) and Omaha. WC completed an Owen-Duluth line, in its last independent days in 1909, that crossed the Hughey Line at Donald. An interlocking tower was installed at the diamond, seemingly an extravagance in Omaha's case. Fountain-Campbell operated from 1902 to 1916, after which Donald disappeared. Donald had a box car body depot in 1920 and several sidings to the mill site that languished in weeds until abandonment.

Cornell Wood Products Company was organized in 1914 to take over Brunet Falls Manufacturing Company at Cornell. Cornell Wood Products went on producing wallboard, pulp and electricity, with a high demand for its products keeping the plant operating into the 1970s. During the lifetime of the Hughey/Hannibal/Cornell Line, the Omaha attended dutifully to its major area customer. In 1945, Omaha handled 2,444 carloads (59,600 tons) out of Cornell. Twenty years before, it was 34,600 tons. Coal shipments in 1945 amounted to 25,000 tons. The plant's importance from the outset was not lost on the Omaha.

Back in 1911, several officers of Brunet Falls Manufacturing Company resided in Eau Claire and took issue with daily mixed Trains 232-233 (out of Eau Claire). They attempted to influence the Omaha to reschedule trains that would dovetail with trolleys between Eau Claire and Chippewa Falls. But if the mixed had switching chores in Chippewa Falls, the delay would make the Brunet men late for work. The railroad had the problem of loading "preference cars" for the branch train, switching produce industries and getting up to Cornell on time. The mixed was powered by 4-4-0s, and an additional car would affect train speeds, and one more stop would affect arrival. One part of the problem had Omaha loading its way freight cars Less-Than-Car-Load, with one car stocked for points north of Cornell and another for points south of town. Omaha officials thought a 9:00 AM arrival at Cornell was realistic, but passenger service to Cornell meant arrival at a village whose leaders continuously complained of barbaric service. This required that Omaha also service humble stations beyond Cornell, bringing their small shipments to the new frontier. Service improved with Trains 234-235, a "switch train," that tied up at Holcombe, five miles north of Cornell. Corporate wisdom had the water supply there, requiring a light engine to run up from the work site. Trains 234-235 also took care of Chippewa Falls work before departure to the Brunet Falls Manufacturing plant. Ultimately, it had a combination car for Eau Claire.

By mid-1912, Brunet Falls Manufacturing Company had levered Omaha to perform two switches each day at Cornell due to plant expansion. The Holcombe tie-up continued, which in turn, might require an enginehouse, something for the motive power

(Above) Cornell Wood Products Company was the industry most responsible for traffic on the Hannibal line. The paper mill and dam at Cornell, 21.5 miles from Chippewa Falls, was the successor to the Brunet Falls Manufacturing Company. *Cornell Wood Products.* (Below) Arnold, located 33 miles from Chippewa Falls, is shown in the heyday of operations on the Hannibal line. Originally named Stillhawn, the village was a junction with the short-lived Wisconsin, Ruby & Southern Railway. Created in 1907, WR&S ran from Holcombe to Arnold, then turned south to the Hawn Lumber Company mill at Ruby. *Larry Easton Collection.*

department to contemplate. Some customers, including the Fountain-Campbell Lumber Company at Donald, clamored for switch train/combination car service, while a Chippewa creamery complained that iced reefers were not being switched to their plant on time. Mail connections could not be ignored either, especially since Train 96, the *Short Line Passenger*, moved BFMCo's mail to Chippewa for the switch train's attention. But, Trains 232-233, the *Hannibal Passenger*, carried 50 passengers per day. Combine No. 427, with just 20 seats, was later replaced by a full smoker coach to handle the rough clientele to Hannibal. Also, there was a need to run light engines from Altoona to Chippewa Falls to cover assignments.

Burnet Falls Manufacturing Company went into receivership in early 1914, with C.O. Frisbie presiding. His complaints to Omaha included leaking car roofs, imperiling wallboard shipments. Late in 1914, Frisbie was agitating to get the branch renamed the "Cornell Line" which would enhance his new Cornell Wood Products Company, the reorganized firm's name. By this time, pressure was mounting due to the war. Autos, the preference of plant management, led to a way out for the commuter service. Mr. Pechin's office worked to segregate passenger cars from log cars, since loose loads often presented dangers. Heavier business, sometimes 75 to 100 log loads at Cornell, further influ-

enced changes. In 1915, another car of immigrants bringing their stock along to Hannibal, arrived on mainline freight Train 78 to brave the new north. The little towns seemed to be growing. Also threatened by change were the small engines, which were becoming outmoded by the loadings they shouldered, including helper service on Chippewa Hill.

Systemwide, Omaha's 4-4-0 engines were overtaxed, and business begged for 4-6-0s. They were dubbed "19 inch engines" in company parlance, the largest of which was the 73 ton F-9 Class built by Schenectady in 1898. Mr. C.D. Stockwell asked the Motive Power office (E.R. Gorman) to make one available. Train 233 was having to leave important loads at Cornell due to inadequate power. Gorman replied that he had nine such engines already assigned on the Eastern Division and that Class E-8 4-4-0 No. 160 (complete with flanger) was the only step upward. At 47 tons, the 160 was still inadequate. Gorman further begrudged the use of the "19 inchers," and he would have to build a flanger (snowplow) if one were assigned. In any event, Gorman was certain an 18 inch engine would handle 800 to 900 tons.

In 1915, Cornell's factory expanded with an expenditure of $200,000. This was a time of labor shortages, and the criticism of passenger service continued. Two years later, a significant line change took place at Lake Wissota due to dam construction. 9.48

(Above) A Stanley, Merrill & Phillips passenger train is powered by Taunton built 4-4-0 No. 4, ex-Omaha No. 214, acquired by SM&P in 1899. The coaches are ex-Pennsylvania Railroad, purchased from a Chicago dealer. SM&P was a common carrier and log line, which operated from Stanley to Jump River via Gilman, with an Omaha junction at Hannibal.

(Right) SM&P Shay No. 10 frequented the north end of the road near Jump River, spotting log cars. Both: *Stanley Historical Society.*

Fairbanks-Morse-Sheffield motor car No. 10 helped to economize SM&P service, but served less than two years due to a fire in 1911. *Stanley Historical Society.*

miles were abandoned in favor of a line out of Norma, 5.89 miles long, which opened in January 1917. Originally, a Minnesota-Wisconsin Light & Power Company project, it was intended to supply power for street car systems in the Twin Cities.

The post-World War I recession in 1920-23 brought further efforts to colonize lands along the Hannibal Line. Wisconsin Colonization Company settled most of its trackside farmlands, although many were far from prosperous. The Omaha looked at the future with some trepidation, due to dwindling forest products and closing mills at Donald. In March 1920, the *Hannibal Limited* carried a smoker-coach (partitioned in the center) seating 32 loungers and 19 first-class passengers. A baggage-express car carried pouch mail. With the recession, a combination car with a large baggage compartment was substituted for the express car, but the smoker-coach was continued. C.D. Stockwell again pushed for a 19 inch engine and two Altoona-Hannibal crews for Trains 234-235. He also observed that the new people in the settlements were accustomed to better passenger service.

In late May 1920, overtime by the Cornell switch train brought a D-11 Class switcher to town, one of Omaha's first 0-6-0s. Gorman's motive power office fussed over extra fuel expense, engine watchmen and housing prospects for the Schenectady switcher. Further problems arose with tardy shipments for Hannibal. A hearing uncovered that three days elapsed before some perishables arrived in Taylor County. This happened due to the several transfer points between Minneapolis-St. Paul and Hannibal. The problems all indicated the motive power situation would have to be solved by using heavier 4-6-0s.

In September 1926, Omaha's service included two trains on the branch, operating at 25 MPH. Special instructions excluded SM&P at Hannibal in favor of lessee Soo Line, because it assigned light power to the shortline. Finally, heavier 4-6-0s began to dominate, at first the F-2 Class, later I-1 and K-1 power, the ultimate branchline engines.

In the Fall of 1934, Omaha presided over the removal of moribund neighbor Stanley, Merrill & Phillips. The Soo Line vacated

SM&P's final 22.4 miles at the end of Owen Lumber Company's cut, and SM&P's C.D. Moon looked for a scrapper. Omaha was approached to operate its heavy K-1s (current 1930s power) on light traffic days over SM&P, delivering empties to trucks, which would tug the gondolas where needed. Foley Brothers of St. Paul, the agent of destruction for Omaha's Wynot, Nebraska, Line, was contacted, but finally, Harry P. Bourke of Escanaba, Michigan, was hired. Bourke was thought to be financially able to buy SM&P and rent the necessary equipment. Unable to run K-1s on SM&P, Bourke cast about for power, and Omaha President C.R. Gray Jr., suggested 4-4-0 No. 171. It was the second instance of a 4-4-0 rental in 1934. SM&P's old Jump River bridge washed out in April 1934, isolating part of the line.

The resurrection of Class E-8 No. 171 from the deadline followed inspections and parts replacement. It was then offered to Bourke for $750, which the Michiganite declined, countering instead with a rent proposal. After some haggling, Bourke was allowed the 4-4-0, together with way car (caboose) No. 6117 and 60 drop-end gondolas. No. 171 left St. Paul Shops under steam on or about September 21, 1934, and proceeded to Altoona. The 1888 Schenectady, then double-headed with the regular Hannibal-bound K-1 power, arriving on September 25 at Hannibal. Omaha engineer Drinkwater then eased the old machine around the SM&P wye to scrapper Bourke.

Abandonment of SM&P continued until late October, while Master Mechanic G.A. Budge stewed about getting E-8 No. 171 back before a costly inspection date. Budge wrote that the engine would be due October 1, 1934, and he wanted it released from the Hannibal work beforehand. It was drained and taken dead in train to Altoona. It returned to St. Paul in the company of big F-8 Class 4-4-0 No. 257, also dead in train, hauled by I-1 No. 345. Within days, SM&P rails were en route to coal mines as far away as Staunton, Illinois. Four years later, the Hannibal Line was cut back to Holcombe, and on April 9, 1943, the last train left Holcombe. Service to Cornell was cut back in the 1970s, and today, the entire line lies abandoned.

Wisconsin, Ruby & Southern Railway had a junction with the Omaha at Arnold, 33 miles from Chippewa Falls. WR&S 0-4-4T engine No. 1 was a Forney-type Vauclain compound that came off Chicago's south side elevated. *Author's Collection.*

(Right) Hannibal's forlorn depot stands abandoned in 1939, just before the track was removed. Hannibal was the Omaha junction with SM&P's line to Jump River. The two roads cooperated with joint depot maintenance. *Curtis Deuel.*

(Below) Omaha E-8 No. 171 was resurrected from the St. Paul deadline to assist in removing the old Stanley, Merrill & Phillips. Shown at St. Paul on July 20, 1934, it subsequently ran for 38 days for scrapper H.P. Bourke of Escanaba, Michigan. The 1888 Schenectady engine was retired in May 1935. *Robert H. Graham.*

Wooden combination cars, like 28 seat No. 424, prevailed on the Cornell branch through 1939. A few of Omaha's wood combines lasted in service into the 1950s. *A. Robert Johnson.*

Above) Omaha Train 232 stops at Holcombe, 26.5 miles from Chippewa Falls, shortly after the line to Hannibal opened in 1903. Thirty-seat combine No. 409 and coach No. 27 trail D-4 Class No. 68, an 1881 Baldwin 4-4-0 engine, which was sold to Bayfield Transfer Railway in 1915. *State Historical Society of Wisconsin.* (Below) Donald is visited by Omaha's mixed train around 1912, with an E-4 Class 4-4-0 heading up a couple of box cars, combine No. 409 and coach No. 5. Located 4.6 miles from Hannibal, Donald was the site of a Fountain-Campbell mill from 1902 to 1916, after which the mill and population evaporated. Soo Line successors still serve Donald's log landing. *Author's Collection.*

The northbound *Namekagon* departs New Richmond, Wisconsin, after its 9:47 AM station stop on September 11, 1948. It will take almost two hours to get to Spooner, nine stops and 64.3 miles away. The train has recently been repainted into C&NW's yellow and green passenger colors, adopted as the system standard for all diesel locomotives and passenger equipment in 1948. *Ken L. Zurn.*

# 14.
## STURGEON RIVER AND THE FISHERMAN

Omaha launched its homemade semi-streamliner *Namekagon* at the beginning of 1939, eight months before C&NW inaugurated its fully streamlined Chicago-Milwaukee-Twin Cities *"400"* passenger train, on September 24th. The little train took its place among uniquely crafted lightweight trains of the day by being a product of the Hudson Shops and not a new purchase. It was named through a contest in conjunction with a northwestern Wisconsin tourist promotion organization. *Namekagon* (pronounced Nam-uh-KAH-gun) is Chippewa for Sturgeon River, the name of the major stream alongside the route of the yellow, red and silver motor train.

Opening day was January 6, 1939, and Omaha's Carl R. Gray Jr., and Passenger Traffic Manager E.L. Pardee were in attendance at Ashland to welcome the new train. Ray C. Gross, winner of the contest to name the train, was also there. *Namekagon's* first run included the adventure of a leaky roof, but it succeeded in bringing a new flare to passenger service from Minneapolis to Lake Superior at Ashland, via the old North Wisconsin line.

Motor car No. 2005 powered the three cars, two of which were converted from conventional gas-electrics, only ten years old. Single engine motor cars 2000 and 2001 were de-engined after various assignments in Minnesota and Wisconsin on routes not far from that of the *Namekagon*. Mid-train car 2000 was converted to a combination baggage-chair car, while car 2001 became *Namekagon's* "Limousine Coach," with its engine room lifted to become a solarium section. To improve the ride, the Limousine received wood-beam swing-motion trucks from another car. The car's rear end featured large windows with appropriate drumheads displayed, both indirectly lighted. Up front, power car 2005's two 300 HP distillate-burning Winton engines were adequate in reeling off the daily 193 miles to Ashland. Three years after inauguration, 25 miles were deleted from the route when the starting point became Hudson.

The aim of *Namekagon* was to stimulate vacation traffic into what was known as Indianhead Country, the imagined outline of northwest Wisconsin that resembled an Indian facing west. While lakes and forests were available to sportsmen since the line's construction in the 1880s, the region had yet to develop as an ultimate retreat. Yet, it was well-known to Omaha employees, as well as to several prominent Wisconsin bankers, industrialists and old money families who had vacation homes in the area.

After a serious layoff at Hudson Shops in 1938, Omaha's Master Car Builder, John M. Ryan, breathed life into the *Namekagon* vision. Perhaps the new motor train was used to rekindle idled skills. Ryan was another Hudson Irishman who had served his apprenticeship above the St. Croix River, gaining his final office in 1933. Shop forces removed the engines and generators from Nos. 2000-2001 and created an attractive pair of lightweight coaches to match power unit 2005's 600 HP. The 40 ton combine No. 2000 seated 28, while 42 ton Limousine Coach No. 2001 accommodated 72. Their appearance was quite modern.

*Namekagon's* regular 9:15 AM departure from Hudson followed Train 508, the *Viking*, just after the latter stormed up the long hill to Northline, a two-mile 1.43% grade. Other hills served to retard *Namekagon's* progress northward, including a 1% knob near Clear Lake and the 1.21% grade into Ashland. Motor trains were not new to this route, and the previous summer, Trains 361-364 ran nearly the same schedule, using similar power.

Operating out of Ashland required turning the three car train on the wye at Ashland Junction, then backing the 4.2 miles to the joint Omaha-C&NW station in town. A tight schedule allowed minimal time between runs as arrival at Ashland was 2:27 PM, with departure set for 2:45 PM. Delays and late running meant Twin Cities passengers could miss their evening connection at Hudson with Train 501.

There were sporadic road failures, and the *Namekagon* had to be replaced by steam power and several 60 foot standard weight coaches. There were no extra lightweight cars.

The crew in the early days was remembered by veterans as Engineer Oliver Bullard and either Mike Kelly or Mike Tierney, conductors. After the tie-up at Hudson became the norm, the crew had some extra duties. The train was "wrong mained" to the depot (on the double-track mainline in front of the depot) where its passengers were discharged. The road crew then ran it around the wye, finally backing the train behind the depot for overnight storage. The motor car was then cut off and moved to the Hudson roundhouse. Their pay claim was 530 miles, which also included 100 miles for terminal switching. This was later challenged by the railroad, especially as the Hudson yard crew would shove the two coaches into a stub end track only a few yards west of the depot.

Steam substitutes were I-1, K-1, G-3 and I-2 Class engines. The more suitable G-3s (4-4-2s) and I-2s (4-6-2s) were mostly phased out after WWII, leaving 4-6-0s to assist the *Namekagon* to its final days in late 1950. Although designed for freight assignments, the universal, practical 63 inch drivered I-1s seldom made the schedules faithfully, but they did standardize motive power, another important requirement.

On summer holidays, the *Namekagon* was often overloaded and required an extra coach, which was beyond the 2005's pulling capacity. Steam was serviced at Hudson and the extra coaches drawn from older stock, usually cars from the 750 series that were spliced in between the regular lightweights, or perhaps a vintage RPO-baggage car when motor car 2005 was in for inspection. The Christmas holidays sometimes brought the car count to four, requiring an I-2 Pacific to make the time and provide adequate steam heat. The extra coaches probably contributed to the arching of car 2000, its platforms distorted by slack action.

The *Namekagon* lasted for nearly eleven years, and its final year was filled with vain attempts to save the service. January of 1950 marked the end of daily runs, and the recently repainted (to standard green and yellow) train became a Monday-Wednesday-Friday affair. On January 12, Omaha filed abandonment documents with the Wisconsin Public Service Commission, indicating losses were $80,000 per year. Zephyr Bus Lines, which had gone into service paralleling *Namekagon's* route, had its representative W.L. Zach appear in favor of the abandonment. Omaha cited excessive costs, and revealed that *Namekagon's* gross revenues equalled the crew's wages. Unknown to the boosters was the general decline of rail passenger service, which their train was but a small part of. Also missing was the vital local patronage.

When 65 year old Albert O. Christopherson retired after 45 years of Omaha service, he did so from the platform of the *Namekagon* on January 28, 1949. He had started as a Waterboy at 14 and entered train service in 1903, rising to passenger conductor in 1941. Christopherson did what so many would in coming years: He took the train with him into retirement. Its expiration left mixed Trains 75-76 as the sole passage to Ashland. Finally, it fell to freight Trains 69-70 to hold down the route with a combination car on the rear. One-by-one, the lights blinked out at on-line depots, as the merger with C&NW brought the harsh reality of modern railroading to seniority rosters.

Other passenger operations on the Ashland-Trego line included summer resort specials running weekends between Eau Claire and Drummond. While the *Namekagon* was a regularly scheduled operation, service to the "Arrowhead Vacationland" was made

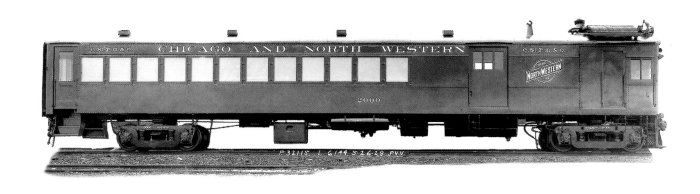

(Top) The Omaha began its gas-electric program May 1928 with the delivery of Pullman-Standard/EMC motor cars 2000-2001, both powered by a Winton 275 HP six cylinder engine. No. 2000 was rebuilt to a baggage-coach for the *Namekagon*. (Center) Motor car 2001 had a much larger seating capacity and later became the "Limousine Coach" in the *Namekagon*. (Bottom) Motor cars 2002-2005 were delivered in July-August 1929 with three different floor plans and passenger space. They were dual-engine, 600 HP units with four traction motors. No. 2005 had no passenger accommodations and became the power car for the 1939 *Namekagon* motor train. All: *Pullman-Standard; Author's Collection.*

available from Chicago, Eau Claire or Spooner as far as Drummond, in response to overflow *"400"* passengers on weekends, or to resort owner's actions. 1935's extra passengers gave way to Trains 1401-1400 in both 1936 and 1937, which were then named the *Arrowhead 400*, a title which echoed the north country's alliance with its native American heritage.

In 1939, North Western added a Spooner-Duluth arm named the *Arrowhead*, serving the Gordon-Solon Springs vacationland with day coach accommodations. It was not repeated after that last, prewar summer. In 1938, a new Chicago-Drummond connection began to run close on the heels of Trains 401-400, and had the weekender in Drummond by 9:50 PM Friday, when it was on time. After a short stay, one could board eastbound Train 402 at Drummond on Sundays at 12:45 PM, running southward to Eau Claire. In prewar days, tight operations had the rider in Chicago at 9:35 PM. Still another accommodation was Trains 310-311, daily except Monday and Tuesday, which connected with Train 511, the *Duluth-Superior Limited,* at Spooner. It was scheduled into Drummond at 7:20 AM, and out at 8:35 PM. With WWII, the *"Fisherman"* was no longer scheduled or requested. Train 311 was equipped with a 10 section sleeper to Drummond, which was put into Train 510 for Altoona, and finally coupled into Train 406, the *North Western Limited,* via Milwaukee for Chicago.

After the war, the odd trains to Drummond returned, finally ending in 1953. Absent, however, was 4-4-0 No. 136, which ran until a wartime scrap drive removed it from the roster. It had been dubbed "the toy Mike" by a less-than-respectful brakeman.

Mr. L.T. Williams, a native of Hayward and a long-time

Motor car No. 2005's dual engines were stenciled for C&NW.
*Pullman-Standard; Author's Collection.*

observer of the Omaha in Sawyer County, remembered No. 136 as regular power on Trains 311-310 between Spooner and Drummond. Williams observed that due to train length, the engine was frequently relieved by I-2 Class 4-6-2 Nos. 383, 384, 385 and 387. Another incident involving No. 136 occurred on Labor Day weekend in 1941, when "the great flood" struck Hayward and washed out track in the town. The previous day, a Saturday, the little 4-4-0 went up to Drummond on Train 311, followed by the *Namekagon* with motor car No. 2005 at noon. Because of track damage, the motor car was barred from returning due to traction motor clearance. It was then necessary for No. 136 to run to Ashland from Drummond for Train 364, Ashland-Hayward, while a train from the south came as far north as the Hayward washout, where a passenger exchange was made. It was perhaps the only time the *Namekagon* actually carried a 10-2-1 sleeper in its consist, brought up from its Train 511 connection.

Early in 1930, President Carl R. Gray Jr., was interested in raising the speed of Trains 311-312, the daily Drummond connection. One problem was turning engines at Drummond, for which the old Wynot, Nebraska, turntable was considered. This would allow a gain in time of 25 minutes. Another possibility was to rent the old Rust-Owen Lumber Company wye, if the lumber firm would upgrade it. Rust-Owen was not interested, plus the wye had only 40-50 pound rail, with stub switches, and Omaha engines never went over it without using idler flats, and then only traversing one leg of the wye. The lumbermen were anxious to close their mill, suggesting Omaha could upgrade the wye. C.D. Stockwell later suggested running power up to Bibon, to turn on the DSS&A wye located there, but it was found that Omaha crews would come under the 80 mile limit operating to Bibon. The Wynot turntable was eventually installed at Drummond.

On August 9, 1953, your author rode one of the last *Fisherman* trains to Drummond, a typical three-car special, behind light Pacific No. 384. After a chance to photograph the old veteran spotted in Spooner that Sunday, I had the pleasure of a cab ride. Certainly, the last of its class on the Eastern Division, it possessed all the old traditions, like a formidable manual reverse "Johnson Bar." Hand-fired No. 384 gave a smooth ride to Drummond, making the appropriate stops at Hayward, Cable and Lake Owen. At the latter station, I transferred back to the cars, as my presence in the cab was unauthorized. Unknown was the fact that this was the last year of operation. The engine's graceful gallop through the woods seemed effortless, yet it was just a few weeks away from retirement. This tourist never had it so good.

While a turntable was located at Drummond, the main reason the trains terminated there was most of the passengers were ticketed to stations south of the old lumber town. Across the tracks, where loaded log gondolas stood, were several old buildings belonging to the Rust-Owen Lumber Company. After appropriate switching, Extra 384 South headed for Spooner and then Eau Claire, the 384 again occupying a quiet stall at Altoona's roundhouse for another week. No. 384's Milwaukee and Chicago passengers were transferred to Train 400 as the old engine cooled down. Comparison between the two accommodations was interesting; one a woodsy, rustic and informal connection, that would soon end, while the other, much more luxurious, would leave the scene just ten years later in an era of major passenger train curtailments.

(Above) This view of the three unit *Namekagon* motor train at Cumberland illustrates the appearance of the two former gas-electrics that were rebuilt specifically for the 1939 train. On the rear is "Limousine Coach" No. 2001, while in the center is baggage-coach No. 2000. The train's "Indianhead" logo was dutifully carried on the rear and up front on both sides of power car No. 2005.

(Right) The interior of the solarium section of No. 2001. This was originally the cab area of the motor car. Both: *Earl Ruhland.*

(Above) The *Namekagon,* in its original silver-red-yellow color scheme, rolls into Cumberland, 22 miles from Spooner, en route to Hayward and Ashland during 1940, its second year of operation. (Below left) Looking toward the rear of Limousine Coach No. 2001. (Below right) The *Namekagon* and crew inside the Minneapolis depot, circa 1940, with engineer Oliver Bullard in the cab doorway, and Brakeman George Corcoran and Conductor Harry Barrett on the ground. A baggage man looks on from behind. All: *Earl Ruhland.*

Heavy holiday patronage often required an additional coach on the *Namekagon*, in which case the motor car would be replaced by a steam engine. On New Year's Day in 1950, I-1 No. 106 pauses at Spooner with a coach and both trailers from the motor train. The RPO didn't run on Sundays or holidays. *William F. Armstrong.*

(Above) Occasionally, G-3 Class 4-4-2 No. 364 powered the *Namekagon*. On Memorial Day in 1949, the 364 is north of New Richmond with a standard coach splitting the *Namekagon* trailers. *Ken L. Zurn.* (Below) A Baggage-RPO car is tucked in behind the tender of the 1906 Alco in this view of the *Namekagon* at its Hayward station stop. The high-drivered Atlantic was retired in April 1952. *L.T. Williams.*

(Above) On May 29, 1949, K-2 Pacific No. 388 lumbers along north of New Richmond with a four car *Namekagon*. Motor car No. 2005 contained a mail compartment, so when the train exceeded its two car capacity, an RPO had to be added to the consist. (Left) Arriving at Spooner from the north, K-2 No. 388 is in charge of a small three car *Namekagon*. Both: *Ken L. Zurn.*

(Below) The arrival of Train 361 at Cumberland, with I-2 Pacific No. 387 on the point, and all heavyweight cars in tow, is enough to make the gentleman on the left glance up from his newspaper. *Earl Ruhland.*

(Above) In the late 1940s, Train 361 stops at Hayward to load passengers and mail, with a standard RPO-baggage car and both of the *Namekagon* trailers in the consist. In the background is a classic Omaha box car. Motor car 2005 is not in service and I-2 No. 384 keeps the schedule. The 1910 light Pacific was retired in November 1953. (Below) Also at Hayward, sister engine 386 is flanked by a 1940s garage scene. No. 386 was from Omaha's last group of I-2s delivered by Alco in December 1910. It was in service until September 1952. Both: *L.T. Williams.*

(Above) The *Namekagon* motor train has arrived at Trego from Ashland in the last couple of years of operation. The tracks on the left go to Superior, and at this point, passengers from the Twin Ports-Eau Claire line could transfer to the *Namekagon* and travel to Hudson, where connections could be made with the *Viking* to the Twin Cities. *C&NW Ry.* (Below) After the *Namekagon* was discontinued on October 1, 1950, only C&NW used the jointly owned Ashland station. This scene is from the late 1950s. *Jim Scribbons.*

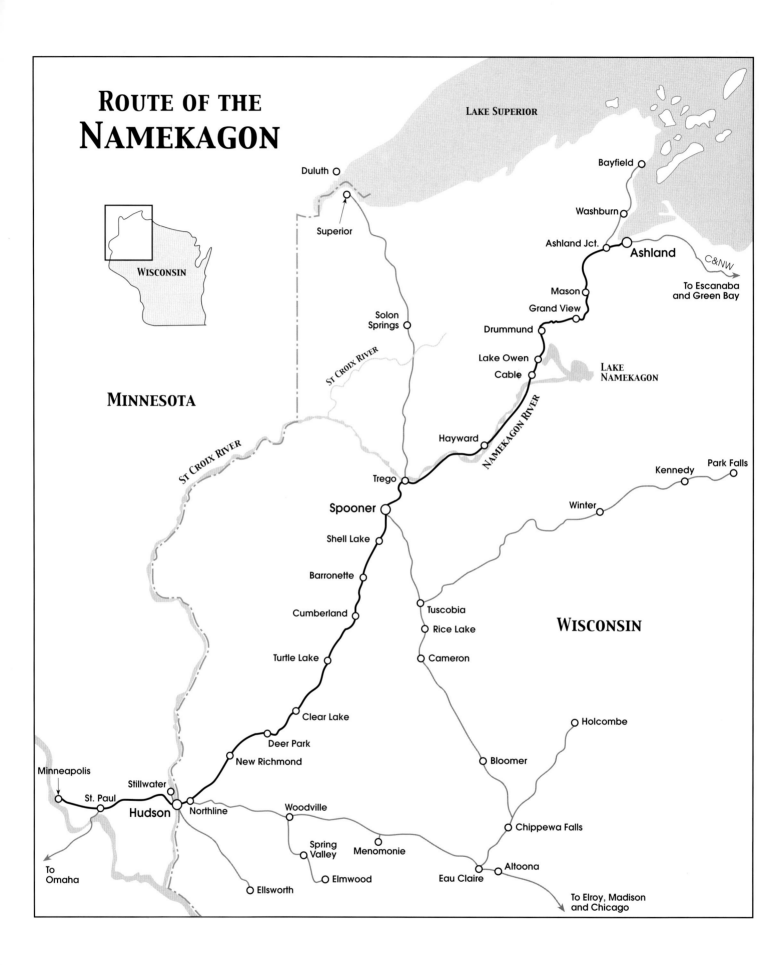

# ROUTE OF THE NAMEKAGON

LAKE SUPERIOR

WISCONSIN

Bayfield

Washburn

Duluth

Superior

Ashland Jct.

Ashland

C&NW

To Escanaba
and Green Bay

Mason

Grand View

Drummund

Solon
Springs

Lake Owen

Cable

LAKE
NAMEKAGON

St Croix River

MINNESOTA

NAMEKAGON RIVER

Hayward

Park Falls

St Croix River

Kennedy

Trego

Winter

Spooner

Shell Lake

WISCONSIN

Barronette

Tuscobia

Cumberland

Rice Lake

Turtle Lake

Cameron

Holcombe

Clear Lake

Deer Park

Bloomer

Minneapolis

New Richmond

St. Paul

Stillwater

Woodville

Hudson

Northline

Chippewa Falls

To
Omaha

Spring
Valley

Menomonie

Elmwood

Altoona

Ellsworth

Eau Claire

To Elroy, Madison
and Chicago

In 1940, the *Fisherman*, with superheated 4-4-0 No. 136 for power, laid over at Drummond. Photographer Ruhland was confronted by weeds, a dead engine and no friendly crew to spot the old timer. *Earl Ruhland.*

(Above) Sometimes Ten-Wheelers handled the *Fisherman*. At Spooner on August 24, 1947, K-1 No.112 has Pullmans at the drawbar instead of coaches. *Author's Collection.* (Below) On August 9, 1953, I-2 No. 384, power for the weekend *Fisherman,* is turned on Drummond's old non-motorized turntable relocated from Wynot, Nebraska. In the distance are surviving Rust-Owen Lumber Company buildings. *Stan Mailer.*

(Above) On Friday, August 7, 1953, Extra 384 West awaits the arrival of Train 401 at Eau Claire for passengers keen on fishing and vacationing at Hayward, Cable and Drummond. The *Fisherman* ran on certain weekends, departing Eau Claire on Friday evening, running to Drummond that night, and then returning on Sunday. (Below) Extra-384 East awaits departure in front of Drummond's weather-worn depot on August 9, 1953. The seasonal Chicago-Drummond weekend train was the last varnish on the Bayfield Line. Both: *Stan Mailer*.

Coming and going at Spooner. (Above) Extra 384 East highballs out of town at Noon on Sunday, August 9, 1953. (Below) The *Fisherman* crosses over from the Hudson mainline to the Altoona mainline at Spooner's south end trackage, with a 540-series diner-lounge on the rear. Light Pacific No. 384 had about four months of life left as it was retired in November that year. Both: *Stan Mailer*.

On August 17, 1949, triumphant Merrillanites celebrate the arrival of the *Twin Cities "400"* making its first postwar stop at the Merrillan depot. More than a thousand turned out to celebrate along with city bands from Neillsville and Alma Center, as well as the Neillsville National Guard. *La Crosse Tribune*.

# 15.

# FINALE

The railroad of Carl R. Gray Jr., and his predecessors reached 1939 with a thin budget, but renewed optimism. The sparse north country road was missing several branches, many red ink passenger locals, and most of its lumber traffic. In its place came the critically acclaimed diesel powered yellow and green *"400"* streamliner, newly upgraded from a steam powered heavyweight high-speed train. On the local scene, the homemade *Namekagon*, despite its detractors, sped along between Hudson and Ashland in silver-red-yellow contrast and continued doing so for the next decade. On the west side, the familiar names of *Nightingale*, *North American* and *Mondamin* linked Omaha with the Twin Cities and were eventually dieselized. The names were reinforcements for the gently rolling prairie lifestyle, which persisted after rough starts for its citizens. In the north, in June 1939, General Superintendent Harry Congdon was enthusiastic about the faster accommodation to Duluth, the *Arrowhead Limited*.

In a report to Gray on May 19, Congdon paid particular attention to the train's speed on curves not yet superelevated (Rockmont to Trego), and instructed Engineer Sidders to use his best judgement. Despite several meets and a missing "19" order, Sidders performed splendidly, losing only 11 minutes on the first run of Train 403. There was also fog, condemning any speed above 10 MPH between Itasca and Duluth, with signals heavily cloaked. The new train was greeted by Duluth's finest, diminishing Congdon's pessimism and making the new service a positive one. He was, however, dubious about the *Limited's* ability to make its schedule.

In contrast, M-1 0-6-0 No. 43, which never strayed west of St. James (according to Mankato's paper), reached 400,000 miles in switching duty. One of five yard engines there, No. 43 typically worked sharp curves from Carney to Minneopa on the west, serving the area quarries as needed. It was retired in September 1945.

Train service to Merrillan and Marshfield, in contrast, was feeling a pinch. One reason was that Merrillan's joint Omaha-Green Bay & Western turntable was hard to operate. It was a manual type that, on occasion, was the victim of frost heaving, making it hard to move. In 1942, Trains 108-109 were in question, between Omaha's mainline and far-off Manitowoc on Lake Michigan. For many years, joint use of equipment prevailed and, in October 1942, C&NW Class D 4-4-2 No. 1017 was actively running into Merrillan. Those called upon to help push the turntable complained bitterly, especially in minus 18 degree weather, not uncommon in Merrillan. One conductor claimed he didn't have to submit to the indignity and, as a result, his brakemen had to roll out the section foreman at 2:00 AM. Engineering forces jacked up the table in December, lubricated it, and pronounced it satisfactory after Omaha I-1 No. 329, off the Mondovi

Job, load-tested it. Three men could move it without undue exertion. The disgruntled conductor was handed a marvelously tactful response to his complaints, suggesting such difficulties might be overcome by applying the veteran's "usual resourcefulness." The bulk of the problem was human, rather than mechanical.

Merrillan's joint enginehouse had two stalls, and Omaha's side was too short for anything but 4-4-0s. In 1925, such power was housed for the Marshfield local, but now only GB&W's Winona way freight power used it. Throughout the later 1930s, Omaha used its superheated F-8 Class 4-4-0s and G-3 Class 4-4-2s on Merrillan-Marshfield-Manitowoc runs. C&NW engines were also used at times. In 1928-29, two daytime trains went to Eland on C&NW, and Omaha power was used six months of the year. Ominously in those times, one two-month period showed a 45% loss in ticket sales. But, as a result of the agreements on the run-through, Omaha power was seen at Green Bay, Kaukauna, New London and Eland. Communities on Omaha's Marshfield stub fought to maintain their passenger service, citing original tie donations as a justification for barring abandonment! After a struggle, Trains 107-128 were discontinued.

Routing for Marshfield Trains 108-109 was changed on July 10, 1938 to Eland-Appleton Junction via Clintonville and New London, instead of through Green Bay and Shawano. The change shorted some of the C&NW communities in their mail service, but generally improved earnings. For the 1940s decade, Omaha continued to share the power and crew responsibilities for Eland-bound Trains 108-109, and supplied I-1/K-1 engines when smaller passenger power was no longer available.

Back in 1912, Marshfield was an important icing station for Swift & Company refrigerator cars. Shipments were directed eastward toward lake ports from Omaha's western territory, and Omaha was asked by the packer to set up an icing station similar to those at Antigo, Green Bay and elsewhere. Marshfield was an important distributing point between the two halves of the North Western systems. Other places were less important, like Waller Pit, near Columbia. In 1911, La Crosse Water Power Company needed a spur near Columbia in conjunction with flood damage at Black River Falls. Later, a gravel pit operator wanted to run his own locomotive over the spur, but was allowed only on the mainline. By 1932, unrepaired bridges into the site were un-passable and trackage was overgrown. The land was sold in 1936.

Marshfield experienced its first J Class Mikado in October 1916. Reports regarding Marshfield's turntable indicated the 60 foot structure wouldn't support the heavy 2-8-2, so preliminary trips to the junction town required a wye to turn the 80 foot engine. Bridges also received attention, and main tracks were adequately conditioned. A roadmaster recommended relaying four curves between Merrillan and Columbia before the 2-8-2s and

(Above) Marshfield's joint Omaha-C&NW engine terminal also serviced Soo Line motive power beginning in 1930. In this view from 1950, Soo Line Consolidation No. 2448 and Alco diesel No. 2109 keep company with a C&NW R-1 Ten-Wheeler and Omaha I-1 No. 358 (on the turntable). *Ken L. Zurn.*

(Right) In its later days, Omaha M-2 No. 50 was a regular at Marshfield, before being retired in June 1956. *John Boose.*

(Below) Omaha F-8 No. 276 is ready to depart C&NW's Manitowoc depot with Train 109 to Merrillan on November 11, 1938. This was the "farthest east" for Omaha motive power, which operated with C&NW crews when in North Western territory east of Marshfield. *Edwin Wilson Collection.*

Marshfield met. Further, C&NW's wye in Marshfield would have to bear the big engines, and the parent road fussed over the fact the wye had just 60 pound rail. They recommended oiling the heel of the outer rail to prevent flanges climbing off. Other tracks had 80 pound rail, and the J (only one operated into Marshfield for some months) was directed to use the heavy leads in the yard. Because of weaker ashpit tracks, the J had to be backed onto a fire-cleaning spot before its tender was replenished. In time, the pit track would be strengthened to take J engines regularly.

In 1921, Omaha faced extra costs at Chili, 9.5 miles west of Marshfield. The flagstop had a population of 200, and Omaha wanted to close its depot at night, since Trains 3 and 8 did precious little after-hours business. Eventually, the railroad was able to cut its nightly losses. An order was handed down by the state railroad commission eliminating the stop, and all was fine until Chili State Bank's cashier mobilized some opinions in opposition. In time, the cashier was visited by a company officer and the railroad was induced to reinstate its night man at a monthly cost of $87.50. A hearing disclosed only 120 cash fares on Train 3, while 164 had been purchased for Train 8 that year. It was held that service was reasonable, but the stop had to be restored, without the open depot or the night man.

Marshfield in the 1940s was a busy place. Passenger service to Lake Michigan was down to the *Fox River Express*, and an every-other-day mixed to Marshfield (Trains 167-168) from Merrillan. Trains 106-129, which were gone by the 1930s, were another passenger entry emanating from the junction town. Altoona yard dispatched a regular time freight, Nos. 169-170, named *Tolake* and *Frolake*, that terminated at Marshfield, but which ran, for a while, to Eland on the C&NW. Marshfield had two yard jobs, some of which worked 15 hour days in the busy 1940s. One of the last steam switchers at Marshfield was M-2 No. 50, according to an observer. At WWII's beginning, F-6 No. 26 handled the work on one shift, which began at 6:30 AM. A saturated slide valve engine, No. 26 was soon scrapped.

Omaha was required to make up the Lake Shore Division's train to Wisconsin Rapids and Nekoosa. This C&NW run was heavily laden with pulpwood, mostly delivered by Omaha extras from Altoona and points north of Spooner. Omaha drags would halt just west of Highway 13 and cut off power, surrendering further duties to C&NW crews. The Omaha train would be brought up to the "New Yard," while the Central Avenue (Highway 13) gates were lowered by a woman operator known as "Butch," a 1950's era regular.

At Marshfield, Omaha, C&NW and Soo Line shared a 12 stall roundhouse, an air-operated crane system for coaling engines, plus a new, modern style depot that still stands. C&NW's line to Wausau and Eland took log shipments to the Wisconsin Valley mill communities, also directing cross-Lake Michigan business to Manitowoc and the car ferries. Statistics regarding train service contracts gave C&NW the majority of cars received in Marshfield's yard: 55.7% versus 44.3% for Omaha in 1931. Omaha Trains 169-170 and C&NW Train 351 were broken up in the old yard, and Omaha way freight No. 167, plus C&NW Trains 354, 170 and 34 began there. The new yard made up Omaha Train 169 and extras, plus C&NW extras, in addition to receiving all Omaha irregulars.

The report for 1946 stated Omaha's income decreased about 40%, from 1945's 16 million to just over 9 million in the first peacetime year. Freight traffic (exclusive of iron ore) decreased 517,000 tons as compared with 1945, evident in grain and grain products, meat and packing house products, coal and coke. Some passenger accommodations were up as Mankato had its depot modernized. Modern coaling plants were installed to replace obsolete structures at Adams and Hudson, even though dieselization was only a decade away. For the entire system, 20 streamlined coaches were scheduled for 1947 delivery, along with 20 passenger diesels.

As improvements developed, a May 1946 coal strike produced an interesting response by the railroad. C&NW arranged for oil burning freight engines to cover its fast freight schedules across Wisconsin. In mid-month, five C&NW J Class oil burners were scheduled to move out of lines west to cover what amounted to a closed railroad as coal reserves ran low. On May 10th, a tank car of fuel oil was sent to Altoona to supply the expected power from Sheboygan on Train 169 to Altoona. Then, on the 11th, Train 483 left Chicago's Proviso Yard with two Class J 2-8-2s double-headed, one of which was an oil burner. At Butler, Wisconsin, the oil fired J was fueled and continued on alone with Train 483 for Minneapolis. Written orders stressed a need to work the engine with light throttle to conserve fuel, as the Adams and Altoona oil shipments hadn't arrived. The oil burner actually reported onto the Omaha about the 12th, accompanied by a traveling engineer. It would be available for Train 484 by the 14th. Four days later, the Federal Government faced a railroad strike on top of a coal stoppage, adding to the mystery of the phantom oil burners. A multiplicity of strikes by railroad crafts ended on May 26, and railroaders were actually drafted into the military, pinching off the conflict. The oil burners disappeared immediately.

Minneapolis-St. Paul's dual terminals reflected the very beginnings of the Omaha. Vital trackage of 10.1 miles from St. Paul's Westminster Street Switch linked St. Paul with Washington Avenue in Minneapolis, the far end of the Great Northern agreement. The large East and West Minneapolis Yards, according to the original 1915 plan, made up the majority of trains for the Western Division, plus some for the east. Two trains were dispatched from Western Avenue, the location of Omaha's St. Paul Shops, over the ancient Minnesota Valley Railroad route toward Mankato. Omaha crews were required to write rule exams for Great Northern, St. Paul Union Depot, and M&StL, along with their own road. After leaving the Minneapolis yards, the trek over GN's freight main eastward included a share of pickups all the way to Westminster Street. Some loads came from Minnesota Transfer Railway, while meat cars came from South St. Paul, the latter during the golden age of the packing house reefer, the offering running to 30 or 40 cars each night. Trains 484 and 488 were often assigned such loads. Another stop at Payne Avenue topped off eastbound trains, which took their cars from the stub-end yard at East St. Paul

Passenger trains from the east made the long descent into St. Paul Union Station, the grade running down past Hazel Park Yard from Midvale (MP 7) to Mile 0. The hill intensified to 1.25% near Westminster Street Switch, just north of St. Paul Union Depot's trackage. After a speedy turning of its power, most Omaha trains were towed backwards up the hill, past Westminster Street Switch, onto GN's 10 mile route westward to Minneapolis Union Station (GN). Empty trains were then dispatched to the Omaha coach yards north of the depot, their power sent to the 30 stall roundhouse alongside the Mississippi River.

The size of the several Twin Cities yards, given in 1915-era 36 to 40 foot cars, is of interest. West Minneapolis had a total capacity of 1050 cars, while East Minneapolis held 2000 cars. East St. Paul took 900 cars, East 7th Street yard held 550 cars, and Hazel Park could handle 800 cars. Omaha's Prince Street Yard, at the freight house, held 270 cars in the 1940s.

The stimulus of WWII brought the Omaha a liberal share of traffic. Patriotism manifested itself in a 29"x 60" *Welcome Home Vets* sign on Marshfield's depot, retained through August 11, 1947, well after the men had returned to Wood County. Nearby Granton, in need of wartime recreation, requested the use of station grounds for an ice rink and the company obliged.

When diesel locomotive manufacturers began capturing the market, Omaha began towing away sizable strings of dead steam power, sending the clanking funeral trains to Valhalla on Rice's Point, Duluth. One wartime group, thus condemned to acetylene flame, included the last superheated 4-4-0s, accompanied by most of the older, Stephenson valve gear equipped I-1 and I-2 veterans. Steam would hold for just a few more years, then it would succumb to another concept of standardization.

In the postwar slump, winter's paralyzing hand would again hobble Omaha operations systemwide. Record cold came to Wisconsin and Minnesota, especially at the end of December 1946. On New Year's Eve, Ashland Junction, virtually on the waters of Chequamegon Bay (and thus Lake Superior), awoke to readings of 30 degrees below zero. Operating in such cold, it was almost forgivable that some trains might not be on time. The early morning hours of New Year's Eve Day, however, conjured up a catastrophe only possible in a near-arctic climate.

Spooner had dispatched Train 75, a double-headed 36 car night freight, with Engineer Arthur Zimmer and Fireman Ed Johnson on I-1 No. 361. Just behind them, 52 year old Ralph Carlson was in charge of K-1 No. 240, fired by Ed Bohn, also a Spooner regular. They were scheduled to tie up at Ashland, but were running two hours late. At the same time, also running two hours late, Duluth, South Shore & Atlantic Train 632 was proceeding eastward with 26 cars (over the Northern Pacific via trackage rights) in the care of 2-8-2 No. 1050. Just before 7:30 AM, as the South Shore train was clattering across the first of two diamonds at 5 MPH, Omaha's Zimmer and Johnson on I-1 No. 361, also traveling at 5 MPH, struck the DSS&A engine, shunting the first Omaha engine off its routing to rest on the NP trackage. The cause of the accident was determined to have been the "failure to properly control speed of CStPM&O train approaching railroad crossing at grade." The tender of Omaha engine No. 240, the second engine, was pushed upward, bringing the coal load down on the cab, trapping Carlson under the pile. Worst of all, the coal pile over Carlson then caught fire. Bohn escaped injury by jumping off at the low speed of impact, as did the crew of engine 361.

Omaha and the C&NW had followed the lead of many railroads in trying different brands of diesels and, by 1947, had 16 switching units on hand. Pioneer diesel No. 55 continued to work at Hudson, and on the branches nearby. ALCO-GE 1000 HP S-2s were used at Altoona, later handling the Cornell job in 1951. Baldwin 660 and 1000 HP yard units showed up at Sioux City, while Fairbanks-Morse 1000 HP power invaded the Twin Cities. Sioux City's imposing passenger station had the services of Whitcomb No. 10, a 380 HP 42 tonner, beginning in mid-1943. In the fall of 1948, at the railroad's eastern end, an ALCO-GE 660 HP S-1 type took on the duties at Elroy, very much a preferred job for its crew during the day. The chief occupation for Elroy's morning switching brigade was to turn the *Dakota 400's* diner for its return trip to Chicago. One summer morning, your author assisted an Omaha engineer by starting the fire in K-1 No. 201, working just one day while diesel No. 69 received its monthly inspection. In contrast, Elroy's night job worked hard on both passenger and freight yard shuffling duties.

In the postwar years, the intention of the company was to expand its streamlined passenger trains, particularly the *400 Fleet*. The ambition nearly brought on a Chicago-Omaha "400," with a Sioux City stub. It generated the world's only single-engine Baldwin passenger diesel with a baggage compartment. Two Omaha Western Division trains, the *Nightingale* and the *North American*, were put on faster schedules and equipped with 4,000 HP diesel power. C&NW signed for fifteen 2,000 HP passenger diesels. Four Fairbanks-Morse units were included for the Omaha, built at Erie, Pennsylvania, by General Electric in early 1947. Nos. 6001A, B and 6002A, B became pool units, in time operating systemwide. In the beginning, however, the 6000s worked between Sioux City and the Twin Cities. As the Opposed-Piston power of the 6000s worked to his advantage, Mr. K.A. Rogers of Chippewa Falls became C&NW's top commuter in terms of miles. By the spring of 1947, he had made 400 trips between Chicago and his hometown on Omaha and C&NW trains. Another commuter farther down the North Western rode twice a week from Reedsburg to Chicago, pursuing his writing career in Chicago radio. The episode was not to last.

Merrillan, at mid-point on the Eastern Division, scored a triumph in November 1949. Amid a weighty celebration, the *Twin Cities "400"* was now scheduled to stop in the town. More than 1,000 residents and visitors observed the ribbon-breaking by a veteran E6 diesel. Mr. and Mrs. John Clune, Merrillanites for 43 years, were present. Clune, at 91, was the oldest living Omaha engineman, retired since 1926 after 57 years of service.

Elsewhere, on July 24, 1949, G-3 No. 364, Omaha's last 4-4-2, powered an excursion train out of the Twin Cities. Protection for the *Namekagon* would afterwards be in the charge of less distinctive engines.

Carl Gray Jr., had returned to the Omaha after his wartime duties as Director General of the U.S. Military Service. As Vice-President of the C&NW system, Gray was appointed by President Harry S. Truman to serve as Veteran's Administrator in 1948, succeeding General Omar Bradley. A struggle with illness forced him to retire from the VA post in 1953, and he returned to St. Paul to live out his last days in retirement. Sixty-six year old Carl R. Gray Jr., passed away in late 1955, almost at the same time his Omaha Road began to draw into its parent company.

For a while, passenger service enjoyed a final expansive time in which great things were expected and often realized. Summer

(Above) Headed for Great Northern's Minneapolis depot, Class I-2 No. 371 clatters over the GN freight line, with a combine and coach, on its way from the Omaha coach yard on July 31, 1933. The first five I-2s, Nos. 371-375, were all retired in December 1937. *Robert H. Graham.*
(Below) At the same location, on July 31, 1949, Class J No. 390 rumbles across the Omaha diamonds enroute to East Minneapolis yard with a freight extra. At far right is the Omaha's West Minneapolis freight house. Western Division freight trains going to Minneapolis came up the Omaha mainline through Mankato, then used Minneapolis & St. Louis trackage for 26.3 miles from Merriam Junction to Holden Street in Minneapolis. There they got on the GN freight line to Minneapolis Junction, finally running south to Omaha's primary Twin Cities yard at East Minneapolis. Engine 390 was built by Alco in 1913. Never rebuilt to a J-A, it was retired in 1952. *John Malven.*

of 1947 found the *Mountaineer* active on C&NW-Omaha Road rails, part of its dash from Chicago to Vancouver, B.C. The tourist train ran partially over the Soo Line and Canadian Pacific, with a third-day arrival at the Straight of Georgia. An engine change at Adams often found a C&NW 2900-series 4-6-2 being replaced by an Omaha E-3 Class 600 for the run to the Twin Cities. The international Pullmans were in good hands.

The *Mountaineer* passed through Milwaukee for its first post-war run June 28, 1947 with old *"400"* stalwart No. 2908 bringing seven cars up the lake shore from Chicago. Its eastbound counterpart was handled by No. 2903, again seven cars behind its big tank, mostly sleepers. One combination car carried checked baggage. Hudson's helper candidate for the International (some were Canadian Pacific cars) was no longer a slogging J-1 2-10-2, as both had been surrendered to the parent road and pressed into Proviso Yard hump duty by 1944. In exchange, Omaha received two Js (hand-fired 2368 and 2371), which were then converted to J-A Nos. 440 and 441. Loss of the J-1s meant that helper and road engines were now evenly matched and both could operate at higher speeds. The Hudson and Knapp helper assignments drew J-As by war's end. After 1949, the *Mountaineer* switched to Soo Line.

Throughout the bleak 1930s, as North Western men were laid off in droves, and others retired, many migrated to far less harsh climates than those native to Omaha or C&NW. In September 1949, 68 veterans of the two companies attended a California meeting. At the same time, dozens more now worked for such calorie-rich roads as Southern Pacific. A chance conversation at Elroy in 1953 found at least 17 men had migrated *en masse* in

(Above) In its youth, F-6 No. 271 works East St. Paul yard in the shadow of Payne Avenue bridge. The clerestory cab roof was a "Gay Nineties" idea that was applied to road power and switchers alike. Built by Schenectady in 1897, No. 271 was retired in 1945. *Robert H. Graham Collection.*

(Right) One assignment for the last of the F-6s was at Hudson Shops. On June 20, 1940, No. 24 was between switching jobs at Hudson. The 1905 Schenectady product lasted into September 1945. *Harold Van Horn.*

276

search of steadier railroading after 1932.

Two years after purchasing the F-M passenger diesels, the Omaha invested in six EMD "covered wagon" freight cab units, Nos. 6500-A, C through 6502-A, C. Delivered in December 1949, they operated in 3,000 HP pairs. In April 1950, six more units arrived, Nos. 6503-A, C to 6505-A, C. Four unusual 800 HP switchers came from General Motors in the spring of 1951. Over the next two years, 23 road switchers arrived, built by three manufacturers, the first of which was Fairbanks-Morse No. 150. The others were numbered from 151 to 172. Omaha's only six traction motor-equipped road switchers were the Fairbanks-Morse group, which operated largely on Western Division branch lines and were familiar sights at Sioux City and central Minnesota points. (Your author can remember, as a C&NW fireman, the sparking brake shoes of units 171 and 172, new and northbound, leaving Beloit in a Madison Division train.) The Pipestone and Currie lines were also host to the F-Ms.

In postwar years, improvements on steam centered on the 600 Class. The big engines lost their steam domes, acquired roller bearings, retired their booster engines, and exchanged feedwater heaters for a more reliable type. A more distinctive appearance was the result, as the familiar Mars light began to grace Omaha's passenger power. Innovative perhaps was the inverted bell bracket on the 600's boiler front. Familiar also in various cases was the employment of 600s on freight trains and use on the Western Division. The E-3s were used on Trains 514-515 which had them visiting Elroy in the wee hours, returning to Minneapolis by mid-morning. No. 601 received a complete set of Boxpok driving wheels, but the company stopped short of equipping all three. In the closing years of steam, the 600s appeared frequently on the *Viking* and made daylight runs to Elroy, hardly challenged by the short trains.

As steam waned, the two companies moved closer to consolidation, especially in the face of diminished earnings. As early as February 1926, C&NW moved successfully to acquire further control of the Omaha by the purchase of its capital stock. This condition occurred because C&NW owned 99.23 percent of Omaha's total outstanding common and preferred stock, and the entire issue of various mortgage bonds. The two companies had officers and directors in common, and when the Interstate Commerce Commission decided in favor of C&NW acquiring the control desired, it looked more and more like a single system.

C&NW moved to lease the Omaha by applying to ICC on July 24, 1956, also leasing other properties owned, leased or utilized by the Omaha. Opposition to the merger came from the Railway Labor Executive's Association over employee protection, which was worked out in the closing months of 1956. Initially at stake were clerical jobs, but the cuts which finally occurred affected all other crafts. The lease was initially arranged to run 50 years, subject to one year's notice of termination. Among other conditions,

Class J-2 No. 424 is southbound with 98 cars at Eagle Point (18 miles north of Eau Claire) on June 20, 1953. The Omaha got four USRA-issue heavy Mikados, Nos. 422-425, from Alco in March 1919. Engine 424 was retired in August 1954. *Joe Collias.*

C&NW had the right to sell, retire or abandon properties no longer required for railroad purposes. This right was used extensively in the coming years.

Omaha's property value, in June 1917, was shown as $87,192,063. On December 21, 1954, Omaha additions and betterments amounted to $23,254,390. In 1955, Omaha reported another $642,856 credit. Omaha faced financial difficulties in its final years, failing to earn its fixed charges. During the 1950s, earnings did not even cover depreciation and retirement charges, and were insufficient to cover roadway and equipment maintenance or replacements. C&NW expected economies of at least $2 million annually, which would inevitably include consolidation of accounting personnel and offices, this saving around $700,000. The $1,300,000 balance would accrue by combining diesel shops and car facilities, and increasing the corporate efficiency.

With many jobs hanging in limbo, opposition was mounted by appropriate labor organizations. On August 30, 1956, the Railway Labor Executive's Association and the Brotherhood of Locomotive Engineers filed a protest and motion to dismiss the railroad's action. On December 8, 1956, C&NW filed an application for supplemental relief, requesting the ICC issue an order directing the company to proceed with integration and unification. Authorization came on December 28, 1956, in the face of a portion of the Railway Labor Act. This was an attempt to circumvent existing labor agreements.

Effective January 1, 1957, C&NW leased all of Omaha's lines in keeping with the December 28 order. It immediately began to integrate its operations, in the absence of an ICC prescription for specific procedures. C&NW tried to confer with the concerned labor organizations over changes in operation. This involved road crew assignments, integration of caboose runs on through trains, and yard operations.

Omaha Road operating contracts at the time of the lease gave its employees seniority rights over all its operating districts. The company proposed to consolidate some seniority districts and revise others. Systemwide, there was to be a reduction of seniority districts from 24 to 8. Successful with its non-operating crafts, C&NW made little headway with the operating employees, who stuck to their guns and insisted on procedures in line with Railway Labor Act rulings. The company declined, stating that such rules were not applicable. Labor next turned to the National Mediation Board, indicating the dispute centered on C&NW's refusal to hold conferences under the Railway Labor Act. The NMB initially advised labor that proper notice of changes was not filed with them. C&NW stated that it would meet with labor, but on a voluntary basis, and not under the aegis of the RLA.

On June 17, 1957, a strike ballot was distributed, to solicit authority to strike if failure to agree followed negotiations. It was a year after the new Heineman Administration had begun to turn the entire system away from certain bankruptcy. Amid strike threats and disgruntled, entrenched employees, the new direction for the company inevitably produced friction and, in the first year and a half, 4,500 employees were laid off. Many under-utilized facilities were closed, Less-Than-Car-Load service was removed, car shops were consolidated and new accounting procedures were introduced. Duplicate facilities, systemwide, were merged into centralized operations. Obvious double facilities, such as Ashland, were soon under one authority, where Omaha's switch engine was replaced with an available ore pool Fairbanks-Morse unit, which idled away the hours until sent out (with Omaha crewmen), sometimes days later. C&NW was able to dieselize virtually overnight in May 1956, as Chicago's Power Board raised utilization and snuffed out steam. In Ashland's case, the utilization went even further, with the F-Ms soon running to Spooner with the night freight train.

All over the road, small groups of pathetically dirty steam power were rounded up. Shopmen were to remove all brass fittings for separate scrapping. On the Omaha, the last I-1/K-1 Ten-

I-1 No. 103 rides the 90' turntable at St. Paul Shops roundhouse after receiving an overhaul and a fresh coat of paint, including a graphite smoke box. C&NW heralds got "System" lettering beginning in 1944. The 1910 Alco was retired in May 1954. *T.S. Martorano Collection.*

(Above) Class E Nos. 506 and 514 bring Train 502, the *Viking,* over to GN's Minneapolis depot from the Omaha's coach yard in July 1936. *George Harris.*

(Left) Class E Nos. 503 and 508 double-head a passenger train at Minneapolis on July 15, 1938. *Robert H. Graham.*

(Below) Approaching Jackson Street in St. Paul on the GN four-track mainline, Class E No. 510 passes GN's Mississippi Street coach yard with a passenger train headed for Minneapolis in 1930. The engine has been turned and is pulling the train from SPUD with its cars in reverse order (note the Pullman 7 Compartment-2 Drawing Room sleeper just behind the tender). At right is the old GN ice house. This building was replaced in 1944 by a new brick power house for the Jackson Street round-house (out of the picture to the right). *Robert H. Graham.*

Wheelers were stripped of their distinctive brass smokebox numberboards, all of which would raise more money than steel scrap for the grim C&NW economy. Almost immediately, Omaha's Hudson Car Shops were closed, many of its senior people transferring to Clinton, Iowa. Many of Omaha's unique passenger cars came trailing down toward busy Chicago scrap yards, red lines painted through number and name, to the great barbecue of steam-era railroad equipment. The move left the Hudson facility abandoned to resale by industrial development people. New car shops at Clinton consolidated work previously done at fourteen older, non-covered yards, which were closed. Land just south of the Hudson facility was sold, including the location of the ancient land department building, which was shortly demolished. Condominiums now stand on the spot where West Wisconsin's affairs were consolidated in 1871.

Many of the last steam runs on the Omaha were found at extreme ends of the road. Omaha tried out an 800 HP switcher on the Park Falls job in April 1956, but up to that time, Trains 245-246 utilized K-1s. In distant Norfolk, Nebraska, the once-a-week assignment still called upon K-1s, at least for a portion of 1956's summer. While Trains 501-508 had steam through 1955, it was nearing a time in which newly rebuilt FP7s would be its final power. For a fleeting while, however, E Class and E-3 Pacifics would bring the forlorn little train down to Elroy, passing way freights 21-22 between Elroy and Altoona. J-As, such as Nos. 417 and 420, would be hold-outs in the remotest part of the Omaha, making stops at Merrillan or Camp Douglas. Other survivors included occasional switch chores by M-5 Class 0-8-0s, with No. 67 operating at Altoona, having been banished from the Twin Cities. Another 0-8-0 was active in Minneapolis as late as September 1956. The last steam engine into Fairmont, Minnesota, happened to be a C&NW R-1, working an extra.

Before steam vanished from the forests of the Omaha, a persevering quintet of railroad fans rode Soo Line Trains 17 and 117, from Waukesha to Park Falls, to chance a ride on the Park Falls Line. On October 8, 1955, Train 246 consisted of seven freight cars, a 440-series combine and K-1 No. 184. Each hamlet was passed in turn, often host to an abandoned log line, which radiated into the forest, ablaze with fall color. The waters of the Chippewa River sparkled in final tribute to the mixed train's passage. The K-1 negotiated the trestles and meadows of the back country, softly emitting its loon-like whistle, an eerie, wilderness sound, unmindful of the impending end with the coming of spring. It joined the mainline at Tuscobia and terminated its run at Spooner in early afternoon. There may have been others bent on a last distillation of things Omaha, whose final days had come. They looked perhaps at mixed trains or occasional freight runs in Nebraska, soon drastically altered with more efficient utilization, and finally at the abandonments which inexorably followed. In the difficult, dieselized 1960s, when the term *Omaha Road* became more archaic and quaint, forest growth took over roadways long since abandoned. It's still difficult to measure the speed at which obliteration came to the Omaha, in the jaws of the parent company's near bankruptcy. Once there were aging old Ten-Wheelers and their combination car consorts, on weedy but serviceable branches. A few years later, only a cinder-ballast trail in the wilderness remained.

We remember the high adventure of a steal-away trip to Altoona, from Elroy, on Train 515. Engine 600, one of the mysterious, grand, newly-discovered (to this observer) north country wonders, never before seen, was up ahead. Train 515 was hardly a challenge for the E-3, pridefully described by a trainman as capable of handling 24 heavy Pullmans and able to easily outpull a North Western 2900. Discussion of several mysterious classes of engines, such as the K-1, only honed our interest. This, the "instructor" was certain, was the better end of the North Western. Long years ago, engine 600 laid a canopy of water vapor over the mainline as the first light of day illuminated the lowland fog in remote, sparse land that had first nurtured the old West Wisconsin Railroad. The short day coach, in which the thoughtful Omaha crew had turned off lights (not so on several C&NW experiences), swayed slightly through high-speed turnouts as gray tuned to bright, blue morning. With hindsight, one could imagine the view outside, of Train 515 making few stops, knifing across the speedway north of Merrillan, through Augusta and Fall Creek, toward Altoona, the heart of Omaha's Eastern Division.

We also remember M-1 No. 9, the lowest-numbered Omaha steamer in 1952, scurrying at remarkable speed across a viaduct in Ashland, just as Soo Line Train 117 passed underneath. There were also rides at Hudson with friend Harold Van Horn, railroad fan and Omaha engineer, as we switched the car shops with K-1 No. 243 in early evening. Not far away was the ancient office building holding perhaps the true key to the Omaha's history. The sound of the "Barksdale Job," heard at 9 PM across Chequamegon Bay from Ashland, herding its powder plant box cars back to the city, each exhaust etched in the night air. Pleasant also was the ride on I-2 Class Pacific No. 384, another mysterious northerner, a fine performer, slicing through the woods along Lake Owen. Omaha's "ponderous pair" of Zulus, migrants from Mankato to Superior and Itasca assignments, worked transfers and switch jobs to the very end. Zulu No. 219 finished out at Spooner in early 1956.

Elroy is now without a railroad. A flat, uneventful field exists where the two halves of a Chicago-Twin Cities mainline met in 1872. The depot, now masquerading as a fire house, stands alone, where once a railroad "beanery" was run by the substantial Ruth Jacobson, representing Union News Company. Once, Elroy's depot and extensive roundhouse were the centerpiece of town activity, for the town was the railroad. Miles northward, Camp Douglas has but one railroad, although it is no longer archrival Milwaukee Road. Wyeville's tower is gone, its ghost accompanying the roundhouse to oblivion. Much of the route to Duluth is a non-entity, and Spooner is no longer a division point with a railroad. The old North Wisconsin Railroad, which once hosted the unique *Namekagon*, has been an empty trail for several decades. The Ashland depot, closed for many years, hosts a fitness club. Sioux City's imposing station and office building were razed in the face of urban renewal. Places like Tuscobia nearly deny their history, yielding the truth only in a telltale row of rough growth toward distant woodlands. Black River Falls lastly stands isolated, its loop line abandoned. Now the Omaha Road seems to exist only in the minds of a few, isolated from the Chicago & North Western long decades ago.

Indeed... there was such a railroad.

# AFFILIATED COMPANY POWER

Minneapolis Eastern Railway, a joint terminal operation with Milwaukee Road, acquired several Omaha 0-6-0s, such as No. 4, shown at Minneapolis on September 25, 1946. The engine was built by Alco in 1912. *Maurice Kunde.*

Lake Superior Terminal & Transfer engine No. 10 was a 44" drivered Baldwin that survived into the mid-1950s. LST&T was formed in 1883 and began operations in the Twin Ports in 1888. Omaha was a one-sixth owner. *Author's Collection.*

Green boiler-jacketed LST&T No. 9 reflects influence of Great Northern, one of the company's major owners. *Maurice Kunde.*

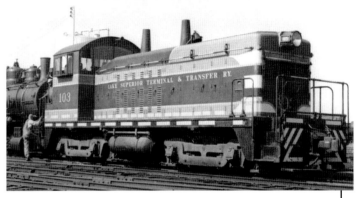

Largely dieselized by 1953, LST&T NW2s in GN livery, were joined by steam during the grain rushes of 1953-55. *Stan Mailer.*

St. Paul Union Depot Company switcher No. 11 was built by Lima. The well-trimmed 0-6-0 works the depot tracks on June 19, 1922. SPUD, along with its trackage and equipment, was jointly owned by the railroads that used the facility. *J. Foster Adams.*

(Above) E-3 No. 602 is in charge of Train 508, the *Viking,* shown departing Great Northern's Minneapolis depot on August 6, 1950. (Below) The overnight *Mondamin,* from Omaha (via Emerson, Nebraska) and Sioux City, approaches the Minneapolis depot on September 4, 1950. The rear of the train is still on GN's Stone Arch bridge (out of the picture to the left). Both: *John Malven.*

(Above) Train 508, the *Viking,* powered by E-3 No. 602, departs St. Paul Union Depot on Labor Day in 1949. The eastbound train came from Minneapolis, via GN trackage, and backed from Westminster Street, 1.6 miles into SPUD. *John Malven.* (Below) Prior to having its tender capacity increased and still relatively new, E-3 No. 600 swings downgrade at Westminster Street in St. Paul with Train 515, the *Victory,* from Chicago on July 30, 1934. After arriving at SPUD, the E-3 will be turned and then will tie onto the rear of the train for the trip back to Westminster Street, with the cars in reverse order, finally arriving at Minneapolis 35 minutes later. *Otto C. Perry; Denver Public Library.*

(Above) Class M-5 No. 60 returns from a transfer run at Hoffman Avenue on joint CB&Q-Milwaukee Road trackage just below Dayton's Bluff in St. Paul. The Omaha received eight of the heavy Baldwin switchers in June 1928, supplanting older 2-8-0 transfer engines in the Twin Cities area. *Lawrence A. Stuckey.* (Below) As seen from the Robert Street bridge, M-5 No. 63 backs through the puzzle switches, just west of St. Paul Union Depot on May 12, 1955. The track curving off to the lower left is the Chicago Great Western line across the Mississippi River. Engine No. 63 survived to 1957 and the end of steam power on the Omaha. *Russ Larson.*

(Left) M-5 No. 61 is at St. Paul in the 1940s. Some 0-8-0s were purged to assignments at Altoona and Superior, and were among the last steam engines to operate. No. 61 was retired in 1957. *Paul Eilenberger.*

(Below) In July 1954, No. 65 steams quietly at Minneapolis. Four of the big M-5 Class switchers were retired in June 1956, Nos. 60, 62, 65 and 66. *Carl Ulrich.*

At East St. Paul yard on April 27, 1946, a switch crew poses alongside M-5 No. 60. The fellow on the left carries the traditional hardwood club used for setting hand brakes. It took two ground men and two "riders" to work the yard, making up transfers for Western Avenue and other points in the Twin Cities. *Robert H. Graham.*

New Year's tragedy. Omaha Train 75 got into trouble on the morning of December 31, 1946, at Ashland Junction, when a collision occurred between an eastbound Duluth, South Shore & Atlantic freight train with 26 loads and an Omaha double-header with 35 cars. The trains met on the junction diamond, with the second Omaha engine (K-1 No. 240) jack-knifed alongside DSS&A No. 1050, a heavy 2-8-2. Ralph Carlson, 240's engineer, was killed in the accident.

(Right) This photo, taken from the U.S. Highway No. 2 overpass, shows the Omaha tracks at the upper left and the position of lead Omaha engine, No. 361, which was shunted by the collision onto the Northern Pacific tracks, the intended path of the South Shore train. *Chick Sheridan.*

(Below) The impact caused Erie box car No. 93754 to shove the tender of the second Omaha engine into its cab and onto the pinned DSS&A engine. *Walter Wilcox.*

286

(Top) Looking north, the wreck scene from ground level shows Omaha I-1 No. 361 having avoided the bulk of the carnage. (Center) Omaha K-1 No. 240 lies mortally wounded up against the DSS&A 2-8-2. All the crew members jumped and survived, except for the engineer of the K-1 who was trapped inside the cab by coal spilled from the tender. (Bottom left) The tender of DSS&A No. 1050 was pinned against the overpass concrete support post. (Bottom right) The cab of the South Shore 2-8-2 was nearly separated from the engine. All: *Walter Wilcox.*

Omaha's Prince Street freight house, near St. Paul Union Depot, was a longstanding landmark that was visible from the Kellogg Street viaduct. The building lasted into the 21st Century before finally being demolished. *William F. Armstrong.*

(Above) In December 1954, a fire at the St. Paul Shops roundhouse (near Randolph Avenue) damaged several Omaha steam engines and one Baldwin diesel switcher. J-A No. 406 is shown on the turntable lead track shortly after, on January 2, 1955. *Wayne C. Olsen.*

(Right) By March 1955, clean-up is beginning to bring order to the scene. *M.P. McMahon.*

288

(Above) A pair of C&NW E8 diesels pause at Merrillan with the eastbound *Twin Cities "400"* in the mid-1950s. After crossing the Green Bay & Western track just south of the depot (in the left background), the train stops with its coaches alongside the passenger platform. Meanwhile, the engineer watches impatiently for the highball. *A. Robert Johnson.* (Below) Class E-3 No. 601 takes on water at Merrillan with Train 508, the *Viking,* in the early 1950s. Engine 601 was the only Omaha E-3 to be upgraded with a full set of Boxpok type drivers. *M.P. McMahon.*

In April 1951, Omaha received four 800 HP SW8 diesel switchers from EMD, Nos. 126-129. The 127 displays its original paint scheme, with promotional lettering touting parent C&NW's *Overland Route* passenger trains at Altoona, around 1958. *A. Robert Johnson.*

(Above) Fairbanks-Morse 1000 HP diesel switcher No. 96 works the Minneapolis yard on June 13, 1957, one of five units (Nos. 94-98) delivered in late 1947 through early 1948. Standard C&NW paint schemes were applied to Omaha diesels, featuring *Route of The "400"* advertising opposite *Route of The Streamliners* slogans. *A. Robert Johnson.* (Below) EMD GP7 No. 155 is shown at Fremont, Nebraska, in 1959. This post-merger diesel has lost its "CStPM&O" corporate initials, but otherwise retains the as-built paint scheme and appearance. Omaha acquired eleven "Geeps" from EMD in two groups. Nos. 151-156 came in August 1951, while Nos. 157-161 arrived in June 1952. *Lou Schmitz.*

(Above) On September 7, 1955, Alco S-1 No. 69 is at Elroy, Wisconsin, where it was the regular depot switcher for most of its life. No. 69 arrived on the property June 8, 1948. *A. Robert Johnson:* (Below) Omaha RS-3 No. 164 is at the head of C&NW Train 515, the *Rochester-Minnesota Special,* at Rochester on July 17, 1953. Six RS-3s came from Alco in August 1952 (Nos. 162-164) and July 1953 (Nos. 165-167). The 164 was one of three Omaha road switchers equipped with a steam generator for passenger service (Nos. 163, 164, 167). *William F. Armstrong.*

(Above) Omaha freight diesel No. 6501-C is paired with younger sister No. 6503-A. The Omaha owned 12 EMD F7 1500 HP cab units that were commonly known as "covered wagons." Nos. 6500-A,C to 6502-A,C were delivered in December 1949 in C&NW's standard green-yellow-black paint scheme. *W.C. Whittaker Collection.*

(Right) In October 1951, Omaha No. 6502-C heads an eastbound time freight at Butler (Milwaukee), Wisconsin. *Ron Albers Collection.*

(Below) Nos. 6505-A and 6505-C were at Omaha in August 1956. Engines 6503-A,C to 6505-A,C came in April 1950 with larger road numbers and Mars lights from retired steam engines. *Lou Schmitz.*

Fairbanks-Morse type H16-66 six axle road switchers were ideal for light branch line rail on the Western Division. Omaha No. 150 was assigned to the Norfolk Line after a brief break-in period at Spooner, where it is shown soon after its February 21, 1951 delivery. *Larry Bohn.*

(Left) In July 1953, the Omaha received five additional H16-66 road switchers from F-M, Nos. 168-172. The engines came with revised cab windows and additional side sill safety stripes. No. 170 awaits duty at East St. Paul on May 19, 1955. *A. Robert Johnson.*

(Below) No. 172 is in iron ore service at Stambaugh, Michigan, on August 14, 1962, still in its original paint scheme, five years after the merger. The units operated with the long end forward. *Fred Ziebe.*

# ACKNOWLEDGEMENTS

The Omaha Road is an outgrowth of territorial trips and newspaper exploration in the railroad's homeland. Photos, the life blood of any such work, accumulated over 40 years. Memorable collections such a Robert Graham's outstanding work detailed CStPM&O motive power, as did the glass plates of J. Foster Adams in another time. The Adams collection is archived by Mid-Continent Railway Historical Society, and called attention to Omaha Road locomotives in a distant time. H.F. Braden, on the road's western end, recorded branch activities just before World War II. M.P. McMahan contributed fine latter-day action shots, alongside others of more modern experience: Jim Scribbins, Ray Buhrmaster, Fred Tonne, Bob Johnson, John Teskey and Lu Williams were able to supply needed photos and data. Bill Armstrong presented invaluable maps and plans. Mike Bartel informed us about recent western conditions and Doug Blegen helped us with Spring Valley. Louise Gervais of Currie, Minnesota. Loaned materials and Altoona's own Gerald A. Hagen, an Altoona vet and former mayor, yielded more information.

Thanks also to Price County Historical Society, University of Wisconsin-Eau Claire, and State Historical Society of Wisconsin, all contributing heavily. Since the Union Pacific takeover, memories and survivors of Omaha's times are faded. Hardly more than the mainline remains in place. Nonexistent too are traditional brass "hooter" whistles and brass numberboards, swept away in Heinemann-era scrap drives. Would that one would appear, voicing a clear, forest-couched tone, now so long gone. It would be a revelation.

*Stan Mailer*

## IN MEMORY OF

Mike Pearsall, who discovered E-3's, and James Kaysen, who wanted to read all about Omaha.

# INDEX

Bold face denotes photograph

## CStP&M Locomotives Acquired 1878-1880

|  |  |  |  |  |  |  |
|---|---|---|---|---|---|---|
|  | (1) | – | 4-4-0 | (BLW.) | (1855) | 12-1/2x20-54 | (note a) |
| D.A. Baldwin | 10 | – | 4-4-0 | BLW. 2390 | 3/71 | 15x22-60-3/4-49000 | Retired 9/92 |
| J. Humbird | 11 | – | 4-4-0 | BLW. 2394 | 3/71 | l5x22-60-3/4-49000 | Sold 1890 Glenwood Mfg. Co. |
| Geo. W. Clinton | 12 | – | 4-4-0 | BLW. 2514 | 7/71 | 15x24-60-3/4-49000 | Sold 1898 Scanlon-Gipson Lum. Co. |
| L.J. Foley | 13 | B-1 | 4-4-0 | BLW. 2598 | 10/71 | 15x22-66-3/4-49000 | Sold 1899 (F.M. Hicks) |
| Matt H. Carpenter | 14 | B-I | 4-4-0 | BLW. 2600 | 10/71 | 15x22-66-3/4-49000 | Sold 1900 (F.M. Hicks) |
| J.G. Thorp | 15 | B-1 | 4-4-0 | BLW. 2608 | 11/71 | l5x22-66-3/4-49000 | Retired 1899 |
| Wm. Wilson | 16 | B-1 | 4-4-0 | BLW. 2609 | 11/71 | 15x24-56-3/4-49000 | Sold 1900 (F.M. Hicks) |
|  | 17 | C-2 | 4-6-0 | BLW. 2677 | 1/72 | 16x24-56-1/2-68000 | Retired 7/12 |
|  | 18 | C-2 | 4-6-0 | BLW. 2680 | 1/72 | 16x24-56-1/2-68000 | Retired 1909 |
|  | 19 | C-3 | 4-4-0 | BLW. 2837 | 6/72 | 16x24-63-68000 | Retired 12/08 |
| G.W. Keyes | 20 | C-3 | 4-4-0 | BLW. 2834 | 6/72 | 16x24-63-68000 | Retired 10/09 |
| Thad Pound | 21 | C-3 | 4-4-0 | BLW. 2968 | 10/72 | 16x24-63-68000 | Retired 1/09 |
|  | 22 | C-3 | 4-4-0 | BLW. 2971 | 10/72 | 16x24-63-68000 | Sold 1900 Northwest Lumber Co. |
|  | 23 | C-3 | 4-4-0 | BLW. 2972 | 10/72 | 16x24-63-68000 | Retired 8/01 |
|  | 24 | C-4 | 4-4-0 | BLW. 3142 | 2/73 | 16x24-59-70000 | Sold 1902 Bayfield Transfer Co. |
|  | 25 | C-4 | 4-4-0 | BLW. 3143 | 2/73 | 16x24-59-70000 | Sold 1903 Superior & S.E. |
|  | 26 | C-4 | 4-4-0 | BLW. 3162 | 3/73 | 16x24-59-70000 | Sold 1899 Upham Mfg. Co. |
|  | 27 | C-4 | 4-4-0 | BLW. 3166 | 3/73 | 16x24-59-70000 | Sold 1900 White River Lumber Co. |
|  | 28 | C-3 | 4-4-0 | BLW. 3242 | 4/73 | 16x24-63-68000 | Sold 1903 Pidgeon River Lumber Co. |
|  | 29 | C-3 | 4-4-0 | BLW. 3243 | 4/73 | 16x24-63-68000 | Retired 2/09 |
|  | 30 | C-3 | 4-4-0 | BLW. 3398 | 8/73 | 16x24-63-68000 | Sold 7/07 Van Dusen Harting Lum. Co. |
|  | 31 | C-3 | 4-4-0 | BLW. 3399 | 8/73 | 16x24-63-68000 | Sold 1903 Bacon & Pettibone |
|  | 32 | D-4 | 4-4-0 | BLW. 4508 | 12/78 | 17x24-61 | Retired 9/10 (note b) |
|  | 33 | D-4 | 4-4-0 | BLW. 4509 | 12/78 | 17x24-61 | Retired 10/10 (note b) |
|  | 34 | D-3 | 4-4-0 | BLW. 4691 | 6/79 | 17x24-59-75000 | Retired 2/13 (note c) |
|  | 35 | D-3 | 4-4-0 | BLW. 4692 | 6/79 | 17x24-59-75000 | Retired 10/08 (note c) |
|  | 36 |  | 0-4-0 | BLW. 4713 | 7/79 |  | Sold 1899 (F.M. Hicks) |
|  | 37 | D-3 | 4-4-0 | BLW. 4805 | 10/79 | 17x24-59-75000 | Retired7/12 (note c) |
|  | 38 | D-3 | 4-4-0 | BLW. 4807 | 10/79 | 17x24-59-75000 | Retired 5/21 (note c) |
|  | 39 | D-3 | 4-4-0 | BLW. 4743 | 8/79 | 17x24-59-75000 | Retired 4/15 (note c) |
|  | 40 | D-3 | 4-4-0 | BLW. 4742 | 8/79 | 17x24-59-75000 | Retired 4/15 (note c) |

Note a ) Ex North Pennsylvania 4.
Note b ) Also listed as 16x24-52.
Note c ) Also listed as 16x24-56.

**Remarks:** First Nos. 1-9 acquired 1868-1871. Details unknown, but all were retired by 1880.

## CStP&M Locomotives Acquired 1878-1880

|  |  |  |  |  |  |  |  |
|---|---|---|---|---|---|---|---|
| (2nd) | 1 | C-1 | 4-6-0 | Pitts. 387 | 1/77 | 16x24-57- Ret | Retired 7/12 (note a) |
| (2nd) | 2 | D-1 | 4-4-0 | BLW. 4899 | 12/79 | 17x24-59-75000 Ret | Retired 8/14 |
| (2nd) | 3 | D-4 | 4-4-0 | BLW. 4905 | 12/79 | 17x24-59-75000 Ret | Retired 9/10 |
| (2nd) | 4 | D-1 | 4-4-0 | BLW. 4941 | 1/80 | 17x24-59-75000 Ret | Retired 9/10 |
| (2nd) | 5 | D-1 | 4-4-0 | BLW. 5294 | 10/80 | 17x24-59-75000 Ret by | Retired by 1917 |
| (2nd) | 6 | D-1 | 4-4-0 | BLW. 5296 | 10/80 | 17x24-59-75000 Ret by | Retired by 1917 |
| (2nd) | 7 | D-1 | 4-4-0 | BLW. 5305 | 10/80 | 17x24-59-75000 Ret by | Retired by 1917 |
| (2nd) | 8 | D-2 | 4-4-0 | BLW. 5303 | 10/80 | 17x24-59-75000 Ret | Retired 10/13 |
| (2nd) | 9 | D-1 | 4-4-0 | BLW. 5338 | 11/80 | 17x24-59-75000 Ret | Retired 8/10 |
|  | 41 | D-3 | 4-4-0 | BLW. 5340 | 11/80 | 17x24-59-75000 Ret | Retired 3/17 |
|  | 42 | D-3 | 4-4-0 | BLW. 5363 | 11/80 | 17x24-59-75000 Ret | Retired 8/14 |
|  | 43 | D-3 | 4-4-0 | BLW. 5366 | 11/80 | 17x24-59-75000 Ret | Retired 7/12 |

Note a ) Ex North Wisconsin 1, *Cumberland*. CStP&M 2nd No. 1 apparently rebuilt to 0-6-0, listed as built by Pittsburg 1/77, wt. 45000.

## St. Paul & Sioux City (acquired 1880), formerly Minnesota Valley (1865-1868)

| | | | | | | | | |
|---|---|---|---|---|---|---|---|---|
| Belle Plaine | 3 | 19 | 219 | | 4-4-0 | Taun. | 390 | 8/66 14x22-54 | Retired 1899 |
| St. Peter | 4? | 20 | 220 | | 4-4-0 | Taun. | 393 | 10/66 14x24-54 | Sold 1890 SC&N 11 (GN) (note a) |
| | | 5 | 205 | | 4-4-0 | Grant | | 10/66 | Retired 1890 |
| Henderson | | 6 | 206 | | 4-4-0 | Taun. | 419 | 10/67 14x24-54 | Sold 1897 Win. Stoddard, St. Paul |
| St. Paul | | 7? | 207 | | 4-4-0 | Taun. | 441 | 9/68 14x22-54 | Rebuilt 1887: 0-4-0 Cl. A-I |
| Sioux City | | 8? | 208 | | 4-4-0 | Taun. | 470 | 8/69 14x24-54 | Rebuilt 1886: 0-4-0 Medelia |
| Pacific | | 9? | 209 | | 4-4-0 | R.I. | 97 | 4/69 15x22-66 | Sold 1899 (F.M. Hicks, Chicago) |
| St. James | | 10? | 210 | | 4-4-0 | R.I. | 128 | 9/69 15x22-66 | Sold 1899 Minn. Sugar Co. |
| Medelia | | 11 | 211 | | 4-4-0 | Taun. | 501 | 7/70 14x24-54 | Sold c. 1890 Fairchild & N.E. 7 |
| (ex SC&StP 2) | 11? | 12 | 212 | | 4-4-0 | (Taun. | 536) | (8/71) 14x24-54 | Sold 1895 Nickerson Lumber Co. |
| (ex SC&StP 3) | 4? | 13 | 213 | | 4-4-0 | (Taun. | 556) | (2/72) 14x22-60 | Rebuilt 1890: 0-4-0 Cl. B-3 |
| (note b) | | 14? | 214 | | 4-4-0 | (Taun. | 560) | (3/72) 14x24-54 | Sold 1899 Jump River Lumber Co. |
| (note c) | | 15? | 215 | | 4-4-0 | (Taun. | 531) | (6/71) | Rebuilt 1890: 0-4-0 Cl. B-3 |
| Wm. Rhodes | (2nd) | 2 | 202 | | 0-4-0 | Taun. | 674 | 6/76 12x224249900 | Sold 1893 (J.T. Gardner, Chgo.) |
| C.H. Bigelow | 3? | 16 | 216 | C-7 | 4-4-0 | Taun. | 690 | 9/78 16x24-64-62200 | Sold 1903 Pan-Amer. Ry. |
| R. Blakely | 4? | 17? | 217 | C-7 | 4-4-0 | Taun. | 691 | 9/78 16x24-64-62200 | Sold 1903 Roddis Lum. & Veneer Co. |
| E.C. Butterfield | (2nd) | 3 | 203 | C-7 | 4-4-0 | Taun. | 708 | 8/79 16x24-60-63000 | Retired 1898 |
| A.H. Wilder | (2nd) | 4 | 204 | C-7 | 4-4-0 | Taun. | 709 | 8/79 16x24-60-63000 | Sold 1899 (F.M. Hicks, Chicago) |
| J.S. Prince | | 18 | 218 | C-7 | 4-4-0 | Taun. | 711 | 9/79 16x24-60-63000 | Retired 1899 |
| | (2nd) | 1 | 201 | | 4-4-0 | (Taun.) | | (1870) | Rebuilt 1890: 0-4-0 Cl. B-2 |

Note a ) 220 listed in Swartz roster ex-SC&StP 4 (Pitts. 168 11/71).
Note b ) Ex North Wisconsin 1, named *New Richmond*.
Note c ) Ex North Wisconsin 2, named *Horace Thompson*.

## Sioux City & St. Paul (acquired 1880)

| | | | | | | | | |
|---|---|---|---|---|---|---|---|---|
| E.F. Drake | I re | 21 | 221 | | 4-4-0 | Taun. | 529 | 5/71 14x24-54-57200 | Sold 1891 Sioux City & No. 12 |
| J.L. Merriam | 2? | - | - | | 4-4-0 | Taun. | 536 | 8/71 14x24-54-57200 | Reno. c. 1873: StP&SC 12 |
| J.E. Lincoln | 3? | - | - | | 4-4-0 | Taun. | 556 | 2/72 14x22-60 | Reno. c. 1873: StP&SC 13 (note a) |
| | 4 | 24 | 224 | | 4-4-0 | Pitts. | 168 | 11/71 15x22-56-55000 | Rebuilt 1892: 4-4-0 Cl. B4 (note b) |
| Geo. H. Mackey | 5 | 25 | 225 | | 4-4-0 | Taun. | 561 | 4/72 14x24-54 | Rebuilt 1890: 04-0 Cl. B-3 |
| Alex. H. Rice | 6 | 26 | 226 | | 4-4-0 | Taun. | 562 | 4/72 14x24-54 | Rebuilt 1890: 0-4-0 Cl. B-3 |
| A. Iselin | 7 | 27 | 227 | | 4-4-0 | Taun. | 567 | 5/72 15x22-60 | Rebuilt 1890: 0-4-0 Cl. B-3 |
| S.T. Davis | 8 | 28 | 228 | A-2 | 4-4-0 | Taun. | 568 | 5/72 15x22-60 | Sold 1899 Bayfield Transfer Co. |
| Geo. A. Hamilton | 9? | 29 | 229 | A-2 | 4-4-0 | Taun. | 578 | 8/72 14x22-64-67400 | Sold 1900 E.H. Hobe Lumber Co. |
| A.W. Hubbard (2nd) | 2 | 22 | 222 | C-7 | 4-4-0 | Taun. | 608 | 4/73 16x24-60 | Sold 1899 Bayfield & Wes. |
| J.W. Bishop( 2nd) | 3 | 23 | 223 | C-7 | 4-4-0 | Taun. | 607 | 4/73 16x24-60 | Retired 1898 |
| T.P. Gere | 10 | 30 | 230 | C-7 | 4-4-0 | Taun. | 614 | 5/73 16x24-64-62200 | Retired 8/01 |
| W.H. Brown | 11 | 31 | 231 | C-7 | 4-4-0 | Taun. | 669 | 2/76 16x24-54 | Sold 1898 Fairchild & N.E. 8 |
| J.C. Boyden | 12 | 32 | 232 | C-7 | 4-4-0 | Taun. | 655 | 2/76 16x24-54 | Retired by 1900 |
| ex SC&N 1? | | 33 | 233 | | 0-4-0T | (Grant) | | (8/69) | Rebuilt 1893: X-O, Scrapped 10/08 |
| StP&SC | | 34 | 234 | | 0-4-0T | BLW. | 4963 | 2/80? | Sold 1893 (J.T. Gardner) |
| StP&SC | | 35 | 235 | C-8 | 4-4-0 | BLW. | 5191 | 7/80 16x24-58-68000 | Retired 12/09 |
| StP&SC | | 36 | 236 | C-8 | 4-4-0 | BLW. | 5192 | 7/80 16x24-58-68000 | Retired 9/09 |
| StP&SC | | 37 | 237 | D-12 | 4-4-0 | BLW. | 5272 | 9/80 17x24-58- | Retired 6/11 |
| StP&SC | | 38 | 238 | D-12 | 4-4-0 | BLW. | 5274 | 9/80 17x24-58- | Retired 9/09 |
| StP&SC | | 39 | 239 | C-8 | 4-4-0 | BLW. | 5217 | 8/80 16x24-58-68000 | Retired 2/09 |
| StP&SC | | 40 | 240 | C-8 | 4-4-0 | BLW. | 5216 | 8/80 16x24-58-68000 | Retired 6/05 |
| StP&SC | | 41 | 241 | D-12 | 4-4-0 | BLW. | 5295 | 10/80 17x24-58- | Retired 12/14 |
| StP&SC | | 42 | 242 | D-12 | 4-4-0 | BLW. | 5297 | 10/80 17x24-58- | Retired 12/14 |
| StP&SC | | 43 | 243 | C-8 | 4-4-0 | BLW. | 5240 | 8/80 16x24-58-68000 | Retired 1909 |
| StP&SC | | 44 | 244 | C-8 | 4-4-0 | BLW. | 5242 | 8/80 16x24-58-68000 | Sold 2/07 (F.M. Hicks) |

Note a ) *J.E. Lincoln* listed in Taunton records as No. 4.
Note b ) 224 listed in Swartz roster ex StP&SC 4 (Taunton 393 10/66).

**St. Paul, Stillwater & Taylor's Falls (acquired 1880 by StP&SC)**

| | | | | | | | |
|---|---|---|---|---|---|---|---|
| | 1 | 45 | 245 | 4-4-0 Taun. | 546 | 11/71 16x24-60 | Sold 1899 (F.M. Hicks) |
| | 2 | 46 | 246 | 4-4-0 Taun. | 547 | 11/71 16x24-60 | Sold 1899 (F.M. Hicks) |

**Covington, Columbus & Black Hills (acquired 1880 by StP&SC)**

| | | | | | | | |
|---|---|---|---|---|---|---|---|
| *Dakota* (a) | 1 | 47 | 247 | 0-6-0 Mason | 560 | 7/76 12x16-33 | Sold 1890 Riverside Land Co. |
| *Dixon* | 2 | 48 | 248 | 0-6-0 Mason | 551 | 7/75 12x16-33 | Sold 1890 Pacific Short Line Co. |
| (Cancelled) | 3 | - | - | 4-4-0 Brooks | 310 | 10/77 | Sold by 1900 LNO&T 204 |

Note a ) Ex Stockton & Lone No. 1.

**Remarks:** Mason engines 1 and 2 originally 3'6" gauge.

**Omaha & Northern Nebraska (formerly Omaha & North Western) (acquired 1880 by StP&SC)**

| | | | | | | |
|---|---|---|---|---|---|---|
| | 1 | 49 | 249 | 4-4-0 Hinkley | 1876 | Retired 1898 |
| (Worth & Sioux Falls 1) | 2 | 50 | 250 D-13 | 4-6-0 BLW. 4824 | 10/79 | Retired 5/15 |

**Sioux City & St. Paul - Additions During 1880**

| | | | | | | |
|---|---|---|---|---|---|---|
| 51 | 251 | C-9 | 4-4-0 Taun. | 741 | 6/80 16x24-63 | Sold 1900 Arpin-Harwood L. Co. |
| 52 | 252 | C-9 | 4-4-0 Taun. | 742 | 6/80 16x24-63 | Retired 1899 Connor |
| 53 | 253 | C-9 | 4-4-0 Taun. | 743 | 7/80 16x24-63 | Sold 1898 R. Conner Lumber Co. |
| 54 | 254 | C-9 | 4-4-0 Taun. | 744 | 7/80 16x24-63 | Retired 1899 |
| 55 | 255 | C-9 | 4-4-0 Taun. | 745 | 7/80 16x24-63 | Retired 1898 |
| 56 | 256 | C-9 | 4-4-0 Taun. | 746 | 7/80 16x24-63 | Sold 1900 Northwest Lumber Co. |
| 57 | 257 | C-9 | 4-4-0 Taun. | 747 | 8/80 16x24-63 | Sold 1898 F. Weyerhaeuser |
| 58 | 258 | C-9 | 4-4-0 Taun. | 748 | 8/80 16x24-63 | Retired 1898 |
| 59 | 259 | C-9 | 4-4-0 Taun. | 749 | 8/80 16x24-63 | Sold 1899 Marshfield & S.E. |
| 60 | 260 | C-9 | 4-4-0 Taun. | 750 | 8/80 16x24-63 | Retired 1898 |
| 61 | 261 | C-9 | 4-4-0 Taun. | 751 | 9/80 16x24-63-66000 | Sold 1901 Laona & Nor. |
| 62 | 262 | C-9 | 4-4-0 Taun. | 752 | 9/80 16x24-63-66000 | Sold 1901 O'Neal Bros. |

**Sault Ste. Marie & Southwestern (acquired 7/1892)**

| | | | | | | |
|---|---|---|---|---|---|---|
| | 1 | | | | | |
| | 2 | | | | | |
| | 3 | | | | | |
| | 4 | | | | | |
| (ex ?) | 5 | 183 | 4-4-0 (Taun.) | (1869) | | Sold 1897 Fairchild & N.E. |
| (ex C&NW 144) | 6 | 184 B-1 | 4-4-0 (Hink. 65) | acq. 1890 | 15x24-64-63000 | Retired 2/09 |

**Minnesota & Wisconsin (acquired 1901)**

| | | | | | | |
|---|---|---|---|---|---|---|
| | 2 | | | | | |
| | 3 | | | | | |
| (ex No. Pac. 44) | 4 | 203 B-5 | 4-4-0 (BLW. 2716) | (2/72) | 15x24-57 | Sold 1903 |
| | 5 | 204 B-6 | 4-4-0 Mason | | | Retired 2/09 |

**Specifications in the class headings:** cylinder bore x stroke - driver diameter - boiler pressure - engine weight - tractive effort

## 0-4-0 SWITCHERS

### 0-4-0 Class C-5: 16x24-51-605000

| 50 | BLW. | 5823 | 9/81 | Retired 6/11 |
|---|---|---|---|---|
| 51 | BLW. | 5832 | 10/81 | Retired 8/10 |
| 52 | BLW. | 5865 | 10/81 | Retired 5/14 |
| 53 | BLW. | 5866 | 10/81 | Retired 7/14 |
| 90 (a) | BLW. | 6731 | 4/83 | Rebuilt 5/14: X-1, Sc 8/19 |
| 91 | BLW. | 6732 | 4/83 | Retired 5/14 |
| 92 | BLW. | 6750 | 5/83 | Retired 11/14 |
| 93 (b) | BLW. | 6759 | 5/83 | Sold 5/21 |

### 0-4-0 Class C-6: 16x22-51-60000

| 107 | Manch. | 1005 | 8/82 | Retired 10/0 |
|---|---|---|---|---|
| 108 (a) | Manch. | 1006 | 8/82 | Rebuilt 12/10: X-1, Sc 5/14 |

### 0-4-0 Class B-3: 15x24-51-58600

| 208 | Rblt from 4-4-0 | 9/86 | Retired 1909 |
|---|---|---|---|
| 213 | Rblt from 4-4-0 | 5/90 | Retired 2/09 |
| 215 | Rblt from 4-4-0 | 2/90 | Retired 2/09 |
| 225 (a) | Rblt from 4-4-0 | 7/90 | Rebuilt 4/07: X-0, Sc 10/16 |
| 226 | Rblt from 4-4-0 | 1890 | Retired 1897 |
| 227 | Rblt from 4-4-0 | 1890 | Retired 1897 |

### 0-4-0 Class A- 1: 14x24-51-59000

| 207 (c) | Rblt from 4-4-0 | 8/87 | Sold 2/07 |
|---|---|---|---|

### 0-4-0 Class B-2: 15x24-51-61500

| 201 (d) | Rblt from 4-4-0 | 10/90 | Sold 12/07 |
|---|---|---|---|

### 0-4-0? Class B-4: 15x2"3V2-63900

| 224 | Rblt from 4-4-0 | 2/92 | Retired 9/09 |
|---|---|---|---|

Note a ) Rebuilt to tank engine for shop transfer service when renumbered to X-series.
Note b ) To Hamm Brewing Co.
Note c ) To Dells Lumber & Shingle Co.
Note d ) To F.M. Hicks, dealer.

## 0-6-0 SWITCHERS

### 0-6-0 Class C-1 - See 2nd No. 1

### 0-6-0 Class D-11: 17x24-51-82000

| 148 | Schen. | 2581 | 6/88 | Retired 8/23 |
|---|---|---|---|---|
| 149 (a) | Schen. | 2582 | 6/88 | Rebuilt 8/19: X- 1, Sc 9/28 |
| 150 | Schen. | 2583 | 6/88 | Retired 8/23 |
| 151 | Schen. | 2584 | 6/88 | Retired 5/26 |
| 152 (a) | Schen. | 2585 | 6/88 | Rebuilt 12/16: X-1 |
| 153 | Schen. | 2586 | 6/88 | Retired 8/23 |
| 180 | Schen. | 3418 | 4/91 | Retired 3/27 |
| 181 | Schen. | 3419 | 4/91 | Retired 3/27 |
| 182 | Schen. | 3420 | 4/91 | Retired 5/25 |
| 185 | Schen. | 3735 | 4/92 | Retired 11/27 |
| 186 | Schen. | 3736 | 4/92 | Retired 3/27 |
| 187 | Schen. | 3737 | 4/92 | Retired 7/28 |

### 0-6-0 Class E-1: 18x24-51-99000

| 10 | Schen. | 3984 | 12/92 | Retired 12/29 |
|---|---|---|---|---|
| 268 | Schen. | 4057 | 3/93 | Retired 12/29 |
| 269 | Schen. | 4058 | 3/93 | Sold for scrap 9/31 |
| 270 re 267 | Schen. | 4059 | 3/93 | Sold for scrap 9/31 |

### 0-6-0 Class F-6: 19x24-51-160-111600-23103

| 270 | Schen. | 4624 | 11/97 | Retired 3/45 |
|---|---|---|---|---|
| 271 | Schen. | 4625 | 11/97 | Retired 3/45 |
| 272 | Schen. | 4626 | 11/97 | Retired 5/35 |
| 13 | Schen. | 5830 | 4/01 | Retired 9/45 |
| 14 | Schen. | 5831 | 4/01 | Retired 1940-1943 |
| 15 | Schen. | 5832 | 6/01 | Retired 9/45 |
| 16 | Schen. | 5833 | 6/01 | Retired 1/44 |
| 24 | Alco-S | 30471 | 6/05 | Retired 9/45 |
| 25 | Alco-S | 30472 | 6/05 | Retired 1940-1943 |
| 26 | Alco-S | 30473 | 7/05 | Retired 1940-1943 |
| 27 | Alco-S | 42620 | 4/07 | Retired 9/45 |
| 28 | Alco-S | 42621 | 4/07 | Retired 1940-1943 |

### 0-6-0 Class F 10: 19x24-51-160-113800-23103

| 22 | BLW. | 20688 | 7/02 | Retired 3/45 |
|---|---|---|---|---|
| 23 | BLW. | 20689 | 7/02 | Retired 1940-1943 |

Note a ) Rebuilt to tank engine for shop transfer service when renumbered to X-series.

## 0-6-0 SWITCHERS

**0-6-0 Class M-1: 18x24-51-200-129800-25920 (note a)**

| | | | | |
|---|---|---|---|---|
| 29 | Alco-S | 45912 | 2/09 | Retired 1/44 |
| 30 | Alco-S | 45913 | 2/09 | Retired 1/44 |
| 31 | Alco-S | 45914 | 2/09 | Retired 3/45 |
| 19 | Alco-S | 47049 | 4/10 | Retired 3/45 |
| 20 | Alco-S | 47050 | 4/10 | Retired 1940-1943 |
| 21 | Alco-S | 47051 | 4/10 | Retired 1940-1943 |
| 32 | Alco-S | 50120 | 7/11 | Retired 3/45 |
| 33 | Alco-S | 50121 | 7/11 | Retired 1940-1943 |
| 35 | Alco-S | 50122 | 7/11 | Retired 8/42 |
| 36 (b) | Alco-S | 50123 | 7/11 | Retired 10/35 |
| 3 | Alco-S | 50928 | 4/12 | Retired 1940-1943 |
| 4 (b) | Alco-S | 50929 | 4/12 | Retired 9/45 |
| 9 | Alco-S | 50930 | 4/12 | Retired 6/53 |
| 12 | Alco-S | 50931 | 4/12 | Retired 8/42 |
| 18 | Alco-S | 50932 | 4/12 | Retired 6/56 |
| 1 (c) | BLW. | 39371 | 2/13 | Rebuilt 9/47 |
| 17 | BLW. | 39372 | 2/13 | Retired 9/45 |
| 37 | BLW. | 39373 | 2/13 | Retired 5/52 |
| 43 | BLW. | 39374 | 2/13 | Retired 9/45 |
| 45 | BLW. | 39375 | 2/13 | Retired 2/55 |

**0-6-0 Class M-2: 2lx28-51-190-173000-39100**

| | | | | |
|---|---|---|---|---|
| 46 | Alco-S | 47369 | 9/17 | Retired 6/56 |
| 47 | Alco-S | 47370 | 9/17 | Retired 6/56 |
| 48 | Alco-S | 47371 | 9/17 | Retired 1949 |
| 49 | Alco-S | 47372 | 9/17 | Retired 11/50 |
| 50 | Alco-S | 47373 | 9/17 | Retired 6/56 |
| 51 | Alco-S | 47374 | 9/17 | Retired 11/50 |
| 52 | Alco-S | 47375 | 9/17 | Retired 1949 |
| 53 | Alco-S | 47376 | 9/17 | Retired 1949 |
| 54 | Alco-S | 47377 | 9/17 | Retired 6/56 |

**0-6-0 Class M-3: 2lx28-51-190-163500-39100 USRA**

| | | | | |
|---|---|---|---|---|
| 75 | Alco-S | 61333 | 7/19 | Retired 2/55 |
| 76 | Alco-S | 61334 | 7/19 | Retired 6/56 |
| 77 | Alco-S | 61335 | 7/19 | Retired 6/56 |
| 78 | Alco-S | 61336 | 7/19 | Retired 6/56 |
| 79 | Alco-S | 61337 | 7/19 | Retired 5/54 |
| 80 | Alco-S | 61338 | 7/19 | Retired 5/54 |
| 81 | Alco-S | 61339 | 7/19 | Retired 6/56 |
| 82 | Alco-S | 61340 | 7/19 | Retired 6/56 |
| 83 | Alco-R | 62615 | 1/21 | Retired 6/56 |
| 84 | Alco-R | 62616 | 1/21 | Retired 6/56 |
| 85 | Alco-R | 62617 | 1/21 | Retired 5/54 |
| 86 | Alco-R | 62618 | 1/21 | Retired 6/56 |

Note a) Originally Class E-10, weight 124,000.
Note b) Sold to Minneapolis & Eastern.
Note c) Rebuilt to 0-6-0T 2151, reno. 1955 to X199900.

## 0-8-0 SWITCHERS

**0-8-0 Class M-5: 25x28-51-200-238950-58400**

| | | | | |
|---|---|---|---|---|
| 60 | BLW. | 60543 | 6/28 | Retired 6/56 |
| 61 | BLW. | 60544 | 6/28 | Retired 1957 |
| 62 | BLW. | 60545 | 6/28 | Retired 6/56 |
| 63 | BLW. | 60546 | 6/28 | Retired 1957 |

**0-8-0 Class M-5 (continued)**

| | | | | |
|---|---|---|---|---|
| 64 | BLW. | 60547 | 6/28 | Retired 1957 |
| 65 | BLW. | 60548 | 6/28 | Retired 6/56 |
| 66 | BLW. | 60549 | 6/28 | Retired 6/56 |
| 67 | BLW. | 60550 | 6/28 | Retired 11/56 |

## 2-8-0 CONSOLIDATION (Transfer Service)

**2-8-0 Class H-1: 22x28-50**

| | | | | |
|---|---|---|---|---|
| 214 | BLW. | 10875 | 5/90 | Retired 12/28 |
| 211 | BLW. | 12328 | 10/91 | Retired 11/28 |
| 267 re 227 | BLW. | 13484 | 6/93 | Retired 10/28 |

**2-8-0 Class H-3: 22x28-50-160-169000-36861**

| | | | | |
|---|---|---|---|---|
| 216 | Alco-S | 30474 | 7/05 | Retired 3/45 |
| 217 | Alco-S | 30475 | 7/05 | Retired 3/45 |

**2-8-0 Class H-2: 22x28-50-160-170425-36861**

| | | | | |
|---|---|---|---|---|
| 209 | BLW. | 16264 | 10/98 | Retired 1940 |
| 210 | BLW. | 16265 | 10/98 | Retired 3/45 |
| 228 | BLW. | 18732 | 3/01 | Retired 12/39 |
| 229 | BLW. | 18733 | 3/01 | Retired 1940 |

**2-8-0 Class Z: 25x32-61-185-243500-51557**

| | | | | |
|---|---|---|---|---|
| 218 | Alco-S | 53092 | 6/13 | Retired 6/56 |
| 219 | Alco-S | 53093 | 6/13 | Retired 6/56 |

## 2-8-2 MIKADO

**2-8-2 Class J: 27x32-64-200-307000-62000**

| | | | | |
|---|---|---|---|---|
| 390 | Alco-S | 52697 | 6/13 | Retired 1952 |
| 391 | Alco-S | 52698 | 6/13 | Retired 1952 |
| 392 | Alco-S | 52699 | 6/13 | Retired 1952 |
| 393 | Alco-S | 52700 | 6/13 | Retired 1952 |
| 394 | Alco-S | 52701 | 6/13 | Retired 1952 |
| 395 | Alco-S | 52702 | 6/13 | Retired 9/50 |
| 396 | Alco-S | 52703 | 6/13 | to J-A 12/39: Retired 8/54 |
| 397 | Alco-S | 52704 | 6/13 | Retired 9/50 |
| 398 | Alco-S | 52705 | 6/13 | to J-A 10/39: Retired 6/56 |
| 399 | Alco-S | 52706 | 6/13 | to J-A 12/41: Retired 2/55 |
| 400 | Alco-S | 54520 | 4/14 | to J-A 10/41: Retired 5/54 |
| 401 | Alco-S | 54521 | 4/14 | Retired 1952 |
| 402 | Alco-S | 54522 | 4/14 | to J-A 2/42: Retired 5/54 |
| 403 | Alco-S | 54523 | 4/14 | Retired 9/50 |
| 404 | Alco-S | 54524 | 4/14 | to J-A 7/41: Retired 6/56 |
| 405 | Alco-S | 54525 | 4/14 | Retired 9/50 |
| 406 | Alco-S | 55562 | 3/16 | to J-A 12/39: Retired 6/56 |
| 407 | Alco-S | 55563 | 3/16 | to J-A 11/38: Retired 6/56 |
| 408 | Alco-S | 55564 | 3/16 | to J-A 6/38: Retired 6/56 |
| 409 | Alco-S | 55565 | 3/16 | to J-A 8/37: Retired 11/53 |
| 410 | Alco-S | 55566 | 3/16 | to J-A 2/41: Retired 1952 |
| 411 | Alco-S | 55567 | 3/16 | to J-A 11/37: Retired 6/56 |
| 412 | Alco-S | 56284 | 10/16 | to J-A 12/37: Retired 1952 |
| 413 | Alco-S | 56285 | 10/16 | to J-A 8/37: Retired 6/56 |
| 414 | Alco-S | 56286 | 10/16 | to J-A 8/39: Retired 6/56 |
| 415 | Alco-S | 56287 | 10/16 | to J-A 1/38: Retired 10/51 |
| 416 | Alco-S | 56288 | 10/16 | to J-A 9/40: Retired 1956 |
| 417 | Alco-S | 56289 | 10/16 | to J-A 3/39: Retired 1956 |
| 418 | Alco-S | 56290 | 10/16 | to J-A 5/39: Retired 6/56 |
| 419 | Alco-S | 56291 | 10/16 | to J-A 11/40: Retired 6/56 |
| 420 | Alco-S | 56292 | 10/16 | to J-A 7/39: Retired 6/53 |
| 421 | Alco-S | 56293 | 10/16 | to J-A 5/40: Retired 1956 |
| 440 (a) | (Alco-S | 55608 | 1/16) | to J-A 1944: Retired 1956 |
| 441 (a) | (Alco-S | 556161 | 1/16) | to J-A 1944: Retired 1952 |

**2-8-2 Class J-2: 27x32-64-200-320000-62000 USRA**

| | | | | |
|---|---|---|---|---|
| 422 | Alco-S | 61034 | 3/19 | Retired 9/52 |
| 423 | Alco-S | 61035 | 3/19 | Retired 6/56 |
| 424 | Alco-S | 61036 | 3/19 | Retired 8/54 |
| 425 | Alco-S | 61037 | 3/19 | Retired 6/53 |
| 426 | Alco-R | 62609 | 1/21 | Retired 11/53 |
| 427 | Alco-R | 62610 | 1/21 | Retired 11/53 |
| 428 | Alco-R | 62611 | 1/21 | Retired 11/53 |
| 429 | Alco-R | 62612 | 1/21 | Retired 6/56 |
| 430 | Alco-R | 62613 | 1/21 | Retired 2/55 |
| 431 | Alco-R | 62614 | 1/21 | Retired 6/56 |

**2-8-2 Class J-3: 27x32-63-200-333000-63000**

| | | | | |
|---|---|---|---|---|
| 432 | Alco-S | 67091 | 10/26 | Retired 8/54 |
| 433 | Alco-S | 67092 | 10/26 | Retired 1952 |
| 434 | Alco-S | 67093 | 11/26 | Retired 1952 |
| 435 | Alco-S | 67094 | 11/26 | Retired 11/53 |
| 436 | Alco-S | 67095 | 11/26 | Retired 1949 |
| 437 | Alco-S | 67096 | 11/26 | Retired 6/56 |
| 438 | Alco-S | 67097 | 11/26 | Retired 1952 |
| 439 | Alco-S | 67098 | 11/26 | Retired 1952 |

Note a ) Ex C&NW Nos. 2363 and 2371, acquired 1944.

## 2-10-2 SANTA FE

**2-10-2 Class J-1: 27x32-57-185-324200-64356**

| | | | | |
|---|---|---|---|---|
| 491 | BLW. | 45976 | 7/17 | Traded to C&NW in 1944: rebuilt to 0-10-2 hump engine |
| 492 | BLW. | 45977 | 7/17 | Traded to C&NW in 1944: rebuilt to 0-10-2 hump engine |

## Eight-Wheeler Classes and Specifications

| Class A-2 | 14x22-64-67400 | See Nos. 228, 229 |
|---|---|---|
| Class B-1 | 15x24-64-63000 | See Nos. 13-16 and 184 |
| Class B-4 | l5x24-63-63900 | See No. 224 |
| Class B-5 | 15x24-57- | See No. 203 |
| Class B-6 | 15x ? | See No. 204 |
| Class C-3 | 16x24-63-60000 | See Nos. 19-23, 28-31 |
| Class C-4 | 16x24-59-70000 | See Nos. 24-27 |
| Class C-7 | 16x24-64-62200 | See Nos. 216, 217, 203, 204, 218, 222, 223, 230-232 |
| Class C-8 | 16x24-58-68000 | See Nos. 235, 236, 239, 240,243, 244 |
| Class C-9 | 16x24-63-66000 | See Nos. 251-262 |
| Class D-1 | 17x24-59-75000 | See Nos. 2-7, 9 |
| Class D-2 | 17x24-59-75000 | See No. 8 |
| Class D-3 | 17x24-59-75000 | See Nos. 34, 35, 37-43 |
| Class D-12 | 17x24-57- | See Nos. 237, 238, 241, 242 |

## 4-4-0 EIGHT-WHEELER

### 4-4-0 Class D-4: 17x24-57
| | | | | |
|---|---|---|---|---|
| 32 | BLW. | 4508 | 12/78 | Retired 9/10 |
| 33 | BLW. | 4509 | 12/78 | Retired 10/10 |
| 44 | BLW. | 5554 | 3/81 | Retired 2/20 |
| 45 | BLW. | 5555 | 3/81 | Retired 3/09 |
| 46 (a) | BLW. | 5556 | 3/81 | Sold 4/15 |
| 47 | BLW. | 5557 | 3/81 | Retired 9/99 |
| 48 | BLW. | 5560 | 3/81 | Retired 7/15 |
| 49 | BLW. | 5558 | 3/81 | Retired 1899 |
| 64 | BLW. | 5907 | 11/81 | Retired 7/12 |
| 65 | BLW. | 5912 | 11/81 | Retired 4/15 |
| 66 | BLW. | 5913 | 11/81 | Retired 4/19 |
| 67 | BLW. | 5914 | 11/81 | Retired 6/22 |
| 68 | BLW. | 5931 | 11/81 | Sold 7/15 |
| 69 | BLW. | 5955 | 11/81 | Retired 9/12 |

### 4-4-0 Class D-5: 17x24-57
| | | | | |
|---|---|---|---|---|
| 54 | BLW. | 5833 | 10/81 | Retired 6/11 |
| 55 | BLW. | 5834 | 10/81 | Ret ired 10/16 |
| 56 | BLW. | 5839 | 10/81 | Retired 4/15 |
| 57 | BLW. | 5836 | 10/81 | Retired 9/13 |
| 58 | BLW. | 5867 | 10/81 | Retired 6/22 |
| 59 | BLW. | 5868 | 10/81 | Retired 9/12 |
| 60 | BLW. | 5873 | 10/81 | Retired 10/10 |
| 61 | BLW. | 5875 | 10/81 | Retired 6/11 |
| 62 | BLW. | 5876 | 10/81 | Retired 4/19 |
| 63 | BLW. | 5881 | 10/81 | Retired 2/13 |

### 4-4-0 Class D-6: 17x24-57
| | | | | |
|---|---|---|---|---|
| 76 | BLW. | 6512 | 12/82 | Ret ired 11/16 |
| 77 | BLW. | 6520 | 12/82 | Retired 6/11 |
| 78 | BLW. | 6514 | 12/82 | Retired 3/17 |
| 79 | BLW. | 6515 | 12/82 | Ret ired 11/14 |
| 80 | BLW. | 6530 | 12/82 | Retired 3/17 |
| 81 | BLW. | 6536 | 12/82 | Retired 8/10 |
| 82 | BLW. | 6569 | 1/83 | Retired 9/15 |

### 4-4-0 Class D-6 (continued)
| | | | | |
|---|---|---|---|---|
| 83 | BLW. | 6573 | 1/83 | Retired 2/17 |
| 84 | BLW. | 6585 | 1/83 | Retired 5/15 |
| 85 | BLW. | 6588 | 1/83 | Retired 5/17 |
| 86 | BLW. | 6621 | 2/83 | Retired 5/14 |
| 87 | BLW. | 6625 | 2/83 | Retired by 6/17 |
| 88 | BLW. | 6654 | 3/83 | Retired S/14 |
| 89 | BLW. | 6656 | 3/83 | Retired 5/17 |

### 4-4-0 Class D-7:
| | | | | |
|---|---|---|---|---|
| 110 | Manch. | ? | 7/82 | Retired 7/12 |

### 4-4-0 Class D-8: 17x24-60
| | | | | |
|---|---|---|---|---|
| 101 | Manch. | 998 | 7/82 | Retired 1899 |
| 102 | Manch. | 999 | 7/82 | Retired 2/09 |
| 103 | Manch. | 1000 | 7/82 | Retired 8/10 |
| 104 | Manch. | 1001 | 7/82 | Retired 2/09 |
| 105 | Manch. | 1002 | 8/82 | Retired 7/07 |
| 106 | Manch. | 1003 | 8/82 | Retired 11/09 |
| 109 | Manch. | ? | 8/82 | Retired 5/13 |
| 111 | Manch. | ? | 8/82 | Retired 12/13 |
| 112 | Manch. | ? | 8/82 | Retired 9/09 |

### 4-4-0 Class D-9: 17x24-63
| | | | | |
|---|---|---|---|---|
| 123 | Schen. | 1699 | 1/83 | Retired 5/14 |

### 4-4-0 Class D-10: 17x24-63
| | | | | |
|---|---|---|---|---|
| 124 | Schen. | 1700 | 1/83 | Retired 11/14 |
| 125 | Schen. | 1701 | 1/83 | Retired 6/11 |

### 4-4-0 Class E-2: 17x24-57 (later 18x24)
| | | | | |
|---|---|---|---|---|
| 70 | BLW. | 6375 | 9/82 | Retired 12/15 |
| 71 | BLW. | 6376 | 9/82 | Retired 5/26 |
| 72 | BLW. | 6413 | 10/82 | Retired 12/26 |
| 73 | BLW. | 6420 | 10/82 | Retired 6/26 |
| 74 | BLW. | 6500 | 12/82 | Retired 8/26 |
| 75 | BLW. | 6501 | 12/82 | Retired 8/14 |

Note a) To Minneapolis, Anoka & Cuyuna Range Railroad.

## 4-4-0 EIGHT-WHEELER

**4-4-0 Class E-3: 17x24-57-**

| | | | | |
|---|---|---|---|---|
| 94 | BLW. | 6737 | 5/83 | Retired 10/26 (18x24) |

**4-4-0 Class E-5: 18x24-62-**

| | | | | |
|---|---|---|---|---|
| 113 | Rhode Is. | 1322 | 11/82 | Retired 11/15 |
| 114 | Rhode Is. | 1323 | 11/82 | Retired 5/25 |
| 115 | Rhode Is. | 1324 | 12/82 | Retired 9/26 |
| 116 | Rhode Is. | 1325 | 12/82 | Retired 9/16 |
| 117 | Rhode Is. | 1326 | 12/82 | Retired 11/26 |
| 118 | Rhode Is. | 1327 | 12/82 | Retired 4/24 |
| 119 | Rhode Is. | 1328 | 12/82 | Retired 9/26 |
| 120 | Rhode Is. | 1329 | 12/82 | Retired 10/26 |
| 121 | Rhode Is. | 1330 | 12/82 | Retired 5/26 |
| 122 | Rhode Is. | 1331 | 12/82 | Retired 10/26 |

**4-4-0 Class E-6: 18x24-63-150-90600-15800**

| | | | | |
|---|---|---|---|---|
| 100 | Schen. | 2051 | 3/86 | Retired 6/22 |
| 126 | Schen. | 2052 | 3/86 | Retired 2/17 |
| 127 | Schen. | 2053 | 3/86 | Retired 5/25 |
| 128 | Schen. | 2054 | 3/86 | Sold 12/27 F. & N.E. 13 |
| 129 | Schen. | 2055 | 5/86 | Retired 5/26 |
| 130 | Schen. | 2056 | 5/86 | Retired 3/27 |
| 131 | Schen. | 2057 | 5/86 | Retired 8/23 |
| 132 | Schen. | 2058 | 5/86 | Retired 5/23 |
| 133 | Schen. | 2344 | 7/87 | Retired 6/22 |
| 134 | Schen. | 2345 | 7/87 | Retired 3/27 |
| 135 | Schen. | 2346 | 7/87 | Retired 12/27 |
| 136 | Schen. | 2347 | 7/87 | Retired 1/44 |
| 137 | Schen. | 2348 | 7/87 | Retired 1/23 |
| 138 | Schen. | 2349 | 7/87 | Retired 8/23 |
| 139 | Schen. | 2350 | 7/87 | Retired 1/23 |
| 140 | Schen. | 2351 | 7/87 | Retired 5/26 |
| 141 | Schen. | 2352 | 8/87 | Retired 12/27 |
| 142 | Schen. | 2353 | 8/87 | Retired 12/27 |
| 143 | Schen. | 2354 | 8/87 | Retired 3/29 |
| 144 | Schen. | 2355 | 8/87 | Retired 1940 |
| 145 | Schen. | 2356 | 8/87 | Retired 2/29 |
| 146 | Schen. | 2357 | 8/87 | Retired 5/26 |
| 147 | Schen. | 2358 | 8/87 | Retired 1/23 |

**4-4-0 Class E-7: 18x22-65-93000**

| | | | | |
|---|---|---|---|---|
| 154 | Schen. | 2575 | 6/88 | Retired 3/27 |
| 155 | Schen. | 2576 | 6/88 | Retired 3/27 |
| 156 | Schen. | 2577 | 6/88 | Retired 3/27 |
| 157 | Schen. | 2578 | 6/88 | Retired 4/27 |
| 158 | Schen. | 2579 | 6/88 | Retired 4/27 |
| 159 | Schen. | 2580 | 6/88 | Retired 12/27 |

**4-4-0 Class E-8: 18x24-63-140-92500-14688**

| | | | | |
|---|---|---|---|---|
| 160 | Schen. | 2587 | 6/88 | Retired 1940 |
| 161 | Schen. | 2588 | 6/88 | Retired 5/35 |
| 162 | Schen. | 2589 | 6/88 | Retired 3/27 |
| 163 | Schen. | 2590 | 6/88 | Retired 12/30 |
| 164 | Schen. | 2591 | 6/88 | Retired 10/29 |
| 165 | Schen. | 2592 | 6/88 | Retired 3/27 |
| 166 | Schen. | 2593 | 7/88 | Retired 12/29 |
| 167 | Schen. | 2594 | 7/88 | Retired 12/29 |
| 168 | Schen. | 2595 | 7/88 | Retired 7/27 |
| 169 | Schen. | 2596 | 8/88 | Retired 12/27 |
| 170 | Schen. | 2597 | 8/88 | Retired 3/27 |
| 171 | Schen. | 2598 | 8/88 | Retired 5/35 |
| 172 | Schen. | 2599 | 8/88 | Retired 3/27 |
| 173 | Schen. | 2600 | 8/88 | Retired 12/29 |

**4-4-0 Class F-8: 19x24-73-190-130700-19103**

| | | | | |
|---|---|---|---|---|
| 275 | Schen. | 4424 | 3/96 | Retired 5/35 |
| 276 | Schen. | 4425 | 3/96 | Retired 12/39 |
| 277 | Schen. | 4426 | 3/96 | Retired 12/29 |
| 278 | Schen. | 4743 | 5/98 | Retired 12/29 |
| 255 | Schen. | 4934 | 12/98 | Retired 5/33 |
| 256 | Schen. | 4935 | 12/98 | Retired 5/33 |
| 257 | Schen. | 4936 | 12/98 | Retired 12/39 |
| 258 | Schen. | 4937 | 12/98 | Retired 12/39 |
| 259 | Schen. | 4938 | 12/98 | Retired 12/39 |
| 260 | Schen. | 4939 | 12/98 | Retired 5/35 |
| 251 | Schen. | 5373 | 12/99 | Retired 5/33 |
| 252 | Schen. | 5374 | 12/99 | Retired 12/29 |
| 253 | Schen. | 5375 | 12/99 | Retired 5/33 |
| 254 | Schen. | 5376 | 12/99 | Retired 12/30 |

## 4-4-2 ATLANTIC

**4-4-2 Class G-3: 20x26-81-200-172000-21827**

| | | | | |
|---|---|---|---|---|
| 367 | Alco-S | 38509 | 12/05 | Retired 1949 |
| 368 | Alco-S | 38510 | 12/05 | Retired 3/45 |
| 369 | Alco-S | 38511 | 12/05 | Retired 11/46 |
| 370 | Alco-S | 38512 | 12/05 | Retired 3/45 |

**4-4-2 Class G-3 (continued)**

| | | | | |
|---|---|---|---|---|
| 364 | Alco-S | 39410 | 6/06 | Retired 4/52 |
| 365 | Alco-S | 39411 | 6/06 | Retired 11/50 |
| 366 | Alco-S | 39412 | 6/06 | Retired 9/45 |

## 4-6-0 TEN-WHEELER

### 4-6-0 Class E-4: 18x24-57-98000

| | | | | |
|---|---|---|---|---|
| 95 | Schen. | 1996 | 8/85 | Retired 12/27 |
| 96 | Schen. | 1997 | 8/85 | Retired 9/27 |
| 97 | Schen. | 1998 | 8/85 | Retired 12/27 |
| 98 | Schen. | 1999 | 8/85 | Retired 9/27 |
| 99 | Schen. | 2000 | 8/85 | Retired 12/27 |

### 4-6-0 Class E-9: 18x24-64-116000

| | | | | |
|---|---|---|---|---|
| 174 | Schen. | 3367 | 4/91 | Retired 7/28 |
| 175 | Schen. | 3368 | 4/91 | Retired 11/28 |
| 176 | Schen. | 3369 | 4/91 | Retired 10/28 |
| 177 | Schen. | 3370 | 4/91 | Retired 12/23 |
| 178 | Schen. | 3371 | 4/91 | Retired 7/28 |
| 179 | Schen. | 3372 | 4/91 | Retired 9/28 |

### 4-6-0 Class F 1: 19x24-56-175-122700-23103

| | | | | |
|---|---|---|---|---|
| 11 | Schen. | 3408 | 3/91 | Retired 12/29 |
| 205 | Schen. | 3409 | 3/91 | Retired 2/29 |
| 220 | Schen. | 3410 | 3/91 | Rebuilt 1923. Retired 5/35 |
| 247 (a) | Schen. | 3411 | 3/91 | Retired 9/29 |
| 248 | Schen. | 3412 | 3/91 | Retired 4/30 |
| 221 | Schen. | 3531 | 7/91 | Retired 12/29 |

### 4-6-0 Class F-2: 19x24-59-170-125100-21219

| | | | | |
|---|---|---|---|---|
| 188 | Schen. | 3729 | 4/92 | Rebuilt 1921. Retired 12/39 |
| 189 | Schen. | 3730 | 4/92 | Sold for scrap 9/31 |
| 190 | Schen. | 3731 | 4/92 | Retired 4/30 |
| 191 | Schen. | 3732 | 4/92 | Retired 12/30 |
| 192 | Schen. | 3733 | 4/92 | Retired 12/30 |
| 193 | Schen. | 3734 | 4/92 | Retired 12/29 |
| 194 | Schen. | 3787 | 6/92 | Sold for scrap 9/31 |
| 195 | Schen. | 3788 | 6/92 | Rebuilt 1921. Retired 12/37 |
| 196 | Schen. | 3789 | 6/92 | Retired 12/29 |
| 197 | Schen. | 3790 | 6/92 | Rebuilt 1921. Retired 12/39 |
| 198 | Schen. | 3791 | 7/92 | Rebuilt 1921. Retired 5/35 |
| 199 | Schen. | 3792 | 7/92 | Rebuilt 1921. Retired 8/36 |
| 200 | Schen. | 3793 | 7/92 | Retired 5/33 |
| 202 | Schen. | 3967 | 1/93 | Rebuilt 1924. Retired 8/36 |
| 206 | Schen. | 3968 | 1/93 | Sold for scrap 9/31 |
| 212 | Schen. | 3969 | 1/93 | Rebuilt 1924. Retired 5/35 |
| 233 | Schen. | 3970 | 1/93 | Sold for scrap 9/31 |
| 234 | Schen. | 3971 | 1/93 | Rebuilt 1924. Retired 5/35 |

### 4-6-0 Class F-3: 19x24-59-

| | | | | |
|---|---|---|---|---|
| 226 | BLW. | 13630 | 8/93 | Retired 3/39 |

### 4-6-0 Class F-4

| | |
|---|---|
| 247 | Converted from Class F-1 (Rebuilt 1895) |

### 4-6-0 Class F-5: 19x24-67-123000

| | | | | |
|---|---|---|---|---|
| 263 | Schen. | 3794 | 7/92 | Retired 7/28 |
| 264 | Schen. | 3795 | 7/92 | Retired 7/28 |
| 265 | Schen. | 3796 | 7/92 | Retired 10/28 |
| 266 | Schen. | 3797 | 7/92 | Retired 12/28 |

### 4-6-0 Class F-7: 19x26-63-156000

| | | | | |
|---|---|---|---|---|
| 273 | Schen. | 4627 | 11/97 | Retired 12/30 |
| 274 | Schen. | 4628 | 11/97 | Retired 5/33 |

### 4-6-0 Class F-9: 19x24-59-190-146300-23715

| | | | | |
|---|---|---|---|---|
| 279 | Schen. | 4754 | 7/98 | Retired 5/35 |
| 280 | Schen. | 4755 | 7/98 | Retired 5/33 |
| 281 | Schen. | 4756 | 7/98 | Retired 5/33 |
| 282 | Schen. | 4757 | 7/98 | Retired 5/35 |
| 283 | Schen. | 4758 | 8/98 | Retired 5/33 |
| 284 | Sclien. | 4759 | 8/98 | Retired 5/33 |
| 285 | Schen. | 4760 | 8/98 | Retired 5/35 |
| 286 | Schen. | 4761 | 8/98 | Retired 5/35 |
| 287 | Schen. | 4762 | 8/98 | Retired 5/33 |
| 288 | Schen. | 4763 | 8/98 | Retired 5/35 |

### 4-6-0 Class G-1: 20x26-63-190-158000-26600

| | | | | |
|---|---|---|---|---|
| 289 | Schen. | 5093 | 7/99 | Retired 5/33 |
| 290 | Schen. | 5094 | 7/99 | Retired 5/35 |
| 291 | Schen. | 5095 | 7/99 | Retired 5/33 |
| 292 | Schen. | 5096 | 7/99 | Retired 5/35 |
| 293 | Schen. | 5097 | 8/99 | Retired 5/33 |
| 294 | Schen. | 5098 | 8/99 | Retired 5/33 |
| 295 | Schen. | 5099 | 8/99 | Retired 5/35 |
| 296 | Schen. | 5100 | 8/99 | Retired 5/35 |
| 297 | Schen. | 5101 | 8/99 | Retired 5/35 |
| 298 | Schen. | 5102 | 8/99 | Retired 5/35 |
| 299 | Schen. | 5401 | 1/00 | Retired 5/35 |
| 300 | Schen. | 5402 | 1/00 | Retired 5/35 |
| 301 | Schen. | 5403 | 1/00 | Retired 5/35 |

### 4-6-0 Class G-2: 20x26-69-  -159000

| | | | | |
|---|---|---|---|---|
| 305 | Schen. | 5837 | 5/01 | Retired 2/29 |
| 306 | Schen. | 5838 | 5/01 | Retired 8/29 |
| 307 | Schen. | 5839 | 5/01 | Retired 4/29 |

Note a) 247 converted to Class F-4.

## 4-6-0 TEN-WHEELER

### 4-6-0 Class 1-1: 2lx26-63-200-179000-30940

| | | | | |
|---|---|---|---|---|
| 302 | Schen. | 5834 | 7/01 | Retired 9/45 |
| 303 | Schen. | 5835 | 7/01 | Retired 1947-1949 |
| 304 | Schen. | 5836 | 7/01 | Retired 11/46 |
| 308 | Alco-S | 25417 | 7/02 | Retired 9/45 |
| 309 | Alco-S | 25418 | 7/02 | Retired 11/50 |
| 310 | Alco-S | 25419 | 7/02 | Retired 11/46 |
| 311 | Alco-S | 25420 | 7/02 | Retired 3/45 |
| 312 | Alco-S | 25421 | 8/02 | Retired 9/45 |
| 313 | Alco-S | 25422 | 8/02 | Retired 1947-1949 |
| 314 | Alco-S | 25423 | 9/02 | Retired 1947-1949 |
| 315 | Alco-S | 25424 | 9/02 | Retired 9/45 |
| 316 | Alco-S | 25425 | 9/02 | Retired 11/50 |
| 317 | Alco-S | 25426 | 9/02 | Retired 11/50 |
| 318 | Alco-S | 27551 | 8/03 | Retired 9/50 |
| 319 | Alco-S | 27552 | 8/03 | Retired 1947-1949 |
| 320 | Alco-S | 27553 | 8/03 | Retired 9/45 |
| 321 | Alco-S | 27554 | 8/03 | Retired 3/45 |
| 322 | Alco-S | 27555 | 8/03 | Retired 1952 |
| 323 | Alco-S | 27556 | 8/03 | Retired 12/39 |
| 324 | Alco-S | 27557 | 8/03 | Retired 11/46 |
| 325 | Alco-S | 27558 | 8/03 | Retired 11/46 |
| 326 | Alco-S | 27559 | 8/03 | Retired 11/46 |
| 327 | Alco-S | 27560 | 8/03 | Retired 11/46 |
| 328 | Alco-S | 27561 | 8/03 | Retired 1947-1949 |
| 329 | Alco-S | 27562 | 8/03 | Retired 1947-1949 |
| 330 | Alco-S | 27563 | 8/03 | Retired 11/50 |
| 331 | Alco-S | 27564 | 8/03 | Retired 3/45 |
| 332 | Alco-S | 27565 | 8/03 | Retired 3/45 |
| 333 | Alco-S | 30468 | 7/05 | Retired 1952 |
| 334 | Alco-S | 30469 | 7/05 | Retired 1947-1949 |
| 335 | Alco-S | 30470 | 7/05 | Retired 11/46 |
| 336 | Alco-S | 39400 | 6/06 | Retired 9/45 |
| 337 | Alco-S | 39401 | 6/06 | Retired 11/46 |
| 338 | Alco-S | 39402 | 6/06 | Retired 6/53 |
| 339 | Alco-S | 39403 | 6/06 | Retired 1947-1949 |
| 340 | AIco-S | 39404 | 6/06 | Retired 11/50 |
| 341 | Alco-S | 39405 | 6/06 | Retired 5/54 |
| 342 | Alco-S | 39406 | 6/06 | Retired 9/50 |
| 343 | Alco-S | 39407 | 6/06 | Retired 11/53 |
| 344 | Alco-S | 39408 | 7/06 | Retired 11/53 |
| 345 | Alco-S | 39409 | 7/06 | Retired 8/54 |
| 346 | Alco-S | 42622 | 8/07 | Retired 9/45 |
| 347 | Alco-S | 42623 | 8/07 | Retired 1952 |
| 348 | Alco-S | 42624 | 8/07 | Retired 12/37 |
| 349 | Alco-S | 42625 | 8/07 | Retired 9/45 |
| 350 | Alco-S | 42626 | 8/07 | Retired 9/45 |
| 351 | Alco-S | 42627 | 8/07 | Retired 1952 |
| 352 | Alco-S | 42628 | 8/07 | Retired 3/51 |
| 353 | Alco-S | 42629 | 8/07 | Retired 8/54 |

### 4-6-0 Class I-1 (continued)

| | | | | |
|---|---|---|---|---|
| 354 | Alco-S | 42630 | 8/07 | Retired 1952 |
| 355 | Alco-S | 42631 | 8/07 | Retired 9/45 |
| 356 | Alco-S | 45915 | 2/09 | Retired 2/55 |
| 357 | Alco-S | 45916 | 2/09 | Retired 2/55 |
| 358 | Alco-S | 45917 | 2/09 | Retired 5/54 |
| 359 | Alco-S | 45918 | 2/09 | Retired 5/54 |
| 360 | Alco-S | 45919 | 2/09 | Retired 1952 |
| 361 | Alco-S | 47040 | 4/10 | Retired 2/55 |
| 362 | Alco-S | 47041 | 4/10 | Retired 3/51 |
| 363 | Alco-S | 47042 | 4/10 | Retired 5/53 |
| 222 | Alco-S | 47043 | 4/10 | Retired 6/56 |
| 223 | Alco-S | 47044 | 4/10 | Retired 1952 |
| 224 | Alco-S | 47045 | 4/10 | Retired 1952 |
| 225 | Alco-S | 47046 | 4/10 | Retired 9/50 |
| 101 | Alco-S | 48948 | 12/10 | Reno. 2nd 364. Retired 11/53 |
| 102 | Alco-S | 48949 | 12/10 | Retired 6/56 |
| 103 | Alco-S | 48950 | 12/10 | Retired 5/54 |
| 104 | Alco-S | 48951 | 12/10 | Retired 2/55 |
| 105 | Alco-S | 48952 | 12/10 | Retired 12/37 |
| 106 | Alco-S | 48953 | 12/10 | Retired 11/53 |

### 4-6-0 Class K-1: 23x26-63-180-186000-33400

| | | | | |
|---|---|---|---|---|
| 107 | Alco-S | 50126 | 7/11 | Retired 2/55 |
| 108 | Alco-S | 50127 | 7/11 | Retired 6/56 |
| 112 | Alco-S | 50128 | 7/11 | Retired 6/56 |
| 230 | Alco-S | 50129 | 7/11 | Retired 6/56 |
| 231 | Alco-S | 50130 | 7/11 | Retired 1947-1949 |
| 232 | Alco-S | 50131 | 7/11 | Retired 1947-1949 |
| 235 | Alco-B | S0947 | 4/12 | Retired 2/55 |
| 236 | Alco-B | 50948 | 4/12 | Retired 6/56 |
| 237 | Alco-B | 50949 | 4/12 | Retired 1947-1949 |
| 238 | Alco-B | 50950 | 4/12 | Retired 2/55 |
| 239 | Alco-B | 50951 | 4/12 | Retired 2/55 |
| 240 | Alco-B | 50952 | 4/12 | Retired 5/54 |
| 243 | Alco-B | 50953 | 4/12 | Retired 6/56 |
| 244 | Alco-B | 50954 | 4/12 | Retired 2/55 |
| 245 | Alco-B | 50955 | 4/12 | Retired 6/56 |
| 246 | Alco-B | 50956 | 4/12 | Retired 12/56 |
| 110 | Alco-S | 52621 | 2/13 | Retired 11/53 |
| 125 | Alco-S | 52622 | 2/13 | Retired 6/56 |
| 183 | Alco-S | 52623 | 2/13 | Retired 6/56 |
| 184 | Alco-S | 52624 | 2/13 | Retired 6/56 |
| 201 | Alco-S | 52625 | 2/13 | Retired 5/54 |
| 203 | Alco-S | 52626 | 2/13 | Retired 12/56 |
| 204 | Alco-S | 52627 | 2/13 | Retired 6/56 |
| 249 | Alco-S | 52628 | 2/13 | Retired 6/56 |
| 261 | Alco-S | 52629 | 3/13 | Retired 6/56 |
| 262 | Alco-S | 52630 | 3/13 | Retired 6/56 |

## 4-6-2 PACIFIC

**4-6-2 Class 1-2: 21x28-75-200-206500-27988**

| | | | | |
|---|---|---|---|---|
| 371 | Alco-S | 27566 | 5/03 | Retired 12/37 |
| 372 | Alco-S | 27567 | 5/03 | Retired 12/37 |
| 373 | Alco-S | 27568 | 5/03 | Retired 12/37 |
| 374 | Alco-S | 27569 | 5/03 | Retired 12/37 |
| 375 | Alco-S | 27570 | 5/03 | Retired 12/37 |
| 376 | Alco-S | 42617 | 4/07 | Retired 1940-1943 |
| 377 | Alco-S | 42618 | 4/07 | Retired 1940-1943 |
| 378 | Alco-S | 42619 | 4/07 | Retired 1940-1942 |
| 379 | Alco-S | 45908 | 1/09 | Retired 3/45 |
| 380 | Alco-S | 45909 | 1/09 | Retired 1940-1943 |
| 381 | Alco-S | 45910 | 2/09 | Retired 9/45 |
| 382 | Alco-S | 45911 | 2/09 | Retired 9/45 |
| 383 | Alco-S | 47047 | 4/10 | Retired 6/53 |
| 384 | Alco-S | 47048 | 4/10 | Retired 11/53 |
| 385 | Alco-S | 48954 | 12/10 | Retired 6/53 |
| 386 | Alco-S | 48955 | 12/10 | Retired 9/52 |
| 387 | Alco-S | 48956 | 12/10 | Retired 1949 |

**4-6-2 Class K-2: 23x28-75-185-220000-31050**

| | | | |
|---|---|---|---|
| 388 | Alco-S | 50124 | 7/11 |
| 389 | Alco-S | 50125 | 7/11 |

**4-6-2 Class E: 25x28-75-200-260000-39700**

| | | | | |
|---|---|---|---|---|
| 500 | Alco-S | 53039 | 5/13 | Retired 6/53 |
| 501 | Alco-S | 53040 | 5/13 | Retired 11/53 |
| 502 | Alco-S | 53041 | 5/13 | Retired 1951 |
| 503 | Alco-S | 53042 | 5/13 | Retired 11/53 |
| 504 | Alco-S | 53043 | 5/13 | Retired 6/56 |
| 505 | Alco-S | 53044 | 5/13 | Retired 1952 |
| 506 | Alco-S | 53045 | 5/13 | Retired 6/56 |
| 507 | Alco-S | 53046 | 5/13 | Retired 1952 |
| 508 (a) | Alco-S | 54516 | 4/14 | Retired 5/54 |
| 509 (a) | Alco-S | 54517 | 4/14 | Retired 6/56 |
| 510 | Alco-S | 54518 | 4/14 | Retired 1949 |
| 511 | Alco-S | 54519 | 4/14 | Wrecked 6/51 |
| 512 | Alco-S | 55540 | 1/16 | Retired 6/56 |
| 513 | Alco-S | 55541 | 1/16 | Retired 11/53 |
| 514 | Alco-S | 55542 | 1/16 | Retired 11/53 |
| 515 | Alco-S | 55543 | 1/16 | Retired 1951 |
| 516 | Alco-S | 56294 | 10/16 | Retired 2/55 |
| 517 | Alco-S | 56295 | 10/16 | Retired 1949 |

**4-6-2 Class E-3: 25x28-75-260-341700-51500 (note b)**

| | | | | |
|---|---|---|---|---|
| 600 | Alco-S | 68516 | 10/30 | Retired 5/54 |
| 601 | Alco-S | 68617 | 10/30 | Retired 6/56 |
| 602 | Alco-S | 68618 | 11/30 | Retired 6/56 |

Note a) 508, 509 rebuilt to Class Ea with booster: 46000TF
Note b) TF 64600 with booster.

**CStPM&O Classification System:** About 1898, the CStPM&O assigned locomotive classes based on cylinder diameter, as follows:

| | |
|---|---|
| Class A - 14" cylinder | Class F - 19" cylinder |
| Class B - 15" cylinder | Class G - 20" cylinder |
| Class C - 16" cylinder | Class H - 22" cylinder |
| Class D - 17" cylinder | Class I - 21" cylinder |
| Class E - 18" cylinder | Class K - 23" cylinder |

After 1913 new locomotives were assigned classes under the Chicago & NorthWestern System, including E Class 4-6-2, J Class 2-8-2, M Class 0-6-0, and Z Class 2-8-0. Nevertheless, the old classification was also retained for older power. All locomotives acquired new by the CStPM&O after it was formed in 1880 are grouped by wheel arrangement.

**Builder Abreviations:**

| | |
|---|---|
| Alco-B for American Locomotive Company Brooks Works | F-M for Fairbanks-Morse |
| Alco-R for American Locomotive Company Richmond Works | Manch. for Manchester |
| Alco-S for American Locomotive Company Schenectady Works | Pitts. for Pittsburg |
| BLW. for Baldwin | R.I. for Rhode Island |
| EMC for Electro Motive Corporation (GM) | Schen. for Schenectady |
| EMD for Electro Motive Division (GM) | Taun. for Taunton |
| GE for General Electric | Whit. for Whitcomb |

## DIESEL LOCOMOTIVES

**EMC 600HP Switcher SW1 196000**

| | | | |
|---|---|---|---|
| 55 | EMC | 1194 | 10/40 |

**EMC 1000 HP Switcher NW2 241000**

| | | | |
|---|---|---|---|
| 70 | EMC | 1195 | 12/40 |

**Alco-GE 1000HP Switcher S-2 219000**

| | | | |
|---|---|---|---|
| 90 | Alco | 69216 | 10/40 |
| 91 | Alco | 72025 | 4/44 |
| 92 | Alco | 72026 | 4/44 |
| 93 | Alco | 72049 | 5/44 |

**Whitcomb 358HP Switcher (44del8A) 84100**

| | | | |
|---|---|---|---|
| 10 | Whit. | 60284 | 6/43 |

**Baldwin 1000HP Switcher VO 232000; 219200**

| | | | | |
|---|---|---|---|---|
| 87 | BLW. | 70149 | 3/44 | (Rblt EMD '58) |
| 88 | BLW. | 72027 | 7/45 | (Rblt EMD '58) |
| 89 | BLW. | 72028 | 7/45 | (Rblt EMD '58) |
| 99 | BLW. | 74088 | 3/49 | (Rblt EMD 5/60) |
| 100 | BLW. | 74089 | 3/49 | (Rblt EMD 5/60) |

**Alco-GE 660HP Switcher S-1 189000**

| | | | |
|---|---|---|---|
| 56 | Alco | 72842 | 11/44 |
| 57 | Alco | 72843 | 11/44 |
| 69 | Alco | 75889 | 5/48 |

**Baldwin 660HP Switcher VO 191500; 189100**

| | | | |
|---|---|---|---|
| 58 | BLW. | 71572 | 6/45 |
| 59 | BLW. | 71573 | 6/45 |
| 68 | BLW. | 71574 | 6/45 |
| 71 | BLW. | 73904 | 3/49 |

**Fairbanks-Morse 1000HP Alt 100.6A 230000**

| | | | |
|---|---|---|---|
| 94 | F-M | L1171 | 12/47 |
| 95 | F-M | 10-L-40 | 2/48 |
| 96 | F-M | 10-L-41 | 2/48 |
| 97 | F-M | 10-L-42 | 2/48 |
| 98 | F-M | 10-L-43 | 2/48 |

**EMD 800HP Switcher SW8 223800**

| | | | |
|---|---|---|---|
| 126 | EMD | 14663 | 4/51 |
| 127 | EMD | 14664 | 4/51 |
| 128 | EMD | 14665 | 4/51 |
| 129 | EMD | 14666 | 4/51 |

**Alco 1000HP Switcher S-4 224000**

| | | | |
|---|---|---|---|
| 101 | Alco | 80621 | 6/53 |

**F-M C-C 1600HP Road Switcher H16-66 273000**

| | | | |
|---|---|---|---|
| 150 | F-M | 16L278 | '51 |
| 168 | F-M | 16L704 | 7/53 |
| 169 | F-M | 16L705 | 7/53 |
| 170 | F-M | 16L706 | 7/53 |
| 171 | F-M | 16L707 | 7/53 |
| 172 | F-M | 16L708 | 7/53 |

**EMD 1500HP Road Switcher GP7 229700; 231000**

| | | | |
|---|---|---|---|
| 151 | EMD | 14667 | 8/51 |
| 152 | EMD | 14668 | 8/51 |
| 153 | EMD | 14669 | 8/51 |
| 154 | EMD | 14670 | 8/51 |
| 155 | EMD | 14671 | 8/51 |
| 156 | EMD | 14672 | 8/51 |
| 157 | EMD | 16891 | 6/52 |
| 158 | EMD | 16892 | 6/52 |
| 159 | EMD | 16893 | 6/52 |
| 160 | EMD | 16894 | 6/52 |
| 161 | EMD | 16895 | 6/52 |

**Alco 1600HP Road Switcher RS-3 (note a)**

| | | | |
|---|---|---|---|
| 162 | Alco | 80137 | 8/52 |
| 163 | Alco | 80138 | 8/52 |
| 164 | Alco | 80139 | 8/52 |
| 165 | Alco | 80519 | 7/53 |
| 166 | Alco | 80520 | 7/53 |
| 167 | Alco | 80521 | 7/53 |

**Fairbanks-Morse-GE 2000HP Pass. A-Unit Alt 100.3A 295600**

| | | | |
|---|---|---|---|
| 6001 A | F-M | L1090 | 5/47 |
| 6001 B | F-M | L1092 | 5/47 |
| 6002A | F-M | L1093 | 5/47 |
| 6002B | F-M | L1095 | 5/47 |

**EMD 1500HP Freight A-Unit F7 224800, 221600**

| | | | |
|---|---|---|---|
| 6500A | EMD | 8578 | 12/49 |
| 6500B | EMD | 8579 | 12/49 |
| 6501A | EMD | 8580 | 12/49 |
| 6501B | EMD | 8581 | 12/49 |
| 6502A | EMD | 8582 | 12/49 |
| 6502B | EMD | 8583 | 12/49 |
| 6503A | EMD | 10558 | 4/50 |
| 6503B | EMD | 10559 | 4/50 |
| 6504A | EMD | 10560 | 4/50 |
| 6504B | EMD | 10561 | 4/50 |
| 6505A | EMD | 10562 | 4/50 |
| 6505B | EMD | 10563 | 4/50 |

Note a) 163, 164, 167 Pass., wt. 234,500, 238,000.

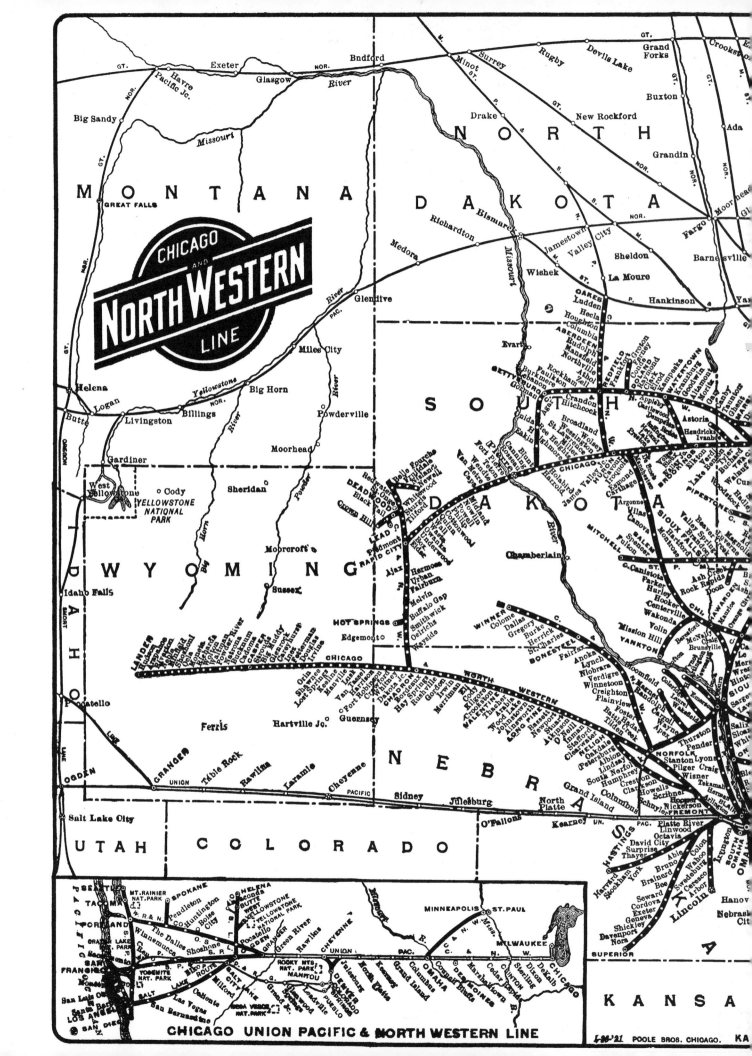